Sea of Glory

ALSO BY NATHANIEL PHILBRICK

The Passionate Sailor

Away Off Shore: Nantucket Island and Its People, 1602–1890

Abram's Eyes: The Native American Legacy of Nantucket Island

Second Wind: A Sunfish Sailor's Odyssey

In the Heart of the Sea: The Tragedy of the Whaleship Essex

NATHANIEL

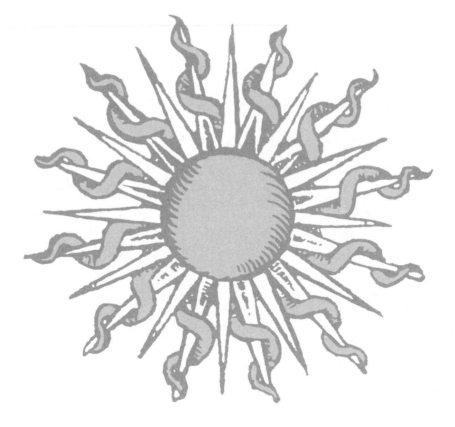

PHILBRICK

Sea of Glory

America's Voyage of Discovery,
The U.S. Exploring Expedition, 1838–1842

VIKING

VIKING
Published by the Penguin Group
Penguin Group (USA) Inc., 375 Hudson Street,
New York, New York 10014, U.S.A.
Penguin Books Ltd, 80 Strand, London WC2R 0RL, England
Penguin Books Australia Ltd, 250 Camberwell Road, Camberwell,
Victoria 3124, Australia
Penguin Books Canada Ltd, 10 Alcorn Avenue, Toronto, Ontario, Canada M4V 3B2
Penguin Books India (P) Ltd, 11 Community Centre, Panchsheel Park,
New Delhi – 110 017, India
Penguin Books (N.Z.) Ltd, Cnr Rosedale and Airborne Roads, Albany,
Auckland, New Zealand
Penguin Books (South Africa) (Pty) Ltd, 24 Sturdee Avenue,
Rosebank, Johannesburg 2196, South Africa

Penguin Books Ltd, Registered Offices: 80 Strand, London WC2R 0RL, England

First published in 2003 by Viking Penguin, a member of Penguin Group (USA) Inc.

10   9   8   7   6   5   4   3   2   1

Illustration of the squadron by Mark Myers
Maps by Jeffrey L. Ward

LIBRARY OF CONGRESS CATALOGING IN PUBLICATION DATA
Philbrick, Nathaniel.
    Sea of glory : America's voyage of discovery : the U.S. Exploring
    Expedition, 1838–1842 / Nathaniel Philbrick.
        p.   cm.
    Includes bibliographical references and index.
    ISBN 0-670-03231-X
        1. United States Exploring Expedition (1838–1842).   2. Ethnological expeditions–
    History–19th century.   3. Ethnology–United States–History–19th century.
    4. Ethnology–Oceania–History–19th century.   5. Wilkes, Charles, 1798–1877.   I. Title.
GN663.P48   2003
910'.973'09034–dc21   2003050178

This book is printed on acid-free paper. ∞

Printed in the United States of America
Set in Caslon Book
Designed by Francesca Belanger

To my father,

Thomas Philbrick

I have ventured . . .
This many summers in a sea of glory,
But far beyond my depth. . . .

—WILLIAM SHAKESPEARE
King Henry VIII 3.2

CONTENTS

Part Four

LIST OF MAPS

PREFACE
Young Ambition

H E WAS NOT YET FORTY-FIVE, but he looked much older, his health broken by four years of hardship and danger. But he had done it. He had successfully completed the voyage of a lifetime–the kind of voyage that had made heroes of Christopher Columbus and James Cook.

The odds had been against him from the start. When his squadron of six sailing vessels set out from the Norfolk Navy Yard in 1838, most of the world's oceans had already been thoroughly explored. That had not prevented the United States from sending him on a bold, some said foolhardy mission: to scour the Southern Hemisphere of the earth for new lands.

Miraculously, he had made discoveries that would redraw the map of the world. He and his officers had surveyed dozens of uncharted Pacific islands. They had completed America's first survey of what would one day become the states of Oregon and Washington. His team of scientists had brought back forty tons of specimens and artifacts, including two thousand never-before-identified species. Most impressive of all, he had established the existence of a new continent. Battling icebergs and gale-force winds in his fragile wooden ships, he had charted a 1,500-mile section of Antarctic coast that still bears his name: Wilkes Land.

But on that September day in 1842, just a few months after his return to the United States, Lieutenant Charles Wilkes was anything but a hero. Instead of being honored with speeches and parades, he had been put on trial in the crowded cabin of the USS *North Carolina* anchored in New York Harbor. Beside him sat his attorney; across from them were the judges–thirteen naval officers who were about to decide whether he was guilty of illegally whipping his men, massacring the inhabitants of a tiny Fijian island, lying about the discovery of Antarctica, and other outrages. Sitting in the gallery were many of his own officers. They whispered among themselves and smiled, confident that their hated commander would soon get his due.

He was a slight man with brown hair and a sharp blade of a nose, his cheeks pitted from smallpox and burned red by the sun and wind. Despite his haggard appearance, there was a fierceness in his eyes. After almost three weeks of testimony, it was now time for him to deliver his defense. He cleared his throat, and in a quavering, indignant voice, he began to tell his side of the story.

America's first frontier was not the West; it was the sea. The United States began as a string of coastal communities dominated by the Atlantic Ocean–a storm-wracked wilderness that made the forests of the interior look like a beckoning refuge. But travel by road was slow and difficult in the early years of the nation, while the sea was a highway that led to just about anywhere in the world. By the late eighteenth century, American mariners had ventured around Cape Horn to the Pacific. In 1792, a sea otter trader from Boston discovered Oregon's Columbia River–thirteen years before the arrival of Lewis and Clark. When the United States did finally send an overland expedition beyond the Rockies in 1803, it was to find a navigable waterway to the Pacific. That was why the Lewis and Clark Expedition was called a *voyage* of discovery. Until the Gold Rush turned the nation's attention to the winning of the West in 1848, America's predominant frontier was still the sea.

A decade earlier, this young nation of sea wanderers became part of an international effort to discover and explore the last unknown portions of the planet. It had begun in 1768, with the voyages of the legendary British navigator James Cook. Earlier explorers such as Columbus and Magellan had been in search of new ways of getting to old, already well-known places–in particular, the spice-rich islands of the East Indies. Their discoveries had been accidental. There had been nothing accidental about Cook's explorations of the South Pacific. When he returned with reports of palm-fringed islands teeming with people, plants, and animals unlike anything ever seen before, the scientists of Europe clamored for more. In the decades to come, England sent out twenty-eight exploring expeditions to the Pacific; France followed with seventeen, while Spain, Russia, and Holland mounted a total of thirteen voyages among them.

In spite of all these efforts to probe the islands of the Pacific, there remained a region that had so far resisted scientific inquiry: the ice-studded mystery at the bottom of the world. Cook had ventured below the Antarctic Circle and found nothing but snow and ice. Given the dangerous conditions and the slender prospect of significant results, further exploration hardly seemed warranted. But by 1838 there was renewed interest in the high southern latitudes. What had once been regarded as a forbidding wasteland was now one of the few places left where a discovery of Cook-like proportions might still be possible. Seventy years after the English explorer's inaugural voyage, the icy waters of Antarctica were just one of the many destinations planned for America's first oceangoing voyage of discovery.

They called it the U.S. Ex. Ex., or simply the Ex. Ex., shorthand for the United States South Seas Exploring Expedition of 1838. It was an unprecedented naval operation, especially for a nation with a navy that was less than half the size of Great Britain's. Whereas most European exploring expeditions comprised two modest-sized ships, the American squadron consisted of six sailing vessels and 346 men, including a team of nine scientists and artists, making it one of the largest voyages of discovery in the history of Western exploration.

No American or European expedition could compare in size to the flotillas launched by the Chinese emperor Yung-lo in the first half of the fifteenth century, some of which included 27,550 men and ventured as far as the east coast of Africa and perhaps beyond. When China chose to disband her fleets of discovery, Portugal became the world's leader in exploration. Under the guidance of Prince Henry the Navigator, Portugal developed a new type of vessel called the caravel, specifically designed for exploration. Based on Egyptian and Greek designs and only seventy feet long, with shoal draft to keep from running aground on unknown coasts, the caravel enabled Portugal to become the first European country to round Africa's Cape of Good Hope and, in 1498, reach the fabled shores of India. By that time, Spain had launched its own expeditions, placing its hopes in an Italian mariner named Christopher Columbus. Columbus insisted that the fastest way to the East was to sail west, and when he subsequently came upon the islands of the Bahamas and the Caribbean, he stubbornly insisted that they were what he had been looking for all along–the Spice Islands of the East Indies. Three hundred and forty-six years later, the history of exploration had come full circle as a nation from the New World Columbus refused to believe existed launched its own voyage of discovery.

With the U.S. Ex. Ex., America hoped to plant its flag in the world. Literally broadening the nation's horizons, the Expedition's ships would cover the Pacific Ocean from top to bottom and bring the United States international renown for its scientific endeavors as well as its bravado. European expeditions had served the cause of both science and empire, providing new lands with which to augment their countries' already far-flung possessions around the world. The United States, on the other hand, had more than enough unexplored territory within its own borders. Commerce, not colonies, was what the U.S. was after. Besides establishing a stronger diplomatic presence throughout the Pacific, the Expedition sought to provide much-needed charts to American whalers, sealers, and China traders. Decades before America surveyed and mapped its own interior, this government-sponsored voyage of discovery would enable a young, determined nation to take its first tentative steps toward becoming an economic world power.

The Expedition was to attempt two forays south–one from Cape Horn, the other from Sydney, Australia, during the relatively warm months of January, February, and March. The time in between was to be spent surveying the islands of the South Pacific–particularly the little-known Fiji Group. The Expedition's other priority was the Pacific Northwest. In the years since Lewis and Clark had ventured to the mouth of the Columbia River, the British and their Hudson's Bay Company had come to dominate what was known as the Oregon territory. In hopes of laying the basis for the government's future claim to the region, the Ex. Ex. was to complete the first American survey of the Columbia, and would continue down the coast to California's San Francisco Bay, then still a part of Mexico. By the conclusion of the voyage–after stops at Manila, Singapore, and the Cape of Good Hope–the Expedition would become the last all-sail naval squadron to circumnavigate the world.

By any measure, the achievements of the Expedition would be extraordinary. After four years at sea, after losing two ships and twenty-eight officers and men, the Expedition logged 87,000 miles, surveyed 280 Pacific islands, and created 180 charts–some of which were still being used as late as World War II. The Expedition also mapped 800 miles of coastline in the Pacific Northwest and 1,500 miles of the icebound Antarctic coast. Just as important would be its contribution to the rise of science in America. The thousands of specimens and artifacts amassed by the Expedition's scientists would become the foundation of the collections of the Smithsonian Institution. Indeed, without the Ex. Ex., there might never have been a national museum in Washington, D.C. The U.S. Botanic Garden, the U.S. Hydrographic Office, and the Naval Observatory all owe their existence, in varying degrees, to the Expedition.

Any one of these accomplishments would have been noteworthy. Taken together, they represent a national achievement on the order of the building of the Transcontinental Railroad and the Panama Canal. But if these wonders of technology and human resolve have become part of America's legendary past, the U.S. Exploring Expedition has been largely forgotten. To understand why, we must look to the Expedition's leader and the young officer who began the voyage as his commander's biggest fan.

It had taken more than a decade to get the U.S. Ex. Ex. under way. By 1838, years of political infighting had severely damaged the Expedition's credibility with the American people. But the turmoil made no difference to a twenty-two-year-old naval officer named William Reynolds. Reynolds was a passed midshipman–the pre-Annapolis

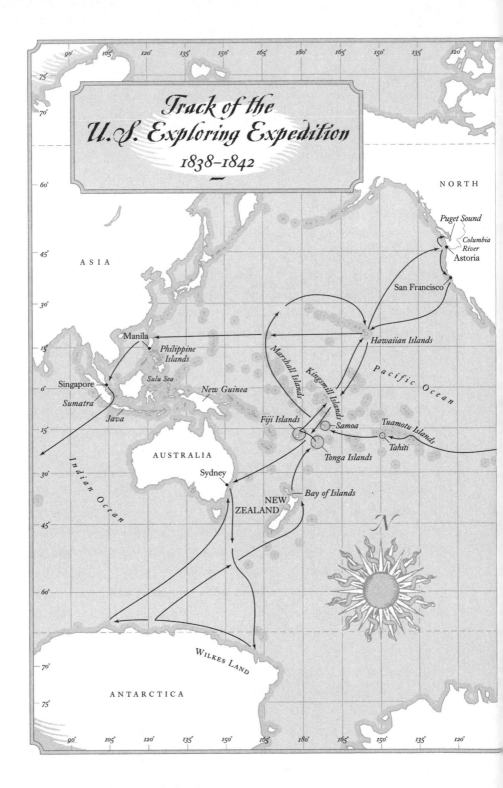

Track of the
U.S. Exploring Expedition
1838–1842

NORTH

Puget Sound
Columbia River
Astoria

San Francisco

ASIA

Manila
Philippine Islands
Singapore
Sumatra
Java
Sulu Sea
New Guinea

Hawaiian Islands

Pacific Ocean

Marshall Islands
Kingsmill Islands

Fiji Islands
Samoa
Tonga Islands
Tuamotu Islands
Tahiti

AUSTRALIA
Sydney

Indian Ocean

NEW ZEALAND
Bay of Islands

N

WILKES LAND

ANTARCTICA

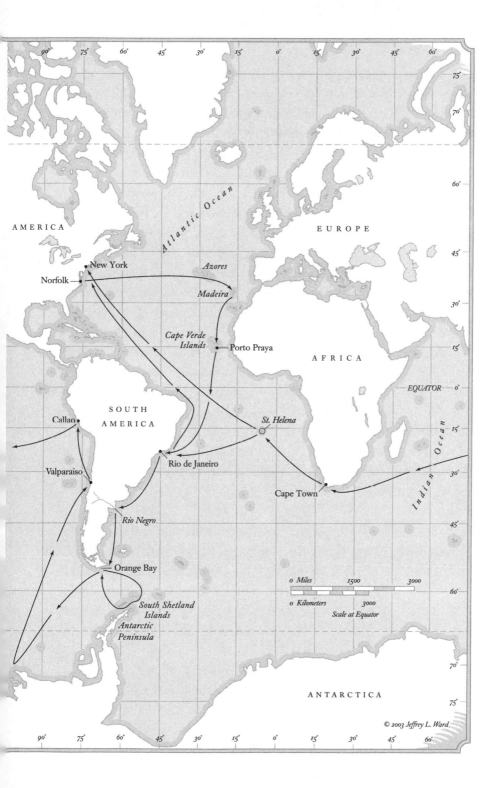

equivalent of a Naval Academy graduate, who after several years of sea duty and study had passed a rigorous series of examinations. For Reynolds, the U.S. Ex. Ex. was the voyage of his young life, and on October 29, 1838–seventy-two days after the squadron's departure–he poured out his enthusiasm into the pages of his journal. "And behold! Now a nation which a short time ago was a discovery itself . . . is taking its place among the enlightened of the world and endeavoring to contribute its mite in the cause of knowledge and research. For this seems the age in which all men's minds are bent to learn all about the secrets of the world in which they inhabit." Reynolds then turned his attention to the Expedition's commander, Charles Wilkes, a controversial choice to lead such an ambitious undertaking. "Captain Wilkes is a man of great talent, perhaps genius," Reynolds declared. After describing his leader's extensive scientific and navigational background, he concluded, "In my humble opinion, Captain Wilkes is the most proper man who could have been found in the Navy to conduct this Expedition, and I have every confidence that he will accomplish all that is expected."

Months later, after the Expedition had rounded Cape Horn, plunged south into the icy Drake Passage, and surveyed the island paradises of Polynesia, Reynolds would return to this passage in his journal. Over the reference to Wilkes he would scrawl, "great mistake, did not at this time know him."

Reynolds would not be alone in changing his opinion of Charles Wilkes. By the end of the voyage, most of the Expedition's officers had grown to despise their commander. The feelings were mutual. Wilkes would bring charges against several of his officers, who then countered with charges of their own, meaning that what might have been the triumphant return of the U.S. Ex. Ex. became clouded by a series of courts-martial.

According to common practice, all the Expedition's officers had been required to keep journals that they were to surrender to their commander at the end of the voyage. Unbeknownst to Wilkes, Reynolds kept two journals: an official log and a secret, far more personal journal that would eventually expand to two volumes and almost 200,000 words. Today these big, twelve-by-twenty-inch unpublished journals reside in the archives of Franklin and Marshall College in Reynolds's ancestral home of Lancaster, Pennsylvania.

Sensitive and well-read, Reynolds was a natural writer, and his journals contain some of the best descriptions of the sea to come from a nineteenth-century American's pen. But the journals are much more than the chronicle of a four-year voyage. Along with the twenty-one letters he wrote to his family back home, the journals tell the story of one man's coming of age amid the ice floes of the Antarctic, the coral reefs of the South Seas, and the giant pines of the Pacific Northwest.

At the center of Reynolds's account is his changing relationship with Wilkes, a relationship that would come to dramatize the tangled legacy of the Expedition. Largely because of its arrogant and uncompromising commander, the Ex. Ex. was never able to shake free of the personal animosities and political intrigue that had plagued it from the start. Even though his journal provides a remarkable window on the Expedition, Reynolds was unable, in the end, to fathom the seemingly inexplicable motivations of his commander. Indeed, for more than a century, Wilkes has stood astride the legacy of the Ex. Ex. like an inscrutable colossus, a forbidding impediment to all who would want to know more.

But there is a way to see past Wilkes's rigid professional demeanor. The dozens of letters he wrote to his wife Jane during the long four years of the Ex. Ex. are full of startling revelations. Just a few months into the voyage, Wilkes almost cracked under the pressures of command. What happened to him over the course of the Expedition is part passion play, part object lesson in how the demands of leadership can at once confirm and transform a person's character.

By all rights, the Ex. Ex. should have become an enduring source of national pride. But Charles Wilkes was no James Cook. Insecure and egotistical rather than self-effacing and confident, Wilkes had a talent for creating discord and conflict. And yet, there was something quintessentially American about Wilkes and the brash, boisterous, and overreaching expedition that he managed to forge in his own makeshift image.

✦ ✦ ✦

Late in life, Mark Twain would remember the excitement he felt when he learned that Wilkes had discovered Antarctica. "When I was a boy of ten, in that village on the Mississippi River which at that time was so incalculably far from any place and is now so near to all places, the name of Wilkes, the explorer, was in everybody's mouth. . . . What a noise it made, and how wonderful the glory! Wilkes had discovered a new world and was another Columbus. . . . [He] had gone wandering about the globe in his ships and had looked with his own eyes upon its furthest corners, its dreamlands—names and places which existed rather as shadows and rumors than as realities."

Henry David Thoreau was also fascinated by the Ex. Ex. "What was the meaning of that South Sea Exploring Expedition," he wrote in the final chapter of *Walden,* published in 1854, "with all its parade and expense, but an indirect recognition of the fact that there are continents and seas in the moral world, to which every man is an isthmus or an in-let, yet unexplored by him, but that it is easier to sail many thousand miles through cold and storm and cannibals, in a government ship, with five hundred men and boys to assist one, than it is to explore the private sea, the Atlantic and Pacific Oceans of one's being alone."

In 1851, Herman Melville published *Moby-Dick,* a novel that in-cludes several references to the U.S. Ex. Ex. More than a decade before, Melville had set out on his own personal voyage of discovery aboard a New Bedford whaleship bound for the very same waters then being plied by the Exploring Expedition. Later, while researching his whaling masterpiece, Melville read Wilkes's narrative of the voyage with great interest. There he learned how Wilkes mercilessly drove his men beyond the edge of their endurance in search of the icy coast of Antarctica. One literary critic has even argued that Melville based his description of Captain Ahab's mythic pursuit of the white whale on Wilkes's search for the white continent.

Every generation has its great men and women, people who, for whatever reason, feel compelled to push themselves to achieve what others might feel is impossible or not worth the effort. Judged by those standards, Wilkes was a great man. But he was also vain, impulsive, and often cruel. Do his personal flaws negate his greatness? As Melville recognized, they were one and the same. "For all men tragically great," Melville writes in *Moby-Dick*, "are made so through a certain morbidness. Be sure of this, O young ambition, all mortal greatness is but disease."

For both Wilkes and Reynolds, the Exploring Expedition would be as much a voyage into the private sea described by Thoreau as it would be a voyage around the world. With their help, perhaps we can gain a new appreciation of an undertaking that should be a recognized and valued part of our nation's heritage. The frontier of Lewis and Clark has long since been civilized out of existence. But as Wilkes and Reynolds came to discover, no one will ever civilize the sea.

A modern rendering of the six vessels of the U.S. Exploring Expedition
assembled at Orange Bay, near Cape Horn, in February 1839. Shown from
the left are the schooner *Sea Gull* at anchor; the flagship *Vincennes* in the
foreground, hoisting out her launch; the schooner *Flying Fish* under way,

shifting her anchoring ground; the sloop-of-war *Peacock* with her hands furling sail; the brig *Porpoise* standing in and shortening sail, preparing to anchor; and the storeship *Relief* in the distance with her upper yards sent down, preparing to distribute provisions.

Part One

CHAPTER I

The Great South Sea

MOST SAILORS did not refer to it as the Pacific Ocean. They called it the South Sea, a name that dated back to 1513 when Vasco Núñez de Balboa ventured across the sliver of mountainous, jungle-choked terrain known as the Isthmus of Panama. The isthmus runs west to east so that when Balboa first glimpsed water, it appeared to extend to the south. Quite sensibly, he dubbed his discovery the Great South Sea.

Seven years later, Ferdinand Magellan and his men, on their way to the first circumnavigation of the world, penetrated the mazelike strait at the craggy bottom of South America. After weathering the terrible gales typical of one of the most inhospitable places on earth, they found themselves in a quiet, vast ocean that Magellan called, with tearful thanks to God, the Pacific—a name that would not catch hold until the mid-nineteenth century.

Balboa found it, Magellan named it, but for any young boy taken with tales of the South Sea—like the young Charles Wilkes—the central figure had to be James Cook. It had been Cook who had first crisscrossed the Pacific, discovering islands at almost every turn. Cook had been a product of the Enlightenment's search for knowledge through the empirical observation of nature. Although not trained as a scientist, he was one of the most expert nautical surveyors in the British navy, a skill that served him well in his voyages to distant lands. First and foremost, however, Cook had been an *explorer*, and the Pacific had served as his route to glory. For the young Wilkes, the South Sea came to represent not only a means of escape from an unhappy childhood but, even more important, a way to win the praise and adulation he had been craving for as long as he could remember.

Wilkes was born to well-to-do parents in New York City in 1798. When his mother died just two years later, he was placed in the care of an aunt, Elizabeth Ann Seton, who would later convert to Catholicism, become an abbess, and eventually be canonized as America's first native-born saint. Wilkes's exposure to sainthood proved short-lived, however. At just four years old, he was sent away to boarding school. When he realized he was about to be abandoned at the school, Wilkes clung to his father's leg and refused to let go. "Young as I was," he wrote, "the impression is still on me & it is the first event of my life that I have any distinct recollection of."

For the next ten years, Wilkes was, in his own words, "a poor castaway boy," attending a series of boarding schools that he hated, always yearning to be at home with the father he loved. The one maternal figure in Wilkes's life was a nanny named Mammy Reed—a fat, dark-eyed Welsh woman who, in stark contrast to his earlier caretaker, had a reputation as a witch. Reed's gaze was so intense that Wilkes claimed, "It was impossible to meet her stare." Reed doted on her "Charley boy," a youngster with a black hole of loneliness at the center of his being. "I had no other companions than my books and teachers," he remembered.

But there was always the sea. Manhattan was surrounded by water, and hull to hull along the waterfront was a restless wooden exoskeleton of ships, their long bowsprits nuzzling over the busy streets, the eyes of even the most jaundiced New Yorker irresistibly drawn skyward into a complex forest of spars and rigging. This was where a boy might turn his back on all that he had once known and step into an exotic dream of adventure, freedom, opportunity, and risk.

The city's wealthiest merchant, John Jacob Astor, had made his fortune with these ships. For Astor, who became known as the Prince of the China Trade, it began, in large part, with sea otter skins procured in the Pacific Northwest—a trade made possible by Wilkes's hero, James Cook. After discovering countless Pacific islands and plunging farther south than anyone else had ever gone, Cook headed out a third and final time in 1776 to find the proverbial Northwest Passage. Earlier mariners had unsuccessfully searched the east coast of North America for a waterway that connected the Atlantic and Pacific Oceans. Cook, by now the most experienced and respected explorer in the world, would try the west coast. As the American Revolution raged on the continent's opposite shore, Cook traded for sea otter skins with Native Americans in the Pacific Northwest. At the time, he had no other intention than to use the skins to manufacture some winter clothing for his crew. Later in the voyage, after Cook was killed by natives in Hawaii, his men sailed for China and were astounded to learn that an otter skin purchased for pennies in Nootka Sound sold for a hundred dollars in Canton.

Internal trade policies made it difficult for English merchants to capitalize on this discovery. Britain's South Sea Company had a monopoly for trade on the west coast of America, while the East India Company controlled the Chinese market. For an English merchant to sell otter skins in China, he had to possess two expensive and hard-to-get licenses. Enter the Americans.

Soon after the secret of sea otter skins was revealed by the publication of the narrative of Cook's final voyage in 1784, American China traders, many of them from Boston and Salem, set out around Cape Horn bound for the Pacific Northwest. In the decades to come, it would be Astor, the New Yorker, who established the first permanent white settlement in the region, known as Astoria on the Columbia River, not far from where Lewis and Clark had wintered in 1805–6. The outpost served as a gathering point for Astor's fleet of ten vessels. One of these ships, the *Tonquin,* became part of the mythology of a frontier that for children of Wilkes's age was what the Wild West would become for subsequent generations of Americans.

On June 5, 1811, the *Tonquin,* under the command of Captain Jonathan Thorn, sailed from Astoria in search of otter skins. Not until more than a year later would the *Tonquin*'s native interpreter Lamayzie make his way to Astoria and tell the tale of what had happened to the missing ship. They had anchored somewhere in the vicinity of Vancouver Island's Clayoquot Sound. Captain Thorn quickly angered the local natives by offering an insultingly low price for their otter skins. The following day, as the *Tonquin*'s crew began to weigh anchor and set the sails, the natives attacked. Almost all the sailors on deck, including Captain Thorn, were bludgeoned and stabbed to death. Some of the men in the rigging were able to lower themselves through an open hatchway down into the ship, where they secured some pistols and muskets and began firing at the natives. Soon they had cleared the decks.

The next morning several canoes made their way to the *Tonquin*. The night before a group of sailors had slipped away in the ship's launch and headed for Astoria. They would never be heard from again. The only man left aboard was a severely injured sailor who did not have long to live. The sailor waited until the *Tonquin*'s decks were thronged with Indians, then took a match to the ship's magazine of gunpowder. The *Tonquin* and approximately a hundred natives were blown to smithereens.

With the outbreak of the War of 1812, when Charles Wilkes was fourteen, a different kind of violence threatened Astor's commercial interests in the Northwest. A British naval vessel was dispatched to the region, and Astor had no choice but to sell his outpost to the English. Closer to home, however, the United States pulled off several stunning victories as the *Constitution* and *United States* bested British frigates in the waters off the East Coast. In the meantime, Captain David Porter rounded the Horn in the U.S. frigate *Essex* and proceeded to wage his own private war in the Pacific. Playing cat and mouse with the British navy, Porter and his men terrorized the enemy's whaling fleet. Porter's swashbuckling exploits climaxed in a bloody encounter with two British frigates off Valparaiso, Chile. Porter was ultimately defeated, but he and his men did much to proclaim America's rambunctious presence in the Pacific.

For a teenager of Wilkes's interests, it was a tremendously exciting time. Today it is difficult to appreciate the level of patriotism commonly felt by those of Wilkes's generation, many of whose fathers were fighting in the War of 1812 and whose grandfathers had fought in the Revolution. Freshly minted naval heroes such as Stephen Decatur and Isaac Hull were regularly fêted in New York, and Wilkes became enamored with the glittering regalia of a captain's dress uniform. Mammy Reed, the Welsh witch, foretold that Wilkes would one day become an admiral. When he pointed out that the U.S. Navy did not grant a rank higher than captain (although the complementary title of *commodore* was used when a captain commanded a squadron), Reed insisted that her prediction would come true.

As the war drew to a close, Wilkes, now sixteen years old, began to press his father to apply for a midshipman's warrant. Under usual circumstances, the Wilkes family had all the social and political connections required to secure such an appointment. Wilkes's mother had been the daughter of William Seton, a wealthy New York merchant; his father was the grandson of an even wealthier British distiller. His father's uncle, John Wilkes, a member of Parliament, had gained international fame for his outspoken support of the American cause during the Revolution. Wilkes's own father, whose middle name was de Pointhieu, had aristocratic relatives in Paris with close ties to the French navy.

But in 1815 not even this impressive pedigree could guarantee a midshipman's appointment. With the end of the war, the navy found itself overloaded with officers. Prospects of peace meant that the number of naval vessels would only decrease. For decades to come the opportunities available to young naval officers would remain disappointingly meager. James Fenimore Cooper, the noted author and a former naval officer who would pen a history of the U.S. Navy, wrote Wilkes's father that there was, Wilkes remembered, "no more likelihood of my being appointed than the heavens should fall to catch larks."

The young Wilkes was receiving little help from his father, who wanted him to become a businessman like himself. By this time, Wilkes was enrolled as a day student at a preparatory school for Columbia College and was showing remarkable promise in mathematics and languages. But no matter how much his father attempted to convince his son that he should stay ashore, dangling before him the prospect of a promising job with his uncle at the Bank of New York, Wilkes's "hankering after naval life & roving life still grew stronger & stronger."

Wilkes began studying with Jonathan Garnett, the editor of the *American Nautical Almanac.* Garnett familiarized the boy with the various mathematical formulae, tables, and solutions associated with navigation; he taught him how to read nautical charts and how to use navigational instruments. He even gave Wilkes his own sextant, which the boy learned how to take apart and put back together. "[B]efore I put my foot on the deck of a vessel," he wrote, "I felt capable of navigating & directing her course." Thus was born an attitude toward the sea that Wilkes would subscribe to in the years ahead: book-learning, at least his version of book-learning, was more than a match for anyone else's practical experience.

Failing to secure an outright commission, Wilkes made an application for a midshipman's warrant contingent on his first gaining relevant sea experience in the merchant marine. Reluctantly, Wilkes's father agreed to let him go, hopeful that the contrast between New York society and the forecastle of a merchant vessel would bring the boy to his senses. "I shall never forget the first time I dressed in my Sailors Jacket & trousers," Wilkes wrote, "the vanity and pride I felt." When he showed the outfit to his father, he was "greatly astonished to see the tears starting from his eyes."

Just a few days into his first voyage aboard the *Hibernia,* one of hundreds of vessels carrying goods and passengers between America and Europe, Wilkes understood why his father had been moved to tears. "A more ignorant and brutal set of fellows could scarcely have been collected together," he remembered. His hands were continually bleeding; his bowels were reacting cataclysmically to the harsh shipboard fare; and even worse, the jacket and trousers he had taken such pride in were smeared with tar. "[C]ould I have set my foot on shore," he wrote, "I never would have again consented to be again afloat."

Despite his suffering, Wilkes could not help but be fascinated by the spectacle of a fully rigged ship under sail. "I had from my reading become acquainted with many of the maneuvers," he wrote, "and took great delight in watching how things were done practically." The captain heard that Wilkes knew how to perform a lunar—a complicated series of observations to determine a ship's longitude that required as many as three hours of calculations and was beyond the abilities of many captains in the merchant service. "[A]lthough I had little practice at sea," Wilkes wrote, "I readily came to take good & satisfactory observations." The captain then proceeded to take credit for the young man's abilities, assuring the paying passengers that he would, in Wilkes's words, "make me a good navigator." Wilkes was infuriated by the captain's deception, but his time would come.

Not long into the voyage, the captain revealed to Wilkes that, incredibly, he had forgotten to bring his charts. He asked the boy if he might be able to draw a chart of the English Channel from memory. Revealing an early willingness to take on a seemingly hopeless task, Wilkes agreed to give it a try. "The next day I was called into the cabin and sheets of letter paper handed me." He hurriedly sketched out a fairly detailed representation of the English Channel—and stunningly, with Wilkes's map in hand, the captain was able to guide the *Hibernia* to Le Havre, France, without incident.

On his return to New York, Wilkes was still angry at the treatment he'd received during the voyage, especially from the captain. He'd been horrified by the ignorance and brutality of his fellow sailors, feeling "great disgust when I looked back on the troubles I had gone through and the low company I was thrown with." For the young Wilkes, it was now a matter of pride. In spite of, or perhaps because of, the adversity he had encountered, he would continue on until he received his commission. Years later he would write, "I have little doubt now that if the treatment I had received had been opposite to what it had been I would have abandoned the idea of following the sea life. I should have seen all its bad features and my tastes were not in unison with it." This was as close as Wilkes would ever come to admitting that his character—at once scholarly, aloof, and condescending—was ill suited to a life at sea.

Not until three years later, after several more merchant voyages, did Wilkes finally receive his appointment in the navy as a midshipman, primarily through the intervention of his father's friend Monsieur Hyde de Neuville, the French minister. After a brief visit to Washington, D.C., to thank de Neuville for his help, Wilkes returned to New York to discover that his father had died. "I never saw him after I entered the

Navy," Wilkes wrote, adding, "I shall not attempt to describe the feelings I experienced . . . and the desolation which home seemed to have undergone." A few weeks later, Wilkes was in Boston reporting to Commodore William Bainbridge and the USS *Independence*.

In Bainbridge, Wilkes found the embodiment of the ideal naval officer. More than six feet tall, Bainbridge radiated an undeniable sense of authority. "His presence was commanding," Wilkes remembered, "and when in full uniform he gave as well as he commanded respect." He was also an officer who was not shy about picking favorites. "He was very decided in his prejudices," Wilkes wrote; "while he encouraged those of whose characters he entertained a high opinion, he was a bitter enemy to the low and vulgar, and no officer could, if he lost his good opinion, expect to regain it." It was a model of command Wilkes would look to for the rest of his life.

Soon after being transferred to the *Guerriere* for a cruise of the Mediterranean, Wilkes discovered that not all naval officers carried themselves with the dignity of Commodore Bainbridge. "Debauchery and drunkenness in a Commander was the order of the day," he later remembered. "[W]hen in port conviviality turned to drunken frolics." In the boisterous camaraderie of steerage, where the midshipmen socialized in "messes," Wilkes–ambitious, solemn, and hardworking–was the odd man out. "I may have had but few friends," he remembered, "but I had no enemies or any that I was not in the best of terms among the officers."

After a nearly fatal bout with what was described as "African fever," Wilkes returned home to New York in 1821. He had been away for more than three years and discovered that since his father's death, "my family had been broken up." His older sister had married and moved to Albany, while two of his brothers, both lawyers, were living in New York. A twenty-three-year-old orphan in search of a home, Wilkes, who as a child had tended to socialize with girls instead of boys, began seeing a woman he had known since he was a child. Jane Renwick, "though not handsome," according to Wilkes, "showed great intelligence . . . and [was] ever open to administer to the wants of others."

The Renwicks had been close family friends of the Wilkeses, and there
had been many times while growing up that young Charles had come
to blows with Jane's brother James over his unmerciful teasing of his sister. For Wilkes, Jane Renwick was the love of his life.

The evenings Wilkes spent over the next few months with Jane and
her mother turned out to be some of the happiest times he had ever
known. "We had a never ending source of amusement," Wilkes remembered. "I often read aloud, and while they read I drew, and the hilarity
and fun was charming." When he received orders to report to the
Franklin for a cruise to the Pacific, Wilkes found it "hard indeed for me
to return to duty and at the same time forego all the delights of the Society of those I was deeply in love with."

The *Franklin* proved to be just the ship for an officer of Wilkes's interests. On the gun deck there was a library, and Wilkes, with the help
of an assistant, became the librarian. But perhaps the best part of the
cruise was its destination: the newly established Pacific Station along
the west coast of South America. Wilkes was about to encounter the
ocean he had been dreaming about since he was a young boy.

When the *Franklin* reached Quilca, Peru, Wilkes was assigned to the
schooner *Waterwitch* with dispatches for General Bolívar in Guayaquil,
Ecuador. They were off the port of Paita when they encountered the
Two Brothers, a whaleship from Nantucket. In most instances naval officers took a dim view of whalemen. Their crews were often as inexperi-
enced as they were undisciplined; the ships smelled of putrid blubber,
smoke, and grease; loaded down with massive brick tryworks, a whaler
presented a most unseamanlike sight as it slogged slowly over the
waves.

The evening before, Wilkes had read an account of the sinking of a
Nantucket whaleship called the *Essex* (not to be confused with the
naval frigate by that name) by an enraged sperm whale. When the captain of the *Two Brothers* introduced himself as George Pollard, Wilkes
realized that he was speaking to the very man he'd been reading about—
the former captain of the *Essex.*

Pollard proceeded to tell the midshipman a story of unbelievable hardship, of how the crew took to their three small whaleboats and, fearful of cannibals on the islands to the west, began to sail against the trade winds for South America, almost three thousand miles away. All three boats would become separated from one another, and as the men began to die of starvation, the survivors realized that they had no alternative but to enact their own worst fears: they must eat the bodies of their dead shipmates. Pollard and a young Nantucketer were eventually rescued almost within sight of the coast of Chile after ninety-four days at sea. "I had by accident become acquainted with a hero," Wilkes wrote, "who did not even consider that he had overcome obstacles which would have crushed 99 out of a hundred."

As it would turn out, several months after his conversation with Wilkes, Captain Pollard once again encountered disaster. At night in a storm to the southwest of the Hawaiian Islands, the *Two Brothers* fetched up on an uncharted shoal. As the ship was being pounded to pieces on the coral, the order was given to take to the whaleboats. Pollard had to be dragged from the deck. The next morning all hands were saved by the whaleship *Martha* and taken to Oahu. Upon returning to Nantucket, Pollard lived out the rest of his life as the town's night-watchman.

What happened to Pollard on his final voyage was a frighteningly common occurrence in the Pacific, an ocean so huge that much of it was not yet adequately surveyed and charted. In addition to unmarked shoals that might crop up almost anywhere, there were hundreds of little-known islands surrounded by reefs of razor-sharp coral. In the absence of a published chart, a captain might rely on a handwritten map given him by a mariner who had recorded his not always trustworthy impressions; often he had only the island's latitude and longitude to guide him.

As a captain approached an unfamiliar shore, he prepared the ship's anchors to be dropped at a moment's notice in case he found himself trapped amid hidden rocks or shoals. He also ordered his men to heave the lead—a tapered cylinder of metal attached to a line marked in fathoms to ascertain the water's depth. In spite of all these precautions, a captain studied the water ahead with an intensity that few landsmen could appreciate, scanning the surface for the dimples and swirls of an otherwise unseen current that might sweep the ship into the coral. He was also on the lookout for a change in color that might presage a sudden and disastrous change in depth. The night Captain Pollard lost his second whaleship in three years, he was standing on the rail, staring down worriedly at the waves after one of his officers reported that "the water alongside looked whiter than usual." Seconds later, the ship slammed into a coral reef that had been impossible to see in the murky darkness.

Two years after Pollard lost the *Two Brothers,* another Nantucket whaleship, the *Oeno,* disappeared without a trace in the Fiji Islands. Nine years later, the ship's cooper, William Cary, returned home to Nantucket and told of how the *Oeno* had been wrecked on an uncharted reef; how the crew had been massacred on Vatoa or Turtle Island, and how only he had escaped by hiding for weeks in a cave. Eventually adopted by a Fiji chief, Cary lived in the islands for several years, doing battle against rival tribes, and meeting, in an incredible encounter, an old schoolmate from Nantucket. David Whippy had deserted from a whaleship several years before and was now an adviser to a chief; and he made it clear to Cary that he was never going back. Not before enduring three more shipwrecks did Cary finally escape the Fijis and return to Nantucket.

Whalemen were not the only ones at the mercy of the uncharted hazards of the South Sea. As the sea otter population in the Northwest dropped catastrophically due to overhunting, New England merchants were forced to look elsewhere for trade goods. In the Hawaiian Islands they found sandalwood, prized by the Chinese for making incense and ornamental boxes. In less than a decade Hawaiian sandalwood was also approaching extinction, so it was on to the treacherous waters of the Fiji Islands, where, in addition to sandalwood, there were plentiful supplies of bêche-de-mer, a sea slug used for soups in China. The deadly reefs surrounding the islands claimed so many ships that it became impossible to buy insurance for a voyage to Fiji. In 1834, the East India Marine Society of Salem made a desperate plea to local and federal governments to provide their sailors with reliable charts: "The Feejee or

Beetee Islands, what is known of them? They were named but not visited by Captain Cook, and consist of sixty or more in number. Where shall we find a chart of this group, pointing out its harbors and dangers? There are none to be found, for none exist!"

American commercial ambition had taken U.S. vessels to parts of the world where not even Cook and dozens of subsequent European exploring expeditions had ventured. Of all the navigators to sail from the United States, it was the sealers who pushed this form of free enterprise exploration the farthest.

Sealers, many of them from Stonington, Connecticut, were a different breed from the sea otter traders. The otter traders never had to get their hands dirty. Sea otters were so difficult to pursue that only Native Americans in their canoes or Aleuts in their kayaks possessed the expertise to capture the fast-swimming creatures. Killing seals, on the other hand, was well within the abilities of any sailor. The rookeries in the Pacific were located on bleak, remote islands where, at least in the beginning, incredible numbers of seals were waiting to be slaughtered and skinned. It is estimated that over three million seals were exterminated on the Juan Fernandez Islands alone in just a seven-year period. In Canton a seal skin sold for in the neighborhood of a dollar, the payment often made in tea.

In the years after the War of 1812, practitioners of what was referred to as "the skinning trade" had reduced the seal population of the Pacific to disastrously low levels, forcing them to sail farther and farther south in pursuit of new rookeries. By 1820, sealers from both Britain and America had reached the South Shetland Islands—an eerie volcanic land of fog, ice, and seals almost six hundred miles below Cape Horn. Although the British claimed the honor of the discovery, the Americans, who subscribed to a policy of secrecy since they knew how quickly an island's seal population could be exterminated, insisted that they had known about the islands all along. In 1820, Stonington sealers took 8,868 skins in the South Shetlands; the next year they returned and killed over 60,000 seals.

It was during this cruise that the twenty-one-year-old Nathaniel Palmer, captain of the forty-seven-foot tender *Hero*, temporarily left the company of the Stonington fleet and headed south in search of new sealing grounds. Not far below the South Shetlands he found a peninsula of rugged land. Surrounded by icebergs and swimming schools of penguins, he followed the coastline south until dense fog—so thick that he could not see the lookout on the forecastle—forced him to turn back. In the early morning hours of February 6, the fog lifted, revealing a surprising sight. On either side of the tiny tender were two Russian exploring ships under the command of Admiral Fabian Gottlieb von Bellingshausen.

The admiral was astounded at the tiny size of the American craft, just a third of the length of his own ship. "It was with great difficulty that I could make the old admiral believe I had come from U States in so small a vessel," Palmer later remembered. Through an interpreter, Bellingshausen told Palmer that previous to being blanketed in fog, he had assumed that he was the first to discover the lands that lay before them. But here was a vessel from America with a captain that was no more than a boy who told of lands even farther to the south. According to one account of the exchange, Bellingshausen told Palmer that "we must surrender the palm to you Americans," adding that he would name the new discovery Palmer's Land in the charts published by his government.

Not until the following century would it be established beyond question that the narrow panhandle of land Palmer had followed south was part of the Antarctic Continent. In the nineteenth century, the general assumption was that what we now call the Antarctic Peninsula was a group of islands just like the South Shetlands above it. There were at least two American sealers, however, who thought differently. In February 1821, Captain John Davis from New Haven and Captain Christopher Burdick from Nantucket independently recorded in their logbooks their suspicions that what they saw to the south was something bigger than an island. On February 15, Burdick wrote, "Land from the South to ESE, which I suppose to be a continent." Eight days earlier, Davis had even gone to the trouble of rowing to shore, and his log provides the earliest documented evidence of a landing on Antarctica. But sealers were more interested in finding seals than in publicizing their naviga-

tional accomplishments. Davis's and Burdick's voyages would go un-
heralded until the 1950s, when their logbooks finally came to the attention of scholars in New Haven and Nantucket.

By the mid-1820s, the South Shetlands had been stripped of seals,
and commercial interest in the region waned. The question of whether
a continent or a group of islands existed to the south would be left un-
resolved for decades to come. In the meantime, the sails of American
whalemen and bêche-de-mer traders continued to whiten the waters of
the Great South Sea. As the need for reliable charts grew stronger, communities up and down the Atlantic seaboard began to insist that it was
time for the U.S. government to catch up to the achievements of its
mariners. In 1828 the citizens of Nantucket drafted a memorial to the
U.S. Congress: "Your petitioners consider it a matter of earnest importance that those seas should be explored; that they should be surveyed
in an accurate and authentic manner, and the position of new islands,
and reefs, and shoals, definitely ascertained."

In the tradition of Cook, it was time America launched an exploring expedition of its own.

CHAPTER 2

The Deplorable Expedition

W ITH THE THREE VOYAGES of James Cook, Great Britain had
set the pattern for future global exploration: two sturdy and
seaworthy ships led by a captain with extensive surveying
experience. By 1804, the exploratory efforts of the world's leading maritime power were coordinated by one man–John Barrow, the second
secretary of the Admiralty. Safely ensconced in his office at Whitehall,
where he remained insulated from the disruptions of political change,
Barrow was free to send out a seemingly continuous stream of won-
drously equipped expeditions. Barrow would remain at the Admiralty
for the next forty-four years, and over that span of time he would dispatch voyages to just about every corner of the world in a deliberate
campaign to extend the bounds of British scientific knowledge and
influence.

The United States, on the other hand, was starting from scratch.
Government-sponsored exploration in America began with Lewis and
Clark in 1803. Although the expedition succeeded in alerting the American people to the promise of the West, no provision was made to do
anything with its results. The journals would remain unpublished for
more than a decade; the botanical collection eventually ended up in England, while other specimens and artifacts were scattered among scientific societies throughout America. From an institutional and policy
point of view, it was as if the expedition had never happened.

In the years after the War of 1812, there were too many distractions
to allow a young, raw-boned nation like the United States to focus on a

project as esoteric as a voyage of discovery in the name of science. There were roads, canals, and railroads to be built, while the obvious sponsor of an expedition–the U.S. Navy–was as conservative an institution as the country possessed. Not founded until 1794, the young navy was reluctant to implement any kind of reform–whether it involved corporal punishment, education, or technology. Even though the United States owed its very existence to the discoveries of Columbus and others, its navy would show a curious and at times infuriating scorn for the concept of exploration.

In 1825 it appeared as if the newly elected president, John Quincy Adams, might goad the nation to action. In his inaugural address he proposed that the United States embark on an innovative program to further the cause of education and science. In addition to a national university and an observatory (which he poetically referred to as a "lighthouse in the sky"), he advocated a voyage of discovery to explore the Pacific Northwest. Congress, unfortunately, refused to fund any of Adams's proposals. If America was ever to follow in the wake of Cook, the impetus would have to come from somewhere beyond the nation's capital.

In 1818, John Cleves Symmes was a thirty-eight-year-old retired army captain living with his wife and ten children in the frontier town of St. Louis. He was a trading agent with the Fox Indians, but his mind was not on his work. Instead, his dreamy blue eyes were often lost in abstraction as he pondered his own theory of the world, a theory that put him at odds with such scientific luminaries as Sir Isaac Newton. But what the largely self-educated Symmes lacked in intellectual credentials, he more than made up for in audacity and pluck.

Symmes had read somewhere that arctic species such as reindeer and foxes migrated north each winter and returned south in the spring, unaccountably well fed and healthy despite having wintered in what most considered an uninhabitable region of frigid temperatures. *Where did these creatures go?* After many years of contemplation, Symmes announced his answer in a single-page circular dated April 10, 1818: "TO ALL THE WORLD! I declare the earth is hollow ..., containing a number of solid concentrick spheres, one within the other, and that it is open at the poles 12 or 16 degrees; I pledge my life in support of this truth, and am ready to explore the hollow, if the world will support and aid me in the undertaking."

Symmes was, by no means, the first to invest the unknown portions of the globe with miraculous properties in the name of science. As late as the midpoint of the eighteenth century, French and English geographers had speculated that an immense and temperate continent known as *Terra Australis Incognita* (The Unknown Southern Land) must exist in the high southern latitudes so as to offset the landmasses to the north and thereby "balance" the earth. But in 1774, when Cook voyaged beyond the Antarctic Circle and found only icebergs and whales, the figment of *Terra Australis Incognita* appeared to have vanished forever.

Symmes believed that beyond the region of ice surrounding each of the poles lay a mild and navigable sea that flowed into a large portal leading to the interior of the earth. He claimed that the crew of a ship sailing to the edge, or "verge," of one of these holes would not even be aware that they had begun to sail down into the earth. On either side of the central hole would be successive layers of land, flourishing with wildlife and, perhaps, people. Because of the earth's tilt, this miraculous new land would be flooded with sunlight. It was up to that former New World, America, to launch the voyage of discovery that would outdo Columbus, Magellan, and Cook.

He was not a particularly good speaker or writer, but Symmes's theory of the "Holes in the Poles" began to find a following. He lectured tirelessly, traveling by horse and wagon across the states of Kentucky and Ohio. There were even some prominent men of science who gave Symmes their cautious approval. Dr. Samuel Mitchell, an astronomer in Cincinnati, Ohio, spoke in support of the theory. A globe patterned on Symmes's ideas became part of the collection at the prestigious Academy of Natural Science in Philadelphia. John J. Audubon sketched Symmes's portrait in 1820, helping to establish his reputation as the "Newton of the West."

In March 1822, Symmes wrote a petition that was presented to Congress by the state of Kentucky. In addition to pronouncing "his belief of the existence of an inhabited concave to this globe," the petition, which was ultimately tabled, called for "two vessels of 250 or 300 tons for the expedition." Thus was born the concept of a voyage that would take another sixteen years to fulfill.

In 1824, during a string of speaking engagements in his native Ohio, Symmes gained the support of an energetic acolyte by the name of Jeremiah N. Reynolds (no relation to Passed Midshipman William Reynolds). Just twenty-four years old, Jeremiah had attended Ohio University before becoming editor of the *Wilmington Spectator.* Soon after meeting Symmes, he decided to scrap his promising newspaper career in favor of a life on the road promoting the notion of a hollow earth. An articulate and charismatic speaker, Jeremiah also had a flair for making influential friends. Symmes's theory began to catch hold as never before, and this improbable duo spoke in sold-out lecture halls all across the United States.

Over time, Jeremiah began to develop a different perspective on his master's theory. Whereas Symmes advocated an expedition north, Jeremiah became increasingly intrigued with the prospect of a voyage south. In 1823, the English sealer James Weddell had sailed farther south than even Cook. Instead of ice he reported to have found open water as far as the eye could see and surprisingly warm temperatures. While Symmes clung to his belief in a hole at the pole, Jeremiah was now willing to entertain the possibility that an American exploring ship might drop anchor at "the very axis of the earth"–an unforgivable heresy as far as Symmes was concerned. In Philadelphia the two visionaries went their separate ways.

Jeremiah continued to broaden his original concept of a voyage of discovery. In addition to searching out the South Pole, the expedition would survey and chart the islands of the South Pacific. This was the voyage that maritime communities in New England and beyond had been pleading for, and Jeremiah soon saw his base of support swell until it had become a force that Washington could no longer ignore. At Jeremiah's urging, marine and scientific societies began to bombard Congress with memorials, and in May 1828, the House passed a resolution requesting President Adams to send a naval vessel to the Pacific. In addition to collecting information helpful to American commercial interests, the expedition was to have a small scientific corps similar to what had accompanied previous European ventures. Jeremiah was designated a special agent to the navy, and in September he filed a report describing more than two hundred uncharted islands and shoals that should be investigated by the expedition. A few weeks later, the 118-foot sloop-of-war *Peacock,* almost completely rebuilt for a voyage of exploration, was launched at the New York Navy Yard.

Despite his earlier connection with the pseudoscientist Symmes (who would die the following year in Ohio, a hollow globe attached to his gravestone), Jeremiah was put in charge of finding a qualified naturalist and astronomer for the voyage. That fall he met with a steady stream of scientists and naval officers interested in joining the expedition. One of the applicants was a thirty-year-old lieutenant named Charles Wilkes.

By the fall of 1828, Charles and Jane Wilkes had been married for two and a half years, their wedding date delayed until Wilkes's promotion to lieutenant in April 1826. Soon after his return from the Pacific in 1823, he attended a public lecture in chemistry. Halfway through the talk, he was startled to see Jane and her mother arriving at the back of the hall. Wilkes sprang to his feet and gallantly offered them his chair and the one next to it. Jane's mother insisted that Wilkes sit with them. "She afterwards told me," he remembered, "that she could no longer endure keeping us apart—our attachment was mutual and of very long standing and had undergone the fullest test."

Wilkes was in no hurry to return to sea. Instead, he was quite content to spend as much time as possible with Jane and her mother while he took in mathematics, languages, drawing, and science. Unlike Cook, Wilkes's pursuit of scientific expertise would keep him on shore. Except for a year-long cruise to the Mediterranean, his voyage to the Pacific as a midshipman would mark his last significant sea experience for the next fifteen years. Instead of the ocean, Wilkes devoted himself to learning how to navigate what was, given the realties of the peacetime navy, the more significant sea: the swirling riptides and shoals of federal politics.

At this time, science in America was largely practiced by amateurs, many of them men of leisure with time to dabble in their favorite disciplines. This meant that someone such as Thomas Jefferson could not only be president of the United States, he could also be one of the foremost scientists in America. No American college offered what we would call today a proper, specialized scientific education. Someone seeking instruction sought out an expert in his field of interest—like Jane's older brother James Renwick, a professor at Columbia College. One of the premier engineers in the United States, Renwick played a large role in Wilkes's education, offering instruction in topics such as astronomy and magnetism as well as introducing him to America's most passionate practitioner of geodesy (the study of the size and shape of the earth), Ferdinand Hassler.

Prior to the War of 1812, the Swiss-born Hassler had been appointed to head the survey of the Atlantic coast—a monumental undertaking for which there was an acute and immediate need. There were no updated charts of the thousands of miles of bays, inlets, and beaches extending from Maine to Florida. In many regions, mariners were still relying on charts created by the British navy prior to the Revolution. But Hassler was much more than a surveyor; he was a proud geodesist who insisted on using the finest instruments from Europe and the latest trigonometric principles to create a survey that would not only be of immense practical benefit but would also represent an important contribution to science.

Such an approach took an enormous amount of time and money relative to the slapdash and often inaccurate chronometric surveys that the nation had, up until this point, relied upon. Hassler's system was based on the creation of a series of huge triangles extending along the entire coastline of the United States. Within these triangles, with sides of approximately thirty miles in length, smaller triangles would be determined, creating the network of reference points required to survey the coast. Before this could be accomplished, however, two baselines of almost nine miles in length had to be established with an accuracy never before achieved in America.

After several years of labor, Hassler had laid the groundwork for a first-rate survey of the coast but had not yet produced a chart. Members of Congress began to insist on tangible results. Hassler's imperious and condescending attitude toward anyone who dared question his methods meant that it was only a matter of time before Congress voted to withdraw its support of the Coast Survey, at least as Hassler had conceived of it, in 1818.

When Wilkes met him in the 1820s, Hassler was struggling to support his large family. With the assistance of Renwick, he had been able to secure some surveying work in the New York area; he also relied on Wilkes's uncle, the banker, to secure emergency loans, using his vast scientific library as collateral. "His forehead was high and his whole expression intellectual," Wilkes remembered. "He was very slovenly in his attire, very old fashioned." Long before there was a national university system to support what would become known as the "mad professor," there was Ferdinand Hassler, and for a number of years he became Wilkes's most influential role model.

In Hassler, Wilkes found a man who refused to succumb to America's long-standing suspicion of the intellectual. "[H]e had a peculiar tone of voice, crackling and Sarcastic, and with a conceit in his knowledge over those who were ignorant of Scientific principles." Although Wilkes saw himself as the rational one in his dealings with the irascible Hassler, the young naval officer seems to have internalized his master's uncompromising arrogance and almost frantic excitability. Just as the strong-willed Hassler had a tendency to create controversy everywhere he went, so would Wilkes develop a similar reputation for inciting turmoil.

Wilkes wanted desperately to be a member of Jeremiah Reynolds's proposed exploring expedition. His unusual naval career was, he felt, ideally suited to such a voyage. In addition to his proven navigational skills and surveying lessons with Hassler, his brother-in-law James Renwick had instructed him in the secrets of the pendulum, a finely tuned instrument used on previous European expeditions to help determine the force of gravity. The fact of the matter remained, however, that Wilkes had not yet established any kind of scientific or, for that matter, naval reputation. And yet, true to his well-to-do background and schooling by Hassler, there was a sense of entitlement about the young naval officer.

Wilkes understood that he was too young to be even considered to command such an expedition. But there had been talk of adding a second vessel. Wilkes made a remarkable proposal to Samuel Southard, secretary of the navy, offering to fund the purchase of an additional vessel—as long as he was given its command *and* was appointed astronomer. "You [may be] unaware that I have commanded a Ship and Schooner towards the same direction the Expedition is to follow," Wilkes wrote, "so I think I am able to take any charge you may assign to me."

When Jeremiah Reynolds finally met Wilkes, he not unexpectedly found him to be "exceedingly vain and conceited." He also complained to Southard that James Renwick had overstated the case for his brother-in-law as an astronomer. "[Wilkes] is [a] deserving young man, and no doubt an enterprising and ambitious officer," he wrote, "but Professor Renwick is puffing him for much more than he is. . . . There is a spirit of dictation about Wilkes and Renwick, that I don't like."

But the expedition of 1828 was not to be. After being delayed into the new year, by which time John Quincy Adams had lost the presidential election to Andrew Jackson, the voyage met the opposition of Senator Robert Y. Hayne from South Carolina, chairman of the Committee on Naval Affairs. Hayne worried that the expedition might encourage the creation of a distant colony, "which could only be defended at an expense not to be estimated." He also pointed out that since the federal government had not yet produced reliable charts of America's own coastline, it was unlikely that an expedition with a handful of men was capable of surveying the entire Pacific. As Lewis and Clark had shown, the country's exploring efforts were best directed toward its own hinterlands. Hayne's views were in keeping with the isolationist sentiment that had brought Jackson to the White House, and the expedition was quickly killed.

That spring Wilkes, by now the father of both a son, Jack, and an infant daughter, Janey, was ordered to join a naval ship sailing for the Mediterranean. In the meantime, Jeremiah Reynolds did his best to put back together the pieces of his shattered dream. If the government would not sponsor a voyage, he would do it through private enterprise. With the assistance and financial backing of Edmund Fanning and some other sealers from Stonington, he formed the South Sea Fur Company and Exploring Expedition. In October 1829, the *Seraph, Annawan,* and *Penguin* set out with Jeremiah, the artist John F. Watson, and the geologist James Eights. Although Eights would eventually publish several important articles based on what he'd observed at the South Shetland Islands, overall, the expedition was a disaster. The seals that were to finance the voyage were few and far between, meaning that the crews, with no prospect of remuneration, had little patience with exploring the frigid waters of the Antarctic Circle. When the men threatened to desert in Chile, the voyage was abandoned.

Wilkes's tour in the Mediterranean proved mercifully brief. Soon after his return to New York, however, he contracted smallpox. Delirious for days at a time, his face a mass of ulcerous lesions, Wilkes, who was confined to his bedroom due to the contagiousness of the disease, "became almost beside myself that I was deprived of the pleasure of my little ones." In December 1831, he was ordered to serve as first lieutenant aboard the *Boxer,* a schooner then at Boston. His poor health made it impossible for him to report for duty, delaying by six years his introduction to a midshipman who had also been ordered to the *Boxer,* sixteen-year-old William Reynolds.

After a convalescence of almost a year, Wilkes received an assignment that was, short of an exploring expedition, the duty he most desired. He was ordered to join a group of five officers working on a survey of Rhode Island's Narragansett Bay. Jane and the children were soon settled in a cottage in Newport. As Hassler's student, Wilkes suggested to the survey's leader, Captain Alexander Wadsworth, that they adopt his master's methods. Before funding had been withdrawn for the proposed exploring expedition back in 1828, Wilkes had been ordered to purchase some surveying instruments. He had taken particular pride in overseeing the construction of a theodolite—a large leg-mounted surveying instrument used to measure horizontal and vertical angles with a telescope. The theodolite was sitting unused at the Depot of Charts and Instruments in Washington, and Wilkes arranged to have the instrument delivered to Newport.

Wadsworth, an officer from the old school, remained reluctant to attempt a survey of the kind Wilkes proposed. Tensions were mounting until Jane interceded on her husband's behalf. Jane was, according to Wilkes, "well posted on the subject," and she soon convinced Wadsworth that her husband actually knew what he was talking about. The couple then offered Wadsworth the use of a room in their cottage as an office for the survey, allowing Wilkes to work up his calculations and draw the charts amid the cheerful bedlam of his young family.

It was during this pleasant interlude in Newport that he responded to a navy circular requesting his ideas on the rehiring of Hassler as director of the Coast Survey. Although praising Hassler's science, Wilkes was highly critical of his teacher's organizational abilities and urged that Hassler be required to report to a board of navy and army officers. When presented with this plan, Hassler refused to work under any supervision. After much discussion, he was eventually hired on his own terms. The reinstated director of the Coast Survey soon learned of Wilkes's disloyalty and let it be known that, in Wilkes's words, "he was not altogether anxious for my services."

Wilkes claimed that he could not have worked with Hassler in any event, but his betrayal of his old friend and mentor would trouble him more than he cared to admit. It also robbed him of a career path that was one of the few in the navy that agreed with his talents and personality. But it was also an object lesson. If the Coast Survey could be resuscitated after a hiatus of more than a decade, then why not the exploring expedition?

✦ ✦ ✦

In the spring of 1833, just a few months after the birth of his third child, Edmund, Wilkes was ordered to Washington to take over the three-year-old Depot of Charts and Instruments. The Depot was where the navy's fifty or so chronometers were tested and maintained. A chronometer is an exceptionally precise timepiece built to withstand the hostile environment of a ship at sea. Set to Greenwich Mean Time, the chronometer enables a navigator to compare the time of the noon sight with the time in Greenwich and then quickly calculate the ship's longitude. Even the most accurate chronometers were not perfect. The trick was to determine how much an individual instrument lost or gained per day, which was known as its "rate," and adjust accordingly. Calculating the rate of a chronometer required several noon sightings at a known location, with the average difference between the chronometer's time and the mean time producing the error of the chronometer. In addition to an office and a room to store the instruments and charts, the Depot included a tiny observatory where the staff could perform the celestial observations for rating chronometers.

Compared to the bustling intimacy of their native New York, Jane and Charles found Washington a virtual ghost town. "There was not an individual stirring," Wilkes remembered, "and the Capitol arose before us in all its blankness, a most uninteresting object it then appeared, lifeless and deserted. . . . The Whole impressed us with the most gloomy foreboding." He and Jane set out to create their own island of happiness within a city that was in 1833 little more than a vast swamp, crisscrossed with dusty dirt roads that became quagmires whenever it rained. Instead of living in the fashionable part of town near the White House, they purchased two large connected brick buildings on windswept Capitol Hill. Built in 1799 with funds provided by George Washington to serve as boardinghouses, the structures possessed more than enough room for a family of five and their servants. Just 1,200 feet from the Capitol, it was the perfect home for a naval officer intent on increasing his influence with the nation's power brokers, and in April, Wilkes moved the entire Depot to his house on the Hill.

At his own expense, he built a new observatory–just a small box, fourteen by thirteen feet and only ten feet high, with two-foot-wide doors on the roof that could be opened to the sky with a system of pulleys. Mounted on granite piers that extended six feet above the floor was a brass transit (an instrument similar to a theodolite that measures horizontal and vertical angles) that Hassler had originally purchased for the Coast Survey back in 1815. The entire building was surrounded by a ditch, five feet wide and deep, to prevent what were termed "the transmission of terrestrial vibrations"–many of them, no doubt, emanating from that big white building atop the hill. Although a meager and unimpressive structure compared to national observatories in England and France, what became known as the Capitol Hill Observatory marked a crucial first step in bringing science to the attention of the federal government.

Wilkes soon found that living on the less fashionable side of town had its advantages. He was able to study at the nearby Library of Congress whenever he wanted, and many members of Washington's society took to stopping to chat with Jane during their morning carriage rides. Perhaps most important to the couple was that this unusual arrangement gave them the opportunity to be a regular part of their children's upbringing. "[W]hat we most valued," Wilkes remembered, "[was that] our Children were Removed from all contact with others, and their lessons & our teaching was Rarely interrupted. This was a great pleasure to us as well as service to them and, as our house was roomy & the garden large, we had the choice of the children to unite with them in their home amusements; at the same time they were under our own eye."

For the next three years, Wilkes and Jane would also make their mark on Washington society, regularly attending parties given by a wide range of foreign dignitaries and government officials. It was commonly said in naval circles that "a cruise in Washington was worth two around Cape Horn," and for Wilkes, this was time well spent.

When Andrew Jackson came to office in 1829 and oversaw the abandonment of John Quincy Adams's exploring expedition, few would have predicted that he would eventually become a fervent advocate of his own voyage of discovery. The president who had railed against the aristocratic merchants of the Northeast, and who portrayed himself as the anti-intellectual advocate of farmers in the South and West, gradually began to see the importance of science and exploration to the United States. Much of his change of heart had to do with the reality of ruling a nation that, like it or not, already had a thriving overseas trade. But there were personal factors as well. Jackson could not help but respect a man like Ferdinand Hassler, who was as ornery and determined as himself. Thus, contrary to all expectations, it was the Jackson administration that presided over the reinstatement of Hassler's Coast Survey. On the diplomatic front, Jackson's combative, highly nationalistic nature made it impossible for him to back away when American interests were challenged abroad, interceding with the firepower required to right any actual or perceived wrongs. It was what one historian has called "a frontier sense of honor" transferred from the backwoods of America to the oceans of the world. And it was the navy that must uphold the nation's international reputation.

In 1831, at Quallah Batoo in Sumatra, a local rajah allowed Malay pirates to attack a Boston ship involved in the pepper trade. Several crewmembers were killed, and the ship was temporarily taken and plundered. In August 1831, Captain John Downes was sent in the frigate *Potomac* to investigate the incident. Instead of demanding restitution and indemnity, Downes chose to launch a full-scale attack. A force of 250 sailors and marines destroyed the fort, burned the town, and killed more than a hundred natives. Although it was clear Downes had exceeded his orders, Jackson publicly praised the mission for having "increased respect for our flag in those distant seas [while providing] additional security for our commerce."

Beating the drum for the United States on this particular operation was none other than Jeremiah N. Reynolds. After the disappointing conclusion of his privately financed exploring expedition, Jeremiah jumped at the chance to serve as secretary to Captain Downes of the *Potomac*. His jingoistic account of the *Potomac*'s mission to Sumatra was published soon after his return to America in 1834. (He would also publish a short story based on a whaling legend he had heard in Chile titled "Mocha Dick, the White Whale of the Pacific," which would later attract the attention of Herman Melville.)

Once back in the United States, Jeremiah seized the day. The nation was in the midst of a period of unparalleled prosperity, and his old friend former navy secretary Samuel Southard was now a senator from New Jersey and head of the Committee on Naval Affairs. The time was right for another attempt at an exploring expedition. As he had done eight years before, he encouraged marine and scientific societies to send petitions of support to Congress, and in March 1836 Senator Southard's committee reported a bill recommending a naval expedition to the Pacific. Two weeks later, on the evening of April 3, Jeremiah addressed Congress in the Hall of Representatives on the subject of the proposed voyage. Fired to an awesome eloquence, he breathed new life into the arguments he had made back in the 1820s. Without once mentioning Symmes, he spoke of the mystery lurking to the south, as well as the continuing need for an expedition as an aid to navigation. But his most passionate plea was in the name of science. His vision of the expedition's civilian corps had expanded well beyond the naturalist and astronomer who were to have sailed on the voyage in 1828.

At a time when a trip to the Pacific was equivalent to a modern-day trip to the moon, a voyage of this kind offered scientists a once-in-a-lifetime opportunity to investigate exotic habitats: rain forests, volcanoes, tropical lagoons, icebergs, and deserts. Before cameras and video equipment, the only way scientists could convey the scope and essence of what had been observed, besides field notes and sketches, was to bring the specimens back with them. Whether it involved shooting and skinning animals and birds, preserving delicate marine organisms in bottles of alcohol, pressing and drying plants, collecting seeds, or accumulating boxes of rocks, soil, fossils, shells, and coral, scientists in European expeditions had inevitably returned with staggering numbers of objects. At the end of the eighteenth century the great German scientist and explorer Alexander von Humboldt had ventured to the interior of South America and proved that a scientist could base an entire career on studying the returns from a single expedition.

Jeremiah Reynolds proposed that America mount an expedition on a scale that had never before been attempted. In keeping with the giant size and boundless ambition of the young nation it represented, the U.S. expedition would "collect, preserve, and arrange every thing valuable in the whole range of natural history, from the minute madrapore to the huge spermaceti, and accurately describe that which cannot be preserved." In addition, the expedition's scientists would study the languages and customs of the many peoples they encountered, while also collecting data concerning weather, navigation, the earth's magnetism, and other fields of interest.

Jeremiah's stirring and patriotic call to science resonated with Congress, and an expenditure of $150,000 was approved in both houses. When a slight ripple of protest arose in the House, his ever-loyal Ohio delegation came to his defense. In response to those who claimed the expedition amounted to a "chimerical and hairbrained notion," Thomas Hamer reminded Congress that the grain-growing states of the West had a "deep interest" in the voyage. America's farmers needed new places to sell their surplus wheat, and the exploring expedition would help to identify potential foreign markets. Hamer's remarks were an indication that all Americans, not just merchants from the Northeast, were beginning to appreciate the importance of the nation's growing economic presence around the world, and it had been the prospect of an exploring expedition to the Pacific that had helped America recognize what its new role had come to be. With his second term ending in less than a year, President Jackson made a personal commitment to seeing that the expedition sailed in the next few months; as early as June 9 he wrote that he was "feeling a lively interest in the Exploring Expedition . . . [and] that it should be sent out as soon as possible."

Jeremiah Reynolds had called for a scientific corps that amounted to a virtual university afloat, with more than twenty scientists engaged in almost as many disciplines. Instead of two ships, the American squadron would have to include at least half a dozen vessels. Assembling a specially equipped squadron of this size would require an immense amount of planning and cooperation on the part of the U.S. Navy. Unfortunately, Secretary of the Navy Mahlon Dickerson shared little of his president's enthusiasm for the voyage. The man who should have been the Expedition's most zealous proponent was, in fact, its principal detractor, applying what little reserves of energy he possessed in deploying strategies to delay its departure.

In 1836, Dickerson, a former governor and senator from New Jersey, was sixty-six years old and in bad health. An amateur botanist and member of the American Philosophical Society, Dickerson did not let his personal interest in science interfere with his commitment to a minimalist navy. In addition to the proposed Exploring Expedition, he successfully fended off efforts to create a much-needed naval academy while offering as little assistance as possible to Captain Matthew C. Perry's nearly singlehanded efforts to demonstate the importance of steam power to the future of the navy.

The Expedition already had a commander, Jackson's old comrade-in-arms Commodore Thomas ap Catesby Jones. A little man who had been permanently disabled by the musket ball he had taken in the shoulder during the Battle of New Orleans, Jones was given sweeping powers by Jackson to assemble the projected squadron, including the flagship *Macedonian*. In a directive that Dickerson would do his best to subvert, Jackson insisted that the secretary not assign any officers to the Expedition to whom Jones had "well-founded objections." Jackson also insisted that Jeremiah Reynolds be included in the Expedition, writing, "this the public expect." Since Jeremiah was a good friend of Dickerson's primary political foe back in New Jersey, former navy secretary Samuel Southard, Jeremiah was a man whom Dickerson was predisposed to loathe. From the beginning, Dickerson did everything in his power to exclude him from the planning of the Expedition.

Dickerson had already asked Lieutenant Charles Wilkes at the Depot to assemble a list of the instruments the Expedition would require. Wilkes, who had been through this once before eight years earlier, quickly drew up the requested list. By the middle of July, he had decided that since the Expedition had taken on a "more enlarged scale than I at first conceived," it would be necessary to go to Europe to procure the necessary instruments. He added that the trip would also provide the opportunity "to obtain a full knowledge of everything that had been already accomplished and attempted in the way of discovery in the Pacific Ocean."

Given that the Expedition was due to leave that fall, a trip to Europe might have seemed out of the question. But Wilkes, who had spent the last four years as the undisputed master of his own private domain at the Depot, was accustomed to getting his way. He also knew that if he could persuade Dickerson to send him to Europe, he–not Jeremiah Reynolds–would become the public face of the Expedition–at least when it came to the European scientific community. On top of that, Wilkes was an ardent Jacksonian Democrat who had carefully cultivated his relationship with the secretary of the navy. Despite Jackson's clearly worded instructions that the voyage must depart soon, Dickerson told Wilkes to sail for England.

When he returned five months later in January 1837, the Expedition was still far from ready. Three vessels had been built, but the large timbers used to strengthen them against collisions with icebergs and coral reefs had made them dreadfully slow and difficult to handle. The selection of officers for the Expedition was going just as badly. Dickerson, in a rare instance of taking the initiative, had recommended two lieutenants–one of whom was Charles Wilkes–to command two of the vessels, but Jones felt that both candidates lacked the necessary sea experience. Although Dickerson finally withdrew his suggestions, in the months ahead he and Jones would continue to squabble over virtually every aspect of the Expedition.

For his part, Wilkes felt that his tour of Europe had been an unqualified triumph. In addition to assembling a first-rate collection of navigational and astronomical instruments from the finest makers in England, France, and Germany, he had become personally acquainted with the scientific greats of Europe, culminating in his being an honored guest at a Royal Astronomical Society dinner. Besides "the great magnetic man," Peter Barlow, known for his pioneering work with compasses, he met Francis Baily, vice president of the Royal Astronomical Society. Baily provided him with two state-of-the-art pendulums and spent several days instructing him in the difficult and painstaking experiments by which the pendulum measures the force of gravity.

Wilkes also met several British naval officers who had led exploring voyages similar to what the United States was contemplating. Robert Fitzroy had recently returned from an expedition to the Pacific that had included a vessel named the *Beagle* and a young naturalist named Charles Darwin. Arctic explorer James Ross, just thirty-five years old, was already known as the discoverer of the earth's magnetic North Pole. In 1831, he had located the place at the edge of the Boothia Peninsula in northern Canada where his dipping needle, a sensitive instrument used to measure the vertical angle of the earth's magnetic field, pointed straight down, and he had planted his country's flag at the magnetic North Pole. Although no one had yet managed to reach the geographical pole, approximately one thousand miles farther north, interest was mounting to find the earth's second magnetic pole, and many felt that Ross was the natural choice to lead a British expedition south.

For an aspiring American scientist and explorer, it was a heady four months among the world's scientific elite. "I feel myself more at ease with *these giants*," Wilkes wrote Jane. He was also convinced he had put together an impeccable collection of scientific instruments. But when he returned to the United States in January, he received little of the praise he had anticipated.

By the winter of 1837, more than a dozen scientists had been chosen for the Expedition. Instead of showering Wilkes with compliments, they were quick to point out that he had neglected to purchase a single microscope, as well as many other instruments required in fields outside the area of his own expertise. After being lionized by the intelligentsia of Europe, it was more than the fiercely proud and sensitive lieutenant could tolerate. When Dickerson finally offered him a position as the Expedition's astronomer, it was under the condition that he report to a civilian scientist who had been a particularly vocal critic of his efforts in Europe. He had been dreaming about sailing on a voyage of discovery for decades, but Wilkes decided he wanted no part of the Expedition as it was presently organized. If he could not go on his own terms, he would not go at all.

✦   ✦   ✦

The spring of 1837 was not good to the Exploring Expedition. In June, Jeremiah Reynolds decided to make public his grievances against the secretary of the navy. In a series of scathing letters published in *The New York Times,* he excoriated Dickerson, eventually forcing the secretary to respond with two letters of his own. This war of words did neither man credit, serving only to further tarnish the image of what one wag renamed "the Deplorable Expedition." In the meantime, the Expedition was denied the services of one of the most talented writers in the country when political infighting made it impossible for the friends of Nathaniel Hawthorne to secure him a position as the voyage's historiographer.

In May, the Panic of 1837 struck the nation's economy. For the last six years, state governments had been piling up huge debts to finance the construction of canals and railroads. Land speculation was rife all over the nation, and imports were outpacing exports. Much of America's economic expansion had been made possible by English capital, and when a financial crisis rocked Europe, many British creditors called in their loans. On May 10, banks in New York suspended the payment of coined money. Soon banks across the country were closing their doors. Just a few months into the presidency of Jackson's handpicked successor, Martin Van Buren, the American economy was in chaos. In this climate of frightening loss and uncertainty, the U.S. Exploring Expedition, a tenuous enterprise in the best of economic times, struggled to become a reality.

Wilkes decided it was time to embark on a new endeavor. That spring he proposed that the Depot of Charts and Instruments sponsor a survey of Georges Bank, a 10,000-square-mile section of tumultuous shoal water approximately a hundred miles off Cape Cod. A prime fishing ground, the Banks were notoriously dangerous. To provide an accurate chart of this serpentine-shaped shoal would be an immense service to mariners throughout the region. For a thirty-nine-year-old lieutenant who had not commanded a ship in *fourteen years,* it was a challenging test. It also happened to be an assignment that would demonstrate whether he had the ability to coordinate a survey of the kind that would make up the primary mission of the Exploring Expedition, and on June 14, Dickerson granted his request.

Saying good-bye to Jane and the children, Wilkes traveled to the navy yard in Norfolk, where the eighty-eight-foot brig *Porpoise* awaited him. He planned to employ what was, for the American navy, a new and revolutionary system of surveying known as the quincunx method. Dickerson had given him permission to borrow some of the instruments he had purchased in Europe. Using two schooners and a fleet of whaleboats, along with specially designed buoys equipped with flags, he and his officers would create a series of interlocking triangles with sides of between a half-mile and three miles in length. Their positions would be established by chronometer and later confirmed by the celestial observations of Professor William Bond at Harvard. The small open boats would be used to measure soundings on shoals that, in some cases, were only a few feet below the water's surface.

It took longer than he had expected, but Wilkes was able to complete the survey in two months. Sometimes deploying all eleven whaleboats at one time, he insisted that his officers and men meticulously survey even the roughest portions of the bank. No one would improve on Wilkes's work at Georges Bank until well into the twentieth century.

In September, he and his officers returned to the Boston Navy Yard to finish the necessary calculations and to work on the chart. Word of Wilkes's survey quickly reached the acknowledged master of American navigation, Nathaniel Bowditch. As a young sailor, Bowditch had taught himself enough mathematics and astronomy to uncover more than eight thousand errors in the leading navigational guide of his day. In 1802 he came out with his own guide, *The New American Practical Navigator,* immediately recognized as the most accurate and comprehensive text on celestial navigation ever published. At sixty-four, he was revered in maritime circles as the paramount navigator in the world.

Wilkes was invited to Bowditch's home in Boston, and once in the presence of his idol, the normally self-assured naval officer found himself "greatly abashed." The two men went for a walk, and Bowditch questioned Wilkes about the survey. Placing his cane in the lieutenant's hand, Bowditch asked Wilkes to draw a diagram in the dirt. "Oh, I see, I see," he replied, nodding his head. "That will do."

Several days later, Bowditch and a friend appeared unannounced at the navy yard to inspect Wilkes's chart. Wilkes would later remember what followed as "one of the most gratifying incidents of my life": "The large and rough chart was spread out on the table with each and every station occupied. He took out from his vest pocket a hand full of small change, five & ten cent pieces, and put them on each station on the chart; these were numerous. Then he explained the whole process [to his friend]. . . . [A]fter fully examining all our work which was recorded in a large volume . . . , he passed a very complimentary speech as to the satisfaction he had derived from the whole." Bowditch subsequently contacted several important government officials about Wilkes's skill as a surveyor. "To him I think I owe, in part," Wilkes later wrote, "my appointment to the Command of the Ex. Ex."

In the months after completing the survey of Georges Bank, some of Wilkes's staunchest advocates proved to be the passed midshipmen who had served under him. Instead of ruling over his officers in a manner that inspired fear and trembling, Wilkes had acted as if he were one of them. He had accompanied them in the whaleboats and had taken the lead when confronting the worst portions of the Bank. A commander usually dined alone in his cabin; Wilkes chose to mess with his officers in the wardroom. This appears to have fostered a remarkable sense of loyalty and enthusiasm, and most of Wilkes's passed midshipmen would follow him to his next assignment—a survey of the waters in the vicinity of Savannah, Georgia.

There was one young sailor, however, who chose not to make the voyage south. Charles Erskine, sixteen, had served as Wilkes's cabin boy. One of five children, whose father had abandoned the family when he was still an infant, Charlie was strikingly handsome, with bright blue eyes and an infectious smile. Late in life, Wilkes would remember him as "one of the most beautiful boys I ever beheld. . . . [T]hough lowly bred, he had a certain refinement of manner and look that drew all hearts towards him." Wilkes took such a keen interest in the boy that for a time aboard the *Porpoise* he became the father figure Charlie had never known.

The falling out came in Boston, Charlie's hometown. They were at the navy yard completing the chart of Georges Bank. Wilkes was anxiously awaiting orders from Washington, and Charlie was directed to make a quick trip to the post office on the other side of the Charles River. On his way back, Charlie decided to stop by his mother's house for a surprise visit. "I shall never forget her fond embrace," he later wrote, "and the 'God bless you, my darling boy!' when I left her." While he waited to cross the river to the navy yard in Charlestown, his hat, along with the letters he had carefully placed inside it, was knocked into the water by a schooner passing through the drawbridge. By the time he'd recovered his hat, the letters were wet but still readable.

When Charlie reached the *Porpoise*, Wilkes was waiting for him, with "a look as dark as a thunder-cloud." Wilkes asked what had taken him so long. Charlie explained that his hat and the letters had been knocked into the river. Wilkes suspected that Charlie had taken the opportunity to enjoy himself in Boston and decided to teach the boy a lesson. Before Charlie knew what was happening, the boatswain's mate had laid him across the breech of a cannon and begun whipping his backside with the colt—a three-foot length of half-inch rope. "[W]e were lying not more than a quarter of a mile in a straight line from where my mother lived," he remembered, "and if she had been at an open window at the front of the house she could have heard my piercing cries." Charlie would not be able to sit for three weeks. His white duck trousers had been cut through by the colt, and threads of cloth were stuck to his ripped and bleeding flesh. "When I shipped [on the *Porpoise*] I had made up my mind to try to be somebody and to get ahead in the world," he wrote, "but now my hopes were blasted. My ambition was gone, yes, whipped out of me—and for nothing."

By the brutal standards of the U.S. Navy, there had been nothing unusual in Wilkes's treatment of Charlie. Many a ship's boy had been whipped for far less. But Wilkes had not consistently operated by the usual standards of the navy. As had been true with the passed midshipmen aboard the *Porpoise,* he had been more of a friend and mentor than a commander to Charlie. When all was going well, this approach made for what was known as a "happy ship." But when a sailor needed to be disciplined, it could all fall apart. Since he considered himself the commander's friend, the sailor tended to resent any attempt to curb his conduct. Long after Charlie had been reassigned to another vessel, he continued to harbor a deep and obsessive hatred for the commander to whom he had once been so close. If he ever got the chance, Charlie vowed he would have his revenge.

Against all odds, the Exploring Expedition seemed about to depart in the fall of 1837. The squadron was now in New York, with more than five hundred officers, sailors, marines, and scientists awaiting orders to sail. The necessary modifications to the overbuilt vessels had been made. The flagship *Macedonian* had been outfitted with an innovative forced hot-water heating system in anticipation of the Antarctic cold. A new kind of foul weather clothing coated with India rubber had been delivered. There was also a new kind of firearm—a pistol equipped with a Bowie knife that could be used both as a form of defense against hostile natives and for hacking through underbrush. For a city suddenly gripped by economic depression, the Expedition was, at least for a time, a welcome distraction. When some of its naval officers made an appearance at a play, the actors stopped the performance to give "the Lions of the day" three cheers.

But no matter how desperately Commodore Jones might labor to bring the Expedition to fruition, a new problem inevitably threatened its dissolution. Distracted by his feuding with Dickerson, he had failed to take note of an important fact. The instruments that Wilkes had assembled more than a year ago were spread out over three cities. Some of the chronometers were at the Depot in Washington. Other instruments were at Professor Renwick's in New York, still others in Philadelphia, and then there were all the chronometers and sextants Wilkes had taken with him to survey Georges Bank. For Jones, this was the last straw. By mid-November his health had begun to suffer from what he called "the pain, expense, and mortification, to which I have been daily subjected for the last eighteen months." He was now regularly coughing up blood. On November 21, he resigned his command.

Jones was the most conspicuous example of how "this great national enterprise" could destroy a person. In the absence of any proper institutional support, the Expedition had become a kind of vortex in which petty personal and professional differences, aggravated by competing political alliances, swirled in a dangerous whirlpool. In waters this fierce, only an individual of extraordinary resilience, passion, and determination had any hope of survival. In his letter of resignation, Commodore Jones complained of "the most determined and uncompromising opposition to me and to my plans up to the latest moment. . . . As regards to myself, I am but the wreck of what I was."

As if to mock the difficult birth of the American Expedition, word reached Washington that a new French squadron had left Toulon in August. In addition to exploring dozens of Pacific islands, the French, under the command of the veteran voyager Dumont d'Urville, planned to sail as close as possible to the South Pole.

By the winter of 1838, President Martin Van Buren had come to the belated realization that his secretary of the navy, Mahlon Dickerson, was not capable of successfully organizing the Expedition. In an extraordinary move, he put his secretary of war, Joel Poinsett, in charge of finding a commander. Poinsett, a former congressman from South Carolina, was well educated and had traveled extensively. As minister to Mexico, he had been responsible for bringing the poinsettia, the flower that bears his name, to the United States. He also had a reputation for getting things done.

But not even Poinsett could easily fix the Expedition. Over the course of the next few weeks, every navy captain he contacted ultimately refused his offer of command. The Expedition had become an embarrassment, a sure way to scuttle a promising career. On February 9, John Quincy Adams visited Poinsett at the War Department. Now a representative from Massachusetts, the former president had seen his dreams of a similar voyage dashed back in 1828. "I told him," Adams recorded in his diary, "that all I wanted to hear about the exploring expedition was, that it had sailed."

Soon after, Poinsett found an officer of suitable seniority willing to consider the possibility of leading the Expedition. Captain Joseph Smith said he'd agree to it if he could have Wilkes as a surveyor. "I think it would be advisable to order Lieutenant Wilkes to report himself to your department at Washington without delay," Poinsett wrote Dickerson on March 1.

Little did anyone suspect that in less than a month, it would not be Captain Smith who would be appointed leader of the nation's first exploring expedition, but a forty-year-old lieutenant who was more accustomed to a desk and an observatory than to the open sea. For Charles Wilkes, the voyage was about to begin.

CHAPTER 3

Most Glorious Hopes

WASHINGTON IN THE SPRING OF 1838 was full of distractions for a young naval officer. But William Reynolds (no relation to the beleaguered Jeremiah N. Reynolds) was a most bookish passed midshipman. Instead of attending the teas and dances to which he received regular invitations, he preferred the Library of Congress. When he wasn't working at the Depot of Charts and Instruments, he could be found, he wrote his sister Lydia, in the "long spacious room" of the nation's library, perusing lavishly illustrated volumes of Audubon, Shakespeare, and Cervantes.

But he was lonely. "[T]his is all very pleasant," he confided to Lydia, "but I want someone to talk to about what I have seen & what I have read." His two best friends in the service, John Adams (nephew to the former president) and William May (son of the Washington doctor who had once been George Washington's personal physician), had recently left town, and he was now "almost totally without society."

Just the year before, the three officers had attended naval school together. Prior to the creation of the academy in Annapolis, midshipmen first went to sea for several years before learning what was known as the "philosophy" of their calling. Reynolds was one of forty-five midshipmen assigned to the Gosport Ship Yard in Norfolk, Virginia, where they attended lectures by day while studying in nearby boardinghouses by night. Adams had been Reynolds's roommate. May had lived in the next room down the hall. Of the threesome, May was the ladies' man. Handsome and impulsive, he had already fought at least one duel. For his part, Reynolds stayed true to his studious self while in Norfolk. In a letter to Lydia, he claimed to be "perfectly indifferent to the attraction of the fair ladies. . . . [W]hile I remain *here*, my book, the immaculate 'Bowditch,' the Midshipman's Bible, will be the only object."

Reynolds's affections may have already been spoken for. In an earlier letter to his sister, he objected to her concern about being seen with a girl named Rebecca Krug, who lived just down the street from the Reynolds family in Lancaster, Pennsylvania. Lydia had explained that if a young woman spent time with the sister of an eligible young man, it was generally assumed that the woman and man must be engaged. "Why Good God," William wrote, "it's absurd to think of such a thing, no one would say so, & if they did, why then, what matter who would believe them on such a foundation." (Despite his protestations, Reynolds would later prove to have more than a neighborly affection for Rebecca Krug.)

By May of 1837, William and the rest of his class were in Baltimore, nervously awaiting their examinations. The first midshipman to be examined failed, or "bilged," after a grueling seven hours of interrogation. As it turned out, both Adams and May bilged, while Reynolds earned the rank of passed midshipman.

The following winter, after a brief stint aboard the newly launched *Pennsylvania*–at 210 feet and 3,104 tons displacement, the largest ship in the U.S. Navy–Reynolds enjoyed an extended stay at home in Lancaster. William was the second oldest of eight children. His father, a former newspaper publisher and state legislator, was now managing an ironworks in nearby Cornwall, Pennsylvania, where the family had taken up residence. It had been his father's good friend Congressman James Buchanan who had secured Reynolds's midshipman's appointment back in 1831, and William's younger brother John was now a cadet at West Point. Of his seven brothers and sisters, it was Lydia, three years his junior, to whom Reynolds was closest. In addition to his usual letters, William often included enclosures for Lydia that were not to be shared with the rest of the family. So it was not unusual that, without his friends Adams and May to talk to in Washington, Reynolds turned to

Lydia soon after reporting to his new assignment: the Depot of Charts and Instruments.

On April 20, the very day Reynolds reported for duty at the Depot, Charles Wilkes was approved by President Van Buren as commander of the U.S. Exploring Expedition. Most members of the service viewed the appointment of so junior an officer as an insult to the navy–even though all previous, more senior candidates had refused the position. But Reynolds was inclined to think differently. His friend William May had served with Wilkes during the survey of Georges Bank. May had nothing but good things to report about his young commander.

Perhaps inevitably, Reynolds began to consider volunteering for the impending Exploring Expedition. Since the Depot was located on the grounds of Wilkes's house, he had already had ample opportunity to meet the new leader of the Expedition. "I like Captain Wilkes," he told Lydia, "which is important (to me)." May was planning to get over a recent love affair by shipping out on the Ex. Ex. "It is most likely, I shall bear him company," Reynolds wrote, "though I may not share his desperate motives."

On May 13, he wrote Lydia from the office of the observatory. "I cannot give up the Exploring Expedition," he declared. "I shall offer myself to Captain Wilkes today or tomorrow, therefore be ye all prepared." As if to emphasize the strength of his resolve, he sealed the letter with Wilkes's own family crest. "The seal," he explained to Lydia, "is Mr. Wilkes coat of arms, a Norman cross bow." With this wax seal the destinies of William Reynolds and Charles Wilkes would be joined for the next four years.

Back in March, when Wilkes had first received orders to return to Washington, he did not want to leave the *Porpoise* and his young and enthusiastic group of officers. After their success at the Georges Bank, they were continuing to do excellent work on Georgia's Calibougue Sound. The orders simply said to proceed without delay to Washington. "What could it mean?" Wilkes wondered out loud. When one of his officers suggested that it might have something to do with the Exploring Expedition, Wilkes shook his head. "Oh no, I have done with it and [am] content to let it alone."

Within a few days, Wilkes was back in Washington, where he learned that Captain Joseph Smith, the latest candidate to lead the Exploring Expedition, had requested that he accompany him as a surveyor. Wilkes would be given command of his own vessel. But he still had his reservations. Smith was not in good health. In addition, many of the officers Smith would inherit from Commodore Jones were senior to Wilkes and would quite naturally object to their junior being elevated to such a high post. After talking it over with Jane, he decided to have nothing to do with an expedition led by Smith.

It is impossible to know if Wilkes anticipated what happened next, but when Smith learned that he would not have Wilkes as a surveyor, he–like so many captains had done before him–declined the offer to command the Expedition. Soon after, Secretary of War Poinsett began to consider offering the post to Wilkes. Even though the lieutenant lacked comparable command experience, he was clearly a competent surveyor. And besides, who else was there? The navy rumor mill would later accuse Wilkes of having schemed to wrest the command from Smith, but Wilkes insisted, "I never thought of such a thing. I was too young an officer to aspire and did not dream of it."

On an evening in March, Poinsett requested that Wilkes meet with him at his home. The two men sat beside the fireplace in Poinsett's parlor. The secretary began by asking Wilkes to describe how he thought the Expedition should be organized. It was, of course, a topic that he had been considering for most of his life. The squadron should be made up of only young officers with the technical training required to conduct a nautical survey. The scale of the Expedition must be reined in. Instead of large and unwieldy ships, a brig similar to the *Porpoise* and several even smaller schooners should be used; they were the only craft suitable for surveying the coral-fringed islands of the South Pacific. As part of this reduction in scale, the scientific corps must be cut by at least two-thirds to less than a dozen men.

Poinsett asked if he thought an expedition along the lines he'd just described could be quickly and successfully organized. Wilkes insisted that it could. Poinsett had been staring at the fire; he now turned to look directly at Wilkes. "I have been authorized by the President," he said, "to offer you the command of the expedition." Wilkes was unable to respond. "Why do you hesitate?" Poinsett asked. "Are you afraid to undertake it?" Wilkes struggled for words. "No sir, but there are very many reasons that crowd upon me why I should not accept it." They continued to talk, and once Poinsett made it clear that he would have almost total control in organizing the Expedition, Wilkes tentatively accepted the appointment. "[I]t was so entirely unexpected," he remembered, "I [told him] I must have time to think the matter over."

That night Wilkes and Jane had what he later described as "a good cry." Jane assured her husband that he had acted honorably throughout these difficult proceedings and that he would "establish a name which both she and our children would glory in." When they finally went to bed, Wilkes almost immediately nodded off. But Jane could not sleep. Her husband would soon be leaving on a voyage that would last at least three years, and Jane, already a mother of three, was five months pregnant.

Almost immediately, enormous pressures came to bear on Poinsett to rescind Wilkes's appointment. The young lieutenant might be one of the navy's top surveyors and a creditable scientist, but this meant nothing to the naval officers who outranked him, almost all of whom, it seemed, joined in a shrill chorus of dissent. Letters of outrage poured into the War Department. "The year Lieutenant Wilkes entered the Navy," Captain Beverley Kennon wrote Poinsett, "I was the third lieutenant of the *Washington* 74; the year he was made a lieutenant, I commanded a ship of war in the Pacific Ocean." Kennon insisted that *he* be given the command. But Kennon had already been offered the position, only to refuse it back when the voyage had become a laughingstock. But now, with a lowly lieutenant given the command, it was no laughing matter. The navy's pride was at stake.

Wilkes was not without his proponents. In a most extraordinary gesture of support, Joseph Smith, the captain under whom Wilkes had refused to serve, wrote to wish the lieutenant well. Smith reported having been roundly criticized by "his brother officers" for providing Wilkes with the opportunity to gain the command. But he assured Wilkes that no "blame can attach to you." "I hope now you will be off & off soon," he wrote. "I have faith in your acquirements of science, in your industry & in what is still more important, *your boldness of purpose & boldness of execution.* I wish you all success & every propitious breeze."

The controversy made its inevitable way to Capitol Hill. During a debate over a naval appropriations bill in April, a congressman brought up Wilkes's appointment, calling it "a violation of rank." Another congressman pointed out that the rules of seniority applied only in a time of war. It was only right that someone of Wilkes's scientific expertise be appointed to the command. Even the sainted James Cook had been "made a Lieutenant for the purpose" of leading an exploring expedition. Yet another congressman claimed that a reputable source had told him that Wilkes had been appointed because he had agreed to dismiss Jeremiah Reynolds, who had become "obnoxious to the Department." So it went, a ceaseless din of outrage that would continue long after the squadron had sailed.

Wilkes might have easily been overwhelmed by the pandemonium. But by keeping the details of the Expedition to himself and Jane and by focusing solely on the tasks ahead of him, he plowed ahead. First he had to determine what vessels were to be included in the squadron. Two sloops-of-war, the 127-foot *Vincennes* and 118-foot *Peacock,* were already slated to be part of the Expedition, as was the 109-foot storeship *Relief,* the only vessel remaining from Jones's original squadron. In keeping with what he had outlined to Poinsett, he added three smaller vessels— the 88-foot brig *Porpoise* and two 70-foot schooners, former New York pilot boats that were rechristened the *Flying Fish* and the *Sea Gull.*

What Wilkes needed to find as quickly as possible were commanders for the *Peacock,* the *Relief,* and the *Porpoise* who did not outrank him, not an easy task given his lowly place on the list. He first appealed to Lieutenant William Hudson from Brooklyn, New York. Although with-

out any surveying experience, Hudson, forty-four years old, had a reputation as an excellent seaman and had already expressed interest in joining the Expedition back when Jones was to be the leader. He was also
one of Wilkes's closest friends in the navy. Unfortunately, even though
Hudson and Wilkes had been promoted to lieutenant on the same day,
Hudson ranked slightly above his putative commander, and to serve
under a junior officer was unheard of. Only after Poinsett had assured
Hudson in writing that the Expedition "was purely civil" did he agree to
take the position.

Wilkes's choice to command the *Relief* was another old friend,
Lieutenant George Blake, who had served with him during the survey
of Narragansett Bay. When it looked like Hudson might not sail with
them, Blake asked Wilkes if he would make him second-in-command.
Wilkes equivocated, and Blake decided to back out of the Expedition altogether. This forced Wilkes to go with Lieutenant Andrew Long, the
man Jones had chosen for the *Relief* and who only agreed to the position once Wilkes had promised that the commander of the *Porpoise*
would not outrank him. Wilkes chose Lieutenant Cadwallader Ringgold, thirty-five, from a prominent Maryland family. With the loss of
Blake, Wilkes was left without a single commanding officer with previous surveying experience.

Wilkes claimed that his most difficult task involved the scientific
corps. He must eliminate twenty of the twenty-seven scientists. First to
go was the head of physical sciences. Wilkes would take over that department, along with all subjects related to surveying, astronomy, meteorology, and nautical science. It was a tall order for one man, even
without the extra burden of leading the Expedition. Wilkes's choices for
the rest of the corps proved to be quite good. The naturalist Titian
Peale, son of the famous painter and museum founder Charles Willson
Peale from Philadelphia, had already accompanied expeditions to
Florida and the West. A capable artist and a crack shot, Peale was a collector par excellence. James Dwight Dana, the Expedition's geologist,
was just twenty-five and had already published his *System of Mineralogy,*
the standard text on the subject. In the weeks before the squadron's departure, he would undergo a sudden religious awakening and, at the

urging of his evangelical parents, join the First Church of New Haven. Dana was destined to become a giant in his field, and while his Christian beliefs would sometimes lead his science astray, the strength of his conversion appears to have made possible the startling breakthroughs that awaited him, encouraging him to look beyond the myriad details of the natural world and seek out the bigger picture. "As a Christian," the geologist James Natland has written, "Dana could now make bold his science."

Dana's friend the botanist Asa Gray was also chosen for the civilian corps, and like Dana, would rise to the top of his field. Unfortunately, after changing his mind several times, Gray would back out of the Expedition at the last minute and be replaced by the lackluster William Rich from Washington. Rounding out the scientific corps was the young philologist, or linguist, Horatio Hale from Harvard; the naturalist Charles Pickering from the Academy of Natural Sciences in Philadelphia; the conchologist (a collector of mollusks and shells) Joseph Couthouy from Boston; and the horticulturalist William Brackenridge, a Scotsman currently living in Philadelphia, who had once supervised Edinburgh's famed botanical garden. It was a young, diverse group that, for the most part, represented the best American science had to offer in 1838.

Over the next five months, Wilkes pushed to achieve what others had failed to accomplish in two years. Each vessel needed to undergo extensive modifications; equipment and provisions must be arranged for; commissioned and noncommissioned officers, as well as sailors and marines, had to be selected. Hundreds of men had already been recruited by Jones, but the months of turmoil and indecision had taken their toll as they bided their time at navy yards in Virginia and New York. But it was the Expedition's officers who were the most disaffected. Indeed, from Wilkes's perspective it sometimes seemed as if the entire U.S. Navy were in league against him. "At times I felt almost overwhelmed at the Situation and the responsibilities upon me," he wrote, "but they were of short lived depressions."

It was in the fitting out of the *Vincennes* and the *Peacock* at Norfolk that Wilkes received the stiffest resistance. The commodore in charge of the navy yard made it clear that he and his officers did not approve of Wilkes's appointment and would do as little as possible to assist in the preparation of the squadron. Appealing to friends at navy yards in New York and Boston, Wilkes was able to procure much of what was denied him at Norfolk. From Boston he received a fleet of whaleboats, while the two schooners were purchased and modified at the New York Navy Yard in just two weeks.

Still, when it came to overhauling the *Vincennes* and the *Peacock*, which were to be equipped with additional spar decks built over the preexisting gun decks, Wilkes had no choice but to deal with the refractory officers in Norfolk. Making it all the more difficult was the temporary loss of his most stalwart advocate, Secretary of War Poinsett. In April, Poinsett was struck down by an illness that, it was feared, might kill him. This meant that Wilkes had no one to turn to when his request to replace some of the vessels' iron water tanks with wooden casks was refused. (If one of the ships was wrecked on a reef, Wilkes argued, the wooden casks would provide more buoyancy than the tanks and could be more easily transferred to shore.) So Wilkes took his grievances to the president of the United States.

Martin Van Buren, known as "the little magician," appeared quite pleased to see Wilkes. He quickly promised to get him his water casks. Then he asked a question: "Why is there such opposition against you?" Wilkes said he thought it had to do with his being so junior a lieutenant. Van Buren told him that over the last few weeks he had been visited by a virtual parade of captains protesting his appointment. Just that morning Commodore Isaac Chauncey, president of the Navy Board, had urged him to suspend Wilkes. The commodore had claimed that "this young Lieut[enant] did not ask nor would he receive any advice which had been proffered him. No one knew what he was doing." Van Buren assured Wilkes that he had his total support and encouraged him to "come direct to me" if he encountered any more trouble.

+   +   +

In addition to preparing six vessels for a voyage around the world and recruiting the necessary officers and men, Wilkes had to prepare the instruments, including twenty-four chronometers. As head of the physical sciences department, he also had several pendulum experiments to conduct before the Expedition could sail. A pendulum is used to determine the force of gravity; by comparing different readings at different locations around the globe, it is possible to determine the contours of the earth, as well as the density of its interior. In the grass field that stretched from the back of his house to the Capitol building, Wilkes erected "Pendulum Houses," temporary shelters that would accompany them on their travels. To assist him, Wilkes assembled a group of six passed midshipmen, including William Reynolds, William May (who had successfully retaken his examination), and several others from the *Porpoise*. For Wilkes, this little community of science on a hill, so near to his own home (where Jane was now almost eight months pregnant), seems to have provided a haven from the storm.

With departure set for August 10, Reynolds wrote his sister Lydia to ask for her help in preparing the clothing he would need. He had left a pair of his red cotton drawers at home, and he requested at least eight more just like it. He also put in orders for eighteen pairs of thin cotton socks, twelve calico shirts, two bedsheets, four pillowcases, and six woolen stockings. He asked that she find his white hat; he would need it to shield himself from the brutal Polynesian sun. He fully expected the voyage to transform him into "a weather beaten, wrinkled, uncouth savage. [M]ay you all have a pleasant time in civilizing me [on my return]."

Every third night, Reynolds and May stayed up until four in the morning, assisting Wilkes with his observations while the other four passed midshipmen split the other two nights between them. "The nights pass most swiftly & pleasantly," he wrote. "Everything is so interesting & occupies the attention so entirely that time flies. I breakfast at the fashionable hour of 12." For Wilkes it meant that he was almost never asleep, and Reynolds and the others developed an almost reverential awe of their commander. "I like Captain Wilkes very much," Reynolds wrote Lydia. "He is a most wonderful man, possesses a vast deal of knowledge, and has a talent for everything."

As he had told Poinsett, Wilkes planned to rely on a corps of young, energetic officers who had just passed their examinations. On most naval vessels, a passed midshipman was relegated to a subordinate role, but on the Exploring Expedition a different standard would prevail. "[T]he Passed Midshipmen will perform the duties of Lieutenants," Reynolds excitedly wrote Lydia. Wilkes felt it was important that the more senior passed midshipmen be given acting appointments, temporary promotions that reflected their increased responsibilities during the voyage. Soon after Poinsett had been struck down by illness, Mahlon Dickerson was replaced by James Paulding as secretary of the navy. In July, Wilkes asked Paulding to grant the rank of acting lieutenant to ten of the passed midshipmen. Unfortunately Reynolds and May were too far down the list to be included.

Wilkes was under the impression that Poinsett had already agreed that he and his second-in-command William Hudson would be given acting appointments as captains. Since it would leapfrog both of them past the rank of commander, the appointments would undoubtedly infuriate the already irate navy hierarchy. But it would have been just as scandalous to place the nation's first exploring expedition, a squadron comprising six vessels and several hundred men, under the command of a mere lieutenant.

The issue of rank had become a matter of deep concern in the U.S. Navy. In Britain and France, an officer could aspire to the rank of admiral, but in the United States he could rise no higher than captain, with the title of *commodore* being given to a captain who commanded a squadron. When an American naval officer encountered a European officer of equivalent age and experience, he was inevitably outranked—a difficult and often embarrassing situation for an officer attempting to uphold the honor of his country. But it wasn't simply a question of creating the proper impression in foreign ports. If an officer was to maintain discipline among his own officers, he needed to outrank them. Due to the backlog in promotions in the peacetime navy, many lieutenants were placed in the unenviable position of commanding officers of their own rank. "It poisons the very fountain of discipline," an anonymous naval officer insisted in a widely read article of the day, "and never fails

to bring forth insubordination—letting loose among the crew those refractory and evil spirits, which discipline alone can chain down." Wilkes
was not out of bounds in expecting an acting appointment to captain.

Unfortunately, Poinsett's illness made it impossible for Wilkes to
confirm his understanding about this critical issue. Assuming the promotions would be forthcoming, he instructed his purser to pay both
himself and Hudson as captains. In the middle of July, Poinsett had recovered enough to resume his former duties. To Wilkes's shock and disappointment, the secretary of war backed away from what Wilkes felt
had been an earlier promise to make him a captain. Wilkes attributed
the change of heart to Poinsett's illness, claiming that his "boldness and
grasping of thought . . . had been greatly weakened." He could only
hope that as the day of the squadron's departure approached, Poinsett
would make it right.

Counseling him on this and many other issues was Jane. It is clear
that her influence extended well beyond mere pillow talk. Wilkes regarded her as his "assistant" and at one point suggested (only half
jokingly) that she and the children might accompany him on the Expedition. "I only wish I could have you as my second in command," he
wrote from Norfolk in July, "and all would go well. What think you of
rigging yourself in men's clothes . . . and all our chicks as little middies
[and then] embarking with me." When on July 19, Jane gave birth to
their fourth child, Eliza, it meant that, at least for a time, she must concentrate on other things besides her busy husband and his voyage.

On the day of Jane's delivery, Wilkes sat down to draft a long and
impassioned letter to Poinsett. Now, more than ever before, Wilkes realized that if he was to bear the full weight of his command throughout
the long, arduous voyage that lay ahead, he needed an acting appointment to captain. He understood why Poinsett was reluctant to give him
the acting appointment he deserved. The secretary had already suffered
the wrath of nearly the entire department by appointing him to lead the
Expedition. But a promise was a promise. "[O]n this I did rely," Wilkes
wrote. If he had suspected he would not be awarded an acting appointment, he would have never agreed to command the Expedition. The
following week, President Van Buren was scheduled to travel to Norfolk

with Poinsett and Paulding to review the fleet. Wilkes felt it would be only appropriate if the acting appointments were made official during that ceremony.

On July 26 President Van Buren and his retinue arrived at Norfolk. Colorful signal flags fluttered from the rigging. All the officers, the full marine detachment, and the marine band were lined up on the quarter-deck of each vessel. Aloft, the enlisted men, in white duck trousers and blue jackets, stood on the yards and booms, facing the president. Since the chronometers had not yet been brought aboard, Wilkes allowed the guns to fire a salute.

About sixty people sat down to a "bounteous lunch" in honor of the Expedition. (Although Commodore Lewis Warrington and the other officers of the navy yard had been invited, none of them chose to attend.) Toasts were delivered. Much wine was drunk. "It was a well timed encouragement," Wilkes remembered, "and showed that, however the officers [of the navy yard] might feel themselves opposed to it, the Gov[ernment]t gave me its full Sanction."

But instead of elation, Wilkes felt a gloom settling over him. Apparently, the acting appointments were not forthcoming–at least not that day. When Poinsett praised the progress that had been made so far, Wilkes responded "that I was not deceived or to be humbugged by such things."

By the beginning of August, Jeremiah Reynolds, the Expedition's original promoter, realized that he was about to be left behind. Dozens of letters, many of them from his supporters in Ohio, had been written insisting that he be included, but Jeremiah's most articulate defender was the writer Edgar Allan Poe. Poe had become so fascinated with Symmes's and Jeremiah's earlier claims about the holes in the poles that he had written several short stories and even a novel, *The Narrative of Arthur Gordon Pym*, that referred to a mysterious opening at the bottom of the earth. Poe would later pay tribute to Jeremiah's role in instigating the Expedition: "Take from the enterprise the original impulse which *he* gave–the laborious preliminary investigation which *he* undertook–the unflinching courage and the great ability . . . by which *he* ensured its consummation–let the Expedition have wanted all this, and what would the world have had of it but the shadow of a shade?" In the years ahead, Jeremiah would insist that Wilkes–that "cunning little Jacob"– had schemed along with Dickerson to deny him his due. But long before Wilkes was named to the command, Jeremiah had been foolish enough to take on the secretary of the navy in the pages of *The New York Times*. As Jeremiah knew better than anyone, the politics of the Ex. Ex. had been part chess game, part internecine warfare, and the only man left standing after a decade of struggle was Charles Wilkes.

In the meantime, the *other* Reynolds was busy preparing for the voyage of his dreams. In early July, Passed Midshipman William Reynolds had briefly visited his family in Lancaster. After picking up his clothing and other supplies, he traveled to Norfolk to join the squadron. By August, the departure date had been pushed back to the middle of the month.

Reynolds was in charge of purchasing food for his mess, the group of officers with whom he would be sharing meals for the foreseeable future. On August 12, he wrote Lydia telling her he had been "most busily and arduously engaged in Expending $1000 for the Mess & $600 for myself: we have a great many stores, and I flatter myself that the mess over which I preside will be the most respectable, tasty, and somewhat stylish." He would be sharing a stateroom with his best friend May on the Expedition's flagship, the *Vincennes*. May, who had been assisting Wilkes, had not yet arrived from Washington, leaving Reynolds to prepare their living quarters. Although it was not yet finished, he claimed the room "will be carpeted, cushioned, curtained (one set crimson damask, one white), mirrored, silver candlesticks, etc. etc.–a little *boudoir*, most exquisitely luxurious in its arrangements."

The squadron was now, for the first time, fully assembled, and Reynolds was delighted by the addition of the two schooners, just delivered from New York. "Passed Midshipmen will command them," he enthused to Lydia. "I wish my rank would entitle me to one. '[T]is something to be a Captain [the title applied by courtesy to any commander of a vessel], and those Boats are large, beautiful & swift–perhaps I may return *Captain* Reynolds."

He was also fascinated by the most unusual passengers who would be accompanying them on the voyage: the "Scientifics." "I like the associates we shall have during the cruise, these enthusiastic artists, and those headlong, indefatigable pursuers & slayers of birds, beasts & fishes & gatherers of shells, rocks, insects, etc. etc." What particularly interested Reynolds about these men was that it was not the promise of glory or wealth that had inspired them to sail on a voyage around the world, but their thirst for knowledge: "They are leaving their comfortable homes to follow the strong bent of their minds, to garner up strange things of strange lands, which proves that the ruling passion is strong in life. . . . We, the ignoramuses, will no doubt take great interest in learning the origin, nature & history of many things, which we have before regarded with curious and admiring eyes." To make sure he had an adequate record of his experiences, he purchased two large journals. "[I]f I fill them," he told Lydia, "I trust I shall make a perusal interesting."

In a hasty addendum written the following evening, his enthusiasm was even greater than the day before. "I am perfectly charmed with everything on board," he gushed, "& have the most glorious hopes of a most glorious cruise. [N]othing could tempt me to withdraw. I am wedded to the Expedition and its fate, sink or swim."

On August 10, it was time for Wilkes to head to Norfolk. "I will not soon forget the scene at the Breakfast table," he wrote Jane the next day, "with your dear self and little Eliza at your breast & those other children around. It was enough to have halted any man [even] if his heart had been made of stone and [has] made me cry a dozen times since. How much comfort & happiness I have left behind." He was leaving not only his wife, but his best and perhaps only true friend, a person with whom he had lived and worked for most of his adult life. Wilkes knew that when he returned in three to four years, his youngest daughter Eliza would have no memory of her father.

By Sunday, August 12, he was in his freshly painted cabin aboard the *Vincennes,* awaiting the sailing orders he had already drafted but which needed to be formally issued by the secretary of the navy. Wilkes would not have been faulted if he had taken time that evening to bask in the glory of his achievement. He had done all that he had promised he would do. Despite almost every kind of opposition, Wilkes had assembled a squadron of six vessels and 346 men. Almost miraculously, he had succeeded in turning around the Expedition's morale. Instead of the nest of intrigue and mistrust it had been just a few months before, the squadron was now characterized by an extraordinary eagerness and zeal. Years later, William Reynolds would remember the astonishing sense of promise he and his fellow officers felt at the voyage's onset.

> The Commander of the Expedition was hailed by all his subordinates, with an *éclat* that must have touched his feelings. The impression in his favour was universal, and the most unlimited confidence as to his abilities as a leader, and his character as a man, was the deep and proper feeling of those who were to trust to him so much. Not a few were bound to him with a personal devotion that was almost chivalrous in its extent, and which had been created by a recent association with him on a perilous service, the survey of a bank in the open ocean. The fervour of these gentlemen, communicated itself to others, who with the ardour of youth, and the impulse of their nature, were ready to believe that the object of such generous promise must be the very *beau ideal* of a Captain for the hazardous enterprise in which they had embarked.

But Wilkes was in no mood to enjoy the marvel he had created. He had heard nothing about his and Hudson's acting appointments. In a final, now blighted gesture of optimism, they had brought with them new captain's uniforms, each equipped with two epaulet straps instead of a lieutenant's one and a round jacket with four buttons over each pocket flap. It was humiliating to have to tell Hudson that they could not yet put them on. It was not a matter of ceremony; the acting appointments were absolutely vital if he was to lead this squadron. With a hurt that still festered decades later, he remembered in his *Autobiography* that he needed the rank of captain "to give force to my position and surround me with, as it were, a shield of protection."

Desperately missing his wife and children, and without this crucial vote of confidence from the secretary of war, Wilkes was being abandoned to his fate, just as his own widowed father had done back when he was four years old. "I hope you will never feel the mortification that I do at this moment," he wrote in a final letter to Poinsett, "at being left now to grapple with things that the Govt. might have put under my entire control by the one act of giving Mr. Hudson and myself temporary acting app[ointment]ts for this service and which I consider was fully pledged to us. . . . I have one consolation left that everything that we do earn by our exertions will be due entirely to ourselves."

By the morning of Sunday, August 18, the squadron had weighed anchor and made sufficient progress that it was time to bid farewell to the pilot. Later, the pilot would report that the sight of six naval vessels, all under full sail in a light breeze on a sunny summer day, was "highly pleasing," especially since he had never seen officers "more bent on accomplishing all within their power for the honor and glory of the navy and of the country."

As he stood on the quarterdeck surveying the squadron behind him, Wilkes could not help but feel self-doubt. Like it or not, he *was* just a lieutenant, with less sea experience than many of his passed midshipmen. "It required all the hope I could muster to outweigh the intense feeling of responsibility that hung over me," he wrote. "I may compare it to that of one doomed to destruction."

Part Two

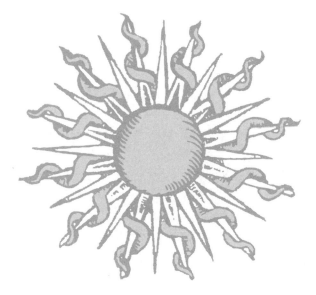

CHAPTER 4

At Sea

WILKES'S FLAGSHIP was one of the most beloved ships in the U.S. Navy. Beamy, yet surprisingly fast, the 127-foot sloop-of-war *Vincennes*, built in 1826, would so impress her new commander in the months ahead that he would boast that she could "do everything but talk." In 1830, the *Vincennes* (named for the Revolutionary-era fort for which the present-day Indiana town is named) became the first U.S. naval vessel to circumnavigate the world; six years later she completed her second trip around the globe. Since then the *Vincennes* had been put in dry dock and given a complete overhaul. Painted black, with a white interior, she was now, according to First Lieutenant Thomas Craven, "the finest looking ship I ever saw." Built atop the *Vincennes*'s original aft cabin, once described as "a pavilion of elegance," was a new thirty-six-foot-long space that significantly increased the ship's functionality. In addition to staterooms for Wilkes and several scientists, this new stern cabin contained a large reception room equipped with drafting tables, a library, and a large conference table. The stern cabin would serve as the command center of the squadron for the duration of the cruise.

Sailing close behind the *Vincennes* was another, slightly smaller sloop-of-war, the 118-foot *Peacock*–named to commemorate the victory of the USS *Hornet* over HMS *Peacock* during the War of 1812. Originally built to be the flagship of the abandoned 1828 expedition, the *Peacock* had seen plenty of hard service over the intervening decade. Just the year before she had been nearly lost at the mouth of the Persian Gulf.

After sixty hours of being pounded on a reef, she had been finally floated free, returning to Norfolk several months prior to the departure of the Ex. Ex. Given the lack of attention the *Peacock* had received at the navy yard, Lieutenant Hudson was deeply concerned about his ship's condition. For now, he took some consolation in the hope that with her armament reduced, the *Peacock* might find an extra knot or two of speed.

The storeship *Relief* was the one vestige of Jones's botched attempt to mount an expedition. To all appearances she was the gem of the squadron. Comfortably fitted out, and with the latest technical innovations, including two Spencer trysails (fore-and-aft sails equipped with gaffes to assist in sailing close to the wind), the *Relief*'s hull shape was that of a packet—the speedy American design developed to carry passengers to and from Europe. Unfortunately, the *Relief,* like the other vessels built specifically for the Expedition, had been woefully overbuilt, and she was anything but fast.

Next, under the command of Lieutenant Cadwallader Ringgold, was the *Porpoise,* the rakish brig that had served Wilkes so well at Georges Bank and Savannah. Almost as new as the *Relief,* the eighty-eight-foot *Porpoise* was having no problem keeping up with the squadron's flagship—a pleasant surprise given that the brig had been outfitted with additional fore-and-aft decks. Bringing up the rear of the squadron were the schooners *Flying Fish* and *Sea Gull,* commanded by Passed Midshipmen Samuel Knox and James Reid, respectively. Some critics had claimed these slender, seventy-foot New York pilot boats, each with a crew of just fifteen men, would never survive the rough waters off Cape Horn. There was no denying, however, that the schooners were just what Wilkes needed when it came to surveying the islands of the Pacific. Equipped with tillers instead of wheels, these highly maneuverable craft were also surprisingly fast, and the *Flying Fish* and the *Sea Gull* were beginning to surge past the much larger *Relief.*

It was an unusual collection of sailing vessels. European exploring expeditions had relied on sturdy but slow ships such as colliers, built to carry coal from the northern ports of England, or, in the case of the latest French expedition, a beamy horse-transport, euphemistically referred to as a corvette. Not only could these vessels bear heavy loads of provisions and men; they could withstand punishment from uncharted hazards such as rocks and ice. Since the initial fleet of heavily reinforced vessels had proven unseaworthy, the Americans had been forced to settle for this eclectic assortment of ships, brigs, and schooners. Sleek and quick, instead of broad and strong, the vessels of the U.S. Exploring Expedition made for an inspiring sight as they glided away from Hampton Roads.

The U.S. Ex. Ex. carried with it the expectations of a young, upstart nation that was anxious to prove it could meet and perhaps surpass what had already been achieved by dozens of European expeditions. But, as all of the Ex. Ex.'s officers and scientists knew, it was very late in the game to be launching an expedition of this scale. The potential for new discoveries in the Pacific was limited, and European scientists were highly skeptical that anyone from the United States might return with significant results. Then there was the potential for disaster—losing a ship, even the entire squadron, in a storm off Cape Horn or on a hidden reef in the Pacific. But it was the prospect of sailing amid the icebergs in this fragile hodgepodge of a fleet that was the most daunting. "On me Rested everything," Wilkes wrote. "I communed with myself under very distressing thoughts."

His instructions called for a three-year dash around the globe. In the next five months alone he was to investigate a group of "doubtful" shoals in the middle of the Atlantic Ocean, provision at Rio de Janeiro, survey the mouth of the Rio Negro in Patagonia, then, after establishing a base of operations at Cape Horn, lead a portion of the squadron on the first of two assaults on the Antarctic regions to the south. To avoid being frozen in for the winter, he was instructed to return to Cape Horn no later than early March 1839.

Then it was on to the Pacific. The squadron would provision in Valparaiso, Chile, then proceed to the Navigator, Society, and Fiji groups—surveying islands all the way—before assembling at Sydney, Australia, in the late fall of 1839 to prepare for yet another push south. By March they would be on their way back north. After provisioning at the Hawaiian Islands, they would continue on to the northwest coast of America in the summer of 1840, where they were to pay particular attention to the Columbia River and San Francisco Bay. But even if they had reached their native continent, they would be farther away from home than at any time during the Expedition since their instructions required them to proceed west to the United States—a voyage of at least 22,000 miles. After stops at Japan and the Philippines, it was on to Singapore, the Cape of Good Hope, and, finally, New York City, which Wilkes hoped to reach by the summer of 1841, almost exactly three years after leaving Norfolk.

As was customary on previous European exploring expeditions, Wilkes kept his instructions a secret throughout the voyage. If circumstances required that he depart from the original plan, he did not want his officers second-guessing him; so he gave them a minimum of information. Even now, with the coast of Virginia rapidly receding behind them, no one except himself and Jane back home in Washington knew where the squadron was headed.

The direction of the prevailing winds required them to sail a zigzag course to Brazil, heading east and south toward Africa, before sailing west and south across the equator to Rio de Janeiro. Wilkes determined to sail first for the island of Madeira, about four hundred miles off Morocco. There the squadron would gather at Funchal Roads before continuing south to the Cape Verde Islands and then on to Brazil.

Wilkes was well aware that if they were to reach Cape Horn by December, time was already running out. Over the next few days it became clear that a fast passage south would be virtually impossible. The *Peacock* was in much worse condition than he and Hudson had originally suspected. Once the squadron had entered the swell of the open ocean, the *Peacock*'s seams began to leak so severely that Hudson was forced to chop a hole in the berth deck to drain it of water. It would require several weeks of repairs at Rio de Janeiro to make the vessel seaworthy. Then there was the matter of the *Relief.* The sluggish storeship soon proved to be a virtual sea anchor, slowing the squadron's progress to a crawl. Just four days out from Norfolk, Wilkes ordered Lieutenant Long to bypass Madeira and the Cape Verde Islands and proceed directly to Rio.

After pushing himself so hard all spring and summer, Wilkes found these new and unexpected problems particularly difficult to bear. The squadron was barely out of sight of land, and already he was exhausted. "[T]he fatigues of all are now and then too much for me," he admitted in a letter to Jane.

Still uppermost in his thoughts was Poinsett's refusal to make Hudson and himself captains. It cast a pall over everything. Wilkes decided that they needed to do something to distinguish them from the other lieutenants in the squadron. If they couldn't wear their captain uniforms (with an epaulet on each shoulder), then they would modify their lieutenant uniforms. Instead of epaulets on their left shoulders, both Wilkes and Hudson would do without epaulets altogether. But if their uniforms were without visible indications of rank, Wilkes insisted that his officers refer to them not as Mr. Wilkes and Mr. Hudson–the way you addressed a lieutenant–but as Captain Wilkes and Captain Hudson.

He then decided he should have a flag lieutenant, an executive secretary who would be responsible for everything from carrying sensitive messages to making dinner arrangements. Overton Carr had been with him at the Depot even before the survey of Georges Bank. Short, boyish, and unfailingly loyal, Carr was the perfect yes-man, and he became Wilkes's flag lieutenant. If the politicians in Washington wouldn't do it, Wilkes would provide himself with the necessary trappings of command.

He soon discovered what so many new captains had learned before him: life was very different in the aft cabin of a man-of-war. For one thing it was lonely. As the leader, he was expected to establish a certain distance between himself and his officers. When he appeared on the quarterdeck, his officers were expected to tip their caps and leave him to the solitude of the weather rail. Except for the occasional nights he invited a few officers to dine with him, he ate alone in his cabin. Most captains had learned how to adjust to the isolation and responsibility of command through years of experience at sea, but Wilkes had seized this position of authority almost overnight. He had not had the time and opportunity to establish a style of command appropriate to a voyage around the world.

There was no right or wrong way to lead a ship and a squadron—every captain had his own approach, depending on his talents and temperament. Some, with Nelson being the most famous example, used the power of their personalities, as well as their considerable skills and physical courage, to inspire their officers and men to do their bidding. Some relied on the threat of the lash; others might employ a well-timed joke. Cook, though he carefully monitored his crew's health, was also renowned for his "paroxysms of passion." A seemingly insignificant incident could cause him to curse, flap his arms wildly about, and stamp repeatedly on the deck. Whatever the command style, consistency was essential to successful leadership. As long as the officers and men knew what to expect, they could adapt to just about anything. But if the officers' and crews' expectations should go unfulfilled in any significant or even insignificant way, the complex interpersonal chemistry of a crowded ship could be quickly and irrevocably altered, transforming a vessel that had once operated like a well-oiled machine into a pressure cooker about to explode.

In the beginning, Wilkes seems to have employed the only command style with which he had any recent experience—the genial approach he had used during the survey of Georges Bank. Just as he had once messed with his officers aboard the *Porpoise,* he frequently left his cabin to socialize in the *Vincennes*'s wardroom. As if to distract himself from the immensity of the challenges ahead, he directed his attention to the more easily managed details of shipboard life. He embarked on a personal campaign to rid the officers' pantries of spiders. Every day the leader of the U.S. Ex. Ex. would venture into his officers' quarters to search out and squish these annoying creatures. When some of the officers began to grow facial hair, he concocted elaborate schemes to convince them of the inappropriateness of the practice without directly forbidding it. When the ringleader, Lieutenant Johnson, finally shaved off his mustache, Wilkes "rejoiced with others that this speck of discord had vanished," adding in a letter to Jane that "I shall be quite adept in studying characters before I get back." It was a petty but telling incident that indicated the lengths to which Wilkes was willing to go to avoid even the hint of conflict with his officers—at least for now.

At this early stage in the voyage, William Reynolds and his compatriots were too enthralled with the grandeur of the undertaking to regard Wilkes as anything but the dashing and inspirational leader of the youngest naval squadron any of them had ever known. "It is so strange to me to look around and find none but youthful faces among the officers," Reynolds wrote Lydia, "a young Captain, with boys for his subordinates—no gray hairs, no veterans among us." Since they were all so young, they were given responsibilities that would have normally been at least three, even four years away. Reynolds was appointed an officer of the deck, an honor usually reserved for a lieutenant. With a speaking trumpet held to his lips, he issued the orders that kept the twenty sails of the *Vincennes* drawing to maximum advantage. "I cannot explain to you the feeling," he enthused to Lydia, "for though we only take advantage of or oppose the wind and waves, it seems as if we directed them. . . . To handle the [sails'] fabric with exquisite skill, to have hundreds move at your bidding, to run in rivalry and successfully with the Squadron and passing vessels, to laugh at the wind and bid defiance to the waves, ah! The excitement is good and glorious. . . . *My* proffession, above any other in the world. Hurrah! For the Exploring Expedition!"

Reynolds also took great interest in the scientists assigned to the *Vincennes:* the bespectacled naturalist Charles Pickering, the broad-shouldered Scottish gardener William Brackenridge, and the bearded collector of mollusks Joseph Couthouy. Although Couthouy had once been a merchant captain, the others were no sailors, and it was taking these studious landlubbers some time to adapt to the cramped quarters of a tossing ship. In spite of all, they created their own wonderfully weird worlds within their staterooms, stuffed till nearly bursting with specimens and artifacts. Reynolds marveled at the "dead & living lizards, & fish floating in alcohol, and sharks jaws, & stuffed Turtles, and vertebrates and Animalculae frisking in jars of salt water, and old shells, and many other equally interesting pieces of furniture hanging about their beds, & around their state rooms." For his part, Reynolds enjoyed slightly more sumptuous quarters. His and roommate William May's stateroom had become the talk of the *Vincennes*. White and crimson curtains now hung from the bulkhead; silver candlesticks and a mirror adorned the bureau; a Brussels carpet lay across the deck while a cutlass and one of the new Bowie knife pistols gave the room a "man of war finish."

Reynolds and May were part of Wilkes's inner circle of half a dozen or so acting lieutenants and passed midshipmen, who had either served with him on the *Porpoise* or assisted at the Depot of Charts and Instruments. During the early days of the voyage, this core group of officers, whom Wilkes referred to as "our Washington folks" since they had spent considerable time that summer making observations on the grounds of his Capitol Hill home, served as a kind of surrogate family for the Expedition's commander. In a letter to Jane he recounted the time when Reynolds and May, who shared a watch together, had breakfast with him in his cabin. The two handsome and dark-haired officers, who looked so much alike that they could have been brothers, insisted that "it was not possible for them to be more comfortable and contented."

In addition to Reynolds, May, Flag Lieutenant Overton Carr, and Wilkes's second-in-command William Hudson, his trusted circle of officers included Lieutenants Robert Johnson, William Walker, and James Alden, along with Passed Midshipmen Samuel Knox, who commanded the schooner *Flying Fish*, and Henry Eld, serving under Hudson in the *Peacock*. Wilkes's most intimate associate on the *Vincennes* was the purser (the naval equivalent of a comptroller), Robert Waldron. Waldron had been with Wilkes on the *Porpoise* and spent an hour of just about every evening in Wilkes's cabin, gossiping about the latest goings on among the officers and men. Also part of this group was the commander's teenage nephew, Wilkes Henry, the eldest son of his widowed sister Eliza. Henry had been his personal clerk aboard the *Porpoise*, and Wilkes had secured a midshipman's appointment for the boy so that he could accompany him on the voyage. Overall, Wilkes was pleased with the group of officers he had assembled. "[Y]ou will be glad to learn," he wrote Jane, "that we have got along very smoothly thus far, and that they one and all exhibit the greatest desire to do their duty."

Charlie Erskine couldn't believe it. Almost a year after being whipped by Charles Wilkes, the boy was once again under his command. That summer Charlie had been reassigned to the *Porpoise,* then at New York and being outfitted for the Expedition. As long as he could stay on the *Porpoise* and have nothing to do with the squadron's leader, he figured he would be safe. But on the morning of August 17, as the squadron prepared to set out from Norfolk, Wilkes's gig came alongside the *Porpoise* with orders for Erskine to join the *Vincennes.* Unaware of his former cabin boy's feelings toward him, Wilkes wanted Charlie to serve on the flagship. "I felt more like jumping overboard than sailing with my worst enemy," Charlie remembered. He begged Lieutenant Ringgold to let him remain on the *Porpoise,* but Ringgold told him he had no choice but to get into the gig.

Once on board the *Vincennes,* Charlie was promoted to mizzen-top man. "I liked my station, the ship's officers, and the crew," he remembered. But at Sunday service the next day he found himself staring across the quarterdeck at Charles Wilkes. "[W]hen I saw him, it made me revengeful," he wrote, "and I felt as if the evil one had taken possession of me."

It was Charlie's first experience aboard a full-rigged ship. Unlike the sloops, schooners, and brigs on which he had previously served, the *Vincennes* possessed three masts and three decks–the spar, gun, and berth decks. The crew of two hundred men was divided into sixteen messes, twelve men in a mess. While the officers ate on tables set with plates, forks, knives, and spoons and employed servants to attend to their personal needs, Charlie and his messmates sat on a piece of canvas spread out on the deck and ate their salt beef out of two wooden tubs known as kids. When not eating or on watch, Charlie slung his hammock from a beam that was just four and a half feet above the deck, with only twenty-eight inches between the sailors on either side of him. As he and the rest of his watch rocked to the creaking sounds of a wooden ship at sea, Charlie found himself reliving the punishment he had suffered at the hands of Wilkes. "I only wish I could forget the past," he wrote, "and that it might not so constantly haunt me."

Eleven days after leaving Norfolk, at midnight on August 29, Charlie came on deck to relieve the lookout on the lee quarter. There was a slight swell, but little wind. While walking the *Vincennes*'s deck, Charlie paused to look down the cabin skylight. Sitting at the table was "the man who had ordered me to be flogged." Even at this late hour, Wilkes was awake, studying a chart. Charlie remembered the sting of the colt as if he had been punished yesterday.

The officer of the deck began to walk forward, leaving Charlie alone beside the skylight. Stacked on a nearby rack were some belaying pins—iron cylinders to which were fastened the ropes of the ship's running rigging. As if in a trance, he found himself reaching for one of the belaying pins and holding it over the skylight. If he waited another second, the roll of the ship would bring Wilkes's head directly beneath the heavy iron pin. But just as he was about to drop the pin through the pane of glass, Charlie was transfixed by a vision of his mother. "My God!" he gasped. "What does this mean?" Greatly shaken, he returned the belaying pin to the rack, unable at first to disengage his fingers. The officer of the deck sang out through his speaking trumpet, "A bright lookout fore and aft!" Charlie blurted, "Ay, ay, sir," and the *Vincennes* sailed on for Madeira, her officers and men oblivious to how close they had come to losing their commander.

On September 6, a low, dark object appeared on the horizon. Word quickly spread through the *Vincennes* that a wreck had been sighted, and soon all hands were on deck. Spyglasses were traded among the officers, each one reporting on what he saw. One claimed he saw a bare mast extending above the waterlogged hull; another said he saw people standing on the deck, waving in distress.

But as the *Vincennes* bore down on the distant object, it was realized to be a huge tree, its sun-bleached branches raised high in the air. It was a cottonwood that had drifted on the Gulf Stream all the way from the Mississippi River. Two boats were dispatched to investigate, and soon the entire squadron had assembled around the tree. The men in the boats discovered a large school of fish hovering among the tree's submerged, barnacle-encrusted branches, and as they harpooned specimens for the scientists, the nimble *Sea Gull* tacked and jibed amid the fleet with what Reynolds called "a graceful beauty in her motion and appearance that is indescribable, but which to the eye of a Sailor is lovely to behold."

The two schooners had come to be regarded as, in the words of another officer, "the *pets* of the squadron." Their refined fore-and-aft rigs not only made them lovely to look at, they enabled them to sail closer to the wind than any other vessel in the fleet. Being a distinctly American type of craft developed in the eighteenth century to negotiate the convoluted coastline of the Atlantic seaboard, the schooners also appealed to the officers' patriotism, and Reynolds predicted that "the English will look upon [them] with jealous eyes." Though the vessels were comparatively small, every lieutenant in the squadron yearned to command one of the schooners, and when Wilkes, at the last minute, had put two lowly passed midshipmen in charge of the vessels, it had caused more than a little grumbling. In answer to queries, Wilkes claimed that the schooners were nothing more than tenders to the *Vincennes* and as a consequence did not constitute independent commands. Given time, he insisted, all the officers would have ample opportunity for glory.

To be sure, Wilkes maintained a tight leash on the schooners. Every morning the *Sea Gull* and the *Flying Fish* were ordered to take up positions on each quarter of the *Vincennes*. As the little vessels wallowed in the man-of-war's wake, the fifteen-man crew of each schooner toed a seam so that Wilkes might inspect them through a spyglass. "That third man, Mr. Reid," Wilkes was heard to shout to the passed midshipman in command of the *Sea Gull*, "his legs are dirty, sir! The next man's head has not been combed! Look at that lubber's neck handkerchief! Stand up, you scoundrels!"

On September 13, Wilkes, in accordance with instructions from the secretary of the navy, ordered all the officers to begin keeping a daily journal. The journals were to include "all occurrences or objects of interest, which may, at the time, be considered even of the least importance." At the end of the voyage, the journals would become the property of the U.S. government. The order was not limited to journals. Everything related to the Expedition—"memorandums, remarks, writings, drawings, sketches, and paintings, as well as all specimens of every kind"—must be turned over to Wilkes at the end of the voyage.

Reynolds had been keeping a journal since the voyage began—a habit that dated to well before the Ex. Ex. "I cannot think of letting this go before any ones eyes but those few at home," he wrote. Even though it was in obvious violation of regulations, he decided to keep the existence of his personal journal a secret and begin keeping another for his commander.

Two days later, Reynolds had the forenoon watch. The *Vincennes* was charging along at ten knots in a stiff breeze. "[W]e all felt elated and excited from the speed at which we were going," Reynolds wrote. Up ahead they spied an unknown brig, and Wilkes told Reynolds to make more sail so that they might catch up to it. After issuing the necessary orders, Reynolds glanced aloft and noticed that something was wrong with the main topgallant sail, the next-to-highest sail on the center mast. Through his speaking trumpet he called out to ease one of the control lines so that the sail would draw properly. A gust of wind blew the sail out with terrific force, causing the released rope to run so quickly that it caught the man at the yard around his neck and yanked him off his feet. "[O]ne awful cry came from his lips," Reynolds recounted. With the rope wrapped around his neck, the sailor, George Porter, swung from the yard, his body "showing terribly distinct against the clear sky."

It was now up to Reynolds to get Porter down. But how? "[D]id we haul on the rope, it would be to choke him instantly," he wrote, "did we slack it, he would be dashed on deck. *There he hung!*" The rigging of the ship was now alive with sailors, making their way toward their helpless shipmate. The first thing to do was to take in the sail. Once the flapping canvas had been tamed, one of the men was able to catch Porter's body, only to have it pulled from his grasp when the ship rolled to leeward. A second attempt proved successful and the rope was immediately cleared from Porter's neck. His face was completely black. "He is dead!" the men shouted down from aloft. But by the time Porter had been brought down to the deck, he was showing signs of life. The rope had wrapped around his jaw and the back of his head, making it impossible for him to breathe but not breaking his neck. The men knew he was going to survive when Porter opened his eyes and worriedly asked the surgeon if this meant he might miss his daily ration of grog. Laughing, one of the sailors claimed that Porter "was not born to be hung, or he would not have missed so good a chance."

By September 16, the *Vincennes* was anchored at Funchal on the south shore of Madeira. For a squadron attempting a quick passage to Rio de Janeiro and then on to Cape Horn, a stop at the already well-known island might seem ill advised, especially since there were not the facilities required to begin repairing the *Peacock*. But Wilkes felt the opportunity to provision and recruit the men would do the squadron good, and Madeira, a lush, volcanic outcropping of stunning beauty a few hundred miles west of Casablanca, was renowned for not only its fresh vegetables and fruits but also its wine.

Perhaps most important, as far as Wilkes was concerned, this 305-square-mile island, much of it devoted to jagged peaks that reached as high as a mile above the surrounding sea, had long been associated with the more than four-hundred-year-long tradition of European exploration. Madeira was first colonized by Portugal in 1434 by one of the knights of Henry the Navigator, the prince traditionally credited with spearheading his country's pioneering voyages down the west coast of Africa and, ultimately, to the East Indies. Several decades later, Christopher Columbus lived for a time at Madeira and the neighboring island of Porto Santo. He married a member of the local lesser nobility, and his conversations with the many sailors who touched at this famous island may have led him to first consider a voyage west. Even the island's eponymous wine was associated with voyages to distant lands. When a trading vessel returned to Madeira from the East Indies with an unopened cask in her hold, the wine was found to have a uniquely sweet, fortified flavor—a consequence of its having been repeatedly baked in the equatorial heat. Thus was born the wine that quickly became a favorite in Elizabethan England and in colonial America. In 1768, James Cook, on his way to his first voyage of discovery, stopped at Madeira, where he took on more than three thousand gallons of wine.

For the next nine days, the officers and scientists fanned out across the island. In emulation of his renowned predecessor, Wilkes secured several casks of choice Madeira, which he and, on occasion, his officers would enjoy throughout the duration of the voyage. The stop was, Wilkes claimed, "of infinite benefit to the officers and crews."

After touching at Porto Praya in the Cape Verde Islands (also visited by Cook), the squadron headed west across the Atlantic. During the long passage to Rio de Janeiro, Reynolds ran into unexpected trouble with the *Vincennes*'s first lieutenant Thomas Craven. Reynolds had served with Craven before and had found him to be a capable and friendly officer. But for no apparent reason during the passage to Rio, Craven accused Reynolds of neglect of duty and gave him a thorough dressing down. "If any one on shore had spoken to me in that way," Reynolds wrote in his journal, "I should have struck him & certainly I felt very much inclined to do to Mr. Craven."

What Reynolds didn't realize was that ever since the Expedition's departure from Norfolk, Craven had become the object of his commander's intense and increasingly vindictive envy. Wilkes was suffering under a deep sense of insecurity. As so many navy captains had already pointed out, he had precious little experience at sea, while Craven was recognized as one of the best seamen in the squadron. If Wilkes hadn't been so insecure about his own nautical ability, he might have recognized how lucky he was to have Craven for a first lieutenant. Instead, he felt threatened by him. Even as Wilkes strove to present an urbane and judicious face to Reynolds and his friends, he covertly worked to undermine Craven. By October, Wilkes's constant harassment and fault-finding had pushed his first lieutenant to take out his frustrations on Reynolds, whom all recognized as one of the commander's favorites.

Reynolds decided he must report the incident to Wilkes. "I understand you, Mr. Reynolds," Wilkes assured him, "& depend upon it, such things shall not happen again." Reynolds felt confident that his troubles with Craven were now over, adding, "Had I not known Captain Wilkes well and been fully aware that he was free from all petty notions such as that my rank will permit [Craven] to inflict insult without fear . . . , I never would have gone to him with my complaint against his First Lieutenant."

"Bah!" Reynolds would later write in the margins of his journal, "he hated Craven & this was the reason he took my part–cove that I was, not to have seen through him then."

As the squadron made its way south and west across the middle of the Atlantic, Wilkes directed a daily search for shoals, islands, and even a volcano that had been reported but had never been independently verified. Spreading out all five vessels from north to south, so that an estimated twenty miles of latitude could be continuously scanned on a clear day, they sailed over the coordinates of these "vigias," or doubtful shoals. Invariably they found no sign of any hazard, and Wilkes would later send a list of these phantom shoals to the secretary of the navy. As the Ex. Ex. was proving, exploration was as much about discovering what did *not* exist as it was about finding something new.

At night during the passage to Rio de Janeiro, the sea seemed to catch fire. Bursts of light sparkled at the vessels' bows while glowing contrails curled in their wakes–a phenomenon known as "the phosphorescence." Referred to today as "bioluminescence," this greenish-yellow light is believed to be caused by tiny dinoflagellates, single-celled marine organisms that undergo a light-producing oxidation process when disturbed. "Every drop that was tossed up shone from its own light," Reynolds recorded, "and as it fell again into the ocean, diffused around rings & circles of the same intense glow, the night being black as Erebus."

On other nights, it was the sky that demanded their attention. As they approached the latitude of Rio de Janeiro, they saw what were known as Magellanic Clouds. The explorer Magellan and his men had recorded sighting these "shiny white clouds here and there among the stars" on the first leg of their voyage around the world. Similar in appearance to the Milky Way, and most easily seen in the Southern Hemisphere, Magellanic Clouds remained a mystery well into the twentieth century–although that did not stop John Cleves Symmes from speculating that they had something to do with his hole at the South Pole. Now known to be galaxies external to our own Milky Way, some as many as 195,000 light-years away, Magellanic Clouds were just one of several spectacular celestial phenomena observed by the Exploring Expedition during the passage to South America. One night, dozens of falling stars lit up the sky. "[A]h! these evenings defy slumber," Reynolds wrote, "and long after the usual hour of rest the upper deck is thronged with ardent gazers, who glow with rapture as they look."

Some of the more ardent gazers in the squadron were the Expedition's two artists, Alfred Agate and James Drayton. In an era before photography, artists were a crucial part of any expedition, providing drawings and paintings that were later used to create illustrations for the published scientific reports and narrative. Although both accomplished artists, Agate and Drayton had the benefit of a relatively new invention, the camera lucida–an optical device that projected the virtual image of an object onto a piece of paper for tracing. In the months ahead, the two artists, as well as the naturalist Titian Peale, would use the camera lucida to create images of hundreds of specimens and artifacts, as well as portraits of the many different peoples they encountered. They also created drawings and paintings depicting important scenes and events during the voyage, often basing their work on sketches provided by the squadron's officers.

On the afternoon of November 23, under full sail, the *Vincennes* stood in for Rio. Soon she had entered a circular bay almost one hundred miles in circumference surrounded by the spurs of a low mountain range. Ships from all over the world were anchored in groups around the bay. As the *Vincennes* sailed up the harbor, she passed the USS *Independence,* the flagship of the Brazil squadron, and Commodore John Nicholson's band struck up "Hail Columbia." Under normal circumstances, naval ceremony required that Wilkes fire a salute in recognition of his superior officer, but because of the delicacy of the chronometers aboard the *Vincennes,* Wilkes decided to forgo this custom. He sent an officer to the *Independence* to explain the reason behind the apparent slight, but Nicholson "appeared somewhat put out," Wilkes remembered, "and it was industriously circulated that I had intentionally treated him with disrespect."

The *Peacock* had preceded the *Vincennes* by three days and was already undergoing repairs, but the *Relief,* which had been sent ahead soon after leaving Norfolk, was nowhere to be seen. Not until four days later, one hundred days after leaving Norfolk, did the storeship arrive, making it one of the longest passages to Rio on record. Instead of following the prevailing breezes east before heading south and west for South America, Lieutenant Long had sailed a more direct, but very slow course. Wilkes already had little confidence in Long (he had been, after all, one of the officers he had inherited from Jones's original expedition), and he took the opportunity to berate him in the presence of the *Peacock*'s Captain Hudson.

Wilkes planned to stay in Rio for at least a month. While the squadron underwent repairs, he would conduct his initial gravity and magnetic experiments. He made arrangements with the Brazilian authorities to create a base at an old convent on Enxadas Island at the mouth of Gunabara Bay facing Rio. Here Wilkes created the same hive of activity that had existed at his Capitol Hill home the previous summer. "[T]he tents are spread," Reynolds recorded, "and the portable houses for the Instruments are put up, and the Instruments are fixed in their stands . . . , and there is a hum and a life and a stirring spirit pervading the usually quiet island."

In addition to supervising his own experiments, Wilkes was responsible for coordinating the scientists' journeys into the Brazilian interior, where they would collect no less than five thousand specimens for shipment back to the United States. Wilkes also supervised the repair of the *Peacock* and the fumigation of the *Porpoise,* and he quickly found himself spread too thin. "I have too much anxiety or rather too many persons depending upon me," he wrote Jane. He knew that his own observations must meet exacting standards since they were to be later integrated with observations being made by Lieutenant Gilliss at the Depot and Professor William Bond at Harvard.

Particularly torturous were the pendulum experiments. Wilkes had procured a sixty-eight-inch-long nonadjustable, or "invariable," free-swinging pendulum from Francis Baily. After suspending the pendulum from an iron tripod, he set up a pendulum clock behind the tripod. Both the clock and the invariable pendulum were swung, and since the two pendulums were different lengths, they swung at different rates. Every so often, however, they would coincide. Observing the two pendulums through a telescope set up on the opposite side of the room, he would record the exact time of the coincidence, repeating the observation over and over again for days on end. Eventually, enough data was accumulated to determine the precise duration of a single swing of the pendulum. With this time and the length of the pendulum, it was then possible to calculate the force of gravity.

As the experiments wore on, Wilkes started to experience terrible headaches. He demanded complete quiet, and when a man mending a sail in an adjacent room of the convent building accidentally made a noise, Wilkes "went off in a minute," according to an officer assisting him in the experiment. "Where is he?" Wilkes screamed. "The son of a bitch. . . . I'll pound him! Where is he? By God, I'll throttle him!" For the officers who had worked with him prior to the voyage's departure, it was a startling change in behavior. "These little outbreaks," Reynolds wrote, "were rather ominous for the future harmony of the squadron."

Wilkes was exhibiting the symptoms of a man who had been stretched beyond his capabilities. The less in control he felt, the more he became fixated on the issue of rank. At one point Commodore John Nicholson, commander of the *Independence* on station at Rio, addressed him as "Mister," instead of "Captain," Wilkes. When Wilkes expressed his outrage in a letter, Nicholson coolly responded, "To call you a Captain or Commander would not make you one." It was a statement that appears to have cut Wilkes to the quick.

Late one night, as he sat alone beside his "wagging pendulum," he burst into tears. "I had a good cry," he admitted to Jane (from whom he would withhold nothing throughout the voyage), "which relieves me not a little. How few, my dear Janie, would believe that the Commdr. Of the Expg Expedn. could be so easily brought to the sinking mood against all the duties that he is surrounded with."

In late December, Wilkes finally finished his pendulum experiments. By then, Lieutenant Long and the *Relief* were already on their way south. It was time, he decided, for some relaxation. With his flag lieutenant, Overton Carr, and a servant, he went ashore to enjoy a heated bath. But when he emerged from the warm water, he collapsed into his servant's arms. "I was conscious," he remembered, "but could not speak." Carr immediately took him to a nearby hotel and put him to bed. When news spread that the commander had fainted and was now catatonic, it "produced a sensation throughout the fleet," Wilkes wrote Jane, "and officers came [running from] all directions." Just three months into the voyage, he was physically and emotionally depleted. Although the surgeon Edward Gilchrist pronounced "the case a very serious one" and suggested a regimen of "restoratives," Wilkes opted for nothing more than a good night's sleep. The next morning he was up and back at work, "to the great surprise of everybody." The fact remained, however, that the commander of the Ex. Ex. was on the edge of a nervous breakdown.

On January 6, the squadron departed from Rio de Janeiro, but not before Wilkes and Nicholson exchanged a final, acrimonious flurry of correspondence. Wilkes accused the commodore of "endeavoring to decry [the Expedition's] National character and destroy its efficiency by not extending to the Commanding Officers the courtesy and etiquette that their situation . . . commands." It all came down to Nicholson's having called him Mr. Wilkes. Baffled and irked by Wilkes's tormented rage, Nicholson asked him a very good question: Rather than pretend to be something he wasn't, why didn't he instead choose to relish the fact that he, a young lieutenant, had been given such a prominent command? "You should feel more highly the honor which has been conferred upon you, as Lieutenant Charles Wilkes, . . . than all the empty and evanescent titles that could be given by either the people or officers of our own Country or any other." Nicholson would ultimately send copies of his correspondence with Wilkes to Paulding at the Navy Department with a cover letter referring to "the wrong impressions he appears to entertain relative to his supposed rank."

Even before the squadron had departed from the United States, Wilkes knew that he would be hard-pressed to reach Cape Horn in time to launch a voyage south before the end of the Antarctic summer in late January. From the beginning, time was of the essence. But Wilkes had shown little inclination to hurry. The squadron had spent a leisurely ten days at Madeira and more than a month in Rio. It was true that the *Peacock* had needed major structural repairs, but Wilkes had chosen to focus on his feud with Commodore Nicholson and his interminable pendulum experiments rather than the pressing need to fix the *Peacock* and be off as soon as possible. Instead of boldly forging ahead, Wilkes had hung back, apparently unable to confront the trial that lay to the south.

They were now more than a week into January and still had at least 1,800 miles between them and the tip of South America. Given the importance of the Antarctic cruise to the Expedition, Wilkes should have dispensed with the scheduled survey of the Rio Negro in Patagonia and sailed with all dispatch for Cape Horn. But to the astonishment of his officers, the squadron proceeded under easy sail and on January 25 dropped anchor at the mouth of the Rio Negro. The next morning, as First Lieutenant Craven directed preparations to begin the survey in the boats, Wilkes retreated to his cabin, where he lay in the grip of yet another one of his debilitating headaches.

By sundown, the boats were more than three miles from the *Vincennes*. The current was so strong that it was almost impossible to row against it, so with night approaching, Craven and his men made for the much closer *Porpoise*. Meanwhile, back on the *Vincennes*, Wilkes, still suffering from a headache, began to suspect that Craven had taken the opportunity to spend a night "in merrymaking" aboard the *Porpoise*.

The next morning, Wilkes determined that Craven must be punished. Even though he had absolutely no tangible proof of misconduct, he sent his trusted flag lieutenant Overton Carr to do his bidding. Craven was ordered back to the *Vincennes* while Carr assumed command of the survey. Craven soon learned that he had been suspended and that Carr had been named first lieutenant.

Craven and his fellow officers were at a loss to know what he had done wrong. As Wilkes would come close to admitting years later in his *Autobiography*, Craven's real sin was not a breach of discipline, but his undeniable competence. By suspending Craven and making Carr the first lieutenant, Wilkes was consciously striking out at an officer whose chief fault was that he "regarded himself as the acting spirit in . . . managing the ship." It was a shabby, duplicitous, and manipulative abuse of power, but Wilkes's actions against Craven may have saved the Expedition. Prior to the incident, he had become stupefied with exhaustion and self-doubt. The leadership style that had worked at Georges Bank was clearly not going to get him through a voyage of this magnitude. Instead of being everyone's friend, he was much better at cultivating his enemies. By lashing out at Craven he had finally roused himself to action. Refreshed and invigorated by his triumph over his first lieutenant, he began to look ahead with enthusiasm for the first time in the voyage.

Soon after Craven's suspension, an onshore gale kicked up, putting the squadron in immediate peril. The surf was breaking on the nearby shore "with tremendous violence," Reynolds wrote, "as if it would wash the sandy barrier away." There wasn't enough time to raise the heavy and cumbersome anchors, so the order was given to slip their cables. Leaving behind buoys to mark the locations of the anchors, the squadron began to claw away from the desolate shore of Rio Negro. Wilkes took great pride in the way that both he and his new first lieutenant responded to the challenge. "I was somewhat pleased to let [Craven] see that there were others quite as competent to perform the duties as he," Wilkes wrote. By suspending his first lieutenant, he had "destroyed within his mind that over Conceit he had in the ability to alone perform and take care of the ship." It was a form of psychological warfare Wilkes would subsequently employ against all officers who, in his judgment, dared to view themselves as indispensable.

Reynolds and his fellow officers were not sure what to think about Craven's suspension. No one liked trouble, and yet a suspension might allow for promotions from below. Perhaps Wilkes had his reasons.

"[T]he friends who were so devoted to the Commander would not suffer a voice to be raised against him," he wrote, "and threatened to quarrel with any one who should say a word to his prejudice. Mr. Wilkes was still an Idol to many, and he knew it."

After retrieving their anchors, the squadron left Rio Negro on February 3. Although Wilkes knew where they were headed, he chose, once again, not to share the information with his officers. Some guessed they were headed for the Falkland Islands; others figured that due to the lateness of the season, they were headed around the Horn for Valparaiso, Chile. Whatever the case might be, for the present they were headed south. When it began to snow on February 6, the quartermaster Thomas Piner, one of the older members of the *Vincennes*'s crew, commented that they were now "getting into the suburbs."

Then it began to blow. "The ship laboured much," Reynolds wrote, "damaging crockery by the wholesale & taking in oceans of water." His ornate bed was not suitable for a gale, so he was forced to spend the night in a hammock in steerage: "[T]o pass the night among such a million of noises, from the tramping & voices of men, the bleating & grunting of the live stock, the workings of the Masts & guns, the creaking of the Ladders, the howling of the winds, the strong dash of the breaking waves, & the continual fetching away of some thing or other about decks, is to suffer more than can be imagined, but which is well known, to all who have weathered out a Gale at Sea."

The next day, warm clothing, including the India rubber jackets originally ordered by Jones, was distributed to the crew. On Saturday, February 16, exactly twenty-four weeks after leaving Norfolk, they sighted the wave-washed outcropping of Cape Horn. Despite the Horn's fierce reputation, the weather was wonderful—warm, sunny, and quiet—and the *Vincennes* sailed on with her studding sails set.

It was soon learned that they were to proceed to Orange Bay, a well-protected natural harbor just inside the Hermit Islands at the southern tip of Tierra del Fuego. Ever since 1616 when the Dutch explorer Willem Schouten named the bleak rock at the end of South America for his hometown of Hoorn in the Netherlands, Cape Horn and its gale-force southwesterly winds had been studiously, often desperately avoided by vessels attempting a passage between the world's two largest oceans. During the War of 1812, navy captain David Porter had rounded the Horn in the American frigate *Essex*. "[O]ur sufferings . . . have been so great," he wrote, "that I would advise those bound into the Pacific, never to attempt the passage of Cape Horn, if they can get there by another route." Wilkes and his men were about to sail into the mythic recesses of one of the most feared places on earth.

Wilkes had instructed Lieutenant Long and the *Relief* to proceed directly to Orange Bay, where he was to have already set up a revolving signal light atop a hill. Since they had no charts of the waters immediately surrounding Cape Horn–a region no mariner in his right mind would choose to visit–they had to be very careful as they felt their way along this rocky, inhospitable tip of the world, especially since, as Reynolds observed, "changes occur here, like lightning–quick & often unexpected."

All that night the wind remained light and baffling. At six in the morning, by which time the sun had already been up for two hours, all hands were called on deck to work the ship through a narrow, rock-rimmed channel. The wind was against them, requiring that they tack the *Vincennes* every five minutes. Repeatedly tacking a seven-hundred-ton square-rigged ship in a confined space required exceptional coordination and skill: The ship's bow was swung quickly into the wind, and with her head yards thrown aback, the bow fell off from the wind until the after yards were swung around so that the sails could fill as the ship settled onto the new tack. Soon after coming up to speed, it was time once again to tack. In light air, there was always a danger that the ship might not have enough momentum to complete the maneuver–known as "missing stays"–a potentially disastrous turn of events when in close quarters with a rock. Tension mounted aboard the *Vincennes,* especially when darkness started to come on. "We were in an unknown place," Reynolds wrote, "we knew nothing of the localities, nothing positive & certain. We had no soundings [due to the extreme depth of the water] & of course could not Anchor."

In hopes of attracting the attention of the *Relief,* they fired guns and rockets. Lookouts strained to see the light that was supposed to have been placed on a high hill. Twice a star rising up over the land was mistaken for the signal.

At midnight the wind began to freshen. In fear of blundering into the rocks, the topsails were reefed, and the *Vincennes* stood offshore and waited for daylight. At four that morning it was light enough to read on deck, and the *Porpoise* was discovered nearby. An hour later, as the sun rose "in fiery splendor," they saw it—the *Relief* at anchor. By six in the morning, they, too, were anchored in Orange Bay.

That afternoon Wilkes finally withdrew "the veil of mystery." "[A]ll hands went to work as if Life & death depended on their exertions," Reynolds wrote. Despite the lateness of the season, they were "to go *South.*"

CHAPTER 5

The Turning Point

THERE WASN'T MUCH that could intimidate James Cook. But on January 30, 1774, the indomitable explorer met his match. Four days after crossing the Antarctic Circle, he reached latitude 71°10' south—farther south than anyone had ever ventured. In front of him stood an immense and impenetrable field of ice, "whose horrible and savage aspect I have no words to describe." He could have pushed east or west in search of an opening to the south, but Cook had had enough. "I whose ambition leads me not only farther than any other man has been before me, but as far as I think it possible for man to go, was not sorry at meeting with this interruption," he later recorded in his journal. He suspected that a large landmass existed to the south, but he was quite content to leave its discovery to someone else. "[W]hoever has resolution and perseverance to clear up this point by proceeding farther than I have done," he wrote, "I shall not envy him the honour of the discovery."

More than sixty-five years later, on February 25, 1839, Charles Wilkes held out hope that he might claim that prize. Unfortunately, it was already a month later in the season than when Cook had reached what had become known as his "Ne Plus Ultra" (Latin for "No Farther"), and Wilkes had not yet left Orange Bay.

The last week had been a mad scramble of preparation. The *Vincennes* was to remain in Orange Bay, where Lieutenant Carr would oversee the collection of meteorological data as well as the celestial observations required to check the rates of their chronometers. Lieutenant

Alden, with Passed Midshipman William Reynolds as his second-in-command, was to survey the rocky coastline of Tierra del Fuego in a thirty-five-foot launch. In the meantime, Lieutenant Long in the *Relief* would take the scientists on a collecting trip into the Strait of Magellan. That left the *Porpoise,* the *Peacock,* and the two schooners for a voyage south.

The Antarctic summer had already turned to autumn–dramatically increasing the risk of becoming trapped in the ice. In the event that they might be forced to winter below the Antarctic Circle, the vessels were loaded with enough provisions to last between eight and ten months. Orange Bay became a scene of near-constant activity. Boxes of provisions were taken from the *Relief* and the *Vincennes* and loaded into the *Peacock, Porpoise, Flying Fish,* and *Sea Gull* as boats bearing firewood and casks of water continually came and went from shore.

Due to the dangerous nature of the duty they were about to undertake, Wilkes decided that lieutenants, instead of passed midshipmen, should be put in command of the schooners. When it was learned that two junior lieutenants, Robert Johnson and William Walker (both part of Wilkes's inner circle), were to command the *Sea Gull* and the *Flying Fish,* respectively, there was an outcry of protest from the senior lieutenants; Hudson's second-in-command, Lieutenant Samuel Lee, even wrote Wilkes a strongly worded letter. Wilkes responded in a manner that was calculated "to astonish everyone." With a stroke of his pen, he dismissed Lee from the squadron, ordering him to report to the *Relief* for passage back to the United States once he reached Valparaiso. This required a complete reshuffling of officers, and in less than an hour, Wilkes had issued the necessary orders, reassigning a total of eleven lieutenants. (Now down an officer, Wilkes reinstated First Lieutenant Craven to active duty aboard the *Vincennes,* but not until Craven had written a letter of apology.)

Wilkes would later describe the suspension of Lieutenant Lee as "the turning point of the discipline of the cruise." Lee, like Craven before him, was one of the senior lieutenants he had inherited from the earlier expedition. He was now convinced that they were part of a "mutinous cabal" that if allowed to continue unchecked would destroy the squadron. "[T]he many headed Hydra is completely overcome," he wrote Jane, "but I have [to] keep a very watchful eye on the boys here-

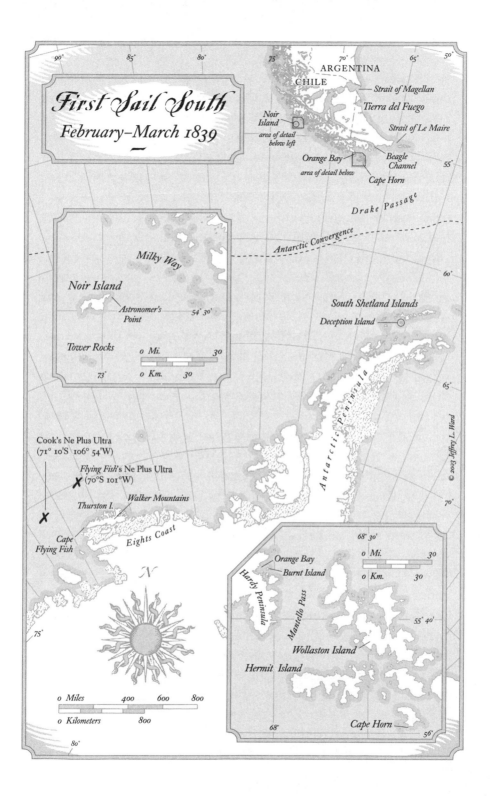

First Sail South
February–March 1839

90° 85° 80° 75° 70° 65° 50°

ARGENTINA
CHILE
Strait of Magellan
Tierra del Fuego
Noir Island
area of detail below left
Strait of Le Maire
Orange Bay
area of detail below
Beagle Channel
Cape Horn
55°

Drake Passage
Antarctic Convergence

Milky Way

Noir Island
Astronomer's Point
54° 30'
South Shetland Islands
Deception Island
60°

Tower Rocks
0 Mi. 30
0 Km. 30
73°
65°

Antarctic Peninsula

Cook's Ne Plus Ultra
(71° 10'S 106° 54'W)
Flying Fish's Ne Plus Ultra
(70°S 101°W)
70°

Walker Mountains
Thurston I.
Cape Flying Fish
Eights Coast

N

0 Mi. 30
68° 30'
Orange Bay
Burnt Island
0 Km. 30
Hardy Peninsula
Mantello Pass
55° 40'
Wollaston Island
Hermit Island

75°

0 Miles 400 600 800
0 Kilometers 800

68°
Cape Horn
56°

80°

© 2003 Jeffrey L. Ward

after." Lieutenant Johnson, the new commander of the *Sea Gull,* had a different perspective on the incident. "Every one says the devilish Schooners are the cause of it all," he wrote. "They ought at first to have been given to the two senior lieutenants when they applied for them."

By February 25, it was time to depart. Wilkes divided the four vessels into two groups. Hudson, in command of the *Peacock,* would sail west and south in the company of the *Flying Fish* in an attempt to better Cook's Ne Plus Ultra in the vicinity of longitude 106° west. Wilkes had taken over command of the *Porpoise* and, along with the *Sea Gull,* would sail south and east toward the South Shetland Islands.

Wilkes's greatest hopes for discovery lay to the east of the South Shetlands. In the more than sixty years since Cook's historic voyage south, only one navigator had bettered his mark. On February 18, 1823, the British sealer James Weddell, sailing from the South Orkney Islands, well to the east of the South Shetlands, had reached latitude 74°15' south, longitude 34°16' west, almost two hundred miles farther south than Cook. Instead of a wall of ice, Weddell had encountered open water and warm temperatures, prompting him to wonder if instead of land, a navigable sea might extend all the way to the pole. Since that time, no explorer had been able to come close to Weddell's achievement. Wilkes theorized that the lateness of the season might actually work to his advantage when it came to reproducing the conditions the British sealer had encountered in what is known today as the Weddell Sea.

The *Porpoise* and the *Sea Gull* were the first to depart Orange Bay at 7:30 A.M. on February 25. "[W]e gave them three hearty cheers," Reynolds wrote, "wishing them, with all our hearts, a prosperous time, and a safe return." At four P.M., a heavy squall pushed the two vessels with a shove out into the fearsome waters of the Drake Passage, the six-hundred-mile stretch of open water between Cape Horn and the South Shetland Islands. The Drake Passage is the only place on earth where the wind can circulate around the entire globe without ever touching land, making it one of the most dangerous places on the planet for a sailing vessel.

The following day, they came upon a whaleship from New York, homeward bound with 3,800 barrels of oil. Realizing that the whalers would soon be back in the United States, Wilkes asked if they'd be willing to take along some letters. The whaling captain cheerfully agreed, and soon the officers of both the *Porpoise* and the *Sea Gull* were scribbling out notes to their loved ones. They were descending into one of the coldest, most perilous parts of the world at a time of year when anyone with any sense would have been headed in the opposite direction. All of them could not help but wonder if these might be the last letters they ever wrote. "I am in excellent spirits," Wilkes assured Jane, "and am living with Ringgold during this trip." He added that their nephew Wilkes Henry "is quite well and grown astonishingly."

With the wind almost directly behind them, they sailed to the southeast at nine knots over huge rolling waves that Wilkes calculated to average thirty-two feet in height. For those aboard the tiny *Sea Gull*, it was proving to be a thrilling and very wet ride as the narrow schooner surfed into the backsides of the cresting seas. On February 28, the jarring strain of several days of wave-riding caused the *Sea Gull*'s gaff to break. Despite the immense seas, Johnson was able to maneuver the schooner to within a few feet of the *Porpoise* and transfer the splintered spar to the brig's carpenter, who had it repaired in a few hours.

That afternoon it began to snow, and they sighted their first cape pigeons or petrels–dark-brown birds lightly spotted with white that are known for following ships in the Southern Ocean for days at a time. Cape pigeons are also regarded as a sign that icebergs are in the vicinity, and sure enough, at dawn the following day, they saw their first "island of ice." Wilkes remarked that the icebergs looked worn, "as if the sea had been washing over them for some time."

They had crossed the Antarctic Convergence, the area where the relatively warm waters from the north meet the cold surface waters to the south. They had entered a region of colder, less salty water, with markedly different flora and fauna. Both the *Porpoise* and the *Sea Gull* were soon surrounded by swimming penguins. "I had not known that the Penguins lived so much in water," wrote Lieutenant Johnson, who was also impressed by the number of whales. "[O]n any part of the Horizon you might be able to sing out 'Spout ho!'"

But it was the icebergs that most impressed all of them. "[W]e met with some large Islands of ice fifty times as large as the Capitol and much whiter," Wilkes wrote Jane, "and a great deal higher. . . . [S]oon we were literally surrounded with them, and a most magnificent sight it was too." On March 1 they sighted several of the South Shetland Islands–volcanic, snow-topped outcroppings that had prompted one sealer to wonder if "Madame Nature had been drinking too much when she form'd this place."

Wilkes had hopes of landing on one of the islands to collect some specimens, but the conditions remained too rough. By March 3, they'd sailed to within sight of the eastern tip of Palmer's Land. By now the icebergs were so numerous that navigation was extremely difficult. Johnson in the *Sea Gull* judged the conditions to be "utterly impassible." But Wilkes remained undaunted. "[M]y little favorite the *Porpoise* showed herself worthy of the affection I have for her," he wrote Jane. With the schooner following in her wake, the brig continued south, the helmsmen of both vessels forced to "put starboard and port every instant to avoid running into [ice]."

Instead of the danger, Wilkes was transfixed by the view. "I have rarely seen a finer sight," he wrote. "The sea was literally studded with these beautiful masses, some of pure white, others showing all the shades of opal, others emerald green and occasionally here and there some of a deep black, forming a strong contrast to the pure white." At one point, with no fewer than two hundred icebergs in sight, Lieutenant Ringgold turned to Wilkes and proclaimed, "This is adventuring with boldness." The two of them laughed, and Wilkes decided to name the three small islands ahead of them the Adventure Islets.

At eight P.M. the fog socked in, forcing them to lay to till daylight. With both the air and water temperature at close to 28°F (the freezing point of salt water), it made for a miserable night, especially since the special cold-weather clothing provided by the government proved next to useless. When on March 5 the wind increased to a heavy gale as the temperature dropped to 25°F, Wilkes realized that it was time to retreat north. Both vessels were coated with snow and ice, but conditions were particularly bad aboard the *Sea Gull*. Every five minutes or so a large wave would break over the little schooner and drench the men. Icicles, "forming with the direction of the wind," hung from the rigging; her fore sheets were so caked with ice that they were "the size of a sloop of war's cable." Wilkes ordered Johnson to return to Orange Bay after first stopping at Deception Island (one of the South Shetlands), where he was to attempt to retrieve a self-registering thermometer left by an earlier British expedition. Although he had no regrets about turning back, Johnson suspected that Wilkes was planning to continue on without him. After beating the ice from the rigging, the crew of the *Sea Gull* made sail for Deception Island.

Wilkes had no illusions about the terrible conditions. To continue south would have been madness given the time of year. While Johnson headed west, Wilkes ordered the helmsman of the *Porpoise* to steer north, along the eastern edge of the South Shetland Islands. Instead of being shaken and dispirited by his brief bout with the Antarctic ice, Wilkes remained jubilant. "[T]hus far," he later reported to Jane, "I may say the Expedition has proved as successful as I could have hoped or expected. . . . I never felt myself so full of energy in my life as I do now." "Adventuring with boldness" apparently agreed with the commander of the Ex. Ex.

To be sure, Wilkes had no reason to apologize for not pushing any farther south. Nine years before, Jeremiah Reynolds and some of the most experienced sealers in America (including the redoubtable Nathaniel Palmer) had not made it beyond the South Shetland Islands, even though the privately funded expedition had left Cape Horn more than a month earlier in the season than Wilkes. Just the year before, the veteran French explorer Dumont d'Urville, whose king had offered each member of his expedition a bonus of a hundred francs if they reached latitude 75° south and an extra twenty francs for every additional degree south, had met with disappointing results. Despite having started in early January, d'Urville had been unable to get beyond 65° south. By the time he sailed for South America, more than half his men had succumbed to scurvy.

D'Urville's experience below the Antarctic Convergence had been so demoralizing that he had chosen to spend the current Antarctic summer months in Polynesia, gathering his men's strength for one last sail south. This meant that even though the French had departed a year ahead of the U.S. Ex. Ex., they had lost their initial advantage. When it came to the race to being the first to identify what lay to the south, it was now a dead heat between the French and the Americans.

But, in actuality, both Wilkes and d'Urville, along with a slew of sealers in the early 1820s, had already glimpsed the Antarctic Continent. What Wilkes called Palmer's Land is now known as the Antarctic Peninsula and has become the primary destination for tourists looking to visit the southernmost continent.

But all that was in the distant future. As far as Wilkes and d'Urville were concerned, the search was still on. And besides, there was always the chance that Lieutenant Hudson had met with unexpected success to the west.

It hadn't started well. Soon after leaving Orange Bay on the morning of February 25, the *Peacock* and the *Flying Fish* had been blasted by a squall that sent them scurrying back for the protection of the bay's outer anchorage. The next morning they were under way in a strong northerly breeze, but an unexpected current from the south of more than eight knots meant that they were barely making any real progress south.

The next day, in a blinding gale, the *Peacock* and the *Flying Fish* were separated. As agreed upon, the *Peacock* waited for twelve hours, but after seeing no sign of the schooner, Hudson ordered that they head to the southwest.

Like any sloop-of-war, the sides of the *Peacock* had been pierced to accommodate her guns; unfortunately, this did not make her a particularly good exploring vessel since the gun ports, which had begun to warp, leaked alarming amounts of the frigid Southern Ocean. Even Hudson's cabin was frequently awash. "I have no doubt," he wrote, "most of us will have to submit to the tortures of Rheumatism as a set off to our curiosity and love of adventure."

Two stoves were set up belowdecks, and hot coffee was served to the men at midnight. In the early predawn hours of March 9, it began to snow, prompting Lieutenant Oliver Hazard Perry Jr. (the son of the

War of 1812 hero) to awaken the naturalist Titian Peale, the only member of the scientific corps to have been included in this first voyage south, and show him an unusual artifact: the snowball he had made while on deck.

A heavy cross-sea made for an uncomfortable ride, particularly for the men up in the ship's rigging, who were ordered to let out the reefs in the topsails for the first time since leaving Orange Bay. Normally the sailors worked barefooted, but given the cold conditions, they'd been given government-issue "exploring boots" that proved to be as leaky as they were cumbersome. That day tragedy struck when William Stewart, captain of the maintop and one of the best seamen aboard the ship, fell from the maintopsail yard, bouncing off the main rigging before plunging into the sea. Sticking out of the water were his two exploring boots. Given the dangerous seas, it would have been impossible to send out a boat for him, but a quick-thinking sailor threw out a bowline and lassoed Stewart's big boots, and he was soon hauled aboard. The surgeon determined that he'd suffered internal injuries during his fall, and two days later Stewart was buried at sea.

On March 11, they saw their first iceberg. "[E]ven the sailors left their breakfast to have a look at it," Peale wrote. Peale busied himself shooting birds—including two albatrosses ("ash colored with sooty heads"), a blue petrel, and a cape pigeon. He hoped the birds would be blown back onto the deck of the *Peacock*, but the winds never seemed to cooperate, and the potential specimens were lost.

On Sunday, March 17, Hudson conducted a religious service on the half-deck. The sea was so high that the men had to lie down on the deck and, according to Peale, "hold on by whatever was near." Hudson thought that this might have been the first time a sermon had been read "within the South Antarctic Circle," adding, "I should indeed rejoice to extend the requirements of the Gospel . . . from Pole to Pole."

The weather was miserable—a wet cold fog that often made it impossible to see the icebergs that loomed ahead until they "popp[ed] up suddenly in your face to bid you defiance." Unlike Wilkes, who seemed to flourish amid the terrors of an iceberg-infested sea, Hudson quickly grew weary of the strain. "This fancy kind of sailing," he confided in his journal, "is not all that it is cracked up to be." But there was one advantage to the steadily falling temperatures. By March 18, the *Peacock* was coated in a thick layer of ice. "Our Antarctic Caulker has so thoroughly performed his duty," Hudson wrote, "that we shall be comparatively dry below."

On March 22, the fog lifted for a moment to reveal an icy barrier similar to what Cook had encountered more than half a century before. Hudson made his way east, hoping for an opening. Heavy squalls battered them on the twenty-fourth, the conditions made all the more dangerous by the presence of dozens of icebergs, some extending as high as two hundred feet above the sea. The next day, the sun broke through the clouds for the first time in almost a week, allowing them to make a noon sight. They were at latitude 68° south, longitude 97°58' west–just a few degrees from Cook.

An hour later, "a strange sail" was sighted to the west. All hands rushed on deck; it was the first vessel they'd seen in almost a month. They hoisted their flag and fired a gun. To their great joy and relief, they soon realized it was the *Flying Fish,* and at three P.M. the schooner passed astern of the *Peacock,* both crews giving each other three hearty cheers. A boat was dispatched to the *Flying Fish,* and soon Lieutenant Walker, along with a sailor whose cracked ribs were in need of medical attention, were on the *Peacock*'s deck. Walker had brought his chart with him and seemed eager to tell his story. Hudson ushered the young lieutenant below to his cabin, and with the chart spread out before them, Walker recounted how the *Flying Fish,* the smallest vessel in the squadron, had just made history.

William Walker had not been particularly happy about commanding the *Flying Fish.* He felt he should have been given the larger *Sea Gull* since he was ahead of Robert Johnson on the list. His friends consoled him with the assurance that the ninety-six-ton schooner "would at least make him an honourable coffin."

Just two days later, on the night of February 26, Walker and his fourteen-man crew began to wonder if that was indeed what the *Flying Fish* was about to become. As they lay to in the squall that had separated them from the *Peacock,* gigantic seas continually broke over the schooner's deck. To continue without the company of the much larger ship seemed like madness. But when the gale moderated the next day, they pushed on to the south.

On the night of March 2, another gale kicked up. The wind shifted direction, creating the same jumbled sea conditions that caused William Stewart's fall aboard the *Peacock.* Aboard the schooner, it was part earthquake, part tsunami. "It was almost impossible to stand on deck without danger of being carried overboard," wrote the surgeon James Palmer, "and below, everything was afloat. Books, clothes and cabin furniture chased each other from side to side; while the bulkheads creaked, and blocks thumped over-head, with a distracting din."

The storm lasted thirty-six hours. On March 6, they experienced their first sunny day of the cruise. Birds followed behind them; a porpoise leaped at their bow; but at midnight it began to blow. "A dreadful night succeeded," Palmer wrote. Huge seas broke across the deck, crushing their two boats and ripping the binnacle, the wooden box containing the compass, off its fastenings and into the ocean. The companion-slide was then torn away by a mountainous wave that flooded the cabin and knocked both the helmsman and lookout off their feet. When a whale rubbed up against the beleaguered schooner and an albatross flapped its wings in the face of one of the men, Walker began to wonder if all of nature had somehow conspired against them.

Three days later, they discovered a leak in the bread-room, requiring that they shift the stores aft. Most of the next day was spent at the pumps. The schooner was now leaking at every seam. Their clothes and bedding were completely soaked. Dispensing with their worthless exploring boots, they wrapped their feet in blankets in an attempt to stay warm. Then it began to sleet, covering the schooner's deck, as well as the jackets of the men, in a glistening shell of ice. When the jib split, the icy conditions made it impossible to take in the sail, which hung over the side by a single hank on the forestay. Five of the men were now so debilitated by cold that they could barely stand. Yet all continued to do their duty without complaint.

On March 14 they reached a prearranged rendezvous point with the *Peacock* at 105° west, just a few degrees of longitude from Cook's Ne Plus Ultra. Once the weather began to ease, Walker and his men took the opportunity to repair their damaged boats and tend to a sailor who had fractured a rib. After waiting a day, with no sign of the *Peacock,* they headed south.

The farther south they sailed, the more astonished they were by the amount of wildlife inhabiting this seemingly barren place. The water was filled with penguins; countless birds swarmed in the air; the many whale spouts reminded the men of smoke curling from the chimneys of a crowded city. At one point a huge right whale, longer than the *Flying Fish,* appeared in front of the schooner and refused to budge, forcing the men to push the creature off with boathooks.

On March 19 they passed between two icebergs that they calculated to be 830 feet high. They hove to beside one of the massive bergs to fill their water casks with meltwater. "Encompassed by these icy walls," Palmer wrote, "the schooner looked like a mere skiff in the moat of a giant's castle." The towering walls of ice and the cold dry Antarctic air created strange acoustics. "The voice had no resonance," Palmer wrote, "words fell from the lip and seemed to freeze before they reached the ear."

Once they'd filled their casks, they continued on through the fog, the deck officer on watch always standing at the forecastle, listening for the roar of breakers. Several times they looked up to discover an iceberg's frozen sides emerging from the mist. At twilight they narrowly averted slamming into a submerged tongue of ice that would have surely sunk them. Although the icebergs were a constant threat, there was yet another, far more insidious danger: becoming trapped in the ice as the temperature began to drop. By this point all their thermometers had been broken, so they mounted tin pots in the rigging and filled them with water. They would continue south until the water started to freeze.

On March 20, the fog suddenly lifted. There, just a few yards ahead of them, was the wall of ice that had stopped both Hudson and Cook. Fifteen to twenty feet high, it extended to both the eastern and western horizons. To the south lay "a vast and seemingly boundless field," wrote

Walker, who proceeded to head west and then east, "luffing and bearing away alternately to avoid dangerous contact with large detached masses."

The next day, at four P.M., they found it–an opening to the south. With all sails set, they were doing eight knots, "flattering ourselves," Walker remembered, "we should get beyond Cook." But by noon of the next day, "our hopes were blasted in the bud." They were hove to in another gale. All around them were icebergs, "whose pale masses just came in sight through the dim haze, like tombs in a vast cemetery."

The next day the skies cleared and the wind disappeared. To the south it seemed as if they could see all the way to the pole. "The eye ached for some limit to the space," Palmer wrote, "which the mind could hardly grasp." Behind them, several giant floes of ice collided, closing them in. The ice shifted again, opening up a sliver of space through which Walker attempted to squeeze his little schooner, sometimes forcing her into the ice. The carpenter ran aft, warning that the vessel was not built for this kind of abuse. "[B]ut there was no alternative except to buffet her through," Palmer wrote, "or be carried to the south." Finally at nine in the morning of March 22, they reached an area of relative safety. They were at latitude 70° south, longitude 101° west.

Two days later, they found themselves once again in a diminishing breeze, with the temperature dropping. It was so quiet that they could hear the water freezing around them. Palmer described it as "a low crepitation, like the clicking of a death-watch" as the sea's surface took on an oily appearance that quickly congealed into a thick, soupy slush known as grease ice. Walker knew that if they didn't break free quickly, they might never break free at all. He headed the *Flying Fish* downwind until he'd established some headway. Then he "gave her the mainsheet," yanking in the large aft sail as the headsails were released and the helm was brought down. The schooner veered into the wind and, amid the crackling of sea ice, shot through the barrier to windward.

But they weren't clear yet. For the next four hours they struggled to the north. The fearful sound of wood grinding against ice prompted the carpenter to attempt a modification to the bow. Borrowing planks from the cabin berths, he tried to reinforce the area of impact at the waterline, but with time running out, Walker refused to wait long enough for him to complete the job. They were constantly adjusting the helm, sometimes tacking, other times jibing, to avoid icebergs that towered over their two masts. Walker was convinced that it was the schooner's small size that saved them. "I do not believe a ship could have passed these dangers," he wrote. They finally reached open water at latitude 70°14' south–less than one degree, or sixty miles, from Cook's Ne Plus Ultra. Behind them to the south, the water had become "a firm field of ice." It was time to head home.

They hadn't surpassed Cook, but they had come very close, and they had done it in a New York pilot boat instead of an overbuilt collier. "I have never known men subjected to equal hardships," wrote Walker, who proudly pointed out that no American vessel had ever sailed farther south.

Geographers would later discover that even if Walker and his men hadn't passed Cook in terms of latitude, they had succeeded in sailing closer to Antarctica. Due to her more easterly position, the *Flying Fish* had come to within 110 miles of Thurston Island, just off the Eights Coast of Antarctica. Today the eastern tip of Thurston Island is called Cape Flying Fish, while the island's interior contains the Walker Mountains–lasting tributes to this truly extraordinary navigational accomplishment.

On March 25, just a day after their narrow escape from the ice, Walker and his men sighted the *Peacock*. After hearing Walker's account of his adventures, Hudson ordered the *Flying Fish* back to Orange Bay at the tip of South America. The *Peacock*, in accordance with Wilkes's instructions, headed north to Valparaiso, Chile, where the entire squadron would soon rendezvous.

It had been a difficult two months for William Reynolds. He had been forced to watch as the *Porpoise*, the *Peacock*, and two schooners left Orange Bay for the mystery that lay to the south. "Next year!" he had consoled himself in his journal, "Will be our turn."

But the duty he had been given was far from a routine surveying assignment. Along with Lieutenant Alden and ten handpicked men, in-

RIGHT: John Cleves Symmes Jr., as sketched by John James Audubon in 1820. Symmes believed that the earth was hollow and contained "holes in the poles." His efforts to launch a voyage to prove his theory initiated the process that resulted, after many stops and starts, in the sailing of the U.S. Exploring Expedition in 1838. *Courtesy The New-York Historical Society*

LEFT: Ferdinand Hassler, first superintendent of the U.S. Coast Survey. Hassler introduced sophisticated European survey techniques to America and was a friend of Charles Wilkes's brother-in-law, James Renwick, a professor at Columbia College. Hassler served as Wilkes's teacher for several years in the 1820s. *Courtesy National Oceanic and Atmospheric Administration*

This humorous lithograph from 1838 reflects the controversy that surrounded the bumbling, protracted attempts to launch America's first exploring expedition, which came to be referred to as the "Deplorable Expedition." *Courtesy Peters Collection, Division of Domestic Life, National Museum of American History, Smithsonian Institution*

Charles Wilkes as painted
by Thomas Sully. *Courtesy
U.S. Naval Academy Museum*

Jane Renwick–the love
of Charles Wilkes's life.
The two were married
in April 1826, just about
the time Wilkes was
promoted to lieutenant.
*Courtesy Naval Historical
Center*

LEFT: Charlie Erskine. Prior to the launching of the Expedition, Erskine served as Wilkes's cabin boy during the survey of Georges Banks in 1837. Although Wilkes described him as "one of the most beautiful boys I ever beheld," he had him whipped for a trivial offense. This image appeared in Erskine's *Twenty Years Before the Mast*, published in 1890. *Author's Collection*

ABOVE: William Reynolds began the Expedition as a fervent supporter of Charles Wilkes but would soon become one of his commander's staunchest foes. *Anne Hoffman Cleaver Collection*

LEFT: William Hudson, second-in-command of the U.S. Exploring Expedition and captain of the *Peacock*. Hudson was one of Wilkes's best friends in the navy and a respected seaman but lacked nautical surveying experience. *From the* Narrative, *courtesy Smithsonian Institution Libraries*

LEFT: The naturalist Titian Peale. As is evident by this self-portrait, painted a few years prior to the Expedition's departure, Peale was, like his father, Charles Willson Peale, a talented artist. *Courtesy Department Library Services, American Museum of Natural History*

RIGHT: James Dwight Dana, just twenty-five years old at the beginning of the Expedition, proved to be the Charles Darwin of the voyage. He would publish several important scientific reports and eventually become a professor at Yale, where he was recognized as America's foremost geologist. *Courtesy Yale University Art Gallery, bequest of Edward Salisbury Dana, B.A. 1870*

LEFT: The botanist Asa Gray was a good friend of the geologist James Dana. He was originally slated to join the Expedition but backed out at the last minute in favor of a teaching position. He later moved to Harvard, where he established himself as the country's preeminent botanist and contributed to several of the Expedition's scientific reports. *Courtesy National Portrait Gallery, Smithsonian Institution*

RIGHT: Charles Pickering (shown here many years after his return from the Expedition) was a scientist of wide-ranging interests, including physical anthropology and botany. *Courtesy Library of the Academy of Natural Sciences of Philadelphia*

LEFT: As the conchologist of the scientific corps, Joseph Couthouy studied mollusks and shells. He and Wilkes had a confrontation in Samoa that would result in his leaving the Expedition in Hawaii. *Courtesy Boston Athenaeum*

RIGHT: William Brackenridge was the Expedition's horticulturalist. After the conclusion of the voyage, he was responsible for the greenhouse of living plant specimens that became the basis of the U.S. Botanic Garden. *Courtesy Smithsonian Institution Archives*

The Expedition's first landfall: Madeira. *From the* Narrative, *courtesy Smithsonian Institution Libraries*

A native of Tierra del Fuego. *From the* Narrative, *courtesy Smithsonian Institution Libraries*

Passed Midshipman Henry Eld's sketch of the squadron at Orange Bay, near Cape Horn. *Courtesy Beinecke Rare Book and Manuscript Library, Yale University*

Orange Bay, near Cape Horn Sa.
25th February 1839.

cluding some of the most experienced sailors in the squadron, he was ordered to explore one of the stormiest coasts in the world in a thirty-five-foot cutter-rigged launch. Although Wilkes appears not to have been fully aware of it, the hazard was huge. The launch, equipped with a small cuddy up forward, was too small and top-heavy to have any hope of weathering the storms that frequented the region. "If they ever get caught in a gale in a sea way...," wrote the scientist Joseph Couthouy, who was also an experienced mariner, "she will play them the slippery trick before they know it." For his part, Reynolds was well aware of the danger: "if we should be caught *'out'* in a S.W. blow, and driven off the Land, we should be *lost!*"

On March 12, just a day after leaving Orange Bay, Reynolds and company were sailing between the Hardy Peninsula, at the southern tip of Tierra del Fuego, for the Wollaston and Hermit Islands, just to the northwest of Cape Horn. They were in the Mantello Pass, a more than sixty-mile-wide stretch of open water, when they saw "heavy masses of dark mackerel clouds" to the south. They had made it to within a half-mile of Wollaston Island when the wind suddenly switched in direction and climbed in velocity, turning the coast that was to be their salvation into a dreaded lee shore. They watched in horror as "the surf broke tremendously [and] saw plainly what would be our fate, unless we could soon find a secure anchorage."

It began to rain; then it began to sleet as the wind continued to build. They had no choice but to make a wild dash for Hermit Island to the south. "[The launch] was pressed with sail," Reynolds wrote, "& bounded from Sea to Sea, with a speed that astonished us." One of the crewmembers was a man named Jim Gibson, a sailor who had once gone to school with Reynolds back in Lancaster. As the waves broke over the sides of the launch, the two old friends, finding themselves in an open boat at the end of the world, talked of "how Comfortable we should be, if [we] were only by his Aunt Hubley's stove, sipping hot punch."

The visibility was so terrible that they couldn't see what lay ahead of them at Hermit Island. With the waves "deluging us fore and aft," they came to within two boat-lengths of a rocky point. Just inside the point was a small cove sheltered from the wind. "[T]he helm was put hard down," Reynolds wrote, "and in another moment we were in calm water, riding quietly at anchor."

For the next two weeks, they would spend most of their time huddled in this and another cove, riding out a series of ferocious gales, one of which was so severe that back in Orange Bay–supposedly the securest anchorage in the Hardy Peninsula–the *Vincennes* dragged her anchors. But they were not alone. There were also the local natives, the Yahgan Indians, who, much like Reynolds and company, traveled from island to island in small open boats. Indeed, the Yahgans were wonderfully adapted to life in a bark canoe. With big torsos, long arms, and spindly legs with flaps of skin hanging down from their knees, they traveled the waters off Tierra del Fuego, often with their entire families in a single canoe: the mother and eldest boy paddling, the father bailing out water and tending the fire that always burned on a few stones and ashes in the center of the hull as the infants and toddlers nestled in a bed of dry grass. Despite the horrendous weather, the Yahgans wore little or no clothing and while on land lived in tiny smoke-filled huts surrounded by heaps of limpet shells.

When Darwin had first seen these people a few years before, he had been so shocked by their primitive state that he had written, "one can hardly make oneself believe that they are fellow creatures, and inhabitants of the same world." Reynolds, on the other hand, quickly discovered that the Yahgans had skills that he and Alden could only envy. After spending an entire night unsuccessfully attempting to light a fire, the naval officers watched in amazement as some Yahgans walked down to the beach the next morning and created a large blaze amid the wet underbrush. "[W]e could not learn by what means they kindled it," Reynolds marveled. The Yahgans were also remarkable mimics, repeating with eerie precision just about everything the Americans said.

One day it began to snow, and the sailors and the Indians enjoyed a snowball fight. "[W]e Skylarked among the snow together, as if we had been old friends: they were naked, & we warmly clad & I just thought that we presented as wide a contrast of person & habit as could be met with any where in the world." But Reynolds, a man who enjoyed his luxuries, was not about to go native. "[I]f *they* be the children of Nature," he wrote, "I am thankful that I am a member of a more artificial community, & will [waive forever] the belief, that those barbarous ones who have the fewest wants, lead a more enviable existence than the great civilized mass."

On March 25, the weather finally began to moderate. Just an hour after leaving their cove, they saw a sail in the distance. It proved to be the *Sea Gull*, and as the schooner approached, the officers on the launch took up a gun and fired a salute. When Reynolds first stepped onto the schooner's deck, he was stunned by its comparative size. "The *Sea Gull* seemed a monster," he wrote. "I thought her almost *too* large." Most of all, however, he felt, for the first time in several weeks, *safe*.

Johnson explained that soon after they returned to Orange Bay from the South Shetland Islands, he had been sent out on a search for the launch by Lieutenant Craven, who had begun to fear the worst. For their part, Alden and Reynolds were eager to hear about the *Sea Gull*'s sail south, and they soon learned about the schooner's stop at Deception Island—how they had anchored in the lagoonlike harbor of a volcano's drowned crater and set out on an unsuccessful search for the self-registering thermometer left by the British explorer Captain Foster. Johnson and his men had walked over the surface of an active volcano, and even as snow and sleet pummeled their heads, they could feel heat radiating up through the thick soles of their boots. At one point Johnson put his ear to the ground and heard a roaring sound, like "a strong draught in a chimney."

Over the next week, as Alden supervised the completion of the survey from the security of the schooner, Reynolds fell in love—not with a woman, but with the *Sea Gull*. He became smitten with everything about this perfectly designed craft. One night as they rode out yet another gale, he could not help but wonder if the *Sea Gull* were, in fact, alive. "I could scarcely believe that all was mechanical," he wrote, "that her nice & regular motion was merely the result of properties bestowed on her by the skillful builder. It seemed much more natural to think that She had a mind, an instinct, a will of her own, & that guided by it, she defied the threatening dangers of the Gale."

By the time they returned to Orange Bay, the squadron was buzzing with excitement. The *Flying Fish* had brought back word of her historic sail south; Wilkes had returned in the *Porpoise,* his initial euphoria tempered by an incident at the Strait of Le Maire just off the eastern tip of Tierra del Fuego. In the same storm that had nearly killed Reynolds and his compatriots, one of Wilkes's officers, Lieutenant John Dale, had been trapped with his boat's crew on the shore of Good Success Bay. The *Porpoise* had been forced to make for the open sea, and it had taken almost a week to retrieve Dale and his men. Wilkes blamed the delay on Dale's incompetence, and a court of inquiry was to be convened once they reached Valparaiso. In the meantime, the *Peacock* was already on her way to Valparaiso while the *Relief* was long overdue from her cruise to the Strait of Magellan. In the sixty days since they first arrived at Orange Bay, they had experienced no less than eleven gales, averaging between two and three days in duration. To be trapped in a storm against a lee shore in the Strait of Magellan was a fate no man wanted to contemplate.

On April 17, Wilkes decided that it was time for the *Vincennes* and *Porpoise* to depart for Valparaiso. He ordered the two schooners to wait another ten days for the *Relief.* If the storeship did return to Orange Bay, Wilkes wanted the schooners to transport the scientists to Valparaiso; otherwise they would be delayed even longer by an interminable passage north aboard the slow-sailing *Relief.* The next time the squadron reassembled, it would be in the warm waters of the Pacific.

The *Vincennes* anchored at Valparaiso on May 15. Wilkes found the *Peacock,* but saw no sign of the *Relief.* From Hudson, who had been at anchor now for close to three weeks, he learned that Lieutenant Long had arrived almost a month earlier and had since sailed up the coast to Callao, Peru, where he was taking on stores. Wilkes also learned why the *Relief* had not returned to Orange Bay.

While the rest of the squadron had headed south, the *Relief* had set out from Orange Bay for the Strait of Magellan on February 26. Long had been instructed to sail west and north, following the rocky coastline to the western entrance to the Strait. He was then to sail the length of the Strait, seeking shelter whenever necessary along its north shore while providing the scientists with every possible opportunity to collect specimens. By the time they returned to Orange Bay, no later than April 15, they would have completed a circumnavigation of Tierra del Fuego. But the voyage did not go as planned.

Instead of hugging the shore on his way to the Strait of Magellan, as Wilkes had advised him to do, Long chose to play it safe, heading well offshore before beginning to work north. Unfortunately a series of storms and headwinds turned what Wilkes had predicted would be a two-day passage to the mouth of the Strait into a seemingly interminable struggle up the coast. On March 17, three weeks after leaving Orange Bay, the *Relief* was finally beginning to approach the western coast of South America. The geologist James Dana looked forward to "fine sport among the guanacos [cousins of llamas], birds and fish of the Straits." But then it began to blow a gale from the southwest.

"The winds howled through the rigging with almost deafening violence," Dana wrote. The sleet and dense haze offered little visibility, but Lieutenant Long knew that somewhere to leeward lay what was known as the "Milky Way," a region of countless rocks and tiny islands that virtually defied navigation. Philip King, the British navy captain whose sailing instructions Long had read with great care, said of the Milky Way: "No vessel ought to entangle herself in these labyrinths, if she does, she must sail by eye. Neither chart, directions, nor soundings, would be of much assistance and in thick weather the situation would be most precarious."

At three P.M. the next day the lookout cried, "Breakers under the bows!" Out of the thick gray mist loomed the hundred-foot-high Tower Rocks, against which the waves of the Southern Ocean broke with such force that the spray shot up higher than the *Relief*'s masthead. The ship was brought about but could make no headway against the tremendous wind and waves. The mist broke clear for a few minutes, revealing Noir Island under the lee bow, just a few miles to the northeast. "[N]ight was approaching," Lieutenant Long wrote, "to claw off or hold our own was impracticable, a portentous sky, and the *'milky way'* close under our lee, warned us that our graves might be made in it." Long resolved to sail for the shelter of Noir Island.

"We could not but admire the coolness and judgment of Captain Long," Dana wrote, "who, through the whole was seated on the fore-yard, giving his orders as quietly and deliberately as in more peaceful times." As the *Relief* bore down on Noir Island, Long ordered the men to prepare the anchors. In a half hour they had rounded the southeastern point of the island, where they found a small, partially sheltered cove. It would have to do. In sixteen fathoms of water, they brailed up their trysails, luffed into the wind, and let go two of their anchors, along with one hundred and fifty fathoms of chain, and furled the sails. "Here we felt comparatively safe," Long wrote. That night, the naturalist Charles Pickering overheard one of the officers remark "that a few such days as this would make a man turn gray." "[T]he sequel proved," Pickering wrote, "that one's hair does not turn gray so easily."

When they awoke the next morning, the wind had diminished. They could see snow atop the six-hundred-foot-high peaks of the island. Some of the scientists, noticing a tiny cove beside them, even talked about going ashore. But then the wind began to build and shifted to the southeast. The island was no longer providing any protection. "A heavy Cape Horn sea was now setting into the harbor," Dana wrote, "and as the ship reared and plunged with each passing wave we feared that every lurch would snap the cables or drag our anchors." An old sailor who had been more than forty-five years at sea told Pickering that he "had never before seen such riding." Behind them was a reef that terminated with a large jagged rock, which now lay directly astern. They watched as the waves thundered against it. That night, the anchors began to drag. Long ordered the men to lower a third anchor, then a fourth. "[T]here seems to be nothing that separates us from eternity," he wrote in his log, "but the sailors semblance of *Hope,* the Anchor."

The next morning, March 20, Long ordered the men to heave in the two larboard chains to see if the anchors were still attached to them. As he had suspected, one of them was gone completely while the other had lost its shank, rendering it worthless. "Our situation may be described," he wrote, "but *I* shan't attempt it." The wind began to build, creating what Long described as "an awful swell." As night approached, Long ordered his officers and men to *"prepare for the worst."* Dana decided that in the event that the *Relief* drifted into the ironbound coast of Noir Island behind them, "his the happiest lot who was soonest dead" since those who weren't drowned or battered to pieces on the rocks could only look forward to dying of exposure on the island, which was now completely smothered in snow. Assuming his time had come, Pickering, the naturalist, decided to retire to his cabin. With a pillow under his head and his cloak wrapped around him, he stretched out on the cabin floor and fell instantly asleep–"a philosophic act," Wilkes later wrote, "that was in keeping with his quiet and staid manner."

No one else aboard the *Relief* appears to have slept a wink that night. "[E]very pitch of the ship was feared as the last," Dana wrote. "How anxiously we followed her motion down as she plunged her head into the water, and then watched her rising from those depths, until with a sudden start she gained the summit of the wave, and reeled and quivered at the length of her straightened cable!" With each one of these upward thrusts, the remaining anchors and chains could be heard dragging across the rocks–an appalling rumble that to Dana's ear sounded like the growling of distant thunder. At nine P.M. the crew was ordered on deck "to await the event." By this time the sound of the dragging anchors had become "almost an incessant peal," Dana wrote, "announcing that the dreaded crisis was fast approaching."

They had drifted to within a ship's length of the reef. One of the anchors finally caught and, for a few brief moments, the *Relief* hovered in the wild surge of the breakers. "[T]he ship rose and fell a few times with the swell," Dana wrote, "and then rose and careened as if half mad: her decks were deluged with the sweeping waves, which poured in torrents down the hatches." The strain on the cables proved too much, and at 11:30 P.M. the anchor chain parted. "[W]e found ourselves," Long wrote, "at God's mercy."

With the remnants of the cables hanging from the bow, the *Relief* began to drift to her apparent destruction. Then a miracle occurred. For the last few hours the wind had been gradually shifting to the east. Just when it looked as if they were about to fetch up on the large rock at the end of the reef, the *Relief*–as if nudged by the hand of God–drifted around the final hazard and out to sea.

Long realized that there was now a possibility for action. He waited until Noir Island's Astronomers Point bore west by south, then ordered the cables slipped. Under fore-trysail and storm-staysail, they wore the ship "short round," Long wrote, "without unnecessary loss of ground." More sail was set, and using the smooth water in the lee of Noir Island to his advantage, Long drove the *Relief* under "a heavy press of sail" to windward. The next morning Pickering awoke to discover that the crisis had passed. The *Relief* had clawed far enough to weather that Long was confident they would soon clear Cape Gloucester and "once more reach the wide waters of the Pacific in safety."

They had made no new discoveries, but the officers and men of the *Relief* had made their mark in the annals of American seamanship. "It is doubtful that in the history of the Navy," one commentator has written, "there has been a more remarkable escape from destruction on a lee shore." Long opened his sealed orders and learned that the squadron was headed for Valparaiso. Although he was supposed to have first returned to Orange Bay, he felt that without any anchors he had no option but to continue on to Chile. At Valparaiso, Long was able to secure an anchor from the British warship *Fly*, and on April 14, the *Relief* sat quietly at rest for the first time in more than a month and a half.

When, a month later, Wilkes learned of the *Relief*'s travails, he was filled not with grateful wonder for her deliverance but with outrage and indignation. Long had committed the same sin that had resulted in the longest passage in recorded history to Rio de Janeiro. Ironically, while trying to play it safe, he had put not only his own vessel but the future of the Expedition at risk. If he had only done as Wilkes had recommended–hug the coast, rather than timidly stand off from it–none of this would have happened.

On May 19, the *Flying Fish*, back under the command of Passed Midshipman Samuel Knox, arrived at Valparaiso. The *Sea Gull* was nowhere in sight. Shortly after leaving Orange Bay, the two schooners had encountered a particularly violent gale, and Knox had fled back to the bay. Knox had last seen the *Sea Gull* riding out the gale in the lee of Staten Island and had assumed she would have beaten them to Valparaiso.

It was too early to leap to any conclusions, but if something *had* happened to the *Sea Gull,* back under the command of Passed Midshipman Reid, Wilkes blamed it on Long. By Wilkes's logic, if the *Relief* hadn't been overdue at Orange Bay, he wouldn't have been forced to order the two schooners to wait for the storeship's return, and the *Flying Fish* and the *Sea Gull* would have sailed safely to Valparaiso. In the meantime all they could do was wait and hope that the little schooner and her fifteen-man crew would be soon sighted sailing into the harbor.

Before he headed for Callao and had it out with Lieutenant Long, Wilkes had other matters to attend to in Valparaiso. On May 20, the day after the arrival of the *Flying Fish,* a naval court of inquiry commenced aboard the *Peacock.* For the next week, Hudson, who was appointed president of the court, presided over a painstaking reexamination of the actions of Lieutenant Dale at Good Success Bay. After close to a dozen witnesses had been called to testify, it was established that Dale had done everything he could to get his boat-crew off the beach but had been thwarted by the rising surf of an approaching gale. Wilkes, who had insisted on the court of inquiry, would later issue a public reprimand accusing Dale of incompetence and cowardice that was completely at odds with the court's findings.

The Dale incident would prove to be a kind of watershed in the Expedition, establishing a pattern that would be repeated over and over again for the next three years. Just as he had done earlier with Lieutenants Craven and Lee, Wilkes had felt compelled to pounce on and attack a seemingly innocent and well-meaning officer. No matter how many times this would happen in the years ahead, Wilkes's officers and men remained at a loss to explain their commander's behavior.

Some leaders have the ability to step back from even the most volatile situation and assess, as best they can, what really happened. Wilkes, on the other hand, epitomized what has been called the "emotional mind." He responded to situations quickly and passionately. Even if subsequent events proved that his initial response was unwarranted, he clung like a bulldog to his first impression. The dismissal of Craven at Rio Negro and Lee at Orange Bay resulted from knee-jerk reactions that a more careful and rational weighing of the evidence would have shown to be completely unjustified. But this is not how the emotional mind works. "Actions that spring from the emotional mind carry a particularly strong sense of certainty," writes Daniel Goleman, "a by-product of a streamlined, simplified way of looking at things that can be absolutely bewildering to the rational mind." Substitute "his officers" for "the rational mind," and you have an excellent description of how the squadron's lieutenants and passed midshipmen responded to these early examples of Wilkes's style of command.

The case of Lieutenant Dale was just as perplexing. Wilkes had watched events unfold on the wave-hammered shore of Good Success Bay from the deck of the *Porpoise.* He had had no direct contact with Dale, and except for a few days of anxious waiting, there had been no long term repercussions from the incident. But Wilkes had been infuriated by Dale's inability to return to the *Porpoise.* From his perspective, Dale's actions amounted to a personal insult–a flagrant crime that required a swift and crushing response. Instead of a commanding officer, Wilkes was behaving much like an indignant child on a playground, and his officers were shocked by his callous bullying of a blameless lieutenant.

"Such a villainous attempt to ruin an unoffending man," William Reynolds later wrote, "opened the eyes of the staunchest admirers of Lieutenant Wilkes to the glaring faults of his character, and to borrow a phrase of his own, [the case of Lieutenant Dale] may be considered as the *'turning point'* of the feelings of the officers, towards their commander. Here forward, there was no affection for his person, and consideration, humanity or justice was no longer hoped for at his hand."

Underlying Wilkes's actions was the conviction that the officers whom he had inherited from Commodore Jones, and who represented the one aspect of the Expedition's organization over which he had had no control, were incompetent. "It is astonishing," he wrote Jane, "that all Commdr Jones men and officers with one or two exceptions are good for nothing." What he did not take into account was that over the course of the last year his inner circle of officers had inevitably gotten to know and respect many of the officers from the previous regime. Reynolds and his friends were becoming less and less willing to stand idly by as Wilkes ran roughshod over their compatriots.

Wilkes, who had not even a smattering of empathetic understanding, remained oblivious to this shift within the squadron. He was convinced that if he could only rid himself of Jones's officers, all would be well. "[A]ll those I have brought into the Expedn. give me no trouble," he assured Jane as late as June 16. "They are improving rapidly under my good tuition and I shall be able to make men of them I hope before I have done with them."

Before the squadron left Valparaiso for Callao in June, Wilkes implemented the first part of a plan "to get rid of many of my worthless officers." Lieutenant Craven had made it clear that he wanted to command a schooner. Well, Wilkes would grant him his wish. He ordered Craven to remain in Valparaiso to take command of the *Sea Gull* when she finally arrived. More than a month overdue, the *Sea Gull* was assumed lost by most officers in the squadron, and Craven made it clear to Wilkes that he knew exactly what his commander was up to. Wilkes insisted, however, that he still held out hope. If, God forbid, the *Sea Gull* did not arrive, then, of course, Craven would be required to return to the United States. Wilkes could now turn his attention to Lieutenant Long.

Once in Callao, Wilkes ordered that the storeship *Relief* be fumigated, a procedure that produced three barrels of dead rats. From Wilkes's perspective, the rats were not the only vermin plaguing the squadron. Long was incompetent and worthy of a court-martial. In addition to Craven, now safely salted away in Valparaiso, and Lee, who had already sailed for the United States on the *Henry Lee* (a ship named for his uncle), there were Lieutenant Dale and an ever-growing list of lieutenants and surgeons whose chief sin was that they had formerly served under Jones. He wouldn't be able to rid himself of all of them, but on June 21, Wilkes consigned a goodly portion to the *Relief.* The storeship, he announced, was too slow to be of use to the squadron. After dropping provisions at Sydney, Australia, and Honolulu, the ship was to return to the United States. "[A]fter I have rid myself of her," Wilkes wrote Jane, "& her useless trash I shall be well off." Long, who had won the respect of all who had served under him, did not take Wilkes's decision well. "Much difficulty & diplomacy" were entailed, Reynolds wrote, "in quieting Captain Long."

It was while the *Relief* was being loaded with provisions for its final swing through the Pacific that some minor trouble erupted. Some of the squadron's marines were ordered to supervise the transfer of whiskey into the storeship's hold, but instead of maintaining proper discipline, the marines joined the sailors in sampling the wares. Wilkes was not amused by the drunken frolic that resulted. The next day, the offenders suffered twenty-four lashes each, even though twelve was the legal limit without the sanction of a court-martial. When three deserters were delivered to Wilkes a few days later, two received thirty-six lashes while the third got forty-one—once again without a court-martial. Wilkes claimed that there was not enough time for normal due process and that the punishments were not unreasonable considering the offenses. It was a judgment that would come back to haunt him several years later.

By now almost all agreed that the *Sea Gull*—which had not been seen in several months—had been lost. Wilkes wrote that her officers, Passed Midshipmen James Reid and Frederick Bacon, "were among the most promising young officers in the squadron." He speculated that the schooner might have tripped her foremast in the gale off Cape Horn, which would have ripped up her deck and caused her to founder. "Poor, poor fellows," lamented Reynolds, who had grown so closely attached to the vessel and her crew at Tierra del Fuego, "what a terrible lot. The two officers were young men of my age, one if he be indeed gone, leaving a wife more youthful than himself and [a] child that [he] has never seen."

With Craven and many of the other senior lieutenants eliminated from the squadron, Wilkes began to reshuffle his officers. For a brief time Reynolds feared he might be transferred off the *Vincennes* to another vessel. Wilkes was now able to reappoint his special favorite

Overton Carr (whom he referred to as "Otty" in his letters to Jane) as his first lieutenant. Wilkes liked to think of himself as coolly objective in his dealings with his officers, insisting to Jane that his lieutenants were "not a little astonished at my decision and impartiality for it makes no matter with me who the individual is that offends, I give him the necessary rebuke." But Otty Carr was the exception. "He is so much in my confidence," he wrote Jane, "from having been my flag Lieutenant and so long with me that it gives me pleasure to aide him in his duties," adding that Carr "has risen further than your dear husband by holding on to my coat."

There was another Wilkes intimate, however, who was giving him no such pleasure. While in Valparaiso, his teenage nephew, Midshipman Wilkes Henry, had been a principal in a duel. Dueling had a long and undistinguished history in the U.S. Navy. One historian has claimed that between 1798 and 1848, thirty-six naval officers were killed in eighty-two duels, approximately two-thirds as many as died in combat during that same period. For a young man whose sense of self-worth was defined by his willingness to die in a noble cause, the dark and romantic tradition of dueling was difficult to resist. Put a steerage full of teenage naval officers together with too much time on their hands, and some sort of trouble was bound to occur. When someone felt his sense of dignity had been slighted, a formal challenge was sure to follow.

When it came to the Ex. Ex., young Wilkes Henry did not have the best of role models. Reynolds's friend William May had fought several duels, including a bloodless square-off four years earlier against another Expedition lieutenant, A. S. Baldwin. (As was often true after a duel, the two former opponents were now good friends.) Wilkes Henry's duel dated back to what Wilkes described as a "foolish quarrel" with Passed Midshipman George Harrison in Rio de Janeiro. Unable to arrange the duel in Rio, they were forced to wait until the squadron's arrival in Valparaiso, where Henry took along fellow midshipman James Blair as his second. Luckily, no one was hurt. "[T]hey took two shots at each other," Wilkes told Jane, "to little effect." Wilkes felt he had no alternative but to dismiss all four officers (the two principals and their seconds) from the squadron, calling them "a pack of young boobies." But it was

Wilkes Henry in whom he was most disappointed. "Oh how I do regret I ever consented to his coming in the Expedition," he wrote Jane.

Knowing that dismissal would ruin his nephew's naval career, Wilkes continued to agonize over the decision. He consulted Hudson, the one man in the squadron whom he felt he could talk to about such matters. "I told him that I should never forgive myself if any accident happened to [Wilkes]," he told Jane. Hudson's own son was a midshipman in the squadron. "[H]e said he could readily enter into my feelings."

On June 22, Wilkes received a letter signed by most of the officers in the Expedition requesting that he not dismiss the duelists and their seconds. The officers promised that they would not allow a similar incident to occur. Wilkes gladly took the opportunity to reevaluate his original decision, especially since it was clear that the officers were most concerned not about Harrison but about his nephew. "[W]hen you know that their fondness for Wilkes has induced them to take this interest for them all," he wrote Jane, "I am sure you will feel as much gratification as I do about it." "[A]ll my troubles about Wilkes are at an end," he happily declared.

The officers' collective plea of June 22 provided an opportunity of another sort for the commander of the Expedition. The letter represented a surprising gesture of support from the officers, especially given Wilkes's most recent actions. He might have used the incident as a rallying point—a way to start to rebuild his officers' morale. He had pared the officer corps down to the extent that it was now dominated by his inner circle. A few nicely timed compliments and promotions would have instilled a renewed sense of purpose and loyalty in a group of men who were yearning for some sign of approval from their commander. Instead, Wilkes listened to Captain Isaac McKeever.

Wilkes had first met McKeever, the commander of the USS *Falmouth*, at Valparaiso and had been immediately seduced by him. Unlike the hated Commodore Nicholson back in Rio de Janeiro (who would later direct the unsuccessful search for the crew of the *Sea Gull*), McKeever immediately referred to him as Captain Wilkes. He also had nothing but praise for Wilkes and the Expedition. Wilkes would later remember that McKeever "gave me encouragement to go forward with resolution and confidence."

Other officers in the squadron took notice of McKeever's attentiveness, particularly when the *Falmouth* followed the squadron to Callao. Once in Peru, McKeever continued his curious wooing of Wilkes, even offering him his ship's launch and a cutter. "Capt. McKeever seems to feel great interest in the Expedition," warily noted Lieutenant Johnson, formerly of the *Sea Gull* and now first lieutenant of the *Porpoise*. "I hope he has no sinister views."

Not until early July did it become generally known what McKeever expected as his part in what Johnson termed the "famous bargain." The removal of so many senior lieutenants from the squadron had created an opening for a sailing master aboard the *Vincennes*. At the very beginning of the Expedition, Wilkes had promised his officers that all promotions would be made within the squadron's own ranks. But it turned out that Captain McKeever had a nephew aboard the *Falmouth*, Lieutenant Edwin DeHaven, who wanted to join the Expedition. Wilkes agreed to make DeHaven his sailing master.

For the junior officers of the Expedition eager for promotion, it was a crushing blow. Reynolds was at the head of the list for the promotion to sailing master, but now he would have to wait. "The Falmouth came in," he bitterly recorded in his journal, "Cap McKeever, gave us his Launch, 1st Cutter and his Nephew: which latter, was heartily wished at the d___l by us." Wilkes would have never acknowledged it, but he was, in effect, continuing the cycle of abuse: just as he had been devastated by Poinsett's refusal to grant him an acting appointment, now he was imposing the same injustice on Reynolds and his fellow officers. "[T]he wound that has been inflicted will rankle all the cruise," Reynolds predicted. "I feel as if my very life had been taken away." For Reynolds and his fellow officers, this was the true turning point of the Expedition.

CHAPTER 6

Commodore of the Pacific

O N JULY 15, 1839, just a day out of Callao, Wilkes did for himself and Hudson what the secretary of the navy had refused to
do. He made the two of them captains. After leaving Norfolk
almost a year before, Wilkes had removed the epaulet from his uniform,
but on that mild clear morning, he appeared on the quarterdeck of the
Vincennes wearing what Reynolds described as "an immense pair of
Epaulettes."

There was more to come. As captain and commander of a squadron,
Wilkes felt he was now entitled to the honorary rank of Commodore of
the U.S. Exploring Expedition. So it was that at precisely 9:00 A.M. the
narrow streamer, known as a "coach whip," at the masthead of the *Vincennes* was replaced by the broad, blue, swallow-tailed pendant, or pennant, of a commodore.

It was an audacious, even outrageous act, without precedent in the
U.S. Navy. Wilkes would later admit that the move could have been
considered "a bold and unwarranted stroke of policy on my part." The
timing was also suspect. Why now, rather than at the beginning of the
Expedition? In a letter to Jane, Wilkes claimed that it was his "excessive
modesty" that had delayed his donning of the epaulets. "It will give
[Hudson and me] much more respect," he wrote, "and I think add to
my influence over the officers and crew." In his official journal, Wilkes
dubiously asserted that he had "assumed the uniform in obedience to
orders of the Secty. Of the Navy. . . . My reasons for not having done
this heretofore [are] but known to myself."

As far as the officers of the U.S. Ex. Ex. were concerned, Wilkes's reasons were quite obvious. The squadron was on the verge of a wilderness larger than all the world's landmasses combined. Once amid the islands of the Pacific, it would take months, perhaps years, for official correspondence to catch up with them. Beyond the reach of the administration, with little chance of encountering another U.S. naval vessel, Wilkes—the self-crowned commodore of the Exploring Expedition—had made it unmistakably clear that he now felt free to do exactly as he pleased.

But could he pull it off? Could he, in the words with which a captain commanded a lieutenant to implement an order, make it so?

As Wilkes's instructions made clear, one of the Expedition's primary goals was to provide charts for the nation's whalemen. America had, by far, the largest whaling fleet in the world. Unlike European merchant vessels, which used the Pacific as a thoroughfare from place to place, the whalemen followed the desultory movements of sperm whales across the full width and breadth of the largest ocean in the world. The vast distances they traveled required the whaling captains to look to the islands of Polynesia for provisions. Since few European mariners had reason to visit many of these islands, previous exploring expeditions had neglected to survey a significant number of the islands in any systematic manner. Indeed, there were entire groups, such as the Fijis, that had not yet been properly surveyed at all. Charting hundreds of Pacific islands was a gargantuan, largely thankless, and incredibly time-consuming task, but it was the chief aim of the U.S. Ex. Ex.

On August 13, after a passage of almost a month, they saw their first Pacific island. Reynolds immediately scampered up the mainmast to the royal yard, where he watched for more than an hour, "entranced with the Singular & picturesque loneliness of that gem of the Ocean." Before him lay one of the easternmost islands of the Tuamotu Group, the largest collection of coral atolls in the world. The island of Reao, known to Wilkes as Clermont de Tonnere, is less than a dozen miles long with the ringlike shape typical of a coral atoll. "[W]here the white beach terminates there is a beautiful fringe of Trees & Shrubbery,"

Reynolds wrote, "hiding from view the Lagoon within, but from aloft, you can look over the quiet lake, the Isles that stud its bosom, and the green strip that encompasses it round about." How an island comprised of coral, which only grows in shallow water, had come to exist in the middle of a vast and deep ocean was a question that greatly concerned the Expedition's scientists. "[E]ven in this enlightened age," Reynolds wrote, "[it] has defied a satisfactory explanation." By the end of the voyage, with a little help from Charles Darwin, the scientists of the Ex. Ex. would have an answer.

Wilkes intended to make Reao an object lesson in what were the Expedition's proper priorities. Surveying, not science, was to be attended to first. All the next day, the scientists watched in indignant disbelief from the decks of the *Vincennes,* the *Peacock,* and the *Porpoise.* After more than a year of anticipation, they were now forced to sit idly by as an island was surveyed, yet remained unexplored. The naturalist Titian Peale called it "a sorry business." Nevertheless, as all of them would begrudgingly come to acknowledge, there was a magnificent precision in the way that Wilkes and his officers undertook a survey.

It was essentially the same system he had developed at Georges Bank. Dividing up the four vessels of the squadron into two groups and assigning each group a specific survey area, he was able to reduce the time normally required to survey an island. One of the more interesting—and ear splitting—aspects of his method was the way he determined the baselines of the survey. The vessels would take up positions along the shore of the island, then begin firing their guns in rapid succession. By noting the time between the gun's flash and report, the officers were able to calculate the distance between the two vessels. (What effect this day-long display of firepower had on the island's native population can only be guessed.) In the meantime, other officers used sextants to measure angles between the vessels and points designated on shore. Once these were completed, the vessels changed their positions and eventually worked their way around the island. It wasn't long before they had roughed out a chart of the island complete with points of "known location along its perimeter."

It was now time for the boat-crews to go to work. One of the sailors

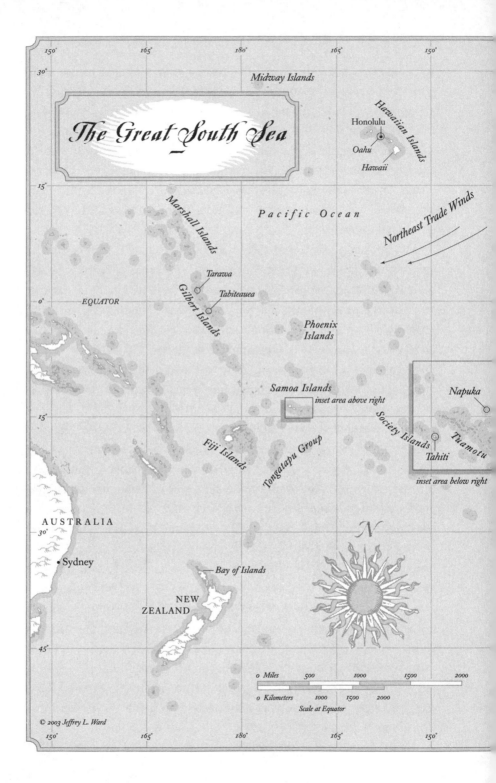

The Great South Sea

Midway Islands

Hawaiian Islands

Honolulu

Oahu

Hawaii

Pacific Ocean

Marshall Islands

Northeast Trade Winds

Tarawa

Tabiteauea

EQUATOR

Gilbert Islands

Phoenix Islands

Samoa Islands

inset area above right

Napuka

Society Islands

Tuamotu

Fiji Islands

Tongatapu Group

Tahiti

inset area below right

AUSTRALIA

Sydney

Bay of Islands

NEW ZEALAND

N

0 Miles   500   1000   1500   2000

0 Kilometers   1000   1500   2000

Scale at Equator

© 2003 Jeffrey L. Ward

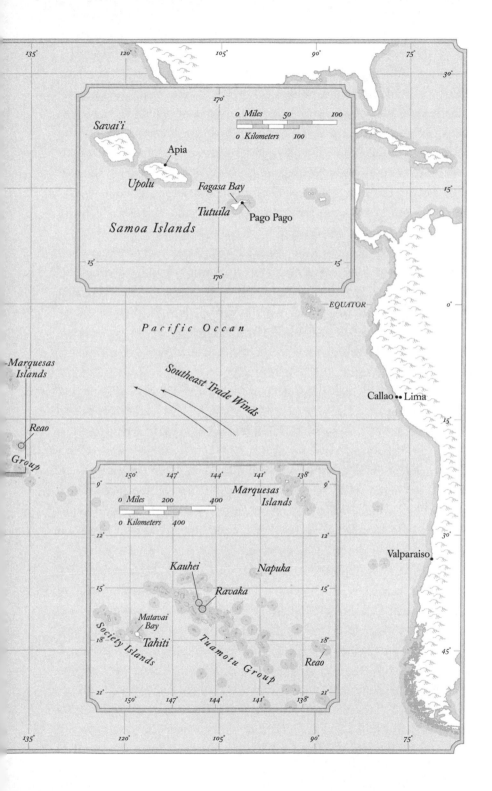

used the sounding lead to determine the water's depth while an officer with a sextant measured horizontal angles to known points on land. Each vessel had what was called a deck-board on which the information was recorded, and at the conclusion of the survey, copies of the data were sent to Wilkes along with a diagram to designate all the control points of the survey. Wilkes and his officers then compiled the various surveys to create a finished chart. The system brought a new level of speed and accuracy to the survey of the Pacific, and Reao was the first of 280 islands to be surveyed by the U.S. Ex. Ex.

But it was punishing work, especially for those assigned boat duty. Wet, sunburned, their eyes scorched from staring through the eyepieces of their sextants and other instruments, the officers and men returned that evening wondering if they would ever be allowed to enjoy the fabled delights of the South Seas. "The Captain has pushed us so with work," Reynolds recorded several nights later, "that we have had scarce time to eat–and there are no signs of a lull as of yet."

Not until the survey had been completed did Wilkes determine that it was time to unleash the scientists. But first he and his officers had to make contact with the island's inhabitants. Soon after departing from Callao he had issued an order insisting that everyone associated with the squadron exhibit "courtesy and kindness towards the natives." To help them achieve this objective, they had an interpreter, John Sac, a minor chief from New Zealand, who after spending some time in Tahiti had lived for a number of years in the United States, where he had been exhibited as a curiosity. As a crewmember aboard the *Sea Gull* during her voyage to the South Shetland Islands, Sac had taken such an enthusiastic interest in killing penguins that Lieutenant Johnson had had difficulty persuading him to relent. For the most part, however, Sac had developed a reputation in the squadron for his "disciplined obedience."

By the time Wilkes and his officers approached the island in a small flotilla of boats, a group of seventeen natives had assembled on the beach, with an estimated hundred or so lurking in the undergrowth behind them. Wilkes was in the lead, flying a white flag of truce, but the natives, "a fine athletic race, much above the ordinary in size," were not in a welcoming mood. Armed with long spears and clubs, the islanders made it clear that they did not want Wilkes to land. The natives in this region had a reputation for cannibalism, and Reynolds claimed that their gestures suggested that if the white men should come ashore "they would certainly be made a meal of."

Even though he had been born many thousands of miles away in New Zealand, Sac was able to understand the islanders, several of whom were chanting in unison. Sac reported that they were telling them, "Go to your own land; this belongs to us, and we do not want to have anything to do with you." At that moment the surf was too high to land, so Wilkes ordered his officers to attempt to appease the natives by throwing them some trinkets. But when the trade goods washed up at their feet, the natives scornfully kicked the baubles aside.

By this point Sac, standing at the boat's bow with a boat hook in his hand, had struck up a conversation with the group's leader. It was not going well. "[Sac] soon became provoked at the chief's obstinacy," Wilkes wrote, "his eyes shone fiercely, and his whole frame seemed agitated. Half naked as he was, his tattooing conspicuous, he stood in the bow of the boat brandishing his boat-hook like a spear with the dexterity of the savage." Although none of them knew what he was saying, Wilkes became concerned that Sac was only making matters worse and ordered him to desist in the negotiations. Reynolds's friend William May and another officer volunteered to swim ashore and attempt to greet the natives personally, but almost as soon as they made it to the beach, they were in full retreat and swimming back to the boats.

This was not the way Wilkes had wanted to begin his tour as commodore. After the scientist Joseph Couthouy also proved unsuccessful in winning the natives' trust, Wilkes ordered several of his officers to shoot off some blank cartridges. Once again, the reaction wasn't what he had hoped. Sac reported that "they hooted at these arms, calling us cowards, and daring us to come on shore." Quickly forgetting his own orders to treat the natives with compassion, Wilkes took up a gun armed with birdshot and fired at the natives on the beach. "[W]hen the Shot struck them," Reynolds wrote, "they brushed away at the spot as if a fly had bitten them, manifesting the utmost unconcern & contempt for us & our weapons, & exhibiting more of the cannibal in their faces

& gestures than was agreeable to witness." Wilkes ordered additional officers, including the naturalist Titian Peale, the best shot in the squadron, to fire on the natives. As the birdshot tore into their legs, backsides, and faces, the natives began to retreat into the interior of the island but with, Reynolds noted, "deliberate dignity."

Now that he had cleared the beach, Wilkes declared that it was safe to land. It was late in the day, but he had some observations he wanted to make, and the scientists would have their first, long-awaited opportunity to collect some specimens. After a mere half hour on the beach, it was time to return to the ships.

Wilkes felt he had provided the natives with "abundant proof of our prowess and superiority." Many of his officers begged to disagree. "I consider the plan of policy pursued here as miserable," wrote the assistant surgeon John Whittle. "[W]e have no doubt left these people in such a state of mind that if a ship should be unfortunately wrecked here, the crew will be murdered."

In the weeks ahead, as the squadron weaved its way among the Tuamotus toward Tahiti, eventually surveying a total of seventeen islands, the frustrations of the scientists only increased. Even when the natives proved friendly or the island uninhabited, Wilkes was reluctant to let them go ashore until after the survey was already well in hand. When no scientists were permitted to land on the island of Raraka, Titian Peale wrote out in bold letters across the page of his journal, "WHAT WAS A SCIENTIFIC CORP SENT FOR?" A few days later, Couthouy finally got the opportunity to collect some sizeable specimens of coral. But when he left them to dry outside his cabin door, Wilkes complained of the smell and ordered that no more coral could be dried below the spar deck. Couthouy insisted that European expeditions "had experienced no difficulty in the preservation of large and numerous specimens." Wilkes replied that "he did not care a damn for what had been done in previous expeditions . . . , and that he should take the responsibility of deciding all matters relative to *our* collections according to his own views." Like it or not, this was going to be the Wilkes Expedition.

If his relations with the scientists had reached a new low, it was even worse with his officers, many of whom had once considered themselves the commander's friends. Like Charlie Erskine before them—the cabin boy who had become so infuriated with Wilkes that he had contemplated murder—they had swung from ardent adoration to an equally passionate hate. "[W]e would have given ourselves to him entirely," Reynolds wrote Lydia, "but he [did] not [know] how to use the men who were so much attached to him and by his own doings he has turned his warmest friends into deathly foes."

As was true on any naval vessel, the officers of the *Vincennes* ate their meals in two different groups or messes, with the lieutenants in the wardroom and the passed midshipmen and midshipmen in steerage. As was also true on any naval vessel, it was common for members of both messes to socialize in their cabins, with Reynolds's and May's carpeted stateroom serving as an especially popular gathering spot. But as relations between the commander and his officers deteriorated, Wilkes began to resent what he saw as an excessive fraternization among his junior and senior officers. On August 20, he issued an order: "The commander has observed with regret, not only a tendency to familiarity among officers of different grades, but that the apartments of all grades of officers have been converted into a lounge by the juniors, which must in the nature of things produce a familiarity having a tendency to destroy . . . discipline."

Reynolds responded with what might be described as the steerage's declaration of independence. "In regard to the Selection of friends, or the privilege of enjoying their Society," he wrote, "so long as we do not impinge on the martial law of the quarter deck, or assemble for seditious purposes, we are strongly & firmly of the belief, that the delicacy of the question should forbid all interference, & must beg to be allowed to follow the sacred bent of our own inclinations." There was no longer any doubt as to how matters stood between the commander and his officers. "From this time forward," Reynolds wrote, "there was 'war to the knife' between Captn. Wilkes & most of his officers."

By mutual agreement, all social contact between Wilkes and his officers ceased. "I have given up inviting the officers to my table," he wrote Jane, "as I found it incompatible with my duties and I was desirous to widen the dividing line between us." Wilkes would later claim that he had, from the very beginning of the Expedition, chosen to remove himself from regular contact with his officers. Reynolds insists, however, that it was only after this bitter exchange that the policy became strictly enforced. "Henceforward the door of the Cabin was only passed on matters of duty," he wrote, "and the commander was left to the delight of his own society." For Wilkes, whose original style of command had involved an unusual amount of interaction with his officers and who had spent much of his professional life working at home in the company of his family, it was going to be a very lonely voyage across the Pacific.

At the island of Napuka (called Wytoohee by the Expedition), the natives once again appeared unwilling to allow them to land. John Sac was in a boat and already conversing with a group on shore when Wilkes rowed up in his six-oared gig with his broad commodore's pennant flying. Thumping his chest, Wilkes shouted out to Sac, "Tell them that *I* am the *Big Chief!*" Sac duly communicated this information, but the natives were apparently unimpressed, forcing Wilkes and his party to return to the *Vincennes* without landing on the island.

What made this incident particularly galling to Wilkes was that, as he and his officers could plainly see, just a short way down the beach Hudson's boat-crews had succeeded in reaching the shore and were engaged in pleasant conversation with the natives. Wilkes ordered one of his officers to inform Hudson that he must immediately vacate the beach. That night he wrote a letter chastising his second-in-command for unreasonably risking his men's lives when, in fact, his only crime had been that he had succeeded where Wilkes had failed.

On the morning of September 2, Wilkes signaled the *Flying Fish* to come within hail. They were just off Kauehi, and he wanted the schooner to transport several of the scientists to the island. The *Vincennes* was lying with her maintopsail aback, moving at a leisurely one knot. The schooner approached from windward and astern, and as she sailed under the ship's stern, Wilkes hailed her commander, Lieutenant Robert Pinkney, to head up and wait, or heave to. Not hearing the order, Pinkney continued on, sailing to leeward of and parallel to the *Vincennes*. Wilkes, irritated that Pinkney had not immediately responded to his hail, ran to the leeward side of his ship and shouted, "Heave to! Mr. Pinkney, I told you to heave to!" Since the schooner was now less than a hundred yards from the ship, there wasn't room for her to heave to in the *Vincennes*'s lee without risking a collision. This did not deter Wilkes, who was now jogging along the gangway so as to keep abreast of the *Flying Fish*. "Why don't you heave to, Mr. Pinkney?" he screamed through the speaking trumpet.

Pinkney could have first headed downwind so as to create a sufficient gap between himself and the ship and then hove to. That was what Wilkes later claimed he had expected him to do. Instead, Pinkney decided to try to sail past the *Vincennes* and, once ahead of the ship, heave to to windward. But when he put the helm hard down, there was not sufficient space between the *Flying Fish* and the *Vincennes,* and the schooner rounded head to wind directly in front of the ship. By this point, Wilkes had made it to the bowsprit. "What do you mean, sir!" he shouted. "What do you mean? I never saw anything of the like! God damn you! I did not tell you to heave to under my bows!" If not for the quick-witted Lieutenant Joseph Underwood, who ordered the foretopsail backed, the *Vincennes* would have surely run down the schooner and very likely killed all hands.

From Reynolds's perspective, it appeared as if Wilkes's excessive badgering of the *Flying Fish*'s commander had pressured him into doing something he would not ordinarily have done. The real fault lay with Wilkes's style of command. As was becoming increasingly clear, even to the youngest boys in the squadron, Wilkes, despite his claims of being "another John Paul Jones," was no seaman. He might be adept at pushing the *Porpoise* through the ice, but he seemed at a loss when it came to the more nuanced intricacies of maneuvering his ship among other vessels. While at Valparaiso the *Vincennes* had become caught up in the rigging of a bark from Hamburg, and Wilkes's "lubberly obstinacy" had deeply embarrassed Reynolds and the other officers. In truth, Wilkes did not have the sea experience or the personality to negotiate a ship in close quarters. His passionate nature made it impossible for him to issue orders in a composed and careful manner, and he was without the natural, ingrained sensitivity to the movements of a sailing vessel that is essential to being an effective seaman.

It didn't help matters that the officer he had chosen as his first lieutenant, Overton Carr, was equally lacking in seamanship skills. But to Wilkes's mind, whatever difficulties he encountered were always the fault of others. He claimed that the incident with the *Flying Fish* had caused the officers aboard the schooner to be "almost beside themselves and nonplused as ignorance is always in such situations." But it had been Wilkes, not the officers of the *Flying Fish,* who had lost control of his emotions, and for the duration of the voyage, he would do everything in his power to persecute the schooner's commander, Robert Pinkney.

Reynolds began to wonder if Wilkes was suffering from some kind of mental imbalance. "We find ourselves entirely at a loss to account for his motives," he wrote Lydia, "or to imagine how any man in a sane mind could be guilty of such wrong headed measures." As far as Reynolds could tell, Wilkes was no longer the same person he had come to admire in Washington. "The nature of the man has become changed," he wrote, "he is as one possessed by a demon."

Wilkes had changed, but less so than Reynolds, who had only known him for a few brief months prior to the Ex. Ex., might have thought. All his life, Wilkes had cast himself as the righteous outsider who must battle against the forces of ignorance and ineptitude to achieve what others thought could never be done. He was the antithesis of the "team player," and as he had proven with Ferdinand Hassler more than a decade before, he was capable of turning on the people closest to him if he thought it served his best interests. For a few brief months, his original corps of passed midshipmen had been an integral part of Wilkes's campaign to prove to Washington, if not the navy, that he was the natural choice to lead the Expedition. Little did Reynolds and the others realize that once they had served Wilkes's initial purposes, all bets were off.

Wilkes's interpersonal skills had always been next to nonexistent, but for much of his professional life he had benefited from the advice of Jane, whom he referred to as "my moderation." Reynolds and his compatriots had become part of Wilkes's world at a time when Jane's influence was at its height; indeed, she seems to have scripted many of the moves that won him command of the Ex. Ex. But now Wilkes was without Jane's steadying hand. On occasion he would consult Hudson, but his good-natured second-in-command was not about to tell him anything he did not want to hear. Without restraint, Wilkes's fanatical and outspoken personality inevitably began to raise havoc with the officers of the squadron.

A year into the Expedition, Wilkes had essentially re-created the environment in which he had always operated: it was he, and he alone, against the rest of the world. It was a turbulent, hurtful, and ultimately wasteful way to conduct one's life, but it was the only way he knew how to do it. Except for his first lieutenant Overton Carr, the purser Robert Waldron, and the surgeon John Fox, there were no officers aboard the *Vincennes* he could trust. This meant that despite being the leader of a nonmilitary expedition, Wilkes conducted himself as if he were in the midst of a war—not with icebergs and uncharted reefs, but with his own officers.

At some point, Wilkes became known as the Stormy Petrel, a nickname that would stay with him for the rest of his life, and as any sailor knows, the appearance of a stormy petrel means that rough weather is ahead. The squadron as a whole, but the *Vincennes* in particular, became a nonstop whirlwind of activity. In addition to their daily surveying duties, the officers and men were constantly harassed by the cry, "All Hands on Deck!"—an order Wilkes issued as many as fifteen times a day. Under these conditions, it was impossible to count on more than an hour's undisturbed sleep a night. But if Wilkes drove his men hard, he drove himself even harder. Every night, he worked well past midnight on his charts. Surgeon John Fox later reported that Wilkes averaged no more than five hours sleep a night and often went for days at a time

with no sleep at all. Sleep deprivation leads to a loss of emotional control as well as a failure to make complex social judgments–just the areas
in which Wilkes's personality was already lacking.

Underlying Wilkes's determination to push himself and his men "to
the wall" was an unshakable sense of dread. "It is almost impossible to
give the constant anxiety I was under," he later wrote, "arising from the
feelings I had of the incompetency of the officers." The true source of
this "constant anxiety" was not a lack of confidence in his officers, but
in himself. Too controlling to adequately delegate his many responsibilities, turned rabid with exhaustion, paranoia, and loneliness even as he
clung pathetically to the tattered notion of his infallibility, Wilkes was in
danger of becoming a caricature of the enlightened explorer. Instead of
his boyhood hero James Cook, the Stormy Petrel was acting more like
that tyrant of legend William Bligh. Whether or not his officers would
go the way of Fletcher Christian remained to be seen.

On September 10, the island of Tahiti came within view. Compared to
the low coral atolls of the Tuamotus, Tahiti's high volcanic peaks were
a wonderful contrast and reminded several of the officers of the Expedition's first landfall, Madeira. But Tahiti was much more than a physical place for the officers and men of the Ex. Ex.; it represented the holy
ground of Pacific exploration–the magical island where European civilization had first come in significant contact with the exotic world of
Polynesia (a term coined in the eighteenth century by the Frenchman
Charles De Brosses, meaning "many islands").

What is remarkable, in retrospect, is how long it took for the two
cultures to meet. Magellan had been the first to sail across the Pacific
in 1521–22. Except for two uninhabited atolls, he had not seen a single island until he'd come across Guam, almost nine thousand miles
from South America. In the intervening years, Spanish galleons regularly sailed from South America to the Philippines, but the route they
followed like a well-worn trail seldom brought them into contact with
the islands and their people. A handful of European mariners had ventured to scattered portions of the Pacific, but for the most part the

ocean remained almost completely unexplored through the middle of the eighteenth century, more than 250 years after Magellan.

That all changed with the voyage of Samuel Wallis, the British naval officer who stumbled on the island of Tahiti in 1768, two years before it was visited by James Cook. The island seemed almost too good to be true. The lush hills and valleys were filled with fruit, vegetables, pigs, and birds; the surrounding waters abounded with fish. With everything they needed at their fingertips, the Tahitians, whose physical size and beauty stunned the Europeans, were free to live a life of apparent ease. Best of all, from the sailors' perspective, the women, wearing little more than the flowers in their hair, were willing to fulfill the men's every desire for the price of an iron nail. When the ready supply of nails ran out, Wallis became concerned that his ship might be pulled to pieces by his sailors' frantic search for additional trade goods.

Even before Wallis returned to England to tell Cook about his discovery, Tahiti was visited by Louis-Antoine de Bougainville, the first Frenchman to circumnavigate the globe. Bougainville's report of a virtual Garden of Eden, which he dubbed "New Cythera," was taken as proof of the Enlightenment's belief in the innate goodness of natural man, uncorrupted by the evils of society. But by the time Cook arrived on the scene a year later, Tahiti was no longer the utopia it had once been. Venereal disease was now rampant on the island, and in a matter of weeks Cook's surgeon reported thirty-three cases among the sailors and marines. In subsequent years a host of European-borne diseases would ravage the native population.

Three decades after its discovery, Tahiti received a visitation of a different sort. Where the French had seen an Eden, the London Missionary Society saw an island of barbarous heathens in desperate need of the Word of God. Not until 1815, when King Pomare II embraced Christianity so as to help him defeat his tribal rivals, did the Society begin to make genuine inroads. Then, with the arrival of a young, charismatic reformed ironmonger named John Williams two years later, Christianity started to spread not only throughout Tahiti but to islands across Polynesia.

By the time the Ex. Ex. arrived at the island, seventy-two years after Cook, the paradise of the South Pacific had become thoroughly
Christian. Hundreds of Tahitians, the women adorned in full-length
dresses and floppy bonnets, the men in a ragged assortment of Western
pants and shirts, made their way to church every Saturday (the holy day
on Tahiti because the first missionaries had forgotten to take into account the time change). Much to the missionaries' dismay, Tahiti had
recently become an occasional provisioning stop for the British and
American whaling fleets, and the boisterous sailors threatened to undermine the natives' tenuous grasp of Christian morality. All the while,
the French and British governments were eyeing each other warily over
control of Tahiti. The island that had once been an icon was in danger
of becoming a colony.

Cook had originally come to Tahiti to observe the transit of Venus
across the sun, and Wilkes, having just reread his great predecessor's
narrative, was intent on re-creating history. "We anchored in Matavai
Bay under Point Venus," he wrote, "perhaps in the very position once
occupied by Captn Cook. . . . The stillness of the harbour with nothing
to disturb its placid surface was refreshing, filled as the air was with the
fragrance of flowers on shore." But instead of lovely women offering
their charms, the squadron was soon surrounded by canoe-loads of natives offering to wash their laundry. In emulation of Cook, Wilkes ordered his officers to erect the squadron's portable observatories on
Point Venus, where several tents, a forge, and a carpenters' work station
were also assembled as a crowd of Tahitians gathered around them.
"[T]hey hovered about us," Reynolds wrote, "as if it was actually necessary to their happiness to be always near us, & never quitted the Point
so long as we remained."

Reynolds was quickly introduced to one of the wonders of the
South Pacific–the coconut. Soon he was drinking as many as thirty of
them a day. "Let me record its praises here," he wrote in his journal, "I
owe my life to the milk of the Cocoa Nut, & like the Natives, I would
rather die, than harm a tree."

The officers and men of the Expedition quickly learned that the
Tahitians' reputation for sexual promiscuity was still well deserved.

Wilkes assured Jane that, unlike former expeditions, whose ships became "floating brothels," he allowed no women on his vessels and required his men to be back aboard by sunset. "This has won great praise from the missionaries," he reported.

Reynolds was shocked by the Tahitians' sexual openness (like "beasts in the fields," he recorded), but he was even more disturbed by the conduct of the missionaries. Instead of striving to teach the natives any substantive religious truths, they ruled by spiritual intimidation. "[T]he only evidence of Religion, that I noticed among the Natives, were the observance of External forms, & a fear of the Missionaries." In the pages of his journal he began to articulate a radical concept for the first half of the nineteenth century—that of cultural relativism. "Who can judge one nation by another?" he wrote. "What man can say, this people shall be my standard, by them I will judge all others? [The Tahitians] differ from us widely, but they are unconscious that *they* are wrong—that, which we could point at, with the finger of Shame & condemn as obscene & sinful, they deem of no harm, but as worthy of commendation & observance." In the months ahead, as the squadron made its way west to the islands of Samoa, Reynolds would find even more reason to question his preconceived notions of the innate superiority of Western society.

Tahiti proved to be an important crossroads for the scientists. Finally, they were set free. Couthouy and Peale would continue to grumble about Wilkes's dictatorial style, but the rest of the scientists found little to complain about as they rushed about the island on various expeditions into the interior. Charles Pickering was designated a "naturalist," but his primary interest was in what we would call today anthropology. He was becoming increasingly fascinated by the stunning variety of peoples he had so far seen—from the African slaves of Rio to the Yahgans of Cape Horn, the Native Americans of the Andes, and now the Polynesians of the Tuamotus and Tahiti. After spending several weeks with the Tahitians, he, like Reynolds, recognized that Western standards did not necessarily apply in the South Pacific. "[T]hese people are not to be judged precisely by the same rule as ourselves," he wrote in his journal. Unlike the Expedition's officers and scientists, who staggered about the underbrush in their thick, sweat-soaked clothes and lugged heavy boxes of provisions and equipment, the nearly naked Tahitians seemed perfectly adapted to the considerable demands of their environment. "Strip [a Tahitian] entirely in the morning and without an implement in his hand, turn him into the woods; then pay him a visit at night. We shall find him clothed from the lace of the Cocoa-nut tree, a garland on his head; a house over him, made of the Wild Bananas; thongs & cordage of all sorts from the bark of the Poorow tree; baskets made by plaiting the segments of a Cocoa-nut leaf; perhaps a mat to sleep on; cups or wash-bowls of Cocoa-nut shell, or even tumblers & casks of the joints of the large Bamboo; a Cap or an Umbrella if it is wanted of the Banana leaf; a fire kindled; [with] provisioning enough for a week."

As the scientists had a field day, Wilkes continued to antagonize his officers. Robert Pinkney, the commander of the *Flying Fish,* was unfairly accused of having neglected the schooner's condition. When Pinkney wrote a letter of complaint to the secretary of the navy, Wilkes refused to forward the correspondence to Washington. As he boasted to another officer, "action could not be taken against *him,* until his return to the U. States"–and that was at least two years away.

On October 11, the *Vincennes* anchored in one of the most unusual harbors in the South Pacific–Pago Pago, a deep, L-shaped canyon in the center of the mountainous island of Tutuila in what is today eastern or American Samoa. Since the prevailing southeasterly trade winds blow directly into the harbor, Pago Pago is easy enough for a sailing vessel to enter but is extremely difficult to leave. About a half-mile from the entrance, the harbor bends almost at a right angle to the west. Here, between precipices that reach as high as one thousand feet, Wilkes reported that the firing of a gun produced "a remarkable reverberation, resembling loud peals of thunder." In a few weeks the harbor of Pago Pago would prove to be an important testing ground for the leader of the Ex. Ex.

Reynolds was assigned surveying duty under Lieutenant Joseph Underwood. With Reynolds in a whaleboat named the *Greyhound* and

Underwood in the larger launch *Leopard,* they were to circumnavigate the island in a clockwise direction, stopping when necessary at villages along the way. The first day of sailing proved as dangerous as anything Reynolds had experienced off Tierra del Fuego. Strong winds and huge waves made surveying, let alone staying upright, extremely difficult. "[T]he Compass whirled like a top," Reynolds wrote, "from the jumping motion of the Boat & the Seas that broke over us [and] drenched all hands." They spent that first night at the village of Leone, where Reynolds was immediately impressed by the gentleness of the natives. "I noticed in the men, a fondness & care displayed towards their children," he wrote, "which I had not expected to find. While on the beach many huge fellows had infants & babbling youngsters in their arms." After picking up their two boats and placing them carefully on land, the natives led Reynolds and Underwood to their village. "There was a deep quiet," he wrote, "& the little scene around me, in the grove of the Magnificent Bread Fruits, was so simply innocent, that my soul was touched. My pride as a white man melted away & I thought in my heart, *these people have more claim to be good than we.* . . . I could not help thinking, what would be the reception of these people in *our Land?*"

At Fagasa, on the northwestern side of Tutuila and only a few miles' walk from the inner reaches of Pago Pago Harbor, which almost cuts the island in half, they found Midshipman Wilkes Henry. Henry had been stationed at Fagasa to measure the tides and make other observations. The commander's falling out with his officers had been as difficult for Henry as it had been for his uncle. Remarkably, the young midshipman had been able to remain on good terms with his fellow officers without being disloyal to Wilkes. Reynolds had nothing but admiration for the boy, and when heavy rains made it impossible to survey the next day, he and Underwood were pleased to spend the morning and afternoon in the village's "big house," talking with Henry and the natives. But the next day, when they returned to the village after surveying the harbor, they discovered that Commodore Wilkes, along with Waldron and nine sailors, had walked across the island to pay Henry a visit. It was time to move on.

A little more than a week later, Reynolds and Underwood had

completed their circumnavigation of Tutuila. The following afternoon the *Vincennes* weighed anchor and began to beat out of Pago Pago. Five days earlier, the *Peacock* and the *Flying Fish,* which had been sent ahead to the island of Upolu in western Samoa, had attempted to do the same thing. Given her fore-and-aft rig, the schooner had had no problem, but it had taken *four hours* for the square-rigged *Peacock* to tack her way out to sea. The large ocean swell at the harbor mouth made it difficult for the ship to carry her momentum through the eye of the wind, and several times it had looked as if the *Peacock* might be in danger of fetching up on the rocks.

From the beginning, it did not go well for the *Vincennes.* Even though the water was as smooth as glass within the inner reaches of the harbor, the ship was unable to complete her first tack—gradually losing all forward motion until she lay motionless in the water with her bow pointed into the wind, known as missing stays. "[B]ut this was not to be wondered at," Reynolds wrote. "Our first Luff [Lieutenant Carr, who was responsible for executing the maneuver] had disgraced himself often before." Luckily, the harbor pilot, an Englishman named Edmund Fauxall, stepped in and issued the orders required to get the ship moving again. The *Vincennes* proceeded along well enough until she reached the swell at the harbor mouth. "Now the greatest care & the nicest skill & judgment were required," Reynolds wrote. "The ship was to be watched & tended, for she had a critical chance to play." They were approaching the western edge of the entrance, a high bluff known as Tower Rock. Wilkes nervously asked the pilot if he thought the *Vincennes* would weather the obstruction. "I do not know yet, Sir" was the response. Soon enough it became clear that another tack would be required. The pilot issued the appropriate order. Wilkes repeated the order, and it was now up to Carr to tack the ship. "Had we gone round then," Reynolds claimed, "all would have been right, but the Ship refused stays." In addition to backing the head yards of the ship, it was often common to lower the headsails and haul the mizzen yard to weather so as to coax the bow through the wind. "Nothing was done to help her," Reynolds bitterly observed; "she lost her way, gathered Sternboard & finally fell off with her head right on the rocks." Like a stalled airplane plummeting to the ground, the *Vincennes* was drifting helplessly to her destruction.

Instead of taking charge of the situation, Carr stood amidships, "his arms akimbo, looking at the sails in utter ignorance what to do." Reynolds and several other officers peered over the gangway, checking to see if the *Vincennes* had begun to drift backward into the rocks. Wilkes asked querulously if the ship was going astern. Normally Carr would have been the one to answer him, but the first lieutenant seemed unable to speak, so Underwood and Reynolds spoke up for him. "Yes!" they shouted.

"This is the last," Wilkes croaked.

But Pilot Fauxall, in Reynolds's words, "knew his business." Barking out the appropriate orders, he was able to manipulate the ship's yards and rudder so that the *Vincennes* came head to wind once again. With Tower Rock to leeward and the swell rolling in from the ocean, it was now "do or die." "We were within the influence of the rollers," Reynolds wrote. "The Surf dashed & broke upon the rocks a few boatlengths under the lee, & looking down beneath the Ship, the rocks *there*, were staring you in the face!"

Although the pilot succeeded in tacking the ship, their troubles were far from over. As the *Vincennes* struggled to gain headway, the ship's slippage to leeward threatened to sweep her sideways back into the rocks. There was nothing left to do but wait and see if the ship could sail herself out of danger. "[T]here was the Stillness of death about the decks," Reynolds wrote. By now all the officers and a considerable portion of the men were lined up along the leeward gangway, "looking fixedly on the foaming breakers that were so close."

Normally Wilkes's "loud, meddling & abusive" voice was an omnipresent part of life aboard the *Vincennes*. But for the last few minutes, he hadn't said a word. He was nowhere to be seen in the vicinity of the helm or along the leeward side of the deck. Then Reynolds saw him. He was off by himself on the weather gangway, leaning on the booms, his face buried in his hands. For the commander of a sloop-of-war, it was an alarming and shameful display of cowardice.

All his life, the high-strung Wilkes had been prone to fainting spells.

In his narrative he would claim to have had "no very precise recollection" of the incident. John Whittle, the assistant surgeon, described Wilkes during the episode at Pago Pago as showing "the strongest symptoms of confusion and alarm and was in fact incompetent for some time to his duties." Whatever the case may be, Wilkes was living the worst nightmare a naval officer could ever dream of. With time slowed to a crawl and with almost the entire crew assembled on deck, his ship was drifting toward disaster, and he was powerless to do anything about it. What's more, his handpicked first lieutenant had also proven a catastrophic failure.

Stray puffs of wind brushed languorously across the *Vincennes*'s sails. Under the pilot's able direction, the ship continued to move ahead, inch by harrowing inch, but the rocks were now directly beneath them. Just then, the breeze freshened, and with a slight gurgle of water at the bow, the *Vincennes* slipped out to sea, with, Reynolds observed, *"nothing to spare!"*

Once it was clear that the ship was no longer in danger, the pilot requested that Wilkes heave to so that he might return to the harbor in his whaleboat, which was tied to the *Vincennes*'s stern. But Wilkes, burning with humiliation and indignation, refused. On and on they sailed in a building breeze, with the bow of the pilot's whaleboat slapping against the big ship's quarter wake. When the order was finally given to heave to, Fauxhall climbed into his boat with a quiet dignity that only infuriated Wilkes all the more. Waving his hand, the pilot mockingly called out, "You may fill away now, sir! Fill away, as soon as you like."

"Captn. W. could have eaten him," Reynolds wrote.

Soon after the pilot had been dismissed, Reynolds went below to bandage his feet; he had burned them in the sun a few days before, and they hurt so badly that he could barely get them into his shoes. But almost as soon as he began to attend to his feet, Wilkes called for "All Hands." One of the *Vincennes*'s whaleboats and a dinghy needed to be brought aboard, an operation that usually required only a few men and took, at the most, five minutes. But as was his wont, Wilkes demanded that the entire crew be on duty.

Reynolds worked as quickly as he could to bandage his feet, but in a few minutes there was another cry for all hands. A few minutes after that, a sailor came below and informed Reynolds that the captain was waiting for him. Reynolds went up on deck and was shocked to see that all two hundred men were standing idly at their stations. Reynolds hobbled to his station and was told that he should consider himself suspended. Outraged by what he perceived to be a calculated effort to humiliate him, Reynolds, despite his blistered feet, paced furiously up and down the leeward gangway as Wilkes glowered at him from the quarterdeck. Then came the next order: "to confine myself to my apartment."

For the next six days, as the *Vincennes* sailed for the island of Upolu in western Samoa, Reynolds remained confined to his windowless, eighty-five-degree stateroom. When he asked Wilkes's secretary when he would learn what the charges against him were, he was told "that it was Cap. Wilkes's way 'to punish first & inquire afterwards.'"

One night, not long after the suspension of William Reynolds, Wilkes was alone on the quarterdeck, leaning against the rail, when he was approached by the *Vincennes*'s quartermaster. Thomas Piner was one of the oldest sailors in the U.S. Navy and was generally recognized, Wilkes wrote, as "a very faithful and tried seaman." Piner apologized for the interruption but said he had "something to tell me which he thought it was important I should know." He then related a conversation he had overheard in the galley involving some officers and the scientist Joseph Couthouy. Couthouy claimed that Wilkes was guilty of exceeding his orders in a manner that endangered the future of the Expedition. He urged the officers present to join him in an effort "to displace" Wilkes from command.

To learn that "almost a mutiny had broken out in my ship" was clearly upsetting to Wilkes, but it was also something of a relief; he could now take action against a person who had become a major thorn in his side. Wilkes thanked Piner for his loyalty and said that he would "see to it." Before leaving, the quartermaster assured him that the men, if not the officers, were happy to serve under him, "for they saw I was up to my business and they had full confidence in myself."

Couthouy was not only a man of science, he was also an experienced sea captain, who had increasing difficulty submitting to the authority of a commander for whom he had lost all respect. A few days later, once the *Vincennes* arrived at Apia on the north side of Upolu, Couthouy learned that the French expedition under d'Urville had been there the year before and that the French flagship, the *Astrolabe*, had been so loaded with shells and coral that her berth deck had resembled "a complete museum." The news drove Couthouy to a desperate, flailing rage. Because of Wilkes's orders concerning the drying of coral specimens, he would never be able to equal the collections of the French.

That night Couthouy regaled the officers in the wardroom with some of the more colorful passages from his journal. The scientist's timing could not have been worse. The walls of the *Vincennes* were thin, and Wilkes, whose cabin was nearby, could hear the theatrical rumble of Couthouy's voice, and in many instances make out the words. Wilkes decided it was time he read the officers' journals.

As he suspected, Couthouy's log proved highly critical of his actions. Much more troubling, however, was the evidence he uncovered of his own officers' disloyalty. "I found no difficulty in ascertaining all who were disposed to give countenance to Mr. Couthouy's Statement," he later wrote. He sent for Hudson, and the two friends had a "long and confidential talk." Wilkes showed him a list he had made of the officers "who were false and true." To put the "cabal" on notice, he would make an example of Couthouy.

Wilkes claimed in his *Autobiography* that he assembled a total of twenty-two officers for his showdown with Couthouy. In reality, however, it was only five: Hudson, Carr, the surgeon Edward Gilchrist, the geologist James Dana, and Couthouy. Wilkes laid out the facts as he knew them and accused the scientist of conspiring to overthrow his command. "I never saw any one so taken aback," he remembered. "He stood convicted before his own party." Wilkes went on to insist that an attack on him was an attack on the Expedition and that it would "not be broken up by any intrigues or Mutinous conduct by any or many, and they might all rely upon it–I should keep My Word." He ended by warning Couthouy that "if I heard any more of his action to this end, I should land him on the first desert island we came to, bag & baggage, and leave him."

Couthouy had been an indefatigable member of the scientific corps. But after this incident, he seemed a broken man. Health problems and his continued difficulties with Wilkes would eventually lead to his detachment from the squadron and his early return to the United States. If Wilkes had appeared vulnerable after the debacle at Pago Pago, it was now clear to all that his almost maniacal will was as powerful as ever.

Wilkes also met with Reynolds, informing the passed midshipman that he had been confined to quarters not for being late to his station but "because I had come on deck in an improper & disrespectful manner & set a bad example to the crew." As Reynolds was well aware, Wilkes was nearsighted. It would have been impossible for him to make out his facial expressions when he came up the fore hatch. When Wilkes said he hoped it would not happen again, Reynolds replied that "I could not amend, while I was not conscious of any impropriety." He was tempted to insist on a court-martial to exonerate himself, but "like many others have done this cruise, I subdued my feelings at whatever sacrifice."

By this time, the squadron had arrived at Upolu's beautiful Apia Bay. The next day Reynolds and Lieutenant George Emmons set out on an overland expedition to survey a harbor on the opposite side of the island. After a week's confinement, Reynolds had difficulty containing his enthusiasm. "I was enraptured with the loveliness around me, & I strode on with a light step, care banished from my mind . . . ; when I behold a glorious prospect, my heart would burst, did I not give way & exult & rejoice aloud!"

They stopped at a village for the night, and before dinner they went to a freshwater pool for a bath. Nearly the entire village followed them, and as Reynolds took off his clothes, one of the natives drew attention to the contrast between his white body and his tanned face, neck, and hands. "Those parts of me, he said were 'Samoa,' the rest 'Papalangi

[Polynesian for white person],' and he proceeded to assure his hearers with an air of triumphant satisfaction, 'that . . . a short time would make us *Samoa all over.*'"

Accompanying Reynolds and Emmons on this journey was the Expedition's philologist, or linguist, Horatio Hale. As the officers faded off to sleep, Hale, Reynolds reported, "sat up late learning the language from pretty lips, both in song & story." Just twenty-three years old, Hale was the son of Sarah Josepha Hale, who as editor of the *Godey's Lady's Book* was one of the most influential women in the United States (not to mention the author of "Mary Had a Little Lamb"). As a student at Harvard, Horatio Hale had visited a group of Native Americans from Maine who had taken up residence near the college grounds. Soon after, he published a vocabulary of the Indians' language that, along with some lobbying on the part of his powerful mother, won him a post on the Ex. Ex.

Unlike his colleague Charles Pickering, who was more interested in what differentiated the various peoples they had so far visited (especially when it came to race), Hale was in search of what these peoples had in common. As it so happened, the vocabularies and oral traditions that he had so far collected from the Tuamotus, Tahiti, and now Samoa pointed to a remarkable similarity among the inhabitants of Polynesia–a fact first observed by James Cook.

In his voyages across the Pacific, Cook had noticed that as far east as Easter Island and as far west as New Zealand and as far north as Hawaii, the people not only looked similar, they spoke only slight variations of the same language. But if they shared a common origin, Cook was hard-pressed to explain how these people managed to scatter themselves across such an immense space. He had seen the natives' ocean-going outrigger canoes. They were capable of incredible speeds and had, on several occasions, literally sailed circles around his pudgy ships. But if the canoes were fast, they could only sail effectively *with* the wind, and the trade winds blew from the southeast. Since the Polynesians looked nothing like Native Americans, he reasoned that they must have come from the west. But how did they sail against the trade winds? And exactly where did they originally come from?

Not until recently have archeologists and ethnographers been able to determine the location of the Polynesian homeland, what is referred to as *Hawaiki* in legends and myths. Between 4000 and 2000 B.C. people began to venture out from the islands of Southeast Asia. The gradual development of the outrigger canoe enabled them to sail farther and farther to the east and south, but it was not until the first millennium B.C. that the distinctive culture of Polynesia first emerged in Samoa and Tonga.

In its pristine state, a Polynesian island was not a particularly good place for humans to live–edible vegetables, especially those containing starch, were nowhere to be found; there were no large animals. The Polynesians' oceangoing canoes became their arks, transporting dogs, pigs, breadfruit seedlings, taro, and, inevitably, rats to islands that had never before seen the like. Once on a new island, the Polynesians set to work re-creating an agricultural society similar to the one they had left behind, a process that led to the extinction of countless indigenous species of animals and plants.

Once a small pioneering outpost was established, there was intense pressure to increase the size of the population. Archeological evidence has suggested that in some instances the population density reached astonishingly high levels. One archeologist working on Upolu claims that the interior portions that were virtually vacant when Reynolds, Emmons, and Hale journeyed across the island once contained between 100 and 242 people per square kilometer–a density that would have had a disastrous effect on the island's ecology. This fostered the development of culturally sanctioned methods of population control–from infanticide to ritual sacrifice to cannibalism, as well as additional voyages of discovery.

Hale would think long and hard about how the early navigators made their way east against the trade winds. Using meteorological data collected by the Expedition, he would eventually be able to demonstrate that, contrary to accepted wisdom, the southeast trade winds are by no means constant. In fact, during the months of January, February, and March, westerly and northwesterly winds prevail all the way to the Tuamotus. If the early Polynesian voyagers ventured east during these months, using the stars to fix their latitude, they knew they could re-trace their steps home during the other nine months of the year.

Around 200 B.C. voyagers set out from Tonga and Samoa for the Southern Cook Islands; soon after that, they were venturing to the So-cieties and Tuamotus; the Marquesas were reached around 100 B.C., while the Hawaiian Islands weren't settled until sometime between A.D. 300 and A.D. 800. New Zealand was discovered last, around A.D. 1000–1200.

Hale and the Expedition had retraced the routes of these early voy-agers back to their starting point in Samoa, an island group where na-tive ways had not been as thoroughly westernized as they had been to the east. But in five years' time, Reynolds predicted, Upolu would be an-other Tahiti. "I could not help thinking," he wrote, "how much better it would be to let them go on their old way. But no, no! we must have all the world like us."

For Reynolds, Upolu would always be the jewel of the South Pa-cific. (He was in good company. Fifty years later the writer Robert Louis Stevenson would decide to live out the rest of his life on the is-land.) What made Reynolds's time on Upolu particularly memorable was his introduction to a chief's daughter named Emma. Just fifteen years old and "the image of faultless beauty, & the pearl of pure & nat-ural innocence," Emma tempted Reynolds with thoughts of leaving the tribulations of the Expedition behind. "I could not help thinking of a life in this Eden," he wrote. "A half wish came in to my head, that I could free myself from my Ship, & under the shade of the delicious groves, form the mind of sweet Emma—ripen the bud into the full bloom of ma-turity—cherish the flower, & wear it forever! What a dream!"

On November 10, the squadron sailed from Apia Bay. Wilkes had hoped to continue on to the Fiji Islands, but time was running out if they were to sail south again in mid-December. They must proceed di-rectly west to Sydney, Australia, where they would undergo the neces-sary preparations. Little did Reynolds realize that his time aboard the *Vincennes* was about to come to an end.

The next day he discovered that First Lieutenant Carr had consigned his India rubber jacket to the lucky bag, the ship's equivalent
of the lost and found, the contents of which were periodically sold at
auction to the crew. Another officer had borrowed the jacket while
Reynolds was away from the ship, and someone had found it on the
gun deck. What particularly rankled Reynolds was that Carr had
known it was his jacket and still ordered it to be placed in this "recepta-
cle of all the old & dirty clothes, blankets, soap, etc. that may be kicking
about the decks."

When Reynolds asked Carr if he could have the jacket back, the
first lieutenant responded "in a short & peculiarly snappish tone, 'You
shan't have it, Sir!'" Reynolds protested and Carr threatened to report
him to Wilkes. Reynolds replied that he would save him the trouble and
report the matter himself.

Reynolds was not surprised when Wilkes informed him that he "entirely approved" of Carr's actions. Wilkes insisted that the orders of the
ship required that all stray clothes be thrown in the lucky bag. Reynolds
pointed out that no such written order existed. "Well, it was *my* order,"
Wilkes blustered, "and if my own coat was found it would share the
same fate!" When Reynolds explained that he had been away from
the ship when the jacket appeared on the gun deck, Wilkes asked for
the name of the officer who had borrowed it. Reynolds indignantly refused to tell him, and the interview was soon ended. Ten minutes later
Reynolds was informed that he had been transferred to the *Peacock*.

It was as if a dagger had been planted in his heart. For almost a year
and a half, the *Vincennes* and his stateroom had been his home. The
members of his mess had become his family. "My mind was utterly dis-
traught!" he wrote. "I never felt leaving Home, with half the force of
grief, that oppressed me, at being thus torn from my happy mess!"

A ship is a total environment—self-contained, isolated from the outside world. The bonds formed within the wooden walls of a ship are as
strong, if not stronger, than anything known on land. For more than a
year, Reynolds had been a proud member of the Expedition's flagship—
his connection to his messmates made all the more resilient by their

shared hatred of their commander. But Wilkes had found a way to hurt him and his friends where it would hurt most. Reynolds was one of the Ex. Ex.'s most popular officers, and his absence would be keenly felt throughout the ship; he had also made no secret of his changed feelings for Wilkes. It was time to get this sensitive and articulate officer off the *Vincennes.*

News of Reynolds's transfer created "a great hubbub." The surgeon John Whittle was disconsolate. "Nothing which has occurred since we left home has given me so much grief as this," he wrote. "He is a fellow of noble soul & has one of the most admirable tempers imaginable. Never have I become more attached to a man after so short an acquaintance." Jim Gibson, the sailor who had been Reynolds's boyhood friend back in Lancaster, came to help him pack. "[He was] in not much better plight than I was myself," Reynolds wrote. "Poor fellow, I was sorry to leave him."

But it was his roommate William May who was the most devastated by the news. "May & I made perfect babes of ourselves," Reynolds wrote. "Twas like the parting of man & wife: like the dissolution of a household!" May vowed that he would not stay aboard the ship with Reynolds gone. All attempts to calm him failed, and he stormed into Wilkes's cabin. "Sir," he shouted, "you have treated my friend, Mr. Reynolds, with great injustice. I am surprised! I am shocked! I am *disgusted,* Sir & I wish to quit the Ship; I cannot stay in her any longer!"

Wilkes ordered May to leave the cabin. May's father was a prominent member of Washington society, and Wilkes appears to have been extremely reluctant to see him go. Soon Robert Waldron, the purser, appeared in steerage to deliver a message from the commander: May had clearly been "very much excited & if he wished to remain in the Ship, he had only to say so"—otherwise, he would be ordered to the *Flying Fish.* "Anywhere!" May exclaimed. In a few minutes his orders were in his hands. The ship was hove to, and the two friends went their separate ways.

Reynolds was received kindly by the officers of the *Peacock* but had some trouble fitting in. For almost a week, he had no assigned duty, and

he didn't know what to do with himself. Finally, when one of the officers became ill, he was given charge of the deck. "[W]henever we came
within hail of the *Vincennes* during my watch," he wrote, "I took great
delight in shaking my trumpet & displaying myself in a most conspicuous manner. Sent away as a convict, banished for punishment, I was
well pleased to show that in my new Ship I occupied a post of honor!"

Eighteen days after the transfers of Reynolds and May, at sundown on
November 29, the *Vincennes* and the *Peacock* were between thirty and
forty miles from Sydney. The shore was not yet in sight. "[W]e gave up
all hope of getting in until the next day," Reynolds wrote, "and were sor-
rowed to think of the breakfast we should miss." Much to everyone's
surprise, the *Vincennes* crowded sail, and Lieutenant Hudson ordered his
men to follow suit. At eight o'clock, they sighted the Port Jackson lighthouse.

The wind was with them, and with time being of the essence, Wilkes
decided to push on even though they were without a pilot. "[O]n, on we
went," Reynolds wrote, "& undertaking rather a critical chance, Captn
Wilkes ran his Ship clear up into the Harbor & we followed, anchoring
off the Town at 11." The next morning the citizens of Sydney were flab-
bergasted to see two American naval vessels sitting quietly at anchor.
"Never had such a thing been heard of," Reynolds wrote. "They
could not credit their eyes, & the Pilots who were looking out for us
were mortified to death!" By arriving at night, they had slipped past the
usually watchful pilots and then proceeded to navigate the difficult,
nine-mile passage to Sydney Harbor. The next day, newspaper articles
appeared, "highly flattering to our nautical skill & daring."

In one bold stroke, Wilkes had put his humiliation at Pago Pago behind him. Suddenly, it was as if the bickering and bad feeling that had
once threatened to destroy the Expedition had never occurred. "[A]ll of
us were perfectly elated," Reynolds wrote, "that the first visit of an
American squadron to the place had been in a manner so well calculated to excite their jealousy & to give us so much *éclat*."

Reynolds later learned that the squadron's arrival at Sydney had not been as dashing and heroic as it had first seemed. Although Wilkes would deny it, he had received more than a little help that night. Standing at his elbow the whole way had been his quartermaster, a former Sydney resident who knew the passage well. "It is just like Lt. Wilkes," Reynolds wrote, "to usurp all the credit for himself."

It was just a hint of things to come.

CHAPTER 7

Antarctica

A T 5.4 MILLION square miles, the Antarctic Continent is roughly the size of the continental United States and Mexico combined. Almost all of it is perpetually covered in ice that in some areas is more than two miles thick. Since the ice reflects as much as 90 percent of the sun's solar radiation, this is the coldest place on earth, with an average annual temperature of -22°F. Between 70 and 80 percent of the world's freshwater is contained in this approximately 6.5-million-cubic-mile reservoir of ice and snow, in which is preserved a climate record that goes back 200,000 years. If the Antarctic ice sheet melted, the sea level of the globe would rise by more than two hundred feet.

Antarctica is also the most inaccessible place on earth. Except for the point where the Antarctic Peninsula reaches toward Cape Horn at the Drake Passage (a gap of six hundred–plus miles), it is surrounded by a moat of more than two thousand miles called the Southern Ocean. In winter, a six-hundred-mile-wide belt of pack ice seals off the continent. In summer, when the ice begins to retreat, the waters surrounding Antarctica become the mariner's equivalent of a minefield. Indeed, an entire vocabulary has been created to describe the appalling variety of icy hazards a navigator encounters as he or she approaches the continent. A "growler" is a piece of sea ice that is about 180 square feet and rises just a few feet above the sea; a "bergy bit" is about the size of a two-bedroom house, while a "floeberg" is described as a "massive piece of sea ice" with a dimpled or "hummocky" surface. But growlers, bergy bits, and floebergs are nothing compared to the vast, flat-topped icebergs that are spawned from the edges of the continent. "Calved" from the fronts of land-based glaciers, these tabular floes are unlike anything seen in the Arctic and are sometimes more than two hundred feet high and *a hundred miles* long. Making these dimensions even more remarkable is the fact that seven-eighths of a typical iceberg is underwater.

As if the danger of ice were not bad enough, the weather in this part of the world is horrendous. Much of this has to do with Antarctica's being the world's highest continent, with an average elevation of 7,550 feet. Cold, very heavy air constantly flows down and north from the high interior; when these gravity-stoked "katabatic" winds collide with the water at the coast, they erupt into blizzards, creating a never-ending series of cyclonic storms that circulates clockwise around the continent. The ocean area from about 40° south to the Antarctic Circle has the strongest sustained winds found anywhere on earth.

Wilkes was not only to penetrate as far as possible into this hazardous region, he was to *explore* it. As James Cook had found back in 1774, this amounted to an almost suicidal endeavor in a sailing vessel. Cook had been well aware that a continent to the south might exist, but given the terrible conditions between himself and a possible discovery, he judged it not worth the effort. Then there was the British sealer James Weddell's claim, backed up by the American Benjamin Morrell, that a navigable ocean existed beyond the icy barrier. Other British sealers had brought back isolated reports of sighting islands in the vicinity of the Antarctic Circle near where the Expedition would soon be headed. The fact of the matter remained, however, that in December 1839, as the U.S. Exploring Expedition prepared for its final push south, no one really knew what was down there at the bottom of the world.

Wilkes was already aware of the French expedition led by Dumont d'Urville. In Sydney he learned that there was yet another expedition headed south. The British had just dispatched James Ross, the discoverer of the magnetic North Pole, on a mission to find the other magnetic pole in the vicinity of 66° south and 146° east—almost directly below Adelaide, Australia, and approximately 250 miles to the north of

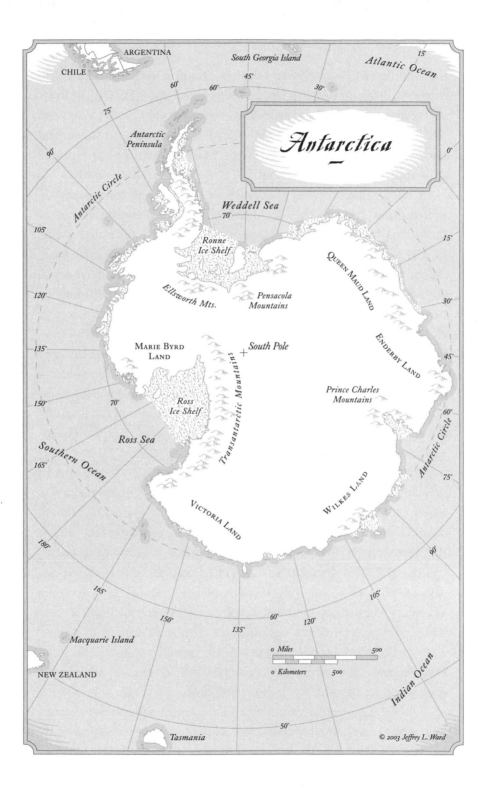

ARGENTINA

CHILE

South Georgia Island

Atlantic Ocean

15

60°

45°

60°

30°

75°

Antarctic Peninsula

90°

Antarctic Circle

0°

Antarctica

Weddell Sea

70°

105°

15°

Ronne Ice Shelf

QUEEN MAUD LAND

120°

Ellsworth Mts.

Pensacola Mountains

30°

ENDERBY LAND

135°

MARIE BYRD LAND

South Pole

45°

150°

70°

Ross Ice Shelf

Prince Charles Mountains

60°

Transantarctic Mountains

Ross Sea

Southern Ocean

165°

Antarctic Circle

WILKES LAND

75°

180°

VICTORIA LAND

90°

165°

105°

150°

60°

120°

135°

Macquarie Island

0 Miles 500

NEW ZEALAND

0 Kilometers 500

Indian Ocean

50°

Tasmania

© 2003 Jeffrey L. Ward

the latitude of Cook's Ne Plus Ultra. In addition, Ross was to attempt to punch through the ice in his heavily reinforced vessels and sail as far as possible south. Ross–whose arrogance may have even surpassed Wilkes's–knew that his rivals had a significant head start; still, he remained confident that he would outdo both of them. The French and Americans didn't stand a chance.

Certainly the people of Sydney would have agreed with at least half of that claim. As far as they could tell the American expedition was, in the words of one observer, "doomed to be frozen to death." While Ross's two ships–converted bomb vessels built to withstand the thunderous recoil of several deck-mounted mortars–had been equipped with an additional layer of eight-inch-thick oak planking, the American vessels were without any significant form of structural reinforcement to withstand the inevitable collisions with the ice. To make matters worse, the *Peacock*'s already poor condition had deteriorated dramatically over the last six months; many key structural components were rotten and in need of replacement. But these repairs would have taken at least two months. After long consultation, Wilkes and Hudson decided that "the credit of the Expedition and the country" demanded that the *Peacock* sail south, no matter how bad her condition might be.

But if the Yanks appeared ill prepared, they had a few factors in their favor. One of them was timing. Ross had left England just a few months before; where he was now was anyone's guess. Although d'Urville's expedition had gotten the jump on all of them, rumor had it that the French, after one unsuccessful push south two winters ago, were on their way back home. The Americans also possessed the advantage of some recent, very valuable experience amid the Antarctic ice. But perhaps most important was that the Americans didn't appear especially bothered by the inadequacies of their equipment and preparation. "[The people of Sydney] saw us all cheerful, young, and healthy," Wilkes wrote, "and gave us the character, that I found our countrymen generally bear, of recklessness of life and limb."

On the day after Christmas, the U.S. Ex. Ex.–minus the scientists, who would continue their researches in Australia, then secure passage to New Zealand, where they would meet up with the squadron in

March—left Sydney Harbor. The wind was light, and the *Vincennes* once again missed stays. Despite his occasional demonstrations of bravado, Wilkes had earned a reputation among his officers and men as an "ignorant and nervous" seaman—not the best qualities for leading a squadron into the terrors of the Antarctic ice. But if Wilkes's seamanship remained in question, his leadership style was no longer in doubt. As early as Rio de Janeiro, when he had been pushed to the verge of a nervous collapse, it had become clear that he needed a persona, what has been called a "mask of command," to hide behind if he was to survive the ordeals that lay ahead. The mask that he chose to assume was that of the martinet, defined by British admiral W. H. Smyth as "A rigid disciplinarian; but one who, in matters of inferior moment, harasses all under him." This was the form of leadership Wilkes would cling to for the duration of the voyage. "The acquirement of being a 'martinette,'" Wilkes later wrote, "when once established goes far to carrying with it authority to induce obedience to command."

But it wasn't all just an act on Wilkes's part. He had become more than a little intoxicated by the sudden influx of power he associated with his self-propelled rise to commodore of the U.S. Ex. Ex. Proper obeisance must be paid. In a letter to Jane he bragged about keeping the American consul in Sydney waiting for two hours while he finished up some experiments. "I am now a *great* man," he wrote, "and others will wait patiently."

In amiable contrast to the Expedition's leader was second-in-command William Hudson. In addition to being an excellent seaman, he had shown no interest in maintaining rigid discipline in this nonmilitary operation. His officers were not required to move to the leeward side of the quarterdeck when he came up from below. His cabin was frequented by his officers, who always seemed to be in excellent spirits. The *Peacock* might be in terrible structural condition, but as William Reynolds could attest, she was a "happy ship." With full confidence in their captain's ability to get them out of the toughest scrape, the *Peacock*'s officers looked with anticipation to the adventures that awaited them. "Antarctic Stock was high!" Reynolds effused in a letter to his mother.

Morale was not so good aboard the *Porpoise*. In Sydney her commander, Lieutenant Cadwallader Ringgold, had become embroiled in a petty feud with a member of his medical staff, Charles Guillou, and the popular surgeon had been transferred to the *Peacock*. Ringgold was also at loggerheads with his first lieutenant Robert Johnson, who along with several other officers had done his best to embarrass Ringgold at a social event prior to the squadron's departure.

For sheer bad feeling, however, nothing could compare to the crew of the *Flying Fish*. Just a few days before, the schooner had lost five of ten men to desertion. Her commander, Robert Pinkney, was able to scare up a few dubious characters from the Sydney waterfront, but the schooner was still down by several men, and Wilkes claimed he had none to spare from the *Vincennes*. "I do not suppose that a vessel ever sailed under the U.S. Pendant with such a miserable crew as we have now," wrote Pinkney's second-in-command, George Sinclair. "It will be a great wonder to me if we return from the southern cruise."

Once the squadron was clear of Sydney, Wilkes insisted that all four vessels sail abreast; every now and then they would be ordered to heave to so that Wilkes could communicate by boat with his commanders. In the event that any of them should become separated, he had designated a rendezvous point: Macquarie Island, a wave-washed, penguin-infested pile of rocks 2,100 miles to the south. For the officers and men of the *Peacock*, who felt that they had the best chance of success, it all seemed like an exasperating waste of time. "Lt. Wilkes evidently did not intend to afford either of his subordinates an opportunity to get *ahead of him* in sailing to the Southward," Reynolds wrote. "For *this* reason most likely, he orders them to keep in company with him." For six days the four vessels succeeded in staying together. Then on January 1 it began to blow. Soon the *Flying Fish* was in trouble.

Scudding before the wind in the gale, Pinkney didn't have the manpower required to shorten sail. The schooner's foresail began jibing back and forth uncontrollably, finally carrying away the jaws of the gaff. Soon the forestay, upon which the vessel's entire rig depended, was broken, and the square yard was in pieces. Giant waves were breaking across the deck. Incredibly, the signal to "make sail" was raised on the

Vincennes. Sinclair was outraged. Instead of helping them, the flagship "kept her course and deliberately left us to whatever fate the Gods of the winds might have in store for us; a few deep toned curses accompanied her."

From the safety of the *Vincennes*'s quarterdeck, Wilkes glanced aft and commented to Reynolds's good friend Lieutenant James Alden that the officers of the *Flying Fish* were clearly "afraid." "[I]t is impossible to describe the disgust with which [Alden] heard such an insinuation," Reynolds later wrote, "from a man who in all times of difficulty and danger was as humble about the decks as a whipped puppy, and as incapable as he was humble." As night came on, the *Flying Fish* disappeared in the darkness. More than a few sailors speculated that the schooner had joined the *Sea Gull* at the bottom of the Southern Ocean.

Three days later the *Vincennes* and the *Porpoise* lost contact with the *Peacock.* Four days later, Wilkes was approaching the latitude of Macquarie Island. He would later claim that they were too far to leeward to reach the rendezvous point without wasting too much time. And so, while Hudson did as his orders demanded and spent the next *three days* beating up to the island, Wilkes pushed on to the south. He had succeeded in giving himself a head start of more than six hundred miles over the two vessels, the *Peacock* and the *Flying Fish*, that had sailed farther south than he had the winter before. When the officers and men of the *Peacock* reached Macquarie Island and found no vessels waiting for them, Wilkes's "miserable double dealing" was obvious to all. After dutifully planting a flag on the island, they set off for the south.

On the evening of January 15, 1840, Reynolds, perhaps the happiest officer aboard the happiest ship in the squadron, saw his first iceberg. It was "glowing with the most vivid & brilliant hues," he wrote; "blue as azure, green as emerald, and, ho! the contrast, whiteness like unto the raiment of an Angel. . . . The imagination cannot picture, neither our tongues convey, the faintest image of so glorious a spectacle."

Soon after sighting the iceberg, Reynolds decided it was time to put on the red flannels that Lydia and his mother had made for him.

"[T]hey are *so* nice & warm," he wrote in his journal, "bless those who made them! Grandmother's stockings too! I feel the good of a Home, away down here!"

They had entered a realm of perpetual daylight. "[W]hat a rooster would do here," he wrote, "I cannot imagine." During his watch from midnight to four A.M., some of the officers were reading Charles Dickens's *Pickwick Papers*. At 2:45 A.M., they watched the sun rise. "It is the funniest thing," he commented, "this never-ending day." Just as strange was the behavior of their compasses. Their proximity to the magnetic South Pole, where the earth's magnetic force field flows in a nearly vertical direction, meant that their compass needles had been rendered virtually useless. An object as small as an iron button was enough to move the compass by as much as twenty degrees. One of Reynolds's fellow officers rightly attributed this phenomenon to "the polar attraction acting in nearly a perpendicular direction upon a horizontal needle." It was graphic evidence that they were approaching the very foundations of the earth.

On the evening of January 15 at latitude 65°25' south, Reynolds climbed to the masthead and saw not a single piece of ice ahead of them. "On the morrow," he wrote, "we would be farther South than the Ship had reached last year. Soon we would pass 70 degrees–eclipse Cook & distance the pretender Weddell. No one hazarded an unfavorable opinion, & we were all in a perfect fever of excitement! I shall never forget that day!"

Around four P.M., fog appeared at the edges of the horizon. Almost simultaneously they saw both the *Porpoise* and a solid barrier of ice looming out of the haze. For the time being they would have to lay aside their hopes of pushing farther south. "There was the low & continuous field of Ice," Reynolds wrote, "running East & West, broken by many Bays & Islands, but effectually stopping any further progress. . . . *Our dreams* were at once destroyed!"

Ringgold informed them that he had been sailing along the edge of the barrier for several days and had found no openings to the south. "We commenced working to windward," Reynolds wrote, "in hope of finding a passage farther to the West, but our overflowing anticipations were checked, gone, broken entirely & we were humbled at the lesson we had received!"

Around noon the next day, Reynolds went aloft with fellow passed midshipman Henry Eld from New Haven, Connecticut. By this point, the *Peacock* had separated again from the *Porpoise*. Reynolds and Eld were up on the crosstrees with the main topmast between them, more than a hundred feet above the surface of the sea, somewhere in the vicinity of 65° south, 160° east. Reynolds, who was nearsighted, had his spectacles on. He and Eld struggled to describe the beauty of what they saw spread out before them, but, as Reynolds wrote, "we had no words. To look over such a vast expanse of the frozen sea, upon which no human eye nor foot had ever rested, & which, formed from the Ocean, now resisted its waves & presented an impassable boundary to the mysterious regions beyond, filled us with feelings, which we were powerless to utter." Then they saw something that suddenly restored their powers of speech. As if with one voice they cried out, "There is land!"

Many miles in the distance, beyond the icy barrier, they saw three distinct peaks—one pointed, the other two more rounded. "They rose to an immense height," Reynolds wrote. "We looked for half an hour at least, & procured a glass to satisfy ourselves that we were not mistaken. We were convinced that our judgment was correct & that we actually beheld the long sought for Terra Firma of the Antarctic continent."

They had come upon the massive, never-before-explored body of Antarctica. If the Antarctic Peninsula below Cape Horn is the continent's panhandle, the wide rounded mass below Australia and extending west along the Antarctic Circle toward Africa is the pan. The *Peacock* was now at the eastern extreme of the pan's northerly edge. The date was January 16.

Both officers scrambled down the rigging to report the sighting. Eld went below to find Captain Hudson, and Reynolds sought out Lieutenant Thomas Budd, the officer of the deck. Although Reynolds could still see the mountaintops from the deck, they were not as clearly defined as they had been from aloft. When he pointed out the land, Budd expressed his doubts and chose not to send anyone to the masthead to confirm the sighting. Reynolds had no alternative but to wait for the appearance of Hudson on the quarterdeck. But Hudson never came.

Reynolds later learned from Eld that Hudson had acted even more oddly than Budd. When told of the discovery, Hudson said that he had no doubt that Eld and Reynolds had seen land; in fact, he was convinced that the large icebergs near them were sitting on the bottom of the sea. But when Eld urged him to come see the mountaintops for himself, Hudson demonstrated an almost bovine lack of curiosity. He would stay by his stove, thank you; he also saw no reason to send an officer aloft to verify their sighting. Assuring Eld that there would be plenty of opportunities to see land in the days ahead, he ordered that the ship be tacked. The wind was light, and he didn't want to run into any trouble amid the ice. Strange conduct indeed for the captain of an exploring expedition.

Both Reynolds and Eld were filled with "disappointment and mortification," especially when they learned that no mention of their sighting had been made in the ship's log. But there was nothing they could do. "I will never give up my belief that this was no deception," Reynolds wrote, "& am perfectly willing to abide by the researches of any future navigators, confident that our discovery will be verified!"

The next day, during Reynolds's watch at 5:30 in the morning, they saw the *Vincennes* for the first time in two weeks. "I remember she passed behind an Ice berg," Reynolds wrote, "& there was an immense discrepancy between its height & that of the Ship." Although Wilkes had been able to sprint ahead at Macquarie Island, Hudson had succeeded in reaching the icy barrier to windward of the *Vincennes,* which had been sailing west along the ice for close to a week. It was an amazing feat of catch-up on Hudson's part. Despite all of Wilkes's machinations, all three vessels—the *Porpoise,* the *Peacock,* and the *Vincennes*—were now within just a few miles of one another.

In contrast to Hudson's loose and buoyant crew, the nerves of the officers and men of the *Vincennes* were drum tight. Wilkes would have it no other way. In true martinet fashion, he rarely spoke with his officers; when an officer dared speak to him, he inevitably dismissed the statement with an insult. It was an unfortunate state of affairs for a vessel in search of any and all indications of land. Even if an officer *thought* he saw land, there was little use in bringing it to the commander's attention since Wilkes would inevitably reject the observation with a sneer.

Over the last two days, however, there had been little opportunity to see much beyond the *Vincennes*'s bowsprit. Dense fog made navigating the icy barrier a particularly hazardous endeavor. Instead of their eyes, the lookouts depended on their ears. When they heard "the low and distant rustling of the ice," they knew it was time to tack. Then there were the times when the usual sounds of a ship at sea—the rhythmic slap of the waves and the comforting creak of the rigging (which always seemed magnified in the fog)—suddenly ceased as the *Vincennes* glided into the eerily quiet lee of an unseen iceberg. "[T]he transition was so sudden," Wilkes wrote, "that many were awakened . . . from sound sleep. . . . [It is] an occurrence from which the feeling of great danger is inseparable." By January 16, the day before the *Vincennes* spoke the *Peacock*, the strain had begun to get the better of Wilkes. "[I]t at times acts on me as if a weight was hung all at once on my heart strings," he wrote in his journal.

With the sighting of the *Peacock*, Wilkes was greatly relieved to have the chance to speak with Hudson, and Reynolds reported that the two captains "had a long yarn." Neither one of them made any mention of sighting land. Wilkes did tell Hudson that he had changed his mind about the necessity of sailing in tandem. Now that he no longer had an advantage to protect, Wilkes was inclined to let each vessel strike out on her own. "I was satisfied that the separation would be a strong incentive to exertion," Wilkes wrote, "by exciting rivalry among the officers and crews of the different vessels." It was a rivalry Hudson and his officers were eager to pursue.

Providing Wilkes with some much-needed distraction from the tensions of the voyage was a new acquisition that he had gained in Australia: a giant Newfoundland dog named Sydney. Newfoundlands, or Newfies, are web-footed, 100- to 150-pound dogs originally bred for swimming, and in the nineteenth century they were such a common shipboard sight that they were known as ship dogs. The Lewis and

Clark Expedition included a Newfoundland named Seaman, and when Napoleon Bonaparte fell overboard during his return from Elba, he was saved by a Newfie. In the months ahead, Sydney became a favorite with the crew of the *Vincennes.*

No one knew it at the time, but the events of January 19–two days after the *Vincennes* spoke the *Peacock*–would be revisited and analyzed countless times in the years ahead. That morning, a Sunday, the *Vincennes* made her way into a deep bay at 154°30' east, 65°20' south. Lieutenant James Alden was the watch officer. For most of the morning it had been quite foggy. A few minutes after eight A.M., Alden heard waves breaking on an iceberg up ahead, and he informed Wilkes of the ship's proximity to the ice. By the time Wilkes came on deck, the fog had lifted to the extent that it was possible to see the ice. Wilkes looked quickly around and said a few barely distinguishable words about managing the ship, then began to go below. At that moment, Alden thought he saw land to the southwest–a barely perceptible rise above the ice. "I said to him," Alden later remembered, "'there's something there,' pointing to it, 'that looks like land.'" Wilkes made no reply and "seemed," Alden recalled, "to treat the report with neglect and went below."

Wilkes had become convinced that his officers were "endeavoring to do all in their power to make my exertions go for nothing." Except for First Lieutenant Carr, he trusted no one, and in his journal entry for January 19 he complained that "There is no one on board My own Ship that I can communicate with." Out of desperation, Wilkes appears to have turned to his noncommissioned officers.

About an hour after his terse conversation with Alden, Wilkes reappeared on deck between nine and ten A.M. By this point Alden had been relieved by Augustus Case as officer of the watch; Case, like Alden, was an officer with whom Wilkes had already had several run-ins. In an extremely unorthodox move, Wilkes left the quarterdeck and wandered over to the port gangway, where the gunner, John Williamson, was standing. "He came to me," Williamson later reported, "and asked me what I thought of the appearance of land. My answer was, if it was not land, I had never seen land, then the conversation ended." Although

Wilkes had found someone to talk to, he had bypassed his watch officer and in so doing, had bypassed the ship's official log, which was the
watch officer's responsibility. As a result, there would be no mention of
sighting land in the *Vincennes*'s log for January 19.

In the meantime, just a few miles to the west, the *Peacock* entered
another large bay in the ice. They pushed south for thirty miles until
they found themselves enclosed on all sides. "The long swell of the
Ocean was shut off altogether," Reynolds wrote, "the water was smooth
and motionless as an Inland Lake and lay like a vast mirror in its frosted
frame." Even though the temperature was only 21°F, he climbed up to
his perch at the masthead. "[T]he whiteness of all this was dazzling and
intense," Reynolds wrote; "unbroken, by the glistening sheet of water
where the Ship floated, idle, quiet and at rest."

This time Reynolds was joined by Midshipman William Clark. As
soon as he'd placed his spectacles on his nose, Reynolds cried out to
Clark, "Do you see that?" Ahead of them was land. "[I]t was of great
height," Reynolds wrote, "of rounded uneven summit & broken sides."
Taking no chances, Reynolds immediately reported his discovery to the
watch officer, Lieutenant Alonzo Davis. Davis cheerfully agreed that it
was land. Soon Captain Hudson and a large number of officers and men
were up in the rigging. "Well it was Land!" Reynolds wrote. As a joke,
they began assigning names to the features they saw before them.
"[O]ne cape was honored with the cognomen of the discoverer,"
Reynolds proudly noted.

What Reynolds didn't learn until later was that by the time Hudson
had returned to the *Peacock*'s deck, he had begun to doubt his own eyes.
"Our land has turned out to be an iceberg," he told Davis, the watch officer. When Davis informed him that he had already recorded the sighting in the ship's log, Hudson told him "that we ought to be very certain"
before mention of land was put down in writing, and he ordered Davis
to remove the offending passage. Hudson was a competent seaman, but
his exceedingly literal cast of mind was ill suited to the challenges of exploration. It was the second time in three days that he had refused to
acknowledge a discovery by William Reynolds.

+ + +

Four days later, at five P.M. on Thursday, January 23, it appeared as if all would soon be forgiven. After continuing west, the *Peacock* had sailed into a bay that was even larger than all the others. The weather was mild and clear; the sea was smooth; and two boats were dispatched to perform magnetism experiments on a nearby chunk of ice as others attempted to find soundings. At 350 fathoms, the sounding lead hit bottom; pebbles and blue mud were found attached to the lead. "Great was the joy & Excitement throughout the ship," Reynolds wrote, "for this was a certain indication of the proximity of Land." As the men in the boats returned to the ship, unaware of the great find, the crew climbed into the rigging and shouted out three cheers. "[N]ow we were sanguine that ere long we should discover 'terra firma,'" Reynolds enthused, "& the prize [of discovery] would be our own."

The already happy crew of the *Peacock* became delirious with excitement. Holding up the mud-smeared lead line, sailors ran about the deck to the music of a fiddle as others burst into song. Taking advantage of the quiet seas, men played shuffleboard below while others rolled tenpins on the gun deck. Hudson gave the order to "splice the main brace," and soon every man had received an extra allowance of grog. "[W]e were a merry ship," Reynolds wrote. "Little did any one think of the change that a few short hours would bring about!"

One of the boat crews had captured a huge penguin on the ice. "[H]e was cruelly put to death," Reynolds wrote, "so that his skin might be preserved for the Satisfaction of those who are content to see the curious things of the world, second hand." Early the next morning Hudson appeared on deck "in the greatest glee." When the penguin's gut had been cut open, they had found thirty-five pebbles inside. Although he had been slow to show much enthusiasm concerning Reynolds's earlier reports of land, Hudson took these pebbles as incontrovertible proof that they were on the verge of a historic discovery. "Poor man!" Reynolds wrote. "He was nearly beside himself with joy."

Reynolds turned in at four that morning, "dreading no evil & confident that we would succeed in finding Land ere we were many days older. True! Even in a few hours, we came nigh to finding it, but at the bottom of the Ocean!!"

When he came on deck at eight A.M., Reynolds discovered that Hudson, in his newfound gusto for exploration, had sailed the ship into an exceedingly perilous position. They were surrounded by ice, but Hudson intended to push on even farther to the very edge of the barrier. There were indications of high land just beyond the barrier, and Hudson wanted to prove that "the indications" were indeed land. It may or may not have been in an effort to make up for his earlier conservatism, but the *Peacock*'s commander was once again demonstrating a disturbing lack of judgment–this time by needlessly risking his ship and men.

By 8:40 A.M. they had gone as far as was possible in a sailing vessel. "We were entirely surrounded by loose Ice," Reynolds wrote, "some pieces were larger than the Ship & they were packed so closely together that we had no room to proceed or maneuver in." It was time to extricate themselves from the ice–if that was still possible. Every now and then a space would open up, but just as Hudson gave the order to tack, a chunk of ice would move in, preventing their escape. Finally, Hudson was able to bring the *Peacock* into the wind, but the resistance offered by the many pieces of ice knocking against the hull slowed the ship until she began to slip backward. Behind them was what Reynolds described as a "huge lump of ice," and the *Peacock* rammed into it, stern first. The collision wrenched the rudder so severely that the head split and tore away the ropes that linked it to the wheel. Soon the entire crew was on deck to watch as the ship once again slammed into the ice, this time completely shattering the rudder, which now dangled from the sternpost like a broken wing.

If they had any hope of escape–let alone sailing more than two thousand miles back to Sydney–they needed a rudder. But to unship and repair the steering device required an open patch of water. To the south, they saw what they needed: a clear area in the lee of a big island of ice. Using the sails to steer the ship, Hudson attempted to maneuver them through the growlers and bergy bits, which inevitably thumped against the hull and banged into the topsides, tearing away a section of the ship's keel as well as the lashing around the port anchor. Once they'd reached open water, a boat was lowered with an ice anchor. If they could secure the *Peacock* to the ice, they might be able to unship the rudder and begin to repair it.

Reynolds climbed into the rigging to assist in furling the sails. The wind began to freshen, and the ice anchor, by now dug into an ice island, started to slip. Reynolds watched from the masthead as the men on the island struggled to keep the anchor in its bed of ice and snow, but in the end there was nothing they could do to stop it from breaking free. Faster and faster, the ship began to slide backward. Up on top of the mast, Reynolds turned and saw a terrifying sight. Behind them was an iceberg of immense dimensions—many miles long and higher than the masts of the *Peacock*. "It rose from the Water, bluff as the sides of a house," Reynolds wrote, "the upper edge projecting like the eaves and when we were under it, it towered above the mast head."

As he held on for dear life, the *Peacock*'s port stern quarter, the weakest part of the ship's frame, slammed into the side of the iceberg. "[T]he Shock & crash & splintering of riven Spars & upper works were any thing but agreeable. For an instant I thought that the Whole Stern *must* be stove, & that a few minutes would send us to the bottom." But instead of being smashed to bits, the twelve-year-old vessel *bounced*, ricocheting off the face of the iceberg. "To strike a second time would be to ensure destruction," Reynolds wrote. "Sail was made at once & the Ship's head paid slowly off from the danger."

Even as the sails were being shaken from their gaskets, he was distracted by the sound of yet another crash. *"Scarcely* had we got from under [the iceberg], when *down came the overhanging ledge of snow."* Tons of snow and ice rained down into the water just behind the ship's quarterdeck, which was soon awash with the resultant upsurge of foam. *"Mercy!"* Reynolds wrote. *"A moment longer and it had crushed us.* I cannot tell you *how* I looked upon that Island as we were leaving it, by inches; there were the marks of the Ship's form and paint, and there at its foot were the tumbled heaps of snow that had so nearly overwhelmed us."

Only now did Reynolds have the opportunity to observe the damage inflicted on the *Peacock:* "the Spanker boom & Stern boat went to splinters, the Boat's davits, Taffrel, & all the Starboard Side of the upper works were Started as far forward as the gangway—these receiving the heaviest Shock, saved the Ship. I shall never forget the look of the old craft . . . , Ice, piled around her, so that we could see nothing Else [on] the Deck—the dark figures of the men & boats were the only relief to the dreary Whiteness."

Even if the disaster was largely his doing, Hudson was now in his element. It had become a fight for survival upon which everything depended on his skill as a seaman. Throughout the ordeal, Hudson remained calm and dignified, and his example inspired his officers and men. "There were no Shrieks," Reynolds wrote, "no Exhibitions of bewilderment, & I verily believe that *had* the old ship settled in the Water, she would have gone down with three as hearty cheers as ever came from an hundred throats."

For the next four hours, Hudson worked his men unmercifully, swinging the yards back and forth in a desperate attempt to steer the *Peacock* through the ice to safety. But all their efforts seemed in vain. "We thumped, thumped . . . ," Reynolds wrote, "making but little progress, & drifting to leeward . . . while the distance between us & the clear Sea was increasing Every moment, from the quantity of Ice brought down by the wind." It was as if the wooden ship were being chewed to pieces by the ice. All of the anchors were stripped of their lashings and hung at the bows by the stoppers; the ship's cutwater was splintered. At one point three of their chronometers were hurled from their beds of sawdust.

Around three P.M. the wind died to almost nothing. They made fast to a bergy bit and attempted to hoist in the broken rudder. It came up in two pieces, and the carpenters went to work. Soon the wind began to increase; once again, the ice anchor did not hold. Hudson determined to make sail and try to force the ship through the ice. But without the rudder, the *Peacock* was, in Reynolds's words, as "helpless as an Infant."

Some of the men attempted to pole the ship through the floes, extending spars over the bow and pushing with all their collective strength against the ice chunks in their path. Others were dispatched in boats to plant anchors in the ice that might be used to guide the ship. But since the ice was all around them, there was little room to use their oars. At one point a boat-crew found itself trapped between two bergy bits that had begun to swing together. The sea "boiled like a caldron" between the two walls of ice, which pressed against the boat's gunwales until water began to spout through the seams. Just when it seemed that the boat was about to be crushed by the ice, the bergs moved apart, and the men pushed their way to safety. Others attempted to *walk* across the ever-shifting ice, laying down planks and lugging the sea anchors from berg to berg.

By six P.M., Hudson and his men had succeeded in working the *Peacock* to within a hundred yards of a large open section of water. Unfortunately, the ship was now wedged into a seemingly impervious barricade of ice. "[W]e had the cruel mortification of seeing the place of comparative Safety so close at hand," Reynolds wrote, "& yet be in as much & more peril, than we experienced through the day."

So far, the wind had remained relatively light. If it should begin to blow, however, they all knew the ship would go down in a matter of minutes as the jagged chunks of ice ripped through the ship's frail sides. That evening, black clouds began to gather in the west. "[T]hey were rolled & curled together in windy looking wreathes," Reynolds wrote, "& they had all the appearance of a coming storm." He climbed aloft to have a better look.

For several minutes, he stared at the clouds. "I watched until I saw the *clouds move*," he wrote. "I saw their *shadow coming over the water*, & now I thought in sad earnest, *'our time has come at last'*!" Convinced that they were all about to die, he could not help but anticipate how it would happen. "[H]ere were one hundred of us, in the full vigour of health & strength," he wrote. "[I]n a few moments not one would be left to tell the tale of our destruction. All must go, without the hope of *even* a *struggle* for life—*there could be no resistance:* when the *crush came, we* should be swept away like the spars & timbers of the Ship."

Hudson gave the order to furl the sails. After that, the men had nothing to do but wait for the coming storm. As the black "funeral Cloud" approached, the breeze began to build. "[M]y feelings were almost overpowering in their force," Reynolds admitted. Suddenly, the cloud's appearance began to change as the wisps dissolved into a harmless mist. Instead of a squall, they found themselves in the middle of a snowstorm. Soon they were back at work, trying to move the ship through the ice.

By one A.M. Hudson realized that they all needed some rest. They had been working nonstop for more than seventeen hours. While one watch remained on deck, the rest went below for some sleep. Reynolds, who was due back on deck in just three hours, fell into his cot. Almost immediately he was in the grip of a terrifying nightmare. "[A]ll the feelings I had mastered during the day," he wrote, "haunted me in dreams. I died a hundred deaths. I was buried under the Ice; & the whole terrible catastrophe of a wreck from the first moment of the Ice striking the deck to the last drowning gasp, occurred with a vividness that I shall never forget!" With every jar of the ship against the ice, he awoke, convinced that he had just breathed his last. "[T]hose 3 hours in my cot," he remembered, "were worse than all the others on deck, with real danger to look upon!"

It was little wonder Reynolds had had such a troubled sleep. While he tossed and turned in his cot, Hudson had decided that he had no choice but to drive the ship through the ice. Setting all available sail and with the wind behind, he repeatedly rammed the *Peacock*'s bow into the obstacles ahead. Soon the foremost piece of the keel, known as the gripe, had been battered to pieces, but Hudson continued on. By the time Reynolds came on deck, the ship had punched her way into a clear channel and was making good progress to the north.

By ten that morning, the carpenters had completed their repair of the rudder. Even though his watch had ended and he was completely exhausted, Reynolds insisted on remaining on deck to witness the reshipping of the rudder. Using a tackle hooked at a point above the rudderpost and secured to the tiller hole, the rudder was lifted high enough so that its upper pintle (a large metal hook) could be lowered into the gudgeon, a metal loop secured to the sternpost. Once this upper pintle was in place, the rudder was held tightly against the sternpost by the rudder chains as it was carefully lowered until the other pintles had been engaged. In the case of the *Peacock*'s jury-rigged rudder, there were just two of the usual five pintles remaining.

By 11:30 A.M., the *Peacock* was on her way again, following a narrow sliver of water that might close in at any moment. By midnight, they had sailed more than thirty miles and were in the open ocean at last. It was Sunday, and after religious service, Hudson called a meeting of the commissioned officers in his cabin. Given the condition of the ship and especially the rudder, it was generally agreed that they had no alternative but to return to Sydney for repairs.

"And so ended our attempt South!" Reynolds wrote. "So vanished our bright hopes, and all that was left for us, was to wish the others better fortunes! True we had seen the Land afar off, & had touched the bottom with our lead, but this was a Lame tale to tell. . . . True we had done all we could, and had nearly become martyrs to our zeal; but disasters never tell much, when productive of defeat, & we were mortified to the very hearts core."

And yet, they had one thing to be thankful for. They were all still alive. If the *Vincennes* had run into similar trouble, Reynolds was sure that Wilkes would have been powerless to save the ship and her crew. "The hero of Pago Pago," he wrote, "was not the man for such terrible occasions as that."

CHAPTER 8

A New Continent

W
HILE THE OFFICERS and men of the *Peacock* had been fighting their way out of the ice and the *Porpoise* pursued her
own course along the edge of the icy barrier, Wilkes, in typical fashion, fell into a squabble with one of his lieutenants. On January
23, a day after passing the opening that would almost claim the *Peacock,*
the *Vincennes* reached a bay in the ice that was about twenty-five miles
wide. By midnight they had ventured almost fifteen miles into the
opening when they encountered a closely packed group of icebergs.
Wilkes determined that it was impossible to go any farther and ordered
that they tack away and continue west. On his chart he called it Disappointment Bay.

But not all of his officers agreed with him, especially Lieutenant
Joseph Underwood. Over the last few days, Underwood was becoming
increasingly frustrated with his commander. He felt that Wilkes had
missed several opportunities to push the ship farther south. When Wilkes
ignored his report of an opening in Disappointment Bay, Underwood
took up a piece of chalk and vented his anger on the log slate, the public record of the ship's course and speed that served as a rough draft for
the ship's log. On the slate he wrote that "an opening had been reported
to the S & W before we tacked ship."

Since the log slate was not erased until noon of the following day,
Underwood's message was waiting for Wilkes when he came on deck
the next morning. He was not pleased. He ordered Underwood on deck
and asked why he hadn't informed him of the opening. When Under-

wood told him that he had done exactly that, Wilkes claimed "he did not recollect the circumstances." He also claimed that he had been aloft just prior to tacking and had seen "a barrier quite round by the S&W." Even though they were now forty miles from Disappointment Bay, Wilkes ordered that they return to the bay so that he could prove Underwood wrong.

It took them an entire day to retrace their steps. Once Wilkes was confident that the bay was, in fact, sealed off by ice, he did his best to humiliate Underwood. "I called all the officers on the deck," he later wrote, "and then addressed Lt. Underwood who was required to point out the opening he had written of." Underwood had no choice but to recant his earlier claims even though it was quite possible that the ice had shifted since they had last visited the bay.

Wilkes saw this as "a heavy stroke upon [the officers'] machinations & deceits." Others saw it as a personal vendetta. Although not aboard the *Vincennes* during the Antarctic cruise, Reynolds had already had sufficient opportunity to witness Wilkes's attitude toward Underwood: "It seemed to be impossible for him sufficiently to gratify his malignant feelings towards that officer, and he pursued him with the most vindictive tyranny." Reynolds attributed Wilkes's behavior to jealousy. In addition to being well liked, Underwood was exceedingly well educated. "In comprehensiveness of mind, in scientific attainments, versatility of talent, and in professional knowledge Lt. Underwood far surpassed Lt. Wilkes," Reynolds claimed. "Jealousy was a fierce passion in the breast of the Commander, and once awoke, it rendered him regardless of humanity, honor, or justice."

Rather than push on to the west, Wilkes decided to dawdle at the scene of Underwood's disgrace. The ship was hove to, a hawser was readied, and they spent the day secured to an iceberg, filling up the tanks with freshwater melted from the ice while others performed magnetic observations on a nearby ice island. Wilkes even took the opportunity to sketch a picture of the *Vincennes* amid the ice. Once back aboard, he issued an order intended to eliminate any future misunderstandings. From now on, the officer of the deck was required to go to the masthead at the end of his watch and "report to me the exact situation of the ice."

Later that day, as they threaded their way through the ice, Wilkes hit upon the notion of charting the icebergs. "[I]t occurred to me," he wrote, "that they might be considered as islands, and a rough survey made of them, by taking their bearings at certain periods, and making diagrams of their positions." Although this struck several of his officers as being of extremely dubious navigational value, Wilkes insisted that they begin surveying the ice. Every few hours the latest batch of diagrams would be inserted into the chart Wilkes was making in his cabin. Wilkes reasoned that if weather conditions should require them to backtrack, he would now have a "tolerable chart" to guide their escape.

At eight A.M. the next day, they sighted the *Porpoise*. Wilkes and Ringgold spoke briefly, comparing their longitudes, but neither one of them seems to have mentioned sighting land. For the first time since they reached the ice, the wind shifted to the southeast, supposedly the prevailing direction. With the wind finally behind them, Wilkes resolved to make up for lost time. With all sails set, the *Vincennes* took off at nine knots through the drift ice, with the *Porpoise* following in her wake. "Sailing in this way I felt to be extremely hazardous," Wilkes wrote, "but our time was so short.... [B]y good look-outs, and carefully conning the ship, [we] were able to avoid any heavy thumps."

At noon the next day, they lost sight of the *Porpoise*. The following day, January 28, was, in the words of James Alden, "as clear as a bell." Alden was the officer of the watch. He was reefing a topsail when he saw what he considered to be his first undeniable glimpse of land. This time Wilkes was willing to listen when Alden reported the sighting. Wilkes climbed up into the rigging with him and, according to Alden, "looked at it for some time and said, 'There is no mistake about it.'" As far as Wilkes's officers were concerned, this was the day, January 28, when they first became convinced that land did indeed exist to the south.

They were in the middle of a vast field of tabular icebergs. At one point they had at least one hundred of them in sight, and by eleven A.M.

they had run more than forty miles through the bergs, with land still in sight to the south. Soon the weather began to thicken; by two P.M. the barometer started to fall; by five, it was blowing a gale. There were huge icebergs in every direction. The last time they'd seen open water was more than forty miles back, and with his chart in hand, Wilkes resolved to retrace their way through the bergs.

By eight P.M., it was, in Wilkes's words, "blowing very hard." It was also snowing, reducing visibility to just a few hundred feet. Even if the surrounding icebergs had been stationary (which, of course, they weren't), it would have been impossible to navigate by chart in these conditions. It was now simply a matter of survival as the lookouts strained to see ahead. Icebergs seemed to be just about everywhere. There "were many narrow escapes," Wilkes wrote; "the excitement became intense; it required a constant change of helm to avoid those close aboard." It was necessary to keep the ship moving at what seemed like

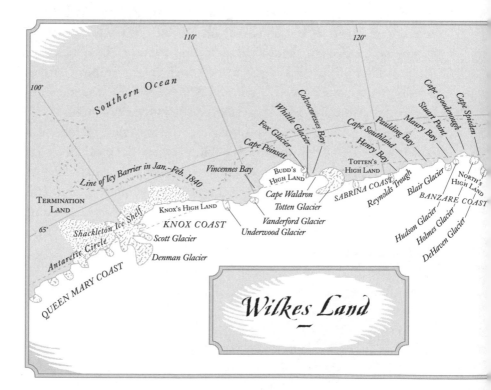

an insanely fast speed given the hazards ahead of them, but it was the only way to maintain sufficient steerage. The *Vincennes* was like a tractor-trailer truck with its accelerator stuck to the floor, weaving its way down a crowded highway. A collision seemed almost inevitable. "I felt that no prudence nor foresight could avail in protecting the ship and crew," Wilkes wrote.

At midnight, all hands were called on deck. The ship was covered with ice, and almost as soon as his feet touched the deck, Gunner Williamson, the man with whom Wilkes had talked about seeing land ten days earlier, slipped and broke several ribs. "The gale at this moment was awful," Wilkes wrote, "large masses of drift-ice and ice-islands became more numerous." In these terrifying conditions, Wilkes's behavior hardly inspired confidence. Alden would later tell Reynolds of the commander's "incoherent and improper orders, his running in frightened anxiety about the decks, his readiness to take suggestion from any-

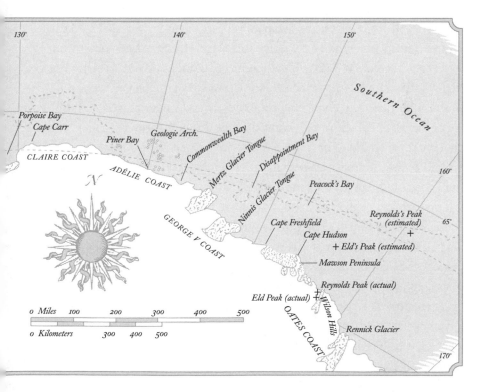

one (no *etiquette* or *isolation then*) and the utter want of reliance in him that was felt, not only by the officers but by the crew."

As the crew struggled to reef the sails, which were coated in a thick layer of ice, a seaman by the name of Brooks became trapped on the lee yardarm. The sail had blown over the yard and prevented him from returning to the deck along with the others. Only belatedly did someone see him, still clinging to the yard. Wilkes and First Lieutenant Carr stared blankly aloft, apparently unable to figure out how to get Brooks down. Alden and Passed Midshipman Simon Blunt leapt into the rigging. By tying a bowline around the sailor's body, they were able to drag him up into the top, then pass him down to the deck and to safety. The surgeons reported he had been within minutes of freezing to death. In addition to Brooks, some of the best sailors on the ship were sent below, overcome with physical and nervous exhaustion as well as the debilitating effects of the cold.

Suddenly a huge berg loomed in front of them. "Ice ahead!" was the cry, followed by "On the weather bow!" and then, "On the lee bow and abeam!" "All hope of escape seemed in a moment to vanish," Wilkes wrote; "return we could not, as large ice-islands had just been passed to leeward: so we dashed on, expecting every moment the crash." Up until now, they had attempted to stay to windward of the bigger bergs, but this time they had no choice but to go below it. As they passed into the lee of the berg, the ship's sails went slack as the hull, formerly heeled so far over that the lee gun ports were underwater, swung upright. All around them the storm was raging; they could hear it roar. But here, in the lee of the berg, it was almost placid, and the officers and men–still frantic with excitement and fear–exchanged wild, desperate glances.

In addition to the iceberg to windward, there was an equally large berg to leeward, and up ahead the channel between the two bergs appeared to be diminishing. As it was, they were in a passage so narrow that they would not have normally dared sail through it even in the finest weather. It was the sounds that first indicated that they had found a way out. The whistling of the wind grew louder as the ship began to lean again to leeward. "We had escaped an awful death," Wilkes wrote, "and were again tempest-tossed."

At 4:30 A.M., they reached a small open area, and the ship was hove to. Wilkes had been on deck for nine straight hours. By seven A.M. the weather appeared to be moderating as the wind shifted from the southeast to the south. By noon it was no longer blowing a gale. "[W]e had escaped," Wilkes wrote, "although it was difficult to realize a sense of security when the perils we had just passed through were so fresh in our minds."

January 30 proved a beautiful day. The breeze had shifted to the east; the sun shone brilliantly, and land was in sight to the south. Under full sail, the *Vincennes* sailed amid the maze of icebergs that had almost sunk the ship the day before. "We wound our way through them in a sea so smooth that a yawl might have passed over it in safety," Wilkes wrote. "No straight line could have been drawn from us in any direction, that would not have cut a dozen icebergs in the same number of miles, and the wondering exclamations of the officers and crew were oft repeated—'How could we have passed through them unharmed?' and, 'What a lucky ship!'"

By eight A.M. they reached the icy barrier. Up ahead there was land, and to the southwest they saw a channel through the broken ice. Crowding all sail, they quickly shot through the opening into a two-mile section of clear water that reached all the way to the shore. Wilkes remarked to one of his officers that this would have been an excellent place to seek shelter in the last storm, little suspecting that in just a few hours that was exactly what they would be doing.

The wind began to increase, and soon they were making nine knots toward the southern part of the bay. Up ahead they could see rocks and icebergs that were clearly aground. With the wind out of the south, they were tacking back and forth in an increasingly confined space. The wind was approaching gale strength, but the quick tacks made it impossible to shorten sail. Soon they were within just a half-mile of land. Dark, volcanic rocks were visible on either side of them. Just beyond the ice, the land rose to a height of approximately three thousand feet and was completely covered in snow. The mountainous ridge extended to the east and west sixty miles or more. On this day, January 30, 1840, at 140°02'30" east, 66°45' south, Wilkes named the land before them "the Antarctic Continent."

He desperately wanted to set foot on his discovery, but the wind was not cooperating. A gale was coming on, and they needed to tack, but it was too windy. With precious little room to leeward, they luffed up, then "wore her short round on her heel." In the midst of the jibe, Wilkes ordered soundings. At just thirty fathoms, they found a hard bottom. Wilkes made a hurried sketch of the inlet and called it Piner Bay for his loyal quartermaster. Fearing that their escape route would soon be closed off by the ice, he reluctantly ordered the helmsman to steer a course north. By noon they were clear of the bay, and the wind was blowing a full gale; by one P.M. they were under storm sails, with their topgallant yards on deck.

"To run the gauntlet again among the icebergs was out of the question," Wilkes wrote. There was too much sea ice to sail through. Wilkes felt they had no alternative but to heave to in the channel they had seen that morning. It was some consolation to know that the ship would drift faster than the bergs, but eventually, after about ten miles, they would run out of channel.

The gale proved to be, in Wilkes's words, "an old-fashioned snow storm," except that these Antarctic flakes "seemed as if armed with sharp icicles or needles." By one A.M., the lookouts saw ice islands to lee-ward; they had run out of channel. They immediately jibed around and made sail. They had no choice but to set out on another wild ride through the ice. There was one essential difference, however. They were now dodging icebergs that were just to windward of the icy bar-rier, and with each tack they drew a little nearer to the frightening wall of ice.

By four A.M., they were getting dangerously close to the edge of the barrier, and the gale was blowing as hard as ever. Wilkes decided it was time to head to the northwest in search of a clear sea. For the next four hours they continued to sail among the icebergs and pack ice. By 8:30 A.M., they had run thirty miles and found, at last, an open sea. Around six P.M., after blowing for a solid thirty hours, their second gale in sev-enty-two hours began to moderate. Once again, Wilkes resolved to sail south. He wanted to land at Piner Bay. But he began to have second thoughts. The bay was now sixty miles away. He wanted to explore as far as possible to the west, and it was getting late in the season. Instead of sailing back into Piner Bay and attempting a landing, Wilkes decided to head west. He was confident that his explorations would provide another chance to set foot on Antarctica.

That day, January 31, the medical officers of the *Vincennes* presented Wilkes with a letter. Although the number of men on the sick list (fifteen) was not especially large, they pointed out that just about everyone aboard was suffering from the cold and lack of sleep. "[I]n our opinion," they wrote, "a few days more of such exposure as they have already undergone would reduce the number of the crew by sickness to such an extent as to hazard the safety of the ship and the lives of all on board."

Soon after receiving the surgeons' letter, Wilkes asked his wardroom officers their opinion. A majority of them agreed with the surgeons: it was time to head north. If he had been so inclined, Wilkes had been given the ideal opportunity to abandon the southern cruise with dignity. Whether it was his innate tendency to disagree with his subordinates or an expression of genuine courage and determination, Wilkes decided to continue to sail west "until the ship should be totally disabled, or it should be evident that it was impossible to persist any longer." He knew that even if *he* was convinced that a continent lay to the south, others might need additional proof. The farther he could extend his survey of the Antarctic coast, the better his chances of being proclaimed the discoverer of a new land.

The next day, February 2, proved blessedly warm, with the thermometer reaching 36°F. The men aired their bedding, and for the first time in days, the deck was cleared of ice. But there remained cause for concern. The sick list was up to twenty men, many complaining of boils and ulcers on the skin. The next day they encountered yet another gale, and the sick list climbed to thirty men, most of whom were, in Wilkes's words, "rather overcome by want of rest and fatigue than affected by any disease." Stoves were placed in the gun and berth decks as the snow continued to fall for another three days. By February 7 the weather had cleared to the point that they could see land in the distance. Wilkes called it Cape Carr; they were at longitude 131°40' east.

On the night of February 9 they saw their first Aurora Australis–the Southern Lights. "The spurs or brushes of light frequently reached the zenith . . . ," Wilkes reported. "[T]here appeared clouds of the form of massive cumuli, tinged with pale yellow, and behind them arose brilliant red, purple, orange, and yellow tints, streaming upwards in innumerable radiations, with all the shades that a combination of these colors could effect." Scientists of the day had various theories as to what was referred to in the Northern Hemisphere as the Aurora Borealis, a term that appears to have been coined by Galileo. Some attributed the phenomenon to comets; others said it was electrical in nature. Scientists have since discovered that the aurora begins with the emission of protons and electrons from the surface of the sun, commonly known as the solar wind. As these particles come under the influence of the earth's magnetic field, which reaches tens of thousands of miles into space, they are drawn toward the two magnetic poles. At around sixty miles from the surface of the earth, the protons and electrons begin to collide with the atmosphere. Much in the same way that a neon light operates, bombarded molecules of oxygen and nitrogen in the vicinity of the poles emit light. Each gas has its own specific color, and the aurora's pattern depends, in large part, on where in the atmosphere the collisions occur. Wilkes claimed that the best way to observe this spectacular display was to lie flat on the ship's deck; he left no report of what his dog Sydney thought of his master's unusual behavior.

For the next four days, they cruised along the icy barrier. Indications of land were now frequent and clear to all, and taking the geographer's prerogative, Wilkes named the more prominent features of what lay to the south for some of his less offensive officers: Totten's High Land and the Budd and Knox Coasts. Wilkes's spirits were so high that he was moved to invite the officers into his cabin to share a bottle of champagne in celebration of their discovery. Not in attendance were those who, in Wilkes's words, "had expressed themselves as disappointed at the result[,] saying I was 'too d—n lucky a fellow' to have this good fortune."

On February 14, Wilkes thought he had a sure chance of finally penetrating the barrier, but just seven miles from the coast they were stopped at the head of what Wilkes dubbed Vincennes Bay. It was a beautiful day, and the incredible clarity of the Antarctic atmosphere, which is virtually devoid of humidity and dust, enabled them to see more than seventy-five miles of coastline.

Wilkes decided to spend a portion of the day performing magnetic observations on a suitable ice island. In addition, the ice might provide some much-needed water. After a brief search, they found an iceberg that was, according to Wilkes's onetime nemesis, Charlie Erskine, "three times larger than the Boston Common."

Charlie had come a long way since the vision of his blessed mother prevented him from dropping a belaying pin on Wilkes's head. While Reynolds and so many of the squadron's officers continued to harbor an almost obsessive hatred for their commander, Charlie had moved on. In Rio de Janeiro, he decided to learn how to read and write. He asked an older sailor to write down the word "mother" on a piece of paper. "I went to work copying," he remembered, "and covered many fathoms of paper with that precious name." By the time the squadron had reached Sydney, he had made much progress. In addition to "mother," he had learned other words and phrases: "home," "sisters," "brothers," "Roxbury," "Boston," and "Hurrah for Jackson, all nations!"

That afternoon on an iceberg in the Antarctic proved to be a highlight of the cruise for Charlie. "We had a jolly time . . . ," he remembered, "sliding and snowballing one another, and playing with the penguins and seals. As we had not got our 'shore legs' on we received many a fall on the ice, which, we found, was very hard and flinty, and caused us to see a great many stars." It was apparent to Charlie that the iceberg had once been aground and then turned over. It was the only way to explain all the rocks and boulders imbedded in its surface. He and his friends collected as many of the stones and pebbles as they could find. "These specimens from the Antarctic Continent were in great demand during the remainder of the cruise," he reported. In the center of the iceberg, beneath a ten-inch-thick skim of ice, they found a three-foot-deep pond of freshwater that was judged to cover at least an acre. Filling large leather bags, they quickly collected five hundred gallons of water.

As Charlie and the other sailors enjoyed themselves, Wilkes and his dog, Sydney, retreated to a corner of the iceberg, where Wilkes set to work on another drawing. It is a revealing picture, particularly since it includes a self-portrait. Wilkes is shown in the foreground with his mittens on, sliding awkwardly down a small ice hill toward Sydney, waiting obediently at the bottom. An officer, who may be First Lieutenant Overton Carr, stands between Wilkes and the others, almost as if he were on guard duty. Although Wilkes probably intended the picture as an inside joke, the contrast between his solitude and the conviviality of the rest of the crew is almost heartbreaking.

For the next week, the *Vincennes* continued west. On February 17, they reached an area where the icy barrier began to curve north. It was a place that Wilkes would call "Termination Land," for on February 21, when the weather once again began to deteriorate, he decided it was time to conclude a cruise that had traced a 1,500-mile section of the newly christened Antarctic Continent–an incredible achievement in any vessel but made all the more remarkable by having been accomplished in a naval sloop-of-war without any significant structural reinforcement. Although he couldn't claim to have reached the magnetic South Pole, he had assembled enough information that, along with data accumulated by the other ships, he had an excellent chance of establishing its location.

Wilkes called the officers and men aft and thanked them for their efforts and informed them that it was time to head north. "I have seldom seen so many happy faces or such rejoicing," he remembered. "For myself, I indeed felt worse for the fatigues and anxieties I had undergone; but I was able to attend to all my duties, and considered myself amply repaid . . . by the important discoveries we had made."

Soon after separating from the *Vincennes* on January 27, Lieutenant Ringgold made an unfortunate decision. Incorrectly assuming that the prevailing winds were from the west, he chose to take advantage of an easterly breeze and sail west and north to 105° east, where he planned to then sail east along the pack ice. The result of this misbegotten strategy was that the *Porpoise* would spend most of her time too far north for her crew to see land. Ringgold's unorthodox course had one benefit, however. He stumbled across the competition.

Out of the haze on January 30 emerged two vessels. At first Ringgold assumed them to be the *Vincennes* and the *Peacock,* but he soon realized that these ships were much smaller than the American vessels. Knowing that Captain James Ross was due to lead an expedition south, Ringgold hoisted his colors and steered for the two ships, "preparing to cheer the discoverer of the North Magnetic Pole."

But it wasn't the English; these vessels were French. When he saw that the leeward ship was flying a broad pennant, he knew that this must be Captain Dumont d'Urville's expedition. Ringgold resolved to pass close astern of d'Urville's ship and exhange "the usual and customary compliments incidental to naval life." Ringgold had all his sails set and was barreling in toward the French when he saw the men aboard d'Urville's ship start to make sail. D'Urville was well aware of the historic nature of this extraordinary encounter, and seeing how fast the American brig was moving, thought it prudent to make sail so that he could keep up with the *Porpoise.* Ringgold, however, convinced himself that the Frenchman intended to leave him behind. Outraged by what he interpreted to be "a cold repulse" and too stubborn to attempt further contact with the French captain, Ringgold hauled down his colors and bore up before the wind. Baffled and somewhat piqued himself, d'Urville and his officers watched the brig sail off into the haze, all of them wondering what the Americans had been thinking.

If Ringgold had been able to contain his overly sensitive notion of "proper feeling," he would have learned that the French had sailed from Hobart Town in Tasmania on January 1. On the afternoon of January 19, they had sighted land. But most important of all, on January 21, they had done what Wilkes had failed to do: they had set foot on a rocky islet in Piner Bay. Opening a bottle of Bordeaux, they had claimed it "in the name of France."

As it was, both Ringgold and d'Urville left their brief encounter none the wiser as to what the other country's expedition had so far accomplished. But all would be revealed soon enough.

+ + +

The squadron was to rendezvous at the Bay of Islands in New Zealand, but as the *Vincennes* sailed north, Wilkes decided to stop first at Sydney. In the meantime, Lieutenant Alden set to work constructing a chart of their discoveries, with Wilkes doing the topographical shading in pencil.

During this long, almost three-thousand-mile sail north, Wilkes began to suffer the inevitable effects of two months of intense emotional and physical hardship. "I had a feeling of exhaustion and lassitude that I could not account for," he wrote, "and the least exertion caused me much fatigue." He began a letter to Jane, in which he characteristically proclaimed that "it has been through my wisdom and perseverance that we have achieved so much in such a short time." These are the words of an egomaniac, but the fact of the matter remained that if Wilkes had not overruled his officers and medical staff on February 1 and continued west, the Expedition's eventual claim to the discovery of a continent would have been difficult to support.

As he had already done several times before, Wilkes had succeeded when just about everyone—including his own officers and men—had assumed he'd fail. Hudson, the most touted seaman of the squadron, had met with disaster. Wilkes, on the other hand, a naval officer with a frightening lack of sea experience but with a will of iron, had accomplished what has to be one of the most extraordinary feats of seamanship of all time. Braving several gales and countless icebergs, he had sailed his ill-equipped wooden man-of-war 1,500 miles along the windiest, least-accessible coast in the world. And he had done it without losing a single man. Today this stretch of the Antarctic coast is known as Wilkes Land.

Even William Reynolds had to give the devil his due: "the *Vincennes* redeemed it all—the splendid success which attended her, in her run of 1500 miles along the Land, was more than even our most sanguine expectations had led us to expect: the great question was set at rest; never before had there been such an immense extent of Land explored in this Latitude." But as had also happened so many times before during the Expedition, Wilkes's subsequent actions would quickly work to undercut all that he had accomplished.

Just a few days prior to their arrival at Sydney, Wilkes called all hands to muster. Once again praising the men for the "brilliant discovery we had made down south," he reminded them that their orders required them to keep the discovery a secret. Almost as soon as they arrived in Sydney on March 11, Wilkes learned that d'Urville had first seen land on the afternoon of January 19 and had set foot on the continent two days later. The news came as a profound shock. "[W]e thought them all on their way home," Reynolds reported, "lo and behold!" But there was no real cause for alarm. Yes, d'Urville *had* effected a landing, but what did that prove? D'Urville had traced only a 150-mile section of coast; after just a month amid the ice, he had decided to quit. "There is no question that it would have been possible to push further west," d'Urville admitted in his journal, "and to chart a longer stretch of the ice barrier . . . , [but] I can frankly admit, I myself was weary of the tough work I had been doing, and I very much doubt whether I could have stood it much longer." Only Wilkes, through sheer determination and nerve, had been able to verify the continental proportions of Antarctica.

What bothered Wilkes and his officers, however, was the date that d'Urville claimed to have first sighted land: the afternoon of January 19. As the Americans well knew, it wasn't until the end of January that they were sure land existed to the south. Soon after their arrival at Sydney, a rueful Lieutenant Alden, having heard the date of d'Urville's discovery, met Wilkes at the gangway of the *Vincennes*. "[I] remarked to him that the French were ahead of us," Alden later remembered. "'Oh no,' said he, 'don't you recollect reporting to me of land on the morning of the 19th?'"

Alden said he didn't remember seeing land on the nineteenth, but after consulting his journal he did recall his half-hearted mention of the appearance of land. As far as he was concerned, however, this did not constitute the date of their discovery. But Wilkes insisted that it did. Wilkes may have even altered his journal. His entry for the nineteenth makes no mention of land except for where the clause "with appearance of Land to the S.S.E." is suspiciously jammed in at the end of a line.

Wilkes had no reason to insist that he had sighted land on the morning of January 19; the important point—that he had been the first to verify the existence of a new continent—was not affected by the French claim. And besides, three days prior to the nineteenth, Passed Midshipmen Reynolds and Eld on the *Peacock* had first sighted land. But Wilkes appears to have not yet been made aware of this crucial piece of information.

The *Peacock* had arrived in Sydney several weeks earlier, and the battered ship, whose stern had been worn to within an inch and a half of the woodends by the ice, was in the midst of repairs. Hudson and Wilkes had an emotional reunion at a house outside Sydney, where the two officers stayed up till four in the morning, talking about their adventures. Hudson spoke in detail about the *Peacock*'s travails in the ice, but he made only a passing reference—if he mentioned it at all—to Reynolds's and Eld's having seen land on January 16. If he were to insist that his ship had been the first to sight land, he would have to explain his inexcusable refusal to acknowledge the passed midshipmen's discovery on the sixteenth. Reynolds summed up the "dilemma" that the *Peacock*'s commander had made for himself: "Captain Hudson would *now* give his head had he paid more attention to the thing; how to get out of the dilemma, he does not know. *His* judgment must be sacrificed & his neglect must be censured, if he now *asserts* that he saw Land on the 16th."

Hudson also knew that Wilkes hungered to have the honor of the discovery all to himself. That night outside Sydney, he appears to have told the Expedition's leader exactly what he wanted to hear. "He said it had all happened as it ought to have done," Wilkes wrote Jane, "he meeting with all the hard luck and I with the success. If anything could have raised him higher in my estimation this has done so. . . . No one could be so fortunate as I have been in having a second like him." It was only a matter of time, however, before the truth of Reynolds's and Eld's discovery—and Hudson's mystifying blunder—would be revealed to the world.

For now, Wilkes was more than willing to take full credit for the discovery. Given the competing claims of the French, he thought it best to go public with his own claim. In the March 13 edition of the *Sydney*

Herald, under the headline "Discovery of the Antarctic Continent," ran a story based on information provided by Wilkes: "we are happy to have it in our power to announce, on the highest authority, that the researches of the exploring squadron after a southern continent have been completely successful. The land was first seen on the morning of the 19 January."

On March 30, the *Vincennes* arrived at New Zealand's Bay of Islands. Wilkes was pleased to find not only the scientists, but also the *Porpoise* and the *Flying Fish.* Many aboard the *Vincennes* had predicted that the schooner would never be seen again. The Antarctic waves had so battered the little vessel that the lookouts had been forced to lash themselves to the foremast when searching for icebergs. The schooner's belowdecks had been almost constantly awash, and on February 5, the men formally requested that Lieutenant Pinkney turn back; by the following day they were on their way to New Zealand.

Both the *Flying Fish* and the *Porpoise* had been at the Bay of Islands for the better part of a month now, and neither of their crews had made any mention of seeing land during the cruise south. But with the arrival of Captain Wilkes, all that changed. When Wilkes first told Ringgold of his discovery, the commander of the *Porpoise* asked Wilkes why he hadn't mentioned seeing land when the two had spoken on January 26. Wilkes then insisted that he *had* mentioned it, but Ringgold apparently hadn't heard him. After all, they had only been within hail for less than half a minute.

Upon hearing of the *Vincennes*'s discoveries, Ringgold's memory began to improve. It might not be in his log, but he now remembered seeing land as early as January 13. Lieutenant Sinclair, perhaps jaded by his horrendous ordeal aboard the *Flying Fish,* remained skeptical of Ringgold's new claim. "It is somewhat strange," he wrote in his journal, "that we did not hear that the *Porpoise* had seen land before the arrival of the Vins but now that the Vins has discovered a new World, it appears that the *Porpoise* saw it before she did. . . . We are a great Nation!" Wilkes had his own doubts about Ringgold's claim. In a letter to Jane, he insisted that both the *Porpoise* and the *Flying Fish* had "made no discoveries although it must have been before their eyes. I was a little surprised at my ship having done nearly all the work but this is entre nous and for all we gained by the others they might as well have been elsewhere employed."

Five days after writing Jane, Wilkes decided to share his findings with a fellow explorer. James Ross had not had sufficient time to sail south that winter; he would soon be in Tasmania, where he would make preparations for a voyage the following season. When he had first met Ross in England during the fall of 1836, Wilkes had been the wide-eyed American without any polar experience. Now *he* was the one who had discovered a continent. It was too good an opportunity to miss. He must write Ross a letter, purporting to offer useful information, but also providing Wilkes the chance to rub in the fact that he had beaten the Englishman to the punch. It made no difference that he was under orders to keep his discoveries a secret. "[A]lthough my instructions are binding upon me relative to discoveries," he wrote Ross, "I am nevertheless aware that I am acting as my govt. would order, if they could have anticipated the case." In this fulsome, at times incoherent letter, Wilkes offers his best guess on the position of the magnetic South Pole; he tells about Piner Bay; about how he secured water from the top of an iceberg; and the weather he encountered. But most remarkable of all, Wilkes chose to include a detailed chart of his discoveries.

It was a letter he would come to regret.

Part Three

CHAPTER 9

The Cannibal Isles

ONCE THE EXHILARATION of having discovered the world's seventh continent had begun to wear off, Wilkes was left with a sobering realization. He had less than a year to perform the two most important surveys of the Ex. Ex.: the Fiji Islands and the Columbia River. If he was to complete the Expedition in the allotted three years, he would have to finish the Fiji survey in under two months, then get the squadron to the Pacific Northwest, a voyage of some six thousand miles, with enough time to survey the Columbia before winter set in. Any delay, no matter how minor, would require him to add another year to the Expedition. In the event of an extended voyage, the sailors' and marines' terms of duty would expire before the squadron returned to the United States. This meant that Wilkes might find himself without a crew if a significant number of the men insisted, as was their right, on quitting the Expedition when their time was up.

Adding to Wilkes's sense of embattled isolation was the lack of news from home. As incredible as it might seem, Wilkes, the leader of the U.S. Ex. Ex., had not received a single letter from his wife and children since the squadron left Rio de Janeiro, almost a year and a half ago. (To make matters worse, Hudson had gotten a letter in Sydney that was just seven months old.) "Don't think for one moment my dear wife [that] I blame you," he wrote Jane. "I am ever aware you have done every thing you ought and I impute it all to mishap." Wilkes could not help but slip into an ever-deepening despair. "[Y]ou must not expect to see the same person that left you," he warned Jane, "but a careworn and broken down old voyager who is and feels that he is doing his duty to his country most faithfully."

His one consolation, besides his faithful dog Sydney, was his nineteen-year-old nephew, Wilkes Henry. Ever since the dueling incident at Valparaiso, the boy had done everything in his power to please his uncle. In addition to fulfilling his day-to-day duties with an alacrity and good humor that endeared him to his fellow officers, he had shown a genuine interest in surveying and cartography. Although Wilkes insisted on treating him as just another officer, he did manage to find a few hours in the week to speak to the boy during his watch, a conversation that inevitably brought Wilkes "great pleasure." "I almost chide myself for suffering the distance to exist between us," he wrote Jane, but given his commitment to playing the part of the martinet, there was nothing else he could do.

As had been true with the race for Antarctica, the United States was locked in a closely contested rivalry with Britain and France when it came to exploiting the economic opportunities available in the Fiji Islands. Although the group's once considerable stands of sandalwood had long since been extirpated, the Fijis continued to offer bounteous quantities of bêche-de-mer, sea slugs that, when properly cured, brought excellent prices in China. Just the year before, Dumont d'Urville's expedition had visited the group and had even burned a village in punishment for the killing of a French captain and the taking of his vessel. Unbeknownst to Wilkes, a British expedition, led by Edward Belcher, was also headed to Fiji.

Over the past decade, captains from Salem, Massachusetts, had dominated the bêche-de-mer trade; in fact, one of Salem's most experienced traders, Benjamin Vanderford, had signed on as a pilot for the Ex. Ex. Vanderford, who had spent ten months shipwrecked on the Fijis, knew better than anyone the challenges of navigating amid the more than 360 islands of this group. No reliable charts existed, and in the last twelve years, eight vessels, five of them from America, had been lost in the region. "[A]s we have so much of the Trade," Reynolds wrote, "it was the duty of the Government to make the Survey; though even at the 11th hour."

Wilkes had picked the island group of Tongatapu, to the south of Samoa and just a three-day sail from Fiji, for a rendezvous point. It wasn't until early May that the newly repaired *Peacock* arrived at Tonga and joined the *Vincennes, Porpoise,* and *Flying Fish* for the first time since the start of the Antarctic cruise five months earlier. Reynolds and his shipmates soon learned of the most recent indignities Wilkes had inflicted on the officers of the Ex. Ex.–despite his recent triumphs.

Reynolds's good friend Edward Gilchrist, the highest-ranking surgeon in the Expedition, had been dismissed for writing a disrespectful letter and sent home to the United States. Lieutenant Alden, who had dared to insist that he had not seen Antarctica on January 19, had been turned out of his comfortable cabin in favor of the more tractable Dr. Fox. The long-suffering commander of the *Flying Fish,* Robert Pinkney, had been confined to quarters aboard the schooner and would soon be following Gilchrist on a vessel bound for home.

Even though Reynolds and his former roommate William May were no longer assigned to the *Vincennes,* Wilkes had found a way to strike out at them too. During the passage from New Zealand to Tonga, he had ordered the carpenter to lay waste to Reynolds's and May's much-loved stateroom, ripping out the walls and furnishings and transforming it into a "stow hole." Reynolds was already looking ahead to the squadron's return to the United States, when Wilkes must face "the honest vengeance of those whom he has so trampled upon." In his journal Reynolds made a solemn pledge: "I have forgotten nothing and nothing will I forgive."

While in Tonga, preparations were hurriedly made for the impending survey of Fiji. The squadron's dozen or more gigs, cutters, and whaleboats were to be used among the coral reefs. Given the violent reputation of the natives, each boat was equipped with not only the necessary surveying equipment but a formidable selection of muskets, rifles, pistols, and gunwale-mounted blunderbusses–heavy shotguns that fired

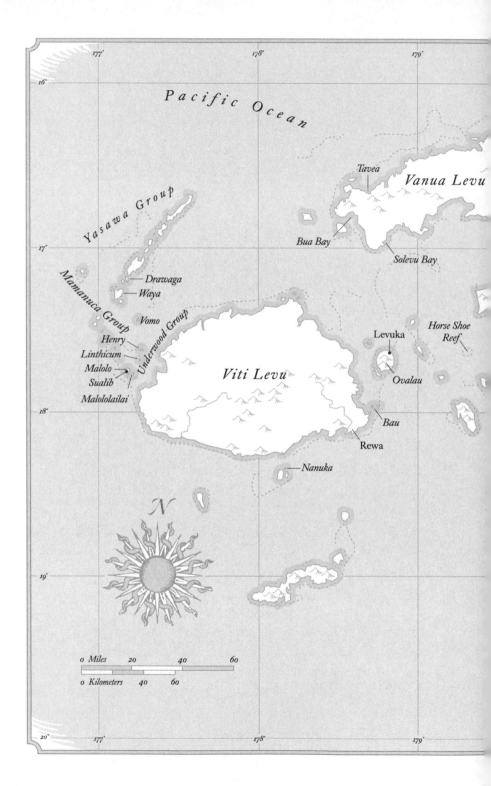

Pacific Ocean

Yasawa Group

Mamanuca Group

Tavea

Vanua Levu

Bua Bay

Solevu Bay

— Drawaga
— Waya
Vomo

Underwood Group

Henry
Linthicum
Malolo
Sualib
Malololailai

Viti Levu

Levuka

Horse Shoe
Reef

Ovalau

Bau

Rewa

— Nanuka

N

| 0 Miles | 20 | 40 | 60 |
| 0 Kilometers | 40 | 60 | |

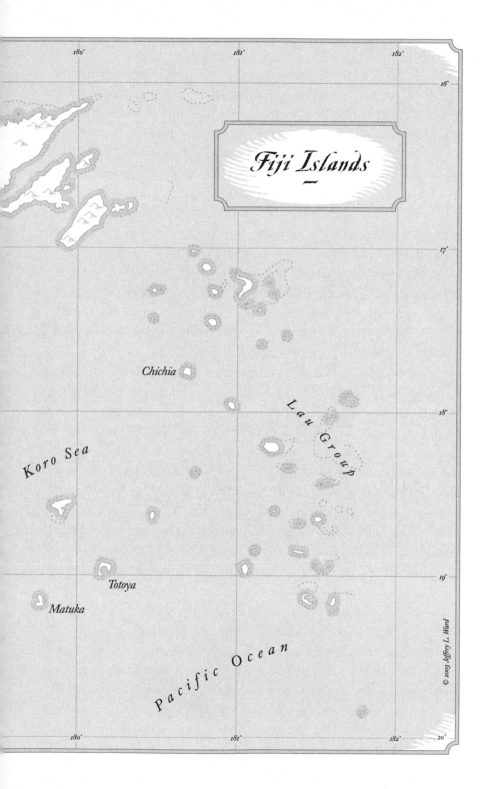

buckshot. Some of the vessels were even equipped with the frames to launch Congreve war rockets, made famous by Francis Scott Key's reference to "the rockets' red glare" during the British attack on Fort McHenry in 1814. When it came to the safety of his officers and men, Wilkes intended to leave nothing to chance. Unfortunately, even these extraordinary measures would not, in the end, prove sufficient.

It had been in Tonga that James Cook had first heard of a land known as "Feejee" (the Tongan name for the island group), where there lived a people feared by the Tongans "on account of the savage practice to which they are addicted . . . of eating their enemies whom they kill in battle." Whether or not the Fijians' reputation for cannibalism had anything to do with it, Cook, like the Dutch explorer Tasman before him, was satisfied with only a fleeting glimpse of the Fijis before the combination of bad weather and a terrifying network of coral reefs persuaded him to move on to a more accessible group of islands.

It wasn't until 1789 that a European navigator made his way into the midst of Fiji, but it was under less than ideal circumstances. William Bligh had just suffered the mutiny on the *Bounty* when he and a handful of supporters, all of them jammed into a tiny ship's launch, found themselves surrounded by unfamiliar islands. Even though they were at one point pursued by two large sailing canoes, Bligh, one of the most skilled surveyors of his generation, was able to sketch a chart of what he had seen. In the intervening decades, others added to Bligh's hurried observations, but by 1840 only a small portion of the hundreds of Fijian islands had been laid down on any chart.

In Tonga, Wilkes decided to construct his own chart of the group based on all available information. Though incomplete, it provided ample evidence of the dangers of these islands. "[I]n addition to the frightful display of rocks & reefs," Reynolds wrote, "[the chart] is garnished here & there, with notices such as 'Brig Eliza lost'; 'Am. Brig lost,' etc. etc.'" Wilkes told his officers that he expected to lose no fewer than two vessels during the survey. Fear of shipwreck and cannibals prompted many of the officers to make out their wills. "[I]t is somewhat amusing to see the dispositions that each one made in case he should be the victim," Reynolds wrote. Four months later, no one would be laughing.

Even though the squadron already had the services of Benjamin Vanderford at its disposal, Wilkes felt it necessary to secure yet another experienced pilot at Tonga named Tom Granby. "You will find when we get to the Islands," Wilkes assured Granby, "that I know as much about them as you do." Granby smiled. "You may know all about them on paper," he replied, "but when you come to the goings in and goings out, you will see who knows best, you or myself."

Two days later, even Wilkes was beginning to appreciate the truth of Granby's words. They were headed to the island of Ovalau, centrally located off the east coast of Viti Levu, the largest island in the group, with the second largest island, Vanua Levu, to the north. To the east was a long necklace of islands known as the Lau Group, and Wilkes sent Ringgold and the *Porpoise* to investigate those islands. The rest of the squadron was approaching what was known as the Koro Sea, a perilous body of water speckled with islands and coral reefs.

At five P.M. on May 6, they sighted the island of Totoya; unfortunately it was thirty miles from the position indicated on Wilkes's chart. The wind had built to a gale, requiring them to take three reefs in the topsails. Prudence would have dictated that they heave to for the night, especially since the *Flying Fish,* now under the command of Lieutenant George Sinclair, was having difficulty in the tumultuous seas. But even with darkness approaching, Wilkes elected to push on, "feeling assured we should thus save much time and probably find smoother water." Wilkes did later admit, however, that "it is by no means a pleasant business to be running over unknown ground, in a dark night before a brisk gale, at the rate of seven or eight miles an hour."

In the early morning hours they almost ran into Horse-Shoe Reef, which the pilot had estimated to be at least twenty miles away. Daylight revealed a dazzling array of islands, all of them "girt by white encircling reefs." But the *Flying Fish* was nowhere to be seen. Impatient to begin his survey, Wilkes continued on toward the high, jagged peaks of Ovalau.

The *Peacock* eventually followed the *Vincennes* into the anchorage at the village of Levuka, and Reynolds was immediately captivated by the view. "The Island was high and clothed in the most luxuriant verdure," he wrote, "with many bold points of rocks and immense forests; and here and there shining waterfalls glanced amid the foliage. . . . We saw many little villages peeping from amidst the trees and scattered huts clinging to the projecting ridges of rocks, clear up to the highest parts of the Island. . . . After the Ice [of Antarctica], we hailed with joy our return to the ever green Isles of the Tropics."

If the landscape was reminiscent of many of the islands they had already seen, the inhabitants were something altogether different. It wasn't just that the Fijians were bigger and more muscular, with darker skin and curlier hair than the Polynesians; it was the way they presented themselves to this already nervous group of *Papalangi,* the Fijian word for white people. With a huge club resting on his shoulder, a Fijian warrior made a most intimidating sight. "[T]hey were fine specimens of men . . . ," Reynolds wrote, "begrimed with dirt, daubed with red paint & soot, the ear slit, & hanging down to the shoulder, with a bone or shell thrust in the hole, hair frizzled out to a most grotesque extent from the head, dyed of various hues & teeming with life; naked, save a girdle of Tappa around the loins, they presented a spectacle of mingled hideousness & ferocity that well becomes the character they have earned for themselves."

Reynolds and his fellow officers began to notice that there were few old people in the village. They later learned that there was a simple reason for this. When it became clear that a man or woman was getting along in years, his or her son dug a grave and strangled the aged parent to death. It was not judged to be an act of cruelty; it was simply the way things were done in Fiji, a place where the value of a human life was said to equal a single sperm whale's tooth. When a chief died, his many wives were put to death. Prior to the launching of a chief's war canoe, the vessel's deck was washed in human blood while the victims' bodies were used as rollers to help launch the canoe into the sea.

If tales such as these had a chilling effect on the officers and men of the Expedition, Reynolds soon discovered that as far as the Fijian children were concerned, *he* was the terrifying one. At one point he approached several youngsters, who ran away screaming to their parents. "And we, who can easily conjure up fright at the sight of a Savage," he wrote, "do not so readily understand why a Savage (even if it be a Baby) should be terrified of us."

Fiji is part of Melanesia, or "the dark islands," a term first coined by Dumont d'Urville to describe the skin color of the inhabitants of the islands stretching from Fiji to New Guinea to the west. The group appears to have been first settled by the same band of proto-Polynesian voyagers who would push on to Tonga and Samoa sometime around 800 B.C. About A.D. 1100, Fiji seems to have undergone a radical change. Whether it was due to the arrival of a new, more aggressive people or the result of a rise in population that led to increasing competition for natural resources, life on Fiji became decidedly more violent. In fact, warfare appears to have become a way of life. Circular forts were built just about everywhere, and cannibalism became one of the fundamental institutions of the islands. In the words of one archeologist, "man was the most popular of the vertebrate animals used for food."

In 1808, Fiji underwent another radical change with the arrival of a Swedish sailor appropriately named Charlie Savage. Along with some shipwrecked pals and a large supply of firearms, Savage and his cohorts introduced a more technologically advanced kind of killing to the islands, eventually hiring themselves out to Naulivou, the chief of the tiny island of Bau, just off the southeastern shore of Viti Levu. Naulivou used his newfound advantage to consolidate his position as the most powerful ruler in Fiji. In just five years, Savage's brutal arrogance caught up with him, and he was killed and eaten at Vanua Levu. But his disturbing legacy lived on, with a succession of sailors serving as what became known as the chiefs' "tame white men."

When Wilkes arrived in Fiji, the most prominent of these white men was a former Nantucketer named David Whippy. Whippy had been living in Fiji for eighteen years and had several native wives. When he paddled up to the *Vincennes* soon after the squadron's arrival at Ovalau, Whippy was accompanied by one of his many children. Despite having begun his career in Fiji as a musket-toting mercenary, Whippy had gained a well-deserved reputation for reliability—not a common trait among the beachcombers of the Pacific. Attaching himself to the chief of Levuka, Whippy had earned the title of "Mata-ki-Bau" or Royal Messenger to Bau, and his close connection to this native power center would enable him to offer Wilkes essential advice during the squadron's stay in Fiji. Wilkes decided to send a message to the current chief of Bau, Naulivou's brother Tanoa, asking that he visit him at Levuka. He then hastily organized a climb up the nearby peak of Nadelaiovalau, so as to introduce the officers and scientists to the geography of the island group.

At 7:30 A.M. the party of twenty-five officers and naturalists, along with Whippy and a large group of natives, began the more than two-thousand-foot climb. Almost two years at sea had left them ill prepared for such a demanding hike. "I have seldom witnessed a party so helpless as ourselves appeared," Wilkes wrote, "in comparison with the natives and white residents, who ran over the rocks like goats." Before long, both Hudson and Passed Midshipman Henry Eld, two of the larger officers in the squadron, were too winded to continue.

As they scrambled up the perpendicular cliffs, Wilkes noticed that the natives would occasionally pull a leaf from a tree and throw it to the ground. Whippy explained that this was done as an act of propitiation wherever a man had been clubbed to death. "Judging from the number of places in which these atonements were made," Wilkes wrote, "many victims have suffered in this way."

By noon they had reached the summit. To the west the interior valleys of Ovalau were dotted with villages and patches of cultivated land, along with groves of coconut and breadfruit trees. In the distance to the north, they could see the "fantastic needle-shaped peaks" of Vanua Levu, almost sixty miles away. Directly below them to the east, the *Vincennes* and the *Peacock* sat quietly at anchor. Wilkes and his officers turned their attention to the sea surrounding the island, where they could easily identify the pattern of reefs extending for miles in every direction. The officers went to work with their instruments, creating a group of preliminary sketches that would prove invaluable in the weeks ahead. Darkness was already approaching when they began the descent, and the natives created torches made of dried coconut leaves to light the way.

Wilkes spent much of the next day organizing two surveying parties, each comprising two boats. The first, led by James Alden, would follow the north shore of Viti Levu, while the second, led by George Emmons, would take the south shore, with the two parties eventually meeting at the island of Malolo to the west of Viti Levu. Word had just reached the squadron that a crewmember aboard the Salem bêche-de-mer vessel *Leonidas* had recently been killed by natives. Adding to Wilkes's concerns for his men's safety was the Fijian custom of taking any vessel that had been driven on shore and killing all on board. Wilkes issued written orders prohibiting the survey crews from landing and requiring that the two boat-crews always remain within signaling distance.

Much to Wilkes's relief, the *Flying Fish* finally arrived at Levuka. The schooner had grounded on a reef and lost part of her false keel but sustained no serious damage. Given that Wilkes had virtually abandoned the vessel in the middle of a gale in the middle of the Fijis, it was remarkable that her commander, George Sinclair, had managed to find his way to Ovalau. This did not prevent Wilkes from giving him "a severe rebuke." Sinclair could only shake his head. "[V]erily I do not know what to make of the man," he wrote; "he can't be pleased."

The next day, Wilkes learned that his diplomatic gamble had paid off. Even though Whippy had doubted that Tanoa, "King of Bau," would accept Wilkes's invitation to call upon him, it was reported that the chief's magnificent, hundred-foot outrigger canoe had been sighted rounding the southern point of Ovalau. With a huge sail made of white mats, the canoe traveled at speeds that were, according to Wilkes, "almost inconceivable." The two hulls were ornamented with thousands of white shells; pennants streamed from the tips of the masts as Tanoa's crew of forty Tongans, renowned for their sailing abilities, maneuvered the canoe through the harbor and landed on the beach.

In becoming Fiji's most powerful leader, Tanoa had gained a reputation for violence and brutality that was matched only by his ambitious son Seru. Several years after a coup temporarily forced his father into exile, Seru had orchestrated the bloody uprising that brought Tanoa back to power in 1837. Just a few months before, Tanoa and Seru had led an attack on the rival town of Verata, killing an estimated 260 men, women, and children. During their return to Bau, the chiefs had ordered that thirty captured children (all of them still alive) be placed in baskets and hoisted to the mastheads of their fleet of war canoes to serve as grim victory pennants. As the canoes tossed in the lumpy seas, the children were slammed repeatedly against the vessels' masts. By the time the fleet reached Bau, the children were dead.

But it wasn't just the acts of violence that had established Tanoa's and Seru's reputations; there were also the inevitable claims of cannibalism. Several of the white residents insisted that they had witnessed these terrifying rituals. Some of the more graphic accounts of cannibalism came from the handful of missionaries who had recently established themselves in Fiji. One of them told how Seru had lopped off and roasted the arms and legs of two captive warriors, then forced them to eat their own body parts.

Many of the Expedition's officers and scientists remained skeptical of these accounts. Then, as now, there were those who insisted that rumors of cannibalism were nothing more than the white man's worst nightmare projected onto an innocent native people. Having heard Captain Pollard's firsthand account of the *Essex* disaster, Wilkes knew better than most that a mariner's obsessive fear of cannibalism began not with the natives of the South Pacific but with the sensational yarns told in the forecastle of a ship. To their credit, the officers and scientists of the Ex. Ex. would delay judgment until they were presented with incontrovertible proof of the practice.

When Tanoa, dressed only in a large turban of white tapa and a small *maro* tied around his loins, appeared on the deck of the *Vincennes,* he hardly seemed capable of the many disturbing acts that had been attributed to him. Thin, with a long gray beard and a high-pitched voice, the king was so unsettled by the gigantic size of the sloop-of-war that he insisted on hugging the ship's taffrail as he made his way to Wilkes on the quarterdeck. With Whippy serving as an interpreter, Wilkes was able to persuade Tanoa to sign a trade agreement similar to one that had been adopted at Samoa. Afterward, several of the *Vincennes*'s cannons were fired for the chief's benefit, followed by a demonstration of the marines' marching skills—performed to the tune of "The King of the Cannibal Islands."

Just a few days later, Wilkes was in the midst of his observations and experiments at Levuka when he was interrupted by a man whom he at first took to be a Fijian, but who turned out to be a deeply tanned former sailor named Paddy O'Connell. Originally from County Clare, Ireland, Paddy had been living in Fiji for more than forty years. He proudly told Wilkes that he had fathered forty-eight children and hoped to reach an even fifty before he died. For reasons Paddy did not want to go into, he had been banished from the community of white residents at Levuka, but was now offering his services to Wilkes and the Expedition.

Upon hearing Paddy's account of some of his adventures, Wilkes informed him that he "did not believe a word of it." But when Paddy claimed he had been an eyewitness to the massacre of the mate and crewmembers of the American bêche-de-mer trader *Charles Doggett* in 1834, the beachcomber soon had Wilkes's attention. It was an incident that had been documented in petitions to the U.S. government, and even though the murders had occurred six years before, Wilkes resolved to bring the perpetrator, a chief named Veidovi, to justice. Veidovi lived at Rewa, a region in Viti Levu to which Wilkes had already dispatched the *Peacock*, and Wilkes instructed O'Connell to set out immediately with a packet of sealed orders for Captain Hudson.

It wasn't long before Hudson had laid his trap. On May 21, he invited the current king of Rewa, along with his three brothers (one of whom was Veidovi), to a special reception aboard the *Peacock*. More than a hundred natives were crowded aboard the warship, but Veidovi was not one of them. Hudson ushered the three chiefs into his cabin for a feast. The natives were in high spirits until Hudson ordered the drum beat to quarters. Sentries suddenly appeared at the cabin door, and the members of the royal party were separated from their attendants. Hudson explained that he had no quarrel with any of them, but that he had been ordered to secure Veidovi for the murder of the white men aboard the *Charles Doggett*.

The king was outraged. *"His blood was up,"* Reynolds wrote, "and it was as much as he could do to keep his passions from breaking out." "Why had he been thus trapped like a bird?" the king asked. "Why had not the Captain asked him for his Brother, when he was free?" Hudson firmly insisted that they would all be released once Veidovi had been delivered to the *Peacock*. Reluctantly the king ordered one of his brothers "to go to the Town & take Veidovi, *alive* if he could, but if he resisted, to *kill him* & bring the body."

Early the next morning a canoe was sighted sailing toward the *Peacock*. Realizing that it was the only way to free his brothers and their wives, Veidovi had agreed to accompany his brother back to the *Peacock*. As soon as he stepped aboard, Veidovi impressed everyone with his regal and solemn bearing. "[H]e was very much dejected," Reynolds wrote, "and this additional gloom threw a more mournful cast over his countenance." Hudson conducted a council in his cabin, where he questioned Veidovi about his role in the killings. The chief freely admitted to the murders, recounting how in hopes of securing some firearms, he had pretended to greet the unsuspecting mate of the *Charles Doggett* in friendship, then grabbed and held him while his warriors clubbed him to death. "All that he had to say," Reynolds wrote, "was 'that he had only followed the Fegee customs & done what his people had often done before.'"

Hudson announced Veidovi's punishment: instead of being executed, he would be taken back to the United States; after several years in America, he would be returned to Fiji, having become "a better man, and with the Knowledge, that to kill a white person was the very worst thing a Feegee man could do." Reynolds had his doubts about the efficacy of the sentence, especially when one of Veidovi's brothers said that "he supposed all he would have to do was to kill white men and then the Men of War would come, carry him to America & bring him back, richer than when they had taken him away."

But for Veidovi, who only a few hours before had been a great chief with fifty-five wives and dozens of children, the sentence was a terrible blow. His brothers were also deeply affected, weeping and kissing him on the forehead. One of Veidovi's attendants asked to remain with his master, but Hudson steadfastly refused. Only after Veidovi had placed both his manacled hands on the young man's head did the attendant finally leave the ship.

The capture of Veidovi had almost immediate repercussions. Word traveled fast in Fiji, and before the end of the day, natives arrived in Levuka with the news. Whippy, whom Wilkes had failed to consult about his decision to take Veidovi, was deeply disturbed. He explained that the chiefs of Rewa and Bau were related through intermarriage, and he thought it likely that Tanoa and Seru might launch a surprise attack and attempt to take Wilkes prisoner, "as it was their custom to retaliate by procuring the capture of the highest chief." In less than a day, he warned, a fleet of canoes with more than a thousand warriors might arrive at Levuka.

Wilkes, the Stormy Petrel, had impulsively, and needlessly, acted to heighten tensions in an island group where even in its most halcyon days the threat of violence was omnipresent. For the duration of their stay in Fiji, the officers and men of the Ex. Ex. would have to be doubly wary of attack.

Wilkes thought it prudent to reposition the *Vincennes* so that the observatory at Levuka might be more easily defended with her guns. Once it had become clear that a strike by Tanoa was not imminent, Wilkes set out on a surveying trip aboard the *Flying Fish*.

In addition to an armory's worth of pistols, muskets, blunderbusses, and cutlasses, Wilkes brought along his own personal deterrent to native violence: his dog, Sydney. Everywhere Wilkes went, whether afloat or ashore, Sydney was never far away. The Newfoundland liked to stand at the gig's bow, and as soon as the boat touched the beach, the dog leaped onto the sand and chased away any nearby natives. As Wilkes conducted his observations surrounded by an armed guard, Sydney prowled about the area, growling menacingly if anyone dared approach. "I think I owe my life to him . . . ," Wilkes later recalled. "The natives were all very much afraid of him, and a word from me would have caused him to seize any of them. . . . It may easily be conceived the attachment I had for him and his love for his master."

+ + +

In the middle of June, Wilkes received word that they were not the only exploring expedition in Fiji. A British squadron led by Captain Edward Belcher had recently arrived at Rewa. One of Belcher's vessels had lost its rudder on a reef, and Wilkes offered to provide some spare gudgeons. The British had spent the previous summer in the Pacific Northwest, and since this was one of the intended destinations of the U.S. Ex. Ex., Wilkes was eager to learn as much as he could about the region. But when Wilkes arrived at Rewa, Belcher appeared less than pleased to see him.

Belcher had just been forced to pay the port charges required by Wilkes's newly instituted trade regulations, and he wasn't happy about it. He was also reluctant to reveal anything about his experience on the west coast of North America. He did say, however, that summer was the only suitable time to visit the region. As it was now already the middle of June, Wilkes realized that he would have to add another full year to the Expedition if he was to survey the Columbia River.

Belcher's lack of candor was a disappointment, but Wilkes's visit with the British commander ultimately proved of immense benefit to him. Belcher was a notorious disciplinarian, and while he and Wilkes spoke in Belcher's cabin, the British officers entertained their American counterparts with tales of abuse and cruelty that made Wilkes's actions seem relatively benign. "[My officers] looked upon me with very different eyes," Wilkes wrote, "and were well satisfied that my discipline was no more rigid than necessary to make my command efficient."

Elsewhere in Fiji, however, there was scant evidence of the supposed efficiency of Wilkes's command. The *Peacock* had recently arrived at Bua Bay on the western tip of Vanua Levu, where two boat-crews led by Lieutenant Perry had been sitting idle for several weeks, waiting for orders from their commander. Although Wilkes would later accuse Perry of laziness, the truth was that Wilkes had forgotten about him, and Perry had no way of knowing where his commander was. Given the tremendous time constraints under which they were all working, this was an inexcusable lapse on the part of the leader of the Ex. Ex.

But if Wilkes's organizational skills might be lacking, at least he was a capable surveyor. As Reynolds was belatedly discovering, Hudson didn't even know the basics of how to conduct a survey, and he wasn't about to learn. Just as he had proven weirdly indifferent to early sightings of the Antarctic coast, Hudson now showed an abysmal lack of interest in the primary mission of the Expedition. For Hudson's officers, who were saddled with the responsibility of carrying out one of the most ambitious survey operations ever undertaken by the U.S. Navy, it was a highly exasperating situation. "Of course we are without a system, and things are done in the most confused disorder," Reynolds fumed, "when they are done at all. It is damnable!"

The *Peacock*'s most recent swing along the west coast of Viti Levu had gone so badly that the sailors had begun to grumble that there was a Jonah aboard the ship. In a single week they had rammed into so many coral reefs that it was a miracle the ship was still afloat. The *Peacock*'s cutter had capsized and sunk before it could be saved. An entire day was lost unsuccessfully attempting to raise the lost boat. But there had been more: one man lost three fingers in an anchor chain; another shot his forefinger in two; yet another nearly amputated his leg; and then there had been the sailor who had crushed his ribs while working the capstan. The once happy *Peacock* had become a ship of gloom.

Reynolds was greatly relieved to be named second-in-command of a two-boat survey of the eastern edge of Vanua Levu. Reynolds and five sailors were to spend the next two weeks in a twenty-eight-foot whaleboat containing a mast, sail, five oars, six muskets, six pistols, four cutlasses, boxes of ammunition, two casks of water, a bag of bread, "a chest of grub," a cask of whiskey, and an anchor and chain. "We had no more room for exercise," Reynolds wrote, "than a chicken in the shell." Since their orders prohibited landing on shore, they were required to find a way to sleep in this overcrowded vessel. Reynolds reserved the boat's stern grating for himself. This put his head in unpleasant proximity with the bilge until he hit upon the idea of using an upside-down bucket for a pillow. His men were left to contort themselves around each other until they were "mixed together so, that to extricate themselves was a matter requiring some care & trouble." When the wind picked up that first night, kicking up a steep chop, sleep became impossible. The next morning, Reynolds "felt as if I had been well cudgeled."

The days were no easier. The weather was beautiful, without a cloud in the sky, but they had no way of shielding themselves from the sun. By noon, the brass portion of Reynolds's sextant had become so hot that he couldn't touch it, and the whaleboat's interior planks were nearly as warm. At times like these, he sometimes sought relief in the water, where a submerged rock might offer a vantage point for his observations. "Often have I been up to my middle," he wrote his family, "screwing away with my sextant upon objects perhaps twenty miles off, with a foothold that I could scarcely preserve from the depth I was in and the swash of the Seas, and surrounded by the men [in the boat] who were holding books, pencils, spy glass, and watch, all of which were used in turn."

All agreed that surveying in an open boat did terrible things to a man's constitution. It was said that two months of this duty was enough to shorten a person's life by one to two years. Some of the officers would spend as many as fifty consecutive days on boat duty. By the end of their stay at Fiji, Hudson calculated that the *Peacock*'s four boats had covered a total of 8,225 miles.

On the evening of July 3, after twelve days of surveying, Reynolds returned for a brief respite aboard the *Peacock*. "[T]he little motion [the ship] had at her anchor," he wrote, "was so different from the quick & irregular jumping of the boats that I tottered, lost my balance & staggered as a drunken man." He soon discovered that the mood aboard the *Peacock* was even worse than when he had left. Yet another accident had occurred. While firing the guns to measure baselines for the boats, a sailor had unwisely slipped a cartridge of powder into his shirt. A spark from the gun's touchhole flew onto the cartridge, and more than three pounds of gunpowder exploded. Reynolds's friend Dr. Guillou didn't give the poor sailor much of a chance. He now lay on a cot on the ship's deck, his horribly scorched skin covered with swatches of oil-soaked linen. "Oh! It was piteous to see him so," Reynolds wrote. "He lingered on, in the most intense pain & groaning continually so that no one could rest in the ship."

As if this weren't enough of a nightmare, the *Peacock*'s officers and men had received an entirely different kind of scare from the natives.

That morning, off the island of Tavea, a young chief and his party of three canoes had come alongside with some news that they wanted to share with the *Papalangi*. The chief's wife excitedly informed Hudson that they had just taken three prisoners from a rival village and had *"roasted them & eaten part!"* What's more, in one of their canoes was a piece of a body, wrapped in plantain leaves. "The infernal devils were eager to show their hellish food," Reynolds wrote, "and they held up the flesh, in the Canoe alongside, that it might be seen. Not content with this, they brought a skull on board, all raw & bloody, with the marks of their teeth, where they had torn away strips of flesh; and one of their Epicures, was crunching *an Eye,* to which was hanging some of the fat & muscles of the face & cheek." Perhaps enjoying the fact that the Americans were so obviously taken aback, the native munching the eye exclaimed, *"Vinaka, vinaka,"* or "Good, good." Hudson turned and vomited over the *Peacock*'s side.

For six feet of cloth, the purser William Spieden purchased the skull for the Expedition's collection. "Everybody in the Ship seemed oppressed with a weight of horror," Reynolds wrote, "& there was a crushing & awfully nervous feeling came over me, which I could not shake off." The next morning, Reynolds went to the forward part of the ship to look at the skull. "God!" he wrote, "to think that *this* had but a day or two ago contained a cunning brain!"

As the officers proceeded with the survey, the scientists were performing some of the most important work of the Expedition. Although the botanist William Rich was, in the words of James Dana, proving "so-so," William Brackenridge and Charles Pickering were more than making up for his lack of expertise. Indeed, the two scientists had become an informal team, with Brackenridge, a broad-shouldered Scot, who had formerly been in charge of the famed Edinburgh Gardens, providing the practical know-how while the diminutive Pickering, whose technical expertise in a variety of fields was unsurpassed, assisted in classification of the 650 different plant species they found in Fiji. It was Pickering who had discovered that as long as they didn't bring any objects of value with them, the natives showed no interest in doing them any harm.

This enabled the two scientists to trek unmolested into the interiors of the islands, where they found a new species of tomato as well as a virulent species of poison ivy that they carefully collected with sticks. In Vanua Levu, Brackenridge found the last remaining groves of sandalwood, which had been previously assumed to be extinct in Fiji.

The philologist Horatio Hale was working up a vocabulary that would ultimately grow to 5,600 words and include five different words for "foolishness." Hale observed that while the Fijians were primarily known for their savagery, they were also the most skilled craftsmen in the Pacific, creating beautifully wrought canoes, houses, and pottery. But it was the geologist, James Dana, who made a truly groundbreaking discovery during the Expedition's stay in Fiji.

While in Sydney, Dana had come upon a newspaper article briefly describing Charles Darwin's new theory of the origin of coral atolls. "The paragraph threw a flood of light over the subject," Dana later wrote, "and called forth feelings of peculiar satisfaction, and of gratefulness to Mr. Darwin." Darwin had hit upon what would become known as the theory of subsidence. The process begins with the rise of a volcanic island. Over time, coral starts to grow in the warm and shallow waters of the new island; then, as the island sinks ever so gradually beneath the waves, the coral continues to grow upward until a lagoon is formed between the coral, now known as a barrier reef, and what is left of the original island. Finally, the island sinks completely below the water's surface, leaving an empty circular lagoon.

Darwin thought it would be difficult, if not impossible, to prove his theory, but in Fiji, Dana found undeniable proof of subsidence. Amid the stunning variety of coral islands in this group, Dana located what would become literal textbook examples of the three stages of coral formation at the islands of Chichia, Matuku, and Nanuku. But for Dana, whose interest in volcanoes dated back to his first voyage as a midshipmen's instructor in the Mediterranean, this was just the beginning. Still to come in the Expedition's tour of the Pacific were the active volcanoes of Hawaii. Besides corroborating Darwin's theory of subsidence, Dana would begin to work toward a sweeping view of geological change that

would anticipate what has been called "one of the great unifying con-
cepts of modern geology"–the theory of plate tectonics.

By the middle of July, both the *Vincennes* and the *Flying Fish* had joined
the *Peacock* at Bua Bay. A gale had been blowing for several days, and
Wilkes used this period of forced confinement to assess the progress of
the survey as his officers plotted and finished their calculations. Wilkes
now realized that another month was needed to finish the survey. Unfortunately, the squadron was running short of food, forcing Wilkes to
cut the men's daily provisions by a third. Although Wilkes would never
officially condone the practice, his officers on boat duty knew that the
only way to feed their men in the days ahead might be to barter with
the natives for food. They also knew that any time they set foot on land,
they did so at their peril.

Earlier in the month, a two-boat survey led by Lieutenant Perry and
Passed Midshipman Knox had been sent to chart Solevu Bay, approximately twenty miles to the south. Around noon on Sunday July 12,
Perry's cutter was sighted sailing toward the anchored squadron. There
was no sign of Knox's boat, but it soon became apparent that two boats'
worth of men were crowded into the launch, along with two native
hostages.

Knox and Perry, it turned out, had been trapped in the bay for several days by the gale. As the boat-crews sat at anchor in the middle of
the bay, the natives on shore left little doubt that if the sailors should
come ashore for any reason, they would not have long to live. When
their provisions finally ran out, Perry and Knox had no choice but to attempt an escape—even though they would have to beat against the gale-
force winds. As soon as they began to tack their way out, Knox's deeply
laden boat missed stays. The strong winds blew the boat ashore, and
the sailors were almost immediately surrounded by natives armed with
clubs, spears, and even a few guns. The boat's blunderbusses and muskets were so soaked with rain and seawater that they were unusable,
and Knox and his men fully expected a hand-to-hand fight to the death.

But for reasons that were not clear, the chief granted them mercy.

(Whippy would later claim that it was the first instance he had ever heard of a grounded vessel's crew not being murdered.) Taking what weapons and equipment they could, Knox and his men abandoned the boat to the natives and waded out to Perry's launch.

Perry knew the wind would have to moderate if he was to sail the launch, now doubly overloaded, out of the harbor. As dusk approached they counted no fewer than fourteen fires along the shore. Every now and then a native would fire off a musket. Around midnight the lookout cried out that the cutter was surrounded by swimming natives. Some of them were diving underwater and attempting to lift the anchor while others tried to cut the anchor cable. The sailors began shooting into the darkness and were eventually able to capture two of the natives, who were quickly tied up and thrown into the bottom of the boat. When the natives on shore realized that they had lost two of their people, "they danced and wailed around their fires," in the words of one sailor, "like so many fiends."

The next morning, Perry decided to try once again to tack out of the bay. As soon as they made sail, the natives began following them along the reef. "[T]he least accident would have thrown our poor fellows ashore," Reynolds wrote, "only to be murdered." There was a steep chop and the boat was soon full of water. The natives had gathered at the edge of the reef, where it looked as if the cutter was sure to run aground. As his men bailed with "Hats, Shoes & buckets," Perry was able to weather the barrier and finally reach the safety of open water.

Upon hearing Perry's report, Wilkes announced that they were going to get the boat back. He and Hudson would be leading a fleet of eleven boats, plus the schooner, in an assault on Solevu. Earlier, Wilkes had ordered Reynolds to resurvey the bay in which the squadron was presently anchored, and when Reynolds headed out at two P.M., he was hopeful that he would be able to complete the work in time to join Wilkes and Hudson. But when he returned to the *Vincennes* at sundown, he was told that they had left two hours before. "I felt as bad as if I had been whipped," he wrote, "& heartily wished Captain Wilkes & his *resurveying* at the ——."

Wilkes and his expedition of eighty men arrived at Solevu the next morning. The tide was low, and there was a wide mudflat between them and the cutter, which had been drawn up into the shallows of a small, winding creek. Using Whippy as his interpreter, Wilkes demanded that the natives hand over the boat and all the articles that had been left in it. "It was a novel position for a Fegee warrior to find himself in," Reynolds wrote. "For never in the annals of his people had so large a body of white men appeared in arms, offering fight, upon their very shores."

The chief agreed to surrender the boat, and it was soon carried down to the water's edge. But after inspecting the boat, Wilkes's officers reported that it was missing the men's personal effects. "My conditions not being complied with," Wilkes wrote, "I determined to make an example of these natives."

That afternoon, the fleet moved in for the attack. The boats grounded in about two feet of water, and the men, all of them armed with muskets, waded the rest of the way to shore under the leadership of Hudson. Wilkes elected to remain in his gig, which had been equipped with a Congreve war rocket.

The village had been left deserted, and the natives, loaded with their possessions, could be seen climbing up a nearby hill, where they paused to watch the ensuing scene. In only a matter of minutes, the entire village was in flames. The popping of burning bamboo sounded so much like the report of a musket, that it was briefly believed the natives were fighting back, but such was not the case. This did not prevent Wilkes from firing a few of his rockets at the natives up on the hill. Partway between a skyrocket and a modern-day missile, the rocket left a smoky contrail before bursting into flame, and the Fijians could be heard shouting out, *"Curlew! Curlew!,"* or "Spirits! Spirits!" Lieutenant Sinclair reported that "we have since heard the most exaggerated accounts of the destructive effect of these 'Flying Devils' as the Natives called the rockets."

That evening aboard the *Flying Fish*, Wilkes and Hudson congratulated themselves on "having punished the insolence of these cannibals without any loss on our side." But, as the geologist James Dana observed, the Fijians probably had a very different view of the incident.

"Burning villages is of no avail as punishment," he wrote in a letter to the botanist Asa Gray. "They only laugh at it. A few weeks will repair all the damage. They have heretofore sneered at men-of-war, as they had done nothing here except burning a town, and it is very important that some more effective mode of exciting their fears should be adopted."

Just eleven days after the burning of Solevu, Wilkes would do as Dana suggested. In addition to reducing yet another beautiful Fijian village to a smoking ruin, he would drench its sands in blood.

CHAPTER 10

Massacre at Malolo

IT WAS TO BE WILKES'S final survey in Fiji—a week-long swing through the westernmost islands of the group. Beginning with the Yasawas to the north, Wilkes would work his way down to the constellation of tiny islands known as the Mamanuca Group, finishing with Malolo, not far from the big island of Viti Levu. Now, with his survey of Fiji almost completed, he could finally begin to look to the future with optimism and pleasure. "I feel I have now got to the top of the hill," he wrote Jane, "and every day shortens the time [until my return]." In typical fashion, he ended the letter with a word about his nephew, who would be accompanying him on the survey: "Wilkes is quite well & a good boy."

The survey party left Bua Bay on July 16. Whippy had warned that they were headed toward one of the most dangerous parts of Fiji—a place where no white man dared reside—so Wilkes made sure that the party had sufficient safety in numbers. In addition to three boats—led by Alden, Emmons, and Underwood—there would be the *Porpoise* and the *Flying Fish,* with the schooner flying his commodore's pennant. The large number of vessels prompted Lieutenant Sinclair to wonder if "we must be bound on some war party"—words that would prove tragically prophetic.

By the second day of the survey, Wilkes had already come close to running the schooner up onto the rocks at least twice. He insisted on overruling the pilot Tom Granby at just about every juncture. "I never, in my life, have seen a man handle a vessel as Capt. Wilkes does," Sinclair wrote. When he wasn't making Sinclair's and Granby's lives miserable, Wilkes continued to harass Lieutenant Underwood. Since publicly vilifying him at Disappointment Bay in Antarctica, Wilkes had suspended Underwood for no apparent reason during the passage to Tonga and was now routinely criticizing his work, even though Underwood was one of the best surveyors in the squadron. At one point Underwood's boat, the *Leopard,* broke its mast, forcing him to return to the *Flying Fish* for a replacement. As Underwood stood on the schooner's deck, working on the mast, Wilkes untied his boat and let it go adrift, requiring Underwood to drop everything and scramble for the boat. But the lieutenant refused to be goaded into anger. "His politeness was not merely external," it would later be said of him, "but that of the heart." Charismatic and kind, with more than a touch of flamboyance, Underwood brought out the worst in a commander who had an astonishing ability to nurse a grudge.

By July 23, a week into the survey, they had reached Drawaqa Island at the southern tip of the Yasawa Group. Wilkes decided to split up the party for the survey of the many small islands of the Mamanucas. Alden and Underwood would proceed ahead in their boats while the *Porpoise* took the western side of the islands and the *Flying Fish,* along with Emmons in the cutter, took the eastern route. The plan was for all five vessels to rendezvous at Malolo the following day.

During a stop at Vomo Island later that afternoon, Tom Granby climbed to the schooner's masthead and saw a large number of canoes heading in their direction from Waya Island to the west. It was time to be off. The wind was from the southwest, forcing them to sail toward the treacherous shore of Viti Levu. Clinging to the masthead, where he had the best possible view of the hazards ahead, Granby guided them through the many reefs and rocks. By sunset the wind had deserted them; as luck would have it, so had the canoes, and they anchored near the shore of Viti Levu. Around two A.M., a light breeze sprang up from the southeast, and under the light of a nearly full moon, they weighed anchor and began sailing for the rendezvous point at Malolo. At eight A.M. the wind once again fell calm. They were near a tiny island that Wilkes named Linthicum for his coxswain. "[N]ot wishing to lose the day," Wilkes decided to land on the island and make some observations. The anchor was lowered, and Wilkes and Passed Midshipman Henry Eld rowed to shore and began connecting the island by triangulation with Malolo, just five miles to the west. "Would to God that we had kept on," Sinclair would later write.

After completing their survey of the Mamanucas, Alden's and Underwood's boat-crews spent the night of July 23 anchored in a bay on the east side of Malolo, bounded on the south by Malololailai, or Little Malolo. That morning the men had only a few yams to divide among them for breakfast. To the east they could see the *Flying Fish* at anchor in the distance, and when Emmons and his boat-crew arrived an hour or so later, Alden and Underwood were hopeful that he had brought some food with him from the schooner. But Emmons informed them that the *Flying Fish* was almost completely depleted of provisions. The officers agreed that they urgently needed to find some food for their men.

That morning, Underwood and a sailor named Joseph Clark were walking the beach, collecting shells, when a group of natives appeared from the island's interior. With the help of the New Zealander John Sac, who served as an interpreter, Underwood began bartering for food. One of the natives claimed there were four big hogs at Sualib, his village on the southwestern side of Malolo, but they would have to bring a boat around the southern point of the island to pick them up. Underwood insisted that one of the natives, who claimed to be the chief's son, serve as a hostage to ensure his own men's safety. The Fijian readily agreed, and Underwood took him back to where Alden's and Emmons's boat-crews were eating their meager breakfast on the beach.

The officers and men were ecstatic to hear that Underwood had found a possible way to get them some food. It was a low, incoming tide, and Underwood volunteered to go to the village on the other side of the island. His boat was considerably smaller than the two cutters, enabling it to sail over shoals that would have grounded the larger craft. To reduce his boat's draft even further, Underwood had elected to leave many of his muskets aboard the *Porpoise*. While this was a clear violation of Wilkes's orders, Underwood was convinced that the risk of attack from the Fijians had been greatly exaggerated. As he had repeatedly told Alden and Emmons, "the best way to gain their confidence was to trust and show that you did not fear them."

Underwood prepared to set out for the village. Instead of the ten muskets he had initially been given, he had only three. In addition to the Fijian hostage, he brought along Sac as an interpreter. As Underwood and his men pushed off from the beach, Alden called out to him, "in a jocose manner, to, 'Look out for the Fijis.'" Emmons added that Underwood had better take a life preserver–after all the water was all of a foot deep.

The *Leopard* soon grounded on the shoals that connected the southern tip of Malolo to Malololailai. While Underwood stayed aboard to guard the hostage, his men jumped out and began dragging the boat over the reef. When a group of natives waded out from shore, the sailor Joseph Clark became fearful that they were about to claim the boat in accordance with Fijian salvage customs, especially when some of them insisted on getting into the boat. "[E]very mark of treachery was apparent in their countenances," Clark insisted.

As sailors often do when performing difficult work, one of the seamen began singing a chantey as they attempted to drag the boat across the shoals. Soon the natives were singing along with them; a few of them even jumped out of the boat and started helping the sailors pull and push the boat over the shallows. "[T]hey had marked us as their victims," Clark wrote. "[But] so great was the effect of the music that they not only *permitted* us to escape, but literally aided us by grasping the rope and attempting to sing with us." As soon as the boat had reached deeper water, Underwood's men leapt back in, and after ejecting the Fijians who were still in the boat, they were on their way to the village of Sualib.

About a quarter mile from the village, the boat grounded on the beach. Leaving the hostage under armed guard in the boat, Underwood and seven men, including Clark and the interpreter John Sac, walked to the village. They found a group of natives waiting for them in the shade of a tree, its branches festooned with an imposing array of war clubs.

The clubs were of two basic types: some had long handles and were used for crushing skulls and breaking bones; others were much smaller and were designed to be thrown at their victims. But of more importance to Underwood and his men were the two skinny pigs tied to the trunk of the tree.

When Underwood asked about the hogs, he was told the chief was away fishing but would return soon to speak to him. About a half hour later, the chief arrived. He wore a white tapa headdress that he drew over his eyes to protect them from the sun. The chief said he would only give them his pigs in exchange for a musket, powder, and ball.

By this time, the tide had risen far enough to enable Alden to sail up beside the *Leopard*. Underwood sent a man to report to Alden that the chief would only trade his hogs for arms. Alden, who did not share Underwood's faith in the natives' trustworthiness, said it was time to cease the negotiations. More than enough time had already passed if the natives really wanted to make a trade.

As the sailor began to wade back to the village with Alden's message for Underwood, Midshipman Wilkes Henry asked if he could go along to assist in the negotiations. Alden hesitated, then allowed the boy to go.

Not long after Henry had left, some natives in a canoe paddled up and spoke briefly with the hostage, who had been transferred to Alden's cutter. Alden noticed that the hostage "displayed a little anxiety to return with them to shore" and even tried to jump out of the cutter when the canoe started back for shore. Alden grabbed the native by the arm and insisted that he remain seated and quiet.

By now, Underwood's protracted negotiations were making Alden extremely apprehensive. He ordered the crew of Underwood's boat to move the vessel in as close as possible to the village. About a half hour later, the sailor Jerome Davis came to Alden with another message from Underwood. All they needed was one more hatchet and they would have their hogs. Alden gave Davis the hatchet, insisting that Underwood "should come off as soon as possible with what he had."

At this point, Emmons arrived. He had sailed over to Malololailai to scout out some possible places where they might enjoy the meal Underwood was trying to arrange for them. Alden was telling him about the hostage's earlier attempt to escape, when the native suddenly leapt over the side and began running for shore. Instead of heading for the village, the hostage ran in the opposite direction, as if to distract them from what was happening on the beach. Both Alden and Midshipman William Clark raised their muskets and aimed at the hostage, who was looking back at them over his shoulder as he ran through about two feet of water. Realizing that a dead hostage would provide them with little leverage with the natives, Alden lowered his musket and told Clark to fire over the hostage's head.

Alden and Emmons would later insist that the escape of the hostage had been the prearranged signal for the killing to begin on shore. But for those on the beach, it seemed as if the bloodbath began with the firing of Clark's musket. As its report echoed over the water, the chief cried out that the *Papalangi* were killing his son and ordered his men to attack. Two natives immediately grabbed Joseph Clark's musket and attempted to rip it out of his hands. Clinging to the firearm with one hand, Clark pulled out a knife with the other and shouted out a question to Underwood: Should he give up the musket or fight? "Fight!" was Underwood's cry. Clark proceeded to stab one of the natives with his knife, then knocked the other down with the butt of his musket.

A mob of natives began pouring out of the nearby mangrove bushes. There were just nine officers and men on the beach, and several of the sailors began to run for the boat. Others fired their muskets and, realizing that they had no chance of reloading, followed their shipmates in a mad dash through the knee-deep water. By now there were close to a hundred natives on the beach, and almost all of them seemed to be hurling some kind of weapon. "The air around our heads was literally filled with clubs and spears," Clark remembered. Underwood shouted out to Midshipman Henry to help him cover the retreat of the men behind them. Henry replied that he had just been hit by a short club and would "first have a crack" at the native who had hurled it. Henry ran into the midst of the natives and killed the man with his pistol. As he ran back to take up his position beside Underwood, he was struck in the back of the head by a short club and fell face-first into the water. He was instantly surrounded by natives, who began stripping off his clothes.

As the rest of the men ran for the boats, only Clark and one other sailor remained to fight beside the two officers. Out of the corner of his eye, Clark saw a native, about fifteen feet away, with a spear in his hand. "[M]y ignorance of the force of these missiles very nearly cost me my life," he later wrote. "It came like a flash of lightning, struck me full in the face, tearing my upper lip into three pieces, loosening my upper fore teeth, and glancing out of my mouth, passed through the left arm of Mr. Underwood." Incredibly, Clark was able to raise his musket and shoot the native through the head before another native came up from behind and knocked him senseless into the water.

The bite of the saltwater on his cut and bleeding face revived Clark, and he was soon back on his feet, only to see Underwood succumb to a blow to the back of the head. Clark did his best to get to Underwood, who was now lying on his left side and using his right arm to fend off the natives' clubs, but Clark was hit on the head and shoulder and once again fell to his knees. He could see blood streaming from Underwood's mouth, nose, and ears; he could also see that a huge native with an upraised club was standing over the fallen lieutenant. Finding reserves of energy he didn't know he possessed, Clark sprang to his feet and attacked the native from behind, stabbing him three times with his knife. He then stooped down and pulled Underwood's head out of the water. "Tell her," whispered Underwood, who had been married just a few weeks before the Expedition sailed, "that I loved her until the last moment."

An eerie change came over the lieutenant's face. "[H]is eyes flashed, and he seemed for a moment to recover himself," Clark remembered, "his countenance gleaming in all the fierceness of the war spirit; he tried to speak, but his mouth was so filled with blood that I could not understand what he wished to say." Clark later realized that Underwood had seen a native approaching him from behind, and "giving *him* that keen, piercing look of defiance, in the last agonies of death, he wished to warn me of the danger." But it was too late. The last thing Clark remembered was an explosion to the head, as if a cannon had been fired a few inches away, then all was blackness.

+   +   +

As soon as the fighting had broken out, Alden and Emmons headed for shore. Riding the newly risen tide, with a fresh breeze behind them, they sailed for the scene of the conflict. They soon came upon the *Leopard,* her terrified crew pushing the boat out into the water as they shouted that Underwood was dead. "The boats had not yet grounded," Alden wrote, "but we immediately jumped overboard, and with all speed hastened to the beach." They were now gripped by the fear that the natives would carry away Underwood's body before they could retrieve it.

But before Alden reached the shore, he came upon a man staggering in the shallows, his face a horrible mess of blood and mangled flesh. It was Joseph Clark. Even as the natives "clubbed and speared us until they supposed that there could be no life in us," Clark had somehow managed to get back on his feet. He was in a state of shock and would have no memory of his actions, but others would later tell him of how he had walked among the natives, his torn lip hanging from his face as he laughed and sang. The natives didn't know what to make of this gruesome apparition and made no further efforts to harm him.

As the others took Clark back to the boats, Alden forged ahead. "When I reached the beach nothing living was to be seen." He found Underwood, stripped of most of his clothing, lying on his back on the shore. Alden cradled his friend's head in his arms and realized that the back of Underwood's skull had been mashed to jelly. "Your poor, poor wife," Alden murmured. "Joe, little is she thinking of this!"

He then turned and saw for the first time the body of Wilkes Henry, almost completely naked. Unlike Underwood, Henry seemed virtually untouched. (It would later be established that he had drowned soon after being knocked unconscious.) By this time Emmons and the men had arrived. The sailors were "excited to fury" and wanted revenge. The bodies of ten Fijians were scattered on the beach, and when one of them proved to be still alive, the sailors immediately set upon him, shooting and stabbing the body with their bayonets and even cutting off the head. Several of the men urged Alden and Emmons to pursue the natives back to the village. Knowing that hundreds of warriors might soon be headed their way, and that there were less than two dozen of them, Alden ordered that they return to the boats.

The bodies were placed in the stern sheets of Alden's cutter, and after covering them with jackets, they set sail for the *Flying Fish*. When Underwood's leg fell from the thwart, it was all Alden could do to lift it back up. For the duration of the eight-mile sail to the schooner, no one said a word.

At that moment Wilkes and Eld were rowing back to the *Flying Fish* after finishing up their observations at Linthicum Island. Eld was the first to notice the three boats sailing toward them from Malolo. He said to Wilkes that it looked as if the boats' ensigns were at half-mast. With what Reynolds called "his usual habit of contradiction," Wilkes replied, "Oh, no, you are mistaken." Eld took another look and said, "They are not only half mast, but they are Union down, & something must have happened."

"No, sir, it can't be," Wilkes shot back, "you are mistaken."

Eld repeated his claim "as peremptorily as he could." Wilkes remained silent for a few moments, then attempted to hail Alden's boat, but his voice failed him.

Wilkes's gig came up to the port side of the *Flying Fish* just as the cutter sailed up on the starboard. Alden was standing at the bow, his face pale and his clothes smeared with blood. "Great God, Sir," he cried out, "Underwood and Henry are murdered. We have been attacked by the natives, and they are both dead."

Wilkes immediately climbed out of his gig and jumped into Alden's cutter. As soon as the jackets were pulled back from the bodies, Wilkes fainted dead away. Eld took Wilkes into the *Flying Fish*'s cabin, and as Dr. Fox tended to Clark's lip, Underwood's and Henry's bodies were moved to the port deck of the schooner and covered with a tarpaulin. Upon regaining consciousness, Wilkes began to weep inconsolably. When he finally emerged from below, red-eyed and sobbing, he made his way to the two bodies and asked that the tarpaulin be withdrawn.

First he knelt beside his nephew. Moaning "the poor boy and his poor mother," he kissed and patted his face. He then turned to Underwood and whispered, "poor fellow."

Alden was still so full of emotion that it was impossible to extract any coherent information from him. But as far as George Sinclair was concerned, "the bloody and bruised bodies of our murdered messmates told a tale [that needed no words]. . . . My whole soul was lost in one all absorbing feeling, and that feeling was anger."

To a man, Wilkes's officers demanded that immediate and crushing action be taken against the natives of Malolo. Although no one had been more personally attached to the victims than Wilkes, it was now his responsibility to, in his words, "prevent a just and salutary punishment from becoming a vindictive and indiscriminate massacre." But before the natives could be punished, the bodies of the victims must be laid to rest. A burial at sea was out of the question. From Paddy O'Connell, Wilkes had learned of what had happened to the victims of the *Charles Doggett* massacre. Not long after the captain consigned them to the shallow, shark-infested water, the decomposing bodies had burst out of their cloth shrouds and floated to the surface. O'Connell claimed that the natives had quickly collected the corpses and feasted on the putrid flesh.

About sixteen miles to the east, Wilkes had seen a beautiful islet that he judged to be far enough away from Malolo that they might bury Underwood and Henry, "without risk of exhumation." That evening Alden, Emmons, and Eld, who was given command of the *Leopard*, took up stations around Malolo to ensure that no natives escaped during the night. Early the next morning, the *Flying Fish* departed on what Wilkes called "our melancholy errand."

They arrived at the island around nine A.M. Dr. Fox and the artist Alfred Agate were rowed to shore to supervise the digging of a common grave. An hour later, they signaled that all was ready. The bodies had been sewed up in two hammocks, which were already soaked with Underwood's blood. Wilkes ordered that the bodies be placed together in his gig and wrapped in the American flag. With Sinclair following in the tender's boat, they rowed for shore.

About twenty sailors, all dressed in white, made up the procession that took the two bodies to a grove of banyan trees in the center of the island. "It was a lonely and suitable spot . . . ," Wilkes wrote, "in a shade so dense that scarce a ray of the sun could penetrate it." The grave had been dug deep into the white sand, which was soon stained red with blood. Agate read the funeral service, and when three volleys were fired over the grave, a flock of birds took wing overhead. "Poor Capt. Wilkes," Sinclair wrote, "his heart seemed nearly broken. He sobbed like a child and I felt for him from the very bottom of my soul." Once the grave had been filled, tree branches were used to erase their footprints from the sand, while footprints were purposely left in an entirely different part of the island in hopes of diverting any natives that might come looking for the burial site. Wilkes decided to name it Henry Island, while designating the islands of which it was a part the Underwood Group.

On their return to Malolo that evening, they found the *Porpoise* anchored in the bay. Emmons had told Ringgold about the killing of Underwood and Henry, and Ringgold's men were already cleaning their muskets and pistols, filling their cartridges with gunpowder, and making other preparations for the impending conflict. Although Wilkes would later claim that he attempted to exercise due restraint in his actions against the natives, the journals of his officers tell a different story. "[W]ar was now declared against the Island," Emmons wrote, "& orders issued by Capt. Wilkes to spare only the women & children."

That night Emmons and Alden patrolled the shores of Malolo in their cutters. It was evident that the Fijians were also preparing for battle. Warriors dabbed with paint and armed with muskets patrolled the shore, shouting out taunts and occasionally firing at the boat-crews. When the sailors had the opportunity to fire back, the Fijians dropped down at the flash of the musket in an attempt to dodge the ball.

The next morning three divisions of about seventy officers and men under the command of Lieutenant Ringgold were rowed to shore at the southern tip of Malolo. Wilkes had instructed them to march across the island to Sualib, the village where the murders had occurred. Sualib was reputed to be an impregnable fortress, and Wilkes ordered Ringgold to kill as many warriors as possible and burn the village. On the north-eastern side of the island was the lightly defended village of Arro (today called Yaro). Wilkes, who led the fleet of boats commanded by Alden, Emmons, and Midshipman Clark, would be responsible for burning Arro while also pursuing any natives attempting to escape by canoe. The *Flying Fish* and the *Porpoise* would stand by with their guns trained on shore.

As the men were being rowed in, three canoes were seen sailing for Malololailai, and Emmons and Alden were sent off in pursuit. Serving as Emmons's interpreter was a Hawaiian known as Oahu Jack. Once they were in firing range, Jack asked the natives where they were from. When they replied "Malolo," Emmons unleashed his blunderbuss, im-mediately killing six natives as the rest dove into the water. "[A]s it was mere slaughter to kill them unresistingly," Alden ordered that the re-maining natives be taken alive. But his men refused to listen. Crying, "Kill! Kill!," they raised their cutlasses and prepared to spear the natives like fish. When one of his men grabbed a Fijian by the hair and drew back his sword, Alden trained his pistol on his own man, who was about to behead a woman. There were also several children, and after putting the male captives in irons, Emmons and Alden returned the women and children to shore.

George Sinclair was in the shore party's second division commanded by Robert Johnson. As he and seventy others took up their positions around the village, he could not help but be impressed by the size and sophistication of the Fijian fortress. It was completely surrounded by a twelve-foot-wide ditch. Behind the ditch was a ten-foot-high palisade built of large coconut tree trunks knitted together by a dense wicker-work. Inside this imposing wall of wood was another ditch, probably dug the night before, with the dirt piled up in front to form a four-foot-wide parapet. Natives were already standing in the ditch, with only their heads exposed, prepared to fire their muskets and shoot their ar-rows through narrow openings in the palisade.

Several chiefs, distinguishable by their white headdresses, stood out-side the stockade, taunting the sailors as they approached. A Congreve war rocket was fired, followed by a volley of gunfire, and the natives quickly retreated into the fort. Waving their spears and clubs in the air, the villagers behind the stockade shouted out, *"Lako-mai!"* or "Come on!"

Ringgold wanted to avoid a direct assault, preferring instead to fire on the fort from a distance in hopes of setting the village aflame with a rocket. Unfortunately, Robert Johnson didn't learn this until some of the people in his division, led by George Sinclair, had already begun to storm the barricade. Sinclair scurried across a narrow causeway that led to a gate. There he saw a warrior about to hurl a long spear. "I gave him the contents of the left barrel of my gun," Sinclair wrote, "fifteen buckshot, which sent him to Kingdom Come."

Ringgold shouted out to Sinclair to return, but Sinclair quickly realized that the gate he had partially entered was constructed like a fish weir—it was easy enough to get in, but getting out was a different matter. He also realized he would be more exposed to enemy fire by retreating back across the causeway than by staying close under the stockade. He could see the natives, "thick as pigs," in the ditch on the other side of the palisade. "The bullets from our men were pouring in thro the Stockade as thick as hail," Sinclair wrote, "but the natives were in a measure protected by this inner ditch." In addition to warriors firing muskets, there were women with bows and arrows. An arrow glanced off a gatepost and struck Sinclair on the lapel of his jacket, but caused him no injury.

He had an easy shot at a native just four feet inside the gate, but when he fired his gun, the native dropped down to the ground, and the ball passed over his right shoulder. Sinclair had heard rumors that the Fijians could dodge a musket ball, and now he knew they were true. When the native sprang back to his feet, William Hayes, captain of the maintop aboard the *Porpoise,* was waiting for him and stabbed the native in the eye with his bayonet.

The action continued at a frantic pace, the air filled with the crackle of gunfire and the angry sizzle of Congreve rockets. Sinclair had just shot a native with his pistol when someone shouted out that a warrior was about to throw a short club at him. He ducked and the club ricocheted off a nearby gatepost. Before the native could get a second club out of the *maro* tied around his waist, Sinclair fired his pistol, and the native dropped to the ground. Suddenly there was much shouting and confusion within the fort as several warriors carried the native's body to a nearby hut. Sinclair later learned that he had killed the chief of Sualib.

All the while, sailors were coming up to the gate, two by two, and firing into the village as Ringgold continued to pepper the village with rockets, but to little effect. About fifteen minutes into the battle, a rocket hit the thatched roof of one of the houses and burst into flame. If the fire should spread, the village would soon become an inferno. A warrior climbed up onto the roof and attempted to dislodge the rocket, but more than a dozen guns were quickly trained on him, and he fell, his body riddled with musket balls.

Soon the fire was spreading throughout the village. An interpreter shouted out that all the women and children would be allowed to escape out the rear gate. As the flames increased, the warriors were forced to abandon the inner ditch, which exposed them to unrelenting fire from the sailors' muskets. Sinclair's double-barrel gun became so hot that he couldn't touch the barrel. "The scene was grand, and beautiful and at the same time horrible," he wrote, "what with the volleys of musketry, the crackling of the flames, the squealing of the Pigs . . . , the shouting of men and women and the crying of children. The noise was deafening, above which you could hear rising now and then, the loud cheers of our men with 'There they go,' 'Down with them,' 'Shoot that fellow,' etc. etc."

A weeping girl was seen stumbling about the village with her arms outstretched. Henry Eld ordered the men not to shoot in the child's direction. Pushing his way through one of the gates, he attempted to reach her, but the scorching heat forced him back.

Soon the entire village was engulfed in flames. Ringgold and his men retreated to a nearby coconut grove where they waited "until the conflagration should have exhausted its fury." After about an hour, some of the men attempted to enter the village. The heat was still so intense that Sinclair feared his cartridge box might explode. They found calabashes of water, hampers of yams, and many pigs, all burned to death;

the villagers had clearly anticipated a long siege. They found spears, clubs, and muskets that had been abandoned by the natives in the ditch. In one of the houses they found Underwood's cloth cap–"all mashed by the blows which had felled him." Most of the dead had been burned to cinders in the fire, with only four or five bodies, including that of the young girl, found lying amid the ashes. One of the victims was identified as the chief whom Sinclair had dispatched with his pistol. "[T]o satiate their revenge," several of the sailors threw the body onto one of the smoldering houses "and roasted him."

The trees surrounding the village were stuck full of arrows, most of them fired by the women of the village. Everyone agreed that the natives had put up a stiff resistance, and yet the sailors had sustained only a single significant injury–one man had received a bad gash in the leg from an arrow. As smoke billowed into the clear blue sky and the inescapable smell of burning flesh filled their nostrils, the sailors attempted to slake their thirst with coconuts. Soon it was time to march to Arro. "We continued as we had commenced," Sinclair wrote, "to destroy every house and plantation that we came across, and as we marched in three lines, I do not think that one escaped us." The villagers who were still alive had fled to the hills, and Ringgold and his men encountered only one native (who was quickly stabbed by several bayonets) during their march to Arro.

They reached the village around sunset. "It must have been a most beautiful place," Sinclair wrote, "situated as it was beneath the shade of a grove of lofty trees." It was now a wasteland. The village had been abandoned by the time Alden had begun the work of burning it. "Thank God we have taught these villains a lesson," Sinclair wrote that night. "[A] load has been taken off my conscience; I hope, however, we have not yet done with them."

Even as Sinclair was writing these words, George Emmons was finishing up the last engagement of the day. He had spent much of the afternoon in pursuit of a group of five canoes sighted leaving Malolo that morning. He figured they must have escaped to Malololailai, and around four P.M., he sailed his cutter in among the mangrove swamps of the

island in search of the missing canoes. Sure enough, there they were—
five canoes making their way along the outer reef of the island. The canoes each contained eight warriors; the vessels' sides had been built up
to shield the natives from attack. Emmons had half his normal crew—
just seven men. "I thought the odds were too great to allow [the Fijians]
any more advantages than they already possessed," he wrote. Emmons
raised the cutter's sails, which enabled the men who had been pulling
oars to take up their muskets, and sailed for the nearest canoe. Once
they were within range, Emmons opened fire with his blunderbuss.
"Many were killed at the first discharge," he wrote, "and others were
thrown in so much confusion that but little resistance was made." One
native, however, was able to throw three spears at Emmons. After successfully dodging all of them, Emmons could see that the native was
reaching for yet another spear. "[H]aving discharged my last pistol," he
wrote, "I jumped into the canoe and jerked [the] spear out of his hands
while Oahu Jack dispatched him with a hatchet."

One of the canoes managed to escape as the rest of the natives
jumped into the water and swam in various directions. After shooting at
a group of four natives who had reached the shallows (killing one and
wounding two), Emmons and his men set to work butchering those still
in the water. He later told Sinclair that the Fijians' "heads were so hard
that they turned the edges of the cutlasses and our men had in some
cases to finish them off with their boat axes." With two of the canoes in
tow, Emmons returned to the *Porpoise* just before midnight.

That night a large number of sharks were seen swimming about the
schooner and brig. "[The sharks] must have had their fill of Fiji meat,"
Sinclair wrote, "as they refused even to taste a piece of fat pork that was
put over for them."

Belowdecks, the officers and men settled into their berths and hammocks and tried, as best they could, to sleep.

Early the next morning a group of natives appeared on the beach near
where the schooner was anchored. Wilkes and an interpreter got in his
gig and pulled for shore. It was low tide, and as they approached the

This diagram demonstrates how the squadron surveyed a Pacific island. Wilkes claimed that the island shown here (which was approximately seven and a half miles in length) was surveyed in just three hours and thirty-five minutes. *From the* Narrative, *courtesy Smithsonian Institution Libraries*

Pago Pago Harbor in Eastern Samoa, where the *Vincennes* was almost lost on the rocks. *From the* Narrative, *courtesy Smithsonian Institution Libraries*

Samoan dance. After more than a year aboard ship, William Reynolds described one of these dances as "highly immodest & indecent; nay, it might be safely termed wanton and lascivious." *From the* Narrative, *courtesy Smithsonian Institution Libraries*

The beautiful Emma. At Upolu, Reynolds, along with most of the officers of the Expedition, became infatuated with Emma Malietoa, the daughter of a Samoan chief. *From the* Narrative, *courtesy Smithsonian Institution Libraries*

ABOVE: In Samoa, the Expedition encountered a tree that had been made to resemble a square-rigged sailing vessel and was known as the *Papalangi* (Polynesian for white man) Ship. *From the* Narrative, *courtesy Smithsonian Institution Libraries*

RIGHT: Reputed to be Henry Eld, who, with William Reynolds, first glimpsed the Antarctic Continent on January 16, 1840. *Courtesy Beinecke Rare Book and Manuscript Library, Yale University*

The *Peacock* crashing into a tabular iceberg. *From the* Narrative, *courtesy Smithsonian Institution Libraries*

BELOW: A sketch by assistant surgeon Charles Guillou, a close friend of William Reynolds's, showing the attempts to extricate the rudderless *Peacock* from the ice. *Anne Hoffman Cleaver Collection*

BELOW: The *Vincennes* at Disappointment Bay, where Wilkes did his best to humiliate Lieutenant Joseph Underwood, who dared to question his commander's resolve. *From the* Narrative, *courtesy Smithsonian Institution Libraries*

The *Vincennes* running before a gale amid the ice. *From the* Narrative, *courtesy Smithsonian Institution Libraries*

The crew of the *Vincennes* relaxes on an ice island–based on a sketch by Charles Wilkes, who is shown in the foreground sliding down a hill toward his Newfoundland dog, Sydney. *From the* Narrative, *courtesy Smithsonian Institution Libraries*

RIGHT: Kotowatowa, a Maori chief from New Zealand. Herman Melville is said to have based his description of Queequeg in *Moby-Dick* on this image. *From the* Narrative, *courtesy Smithsonian Institution Libraries*

The giant sailing canoe
of the Fijian chief
Tanoa. *From the*
Narrative, *courtesy
Smithsonian Institution
Libraries*

The Cannibal King: Tanoa, chief of Bau.
From the Narrative, *courtesy Smithsonian
Institution Libraries*

Rewa, where William Hudson
abducted the chief Veidovi.
From the Narrative, *courtesy
Smithsonian Institution Libraries*

RIGHT: Veidovi (known as Vendovi to the officers and men of the U.S. Ex. Ex.) as he appeared at the time of his abduction. BELOW: Veidovi as he looked after being shaved by the *Vincennes*'s barber. *From the* Narrative, *courtesy Smithsonian Institution Libraries*

RIGHT: A club dance in Fiji. *From the* Narrative, *courtesy Smithsonian Institution Libraries*

BOTTOM RIGHT: Some of the Fijian war clubs brought back by the Expedition. The smaller ones were hurled end-over-end at the enemy. *Courtesy Smithsonian Institution, National Museum of Natural History, photo by Victor Krantz*

Necklaces, some of which feature human teeth, from the Expedition's collection of Fijian artifacts. *Courtesy Smithsonian Institution, National Museum of Natural History, photo by Victor Krantz*

Lieutenant Joseph Underwood, the charismatic officer who became the object of Wilkes's jealousy and wrath. Underwood was tragically killed, along with Wilkes's nineteen-year-old nephew, Wilkes Henry, at Malolo. *Courtesy the U.S. Naval Academy Museum*

BELOW: The massacre at Malolo, from the narrative written by George Colvocoresses. *Author's Collection*

A map of the Expedition's activities at Malolo. *From the* Narrative, *courtesy Smithsonian Institution Libraries*

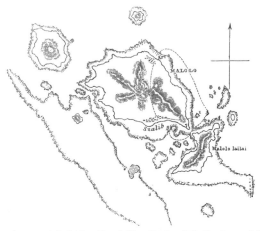

The anchor represents the brig's position. 1. Place of landing. 2. Boats' anchorage. 3. Position of boats off Sualib. 4. Point where the two canoes were captured. 5. Where Lieutenant Emmons met the canoes. 6. Sand-bank. 7. Hill on which the natives sued for mercy. ------ Track of boats and shore party.

LEFT: The retaliatory strike on the village of Sualib as sketched by Henry Eld, who participated in the attack. *Courtesy Beinecke Rare Book and Manuscript Library, Yale University*

BELOW LEFT: Lieutenant George Emmons in his blunderbuss-equipped ship's launch attacks several canoes from Malolo, an encounter that killed more than a dozen Fijians. Sketch by Henry Eld. *Courtesy Beinecke Rare Book and Manuscript Library, Yale University* edge of the reef, the men withdrew, leaving a woman with a white chicken in her hands, which she offered to Wilkes as a token of peace. She also had several articles that had belonged to Underwood and Henry.

Wilkes took the personal effects but refused the bird. He had learned that it was Fijian custom for a defeated people to sue for mercy before "the whole of the attacking party, in order that all might be witnesses." He felt that if he didn't insist on these terms, the people of Malolo would "never acknowledge themselves conquered." Wilkes told the woman that he would assemble his men on a hill in the southern part of the island around noon. If her chiefs and her people did not appear soon after, the attack would begin again.

Late that morning Wilkes and close to a hundred officers and men climbed the hill. "The day was perfectly serene," he wrote, "and the island, which but a few hours before, had been one of the loveliest spots in creation, was now entirely laid waste, showing the place of the massacre, the ruined town, and the devastated plantations. The eye wandered over the dreary waste to the beautiful expanse of waters beyond and around, with the long lines of white sparkling reefs, until it rested, far in the distance on the small green spot where we had performed the last rites to our murdered companions. A gentle breeze, which was blowing through the casuarina trees, gave out the moaning sound that is uttered by the pines of our own country, producing a feeling of depression inseparable from the occasion, and bringing vividly to my thoughts the sad impression which this melancholy and dreadful occurrence would bring upon those who were far away."

About four P.M. Wilkes heard the sound of "distant wailings." A long line of natives could be seen making their way over the hills toward them. When the line stopped at the foot of the hill, Wilkes threatened to destroy them with his war rockets if they did not climb the hill to do obeisance. Falling to their hands and knees, with their faces toward the ground, the natives crawled up the hill to within thirty feet of Wilkes and his officers. As the natives behind him uttered "piteous moans," an old man stood and begged Wilkes for mercy, "pledging that they would never do the like to a white man." Offering Wilkes two young girls, which were quickly refused, the old man said that they had lost close to eighty men, and that they considered themselves a conquered people.

Through an interpreter, Wilkes lectured them about the power of the white man, insisting that if anything like this should ever occur again, he would return to the island and exterminate them. He also insisted that early the next day they must come to the town of Arro with all the provisions they could gather and that they would spend the entire day filling casks of water for his ships. Wilkes later claimed that "this was according to their customs, that the conquered should do work for the victors."

The next morning the *Flying Fish* and the *Porpoise* were brought to Arro, where seventy natives were already waiting for them. By the end of the day, three thousand gallons of water had been loaded into the brig and schooner, along with twelve pigs and about three thousand coconuts. The natives also produced Underwood's pocket watch, which had been melted in the fire at Sualib, and Henry's eyeglasses.

With the task of revenge completed, Wilkes was left with nothing but the enormity of his loss. For the next few days he would be, by his own admission, "unfit for further duty."

On Friday, July 31, Reynolds was aboard the *Vincennes,* at anchor beside the *Peacock* off Vanua Levu, talking with William May. May was at work on a chart of the harbors of Tutuila in Samoa, which Reynolds had surveyed with Joseph Underwood. The two men got to talking about Underwood and began to speculate about when the surveying party might return.

Soon after, Reynolds was seated beside the stern window of the *Vincennes*'s cabin, working on a chart of Bua Bay, when a boat, followed by several others, rowed past the ship's stern. He knew it must be the surveying party, but chose to continue with his work, being in the middle of a particularly difficult calculation. Suddenly May burst into the cabin, shouting, "Oh, Reynolds! Underwood and Henry are killed, murdered by the natives."

That night, Alden told his tale—recounting the slow, agonizing unfolding of events that had led to the massacre on the beach and then the swift and overwhelming response. Like all of them, Reynolds felt nothing but anger and hatred for the natives of Malolo. "[L]et no one say that there was one life too many taken," he insisted.

For Wilkes, the need for retaliation had not yet been laid to rest. Privately, he blamed Alden for allowing Underwood and Henry to go on shore and for not keeping better track of the hostage. "[I]t is extremely difficult after such a distressing calamity to find fault," he wrote Jane, "particularly when one is so nearly interested as I am in its results and when no possible good could come from the investigation."

But it was Underwood whom he blamed the most. "[I]t was owing to the overconfidence of Lt. Underwood," he wrote Jane. "[He] must have perceived the suspicious appearances about the natives but did not act upon them until it was too late." Underwood was dead, but Wilkes would have his revenge. He ordered that the lieutenant's personal effects be put up for auction. "There was a general feeling of indignation among the officers when this order was known," Reynolds wrote. "They felt it would be sacrilege to deprive the widowed wife of the relics of her lost husband." Underwood had been one of many officers who had drawn up his will prior to the Fiji survey, and the executor of that will, James Blair (who had been Wilkes Henry's second during the duel at Valparaiso), protested Wilkes's actions as "illegal and without precedent." Wilkes's malice and hurt would not be thwarted, however, and the auction went forward. "Decency and humanity were outraged in the Exhibition that followed," Reynolds wrote.

But Wilkes was not finished. Upon the completion of the survey, Veidovi was transferred from the *Peacock* to the *Vincennes*. Under Hudson's charge, the Fijian chief had been allowed on deck and had spoken frequently with the officers. But everything changed when he arrived on the *Vincennes*. "He soon found that Lieut. Wilkes was a very different white man from the humane Lieut. Hudson," Reynolds wrote. Wilkes ordered that Veidovi be kept in confinement. Like any Fijian chief, he took great pride in his immense crop of hair, which extended as many as eight inches from his head. Before being taken prisoner, he had more than a dozen barbers to attend him; instead of a pillow, he had slept on a finely crafted neck-stand that prevented his hair from being crushed at night. Wilkes decided it was time to remove this last vestige of his former life. "A close crop was made of his head by our ship's barber," Wilkes wrote, "who was much elated by the job and retained locks for presentation." Veidovi, on the other hand, was devastated. "[I]t was some time before he became reconciled to his new costume," Wilkes wrote, "and the mortification he experienced in having his huge head of hair [chopped] off."

None of these actions seemed to quell Wilkes's anger and anguish as the squadron set out from Fiji in the middle of August. As late as October, he wrote Jane that "the fate of poor Wilkes . . . continues to grieve and depress me. I have borne up against the shock it gave me as well as I could but I feel so in the land of strangers even in my own ship that I have little if any communication with my officers."

Whether it was by death or by dismissal, the squadron had lost its best and most capable officers. Reynolds didn't know how the rest of them could continue under Wilkes's spiteful and vindictive leadership. Making matters worse was the addition of another year to the cruise. "[T]his slapping on an additional twelvemonth, makes a horrible abyss," he wrote, "the bottom of which no one can see, or have the heart to look for. Our spirits are broken."

Under partial rations, against light and baffling headwinds, the squadron sailed for Hawaii.

CHAPTER 11

Mauna Loa

O VER THE LAST FEW DECADES, the Hawaiian Islands, known to Wilkes as the Sandwich Islands, had become the epicenter of American whaling in the Pacific. Five of six whalers that passed through Honolulu were from New England or New York. That fact, combined with the strong American missionary presence throughout the island group, made Hawaii one of the few places in the Pacific where the United States exerted more of an economic and cultural influence than her European rivals. But not even this most American of Polynesian communities knew what to make of the U.S. Exploring Expedition when the squadron arrived in late September 1840–especially when several hundred sailors, all dressed in white shirts and pants, with handkerchiefs around their necks, black tarpaulin hats on their heads, and Spanish dollars in their pockets, descended on Honolulu.

It was an ideal town for a sailor. Years of catering to the crews of whaleships had schooled the inhabitants in the fastest way to separate a sea-weary mariner from his money. Dance halls with fiddlers, prostitutes, and plenty of alcohol were open at almost all hours, and the Expedition's sailors and marines quickly availed themselves of the local attractions. There was, however, an important difference between the Expedition and the whaling fleet. The sailors of the Ex. Ex. were proud to be representing the United States of America, and the more they drank, the more patriotic they became. A group of them procured a giant ensign and began to march through the streets of Honolulu, shouting, singing, waving the flag, and at every corner, pausing to give three hearty cheers for their native land. "It was glorious fun for them," Reynolds wrote. "Two weeks liberty, plenty of money & their own masters. No wonder they went into such half-crazy excesses."

Of these sailors, Charlie Erskine had perhaps the best reason to celebrate. For the last year and a half he had been struggling to teach himself to read and write. In Honolulu he wrote the first letter of his life. "Mother, Mother, Dear Mother," it began, "While fair away a cruseing amoung the islands of the sea, I never, Oh no Dear mother, I never, never will forget to think of thee. By going to Mr. F.D. Quincy 25 Commercial Street you will get one hundred dollars from Your absent son Charlie."

Soon after the *Peacock*'s arrival in Honolulu, Reynolds received his mail from Captain Hudson. "I got such a pile of letters and papers as I could scarcely carry—my arms were full," he wrote. "I was completely puzzled, I did not know which seal to crack first, and after inspecting and turning and tossing I found it was no use to select and so picked them as I could." After several delightful hours of reading, he turned in for the night. "All that I had learned was floating through my head," he wrote, "and it was near 3 before I fell asleep."

For Reynolds it was a joyous relief to know that his family was, as of ten months ago, "all well and happy and had not forgotten or neglected me." He good-naturedly scolded Lydia for dashing off letters that "were not any too lengthy," insisting, "There is nothing about Home too trifling to be overlooked." During the long passage to Honolulu, he had begun to think about his standing in the navy, and he felt nothing but pessimism concerning the chances of his getting a promotion any time soon. "I shall be *30 years of age*," he wrote his family, "when, by the present method of filling the vacancies occasioned by *deaths* and resignations, I *may* be made a Lieutenant. . . . *What* a prospect *is this!* It is enough to drive one crazy." But he didn't want them to worry and assured them with characteristic cheerfulness, "I am far from being miserable."

He gave his family detailed mailing instructions for the duration of the Expedition. Although Wilkes kept the future movements of the

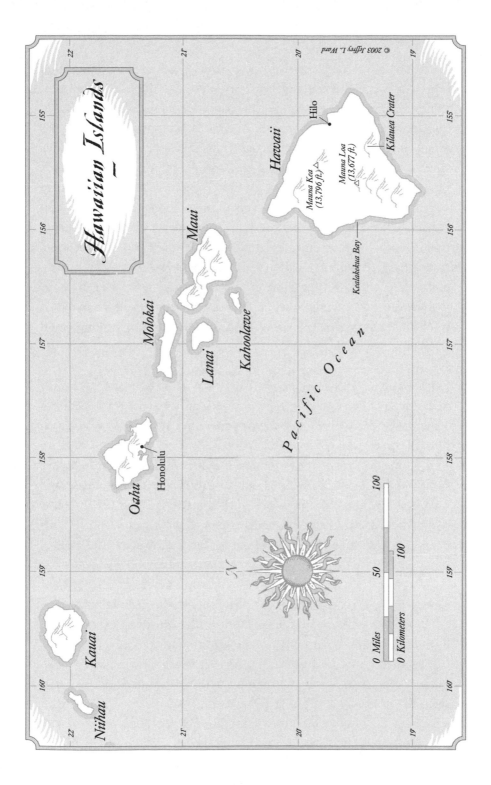

Hawaiian Islands

© 2003 Jeffry L. Ward

Hawaii

Hilo

Mauna Kea
(13,796 ft.)

Mauna Loa
(13,677 ft.)

Kilauea Crater

Kealakekua Bay

Maui

Molokai

Lanai

Kahoolawe

Pacific Ocean

Oahu

Honolulu

N

0 Miles   50   100

0 Kilometers   100

Kauai

Niihau

squadron "a profound mystery," the officers generally assumed that they would spend the summer of 1841 surveying the Columbia River, then return to America via the Cape of Good Hope after stopping at Singapore. Reynolds had learned of three different routes for getting letters to the Hudson's Bay Company's Fort Vancouver on the Columbia River—by way of Montreal, St. Louis, and New Orleans. After that, it would be a little trickier. "You must write by every chance to the Cape of Good Hope and to Batavia or Singapore, up to October 1841," he directed. "Boston and Salem vessels are most numerous in the East Indian trade, and if you see none advertised, why be sure and send a package to the Navy Department and to the Lyceum at Brooklyn *every* month, and I cannot help getting some of them." Finally, he wanted to be remembered to his youngest sister, now approaching three years old. "I send Elly some kisses," he wrote, "and would give *all* my money for a sight of her sweet little face."

By the time he reached Honolulu, Charles Wilkes had begun to emerge from the cocoon of sorrow, rage, and despair that had enveloped him since the death of his nephew. Forty letters from Jane were waiting for him. But instead of softening the jagged edges of his psyche, the news from home only made the bitterness of his recent loss all the more difficult to bear. Inevitably, he took out his frustrations on his officers and men. As early as the dismissal of Lieutenant Lee at Cape Horn, he had complained to Secretary of the Navy James Paulding of a "cabal" of officers that was attempting to undermine the Expedition. In Honolulu, he appears to have received a private letter of encouragement from Paulding that he interpreted as a carte blanche. "Cabals of discontented officers must be promptly arrested," Paulding insisted, "and their leaders either kept in subjection or detached from the squadron, as it is not to be endured that the purposes you are sent to attain are to be defeated."

In the months ahead, Wilkes launched into a virtual rampage, dismissing officers at a rate that outdid anything the squadron had seen since the detachment of the *Relief* in Callao. Lieutenant Pinkney, who had spent the last five months confined to quarters aboard the *Peacock*, was soon on his way back to the United States. When Wilkes discovered that Dr. Guillou had torn out several pages from his journal (claiming that they were of "a personal nature"), Wilkes took the opportunity to dismiss the surgeon, who would remain as an unpaid passenger aboard the *Peacock.* "[T]hey, of course, have complaints to make against me," Wilkes wrote Jane, "but [they] are so absurd & silly that they will go to work in my favor & show how strictly I have maintained the discipline of the Squadron."

When Joseph Couthouy appeared in Honolulu fully recovered from illness and expecting to resume his duties as conchologist, Wilkes acted quickly to remove the headstrong scientist, once and for all, from the squadron. Wilkes was convinced that Couthouy had been writing letters to Jeremiah Reynolds and others back in the United States that were critical of him. Soon after seeing a copy of the *Niles Register* that contained a letter from an unnamed participant in the Expedition who claimed that the commander of the squadron was "getting delirious," Wilkes insisted that the conchologist turn over all his specimens and notes before returning to the United States. "Couthouy says he will publish [reports against] me when he goes home and all this sort of stuff," Wilkes wrote Jane. "Be it so, he will find I am all marble as far as . . . his influence."

Wilkes's claims of invulnerability were more than mere bravado. It was extremely difficult for an officer to bring charges against a superior. He had to wait until the end of the cruise, which could be years after the incident, then risked endangering his reputation in the service if he still insisted on preferring charges. As a result, few subordinates went to the trouble of attempting to bring a superior to justice. This meant that captains and commodores were, in the words of a leading naval historian, "virtually immune to any serious punishment."

But by dismissing so many officers from the squadron, Wilkes was creating a problem for himself. When the angry and disaffected officers returned to Washington, they would inevitably corroborate each other's account of a commander run amok. Wilkes, on the other side of the world, would be unable to counter their claims. By the time the squadron returned to the United States, he would belatedly begin to realize that he had laid the groundwork for his own undoing.

The commander of the Ex. Ex. had yet another chink in his supposedly impregnable armor. Wilkes might wear the uniform of a captain and fly the pennant of a commodore from his flagship's masthead, but the fact remained that the secretary of the navy still addressed him in official correspondence as a lieutenant. But none of this seemed to trouble Wilkes. Ever since Mammy Reed had predicted he would one day become an admiral, he had been driven by a sense of election. "[T]here is an all protecting care over me," he assured Jane even before the squadron set out from South America, "and both you and I must strive to deserve it." Like that other self-crowned hero of the age, Napoleon, Wilkes did not feel bound by the rules that governed most men, and it annoyed him that others were so slow to appreciate that destiny had earmarked him for greatness. When his replacement at the Depot of Charts and Instruments, Lieutenant James Gilliss, wrote him as a friend instead of a superior, Wilkes was outraged. "I am now of different flesh & blood from him," he told Jane. "The idea of a Lt. in the Navy writing to me on terms of familiarity–that day has gone by and I hope you will carry yourself with all due dignity to these jackanapes and vulgar upstarts. . . . I cannot my dear Jeanie any longer think and feel as a Lieutenant. I am only opposed to them and goading of them to their duty."

These are extraordinary words coming from a man who was still, by all rights, a lieutenant, suggesting that Wilkes was delusional if not delirious. But as Reynolds recognized, there was more than a little method to Wilkes's madness. "I wish almost, that the plea of insanity could be advanced for him," Reynolds wrote, "for his acts proclaim him to be either crazy, beyond redemption, or to be a rascally tyrant & a liar." Wilkes's unswerving belief in himself had led him down a dangerous, potentially catastrophic path, but his claims of being a captain were more than mere wish fulfillment. As always, he had a plan.

As the news of his many accomplishments reached the United States, he was convinced that the secretary of the navy would have no choice but to promote him to captain. In fact, Wilkes would later claim that both Paulding and Secretary of War Poinsett had promised him a captaincy before the completion of the voyage. As long as the promotion came through, he could safely return to the United States with his commodore pennant flying. By extending the duration of the voyage by a year, Wilkes felt he had made this a virtual certainty. "[I]t will enable me to add many [things] to increase the glory of the cruise," he wrote Jane. "I shall certainly make it a brilliant one."

That fall, a vessel from Mexico arrived in Honolulu with the latest news from the United States. Wilkes was pleased to learn that the discovery of Antarctica "was received with great Enthusiasm." He was also pleased to learn that as of the middle of September Congress was still in session. "[I]f the American Nation could be depended upon," he wrote Jane, "I should think they would have passed our promotions before the adjournment of the Senate." In the meantime, he continued to conduct himself as if his promotion had already occurred.

If Wilkes felt free to oppress his officers, he was under even fewer constraints when it came to the sailors and marines. The Ex. Ex. was a nonmilitary operation, but a naval code of discipline still prevailed. Buttressed by the Articles of War, a naval captain ruled with what Herman Melville called "a judicial severity unknown on the national soil." But there were limits. Unless formally sentenced in a court-martial, no sailor could receive more than twelve lashes. So far, however, this had not deterred Wilkes. Since the squadron left Norfolk, there had been no less than twenty-five instances in which men had received double the legal limit, and in Honolulu Wilkes's enthusiasm for the lash reached new, appalling heights.

His decision in Fiji to add another year to the Expedition had created a problem. The sailors' and marines' terms of duty expired in November, and Wilkes was required to provide them with transportation home if they chose not to reenlist. After their raucous two-week fling in Honolulu, most of the sailors opted to remain with the squadron. Those who did decide to leave were replaced with native Hawaiians, who would be returned to Honolulu after the squadron's visit to the Pacific Northwest. When it came to the marines, Wilkes adopted a different policy. The marines functioned as the squadron's police force, and Wilkes knew that it would be difficult to find adequate replacements in

Hawaii. He therefore demanded that they remain with the Expedition until its conclusion. When four marines refused to reenlist, Wilkes responded by placing them in solitary confinement in a rat-infested fort in Honolulu. Twelve days later, he cut their meager rations of taro and goat's milk in half. A week after that, the marines, all of them in double irons and deathly pale after almost a month's imprisonment, were brought back to the *Vincennes*. Wilkes asked if they were now willing to return to duty. When they refused, he threw them in the ship's brig. Two days later he brought all four to the gangway and asked if they had changed their minds. After they once again insisted that their enlistments had expired, Wilkes gave each of them a dozen lashes, then threw them back in the brig.

Marines were in a peculiar situation when it came to flogging. The U.S. Army had outlawed the practice back in 1812; but it was still legal in the navy. This meant that a marine on land couldn't be flogged; but if he should be unlucky enough to serve aboard a naval vessel, he, along with the sailors, must fear the lash. Three days later, Wilkes ordered the marines back to the gangway, where they were each given another twelve lashes. Only then, "for the preservation of their lives," did the marines agree to reenlist.

Wilkes would save the most horrendous display of brutality for two marines and a sailor who had been tried by courts-martial aboard the *Peacock* in October. The marines had gotten drunk and threatened to kill Hudson's steward along with several officers. The sailor, an Englishman named Peter Sweeney who had joined the *Vincennes* in New Zealand, had been guilty of a variety of outrages stemming from a seemingly pathological hatred of all things American. The punishment Wilkes chose to inflict on Sweeney would only strengthen his prejudices.

That fall there were nine American whaleships at Honolulu. When the American consul complained of the whalemen's "unruliness," Wilkes determined "to show the crews of all these vessels that authority to punish offences existed." Sweeney and the two marines would be flogged "round the fleet," in which a man was tied to a gallows mounted on a boat and towed alongside each ship in a squadron, where he received a portion of the lashes sentenced him by court-martial.

In the British navy, flogging round the fleet was regarded as "a diabolical punishment" and "the equivalent to a death sentence." Precious little is known about its use in the U.S. Navy, primarily because it was rarely resorted to. But Wilkes, who appears to have taken an almost sadistic pleasure in punishing his men, described it as "the usual manner in such cases."

When the time for punishment arrived on October 31, the Honolulu waterfront was thronged with people. The *Vincennes* was moored with her stern to the wharf, and thousands of natives, along with a sprinkling of American and European merchants and sailors, lined the shore. Many had climbed to the rooftops of the houses so that they could get a better view. The decks and rigging of the whaleships also provided good places to watch as a disorderly flotilla of native canoes jockeyed for position beside the *Vincennes,* the *Peacock,* and the *Porpoise.*

The ship's launch had been fitted out with a platform of square gratings and a gallows sufficient to accommodate three men. Under the direction of Lieutenant Robert Johnson, the boatswain's mate and several quarter-gunners prepared the prisoners for punishment. First, the prisoners' shirts were taken off and draped over their shoulders. Then shot-boxes were placed between their feet as their ankles were tied to the gratings and their wrists were raised above their heads and secured to the gallows. The launch was brought alongside the *Vincennes,* where Wilkes, in full dress uniform, read the sentences: the launch would take the prisoners from the *Vincennes* to the *Peacock* and to the *Porpoise;* at each vessel, the men would receive a portion of their total lashes–thirty-six and fifty for the marines Ward and Riley, respectively, and twenty-four for Sweeney. With the order, "Boatswain's mate, do your duty," the punishment began.

As the quarter-gunners removed the shirts from the prisoners' backs, the boatswain's mate took the cat-o'-nine-tails out of its bag. After drawing the nine cotton cords of the cat (each of which ended with a knot or a lead pellet) through his fingers, the boatswain's mate raised the cat above his head and brought it down hard across the first prisoner's back. The bite of the cat was said to burn like hot lead. Not until the cat had fallen a total of 110 times was the punishment completed.

But the men of the *Vincennes,* all of them assembled at the gangway on the spar deck, were not finished with Peter Sweeney. When the blood-spattered launch returned to the flagship, one of the sailors handed First Lieutenant Carr a letter requesting that Sweeney be discharged from the squadron. Carr passed the letter to Wilkes with the recommendation that the men's request be granted. After reading the letter aloud, along with the names of those who had signed it, Wilkes declared that "he was glad that they had manifested such a desire." Sweeney, the blood seeping through the back of his white navy-issue shirt and with his hands tied behind him, was transferred from the launch to a small dinghy. While one man tied him to the thwart, another cut the eagle buttons from his shirt collar. Once Sweeney's bag and hammock had been tossed into the boat, Wilkes ordered the men to give him "three hearty cheers," to which Sweeney responded with three angry cheers of his own. A fife and drum struck up "The Rogue's March," and the dinghy was towed stern-first around the harbor. The boat was eventually taken to shore; Sweeney was cut free; and, with his bag and hammock in hand, the English sailor staggered across the beach before disappearing into the crowd.

Taking a special interest in the proceedings was a boy who had firsthand experience with Wilkes and the lash. "This example was set before a half-civilized people," Charlie Erskine wrote, "who were just emerging from heathen darkness into Christian light! Well might it have been asked, 'Where is our Christianity? Where is our civilization?'"

By November, the squadron had succeeded in surveying most of the islands in the group. Near Honolulu, they surveyed the Pearl River, which Wilkes predicted would one day be "the best and most capacious harbor in the Pacific." Today it is known as Pearl Harbor. In the months ahead, Wilkes planned to send the *Peacock* and the *Flying Fish* to the islands to the west, including the Gilbert, Marshall, and Caroline groups. The *Porpoise,* on the other hand, was to sail to the southeast, back to the Tuamotu and Society Islands, where Ringgold was to survey islands that the squadron had not been able to visit during its first swing through the region.

While Hudson and Ringgold spent the winter sailing hither and yon across the Pacific, Wilkes would remain in the Hawaiian Islands. He planned to sail the *Vincennes* to Hawaii, the largest island in the group, where he hoped to "swing the pendulum" atop the huge volcano of Mauna Loa. In March, he would return to Honolulu to meet up with the *Porpoise* before departing for the Columbia River, where they would rendezvous with the *Peacock* and the *Flying Fish* in May.

In anticipation of the *Peacock*'s five-month cruise to the Central Pacific, Reynolds spent much of November purchasing provisions. "I had crammed every stow hole full," he wrote, "& felt that I had no more to do, when on the last day of November, I was thrown into despair." A day before Reynolds was to depart, Wilkes transferred him to the *Flying Fish*. In contrast to the *Peacock*, the schooner, now under the command of Passed Midshipman Samuel Knox, had been poorly provisioned. "I regarded with a sad stomach," Reynolds wrote, "the very scanty supply upon which I was to depend while others [aboard the *Peacock*] were feasting on the bountiful store, which I had taken so much trouble to procure." Gone were the days of falling in love with a schooner's fine lines.

By December 3, Wilkes and the *Vincennes* were on their way to Hilo Bay on the eastern shore of Hawaii. Larger than the other seven islands of the group, Hawaii is also the youngest island of the group, having come into existence approximately a million years ago (a blink of the eye in geological time) and is made up of five distinct volcanoes. Of these volcanoes, Mauna Loa is by far the biggest. Its summit is 13,677 feet above sea level—over two and a half miles high—but this statistic does not do justice to the volcano's proportions. Measured from the seafloor, Mauna Loa is more than five and a half miles high, higher than even Mount Everest and K-2. Mauna Loa is also astonishingly broad, containing an estimated ten thousand cubic miles of rock, making it the most voluminous volcano on earth. Indeed, Mauna Loa is so heavy that it has depressed the seafloor by almost *five miles*. Measured from its base below the seafloor, Mauna Loa is ten and a half miles high—almost twice the height of Mount Everest.

Prior to the visit of the U.S. Ex. Ex., there had been only three recorded ascents of Mauna Loa. The first unsuccessful attempt had been made in January 1779 by a party from Cook's final expedition. Just a few weeks before Cook's death in Kealakekua Bay on the western side of Hawaii, four men, including the American corporal of marines, John Ledyard, attempted to scale the volcano. After two days of climbing, Ledyard and his companions encountered a thicket so dense that they were forced to turn back. Fourteen years later, Archibald Menzies, a botanist with George Vancouver's expedition, encountered the same thicket and also decided to abandon his attempt. Not until his third try, on February 1794, when he followed the advice of Hawaii's ruling chief Kamehameha I, who suggested he approach the mountain from the southeast, did Menzies and three others reach the snow-covered summit. Menzies, an experienced and hardy naturalist, described the climb as "the most persevering and hazardous struggle that can possibly be conceived."

Since Menzies's ascent, which Vancouver failed to mention in his narrative of the expedition and which was therefore unknown to Wilkes, two other scientists—the Scottish botanist David Douglas in 1834, and the scientist M. Isidor Lowenstern in 1839—had reached the top of Mauna Loa. In both instances, dreadful weather conditions reduced the naturalists' time at the summit to a few hours. Wilkes, on the other hand, intended to create a temporary observatory atop Mauna Loa. This required that he bring the necessary equipment and provisions, including the panels of his pendulum house as well as his cumbersome and extremely delicate pendulum clock.

Ever since the Frenchman Pierre Bouguer had conducted pendulum experiments in the Andes Mountains in Peru in 1737, scientists had been using pendulums, which measure the force of gravity, to determine the density of the earth's more dramatic topographical features. Bouguer had found that the rocks of the Andes appeared to be less dense than the rocks of the Peruvian lowlands, thus becoming the first to realize that the density of the earth's crust is variable. (Today these density variations are known as Bouguer anomalies.) Wilkes planned to take gravity readings not only atop Mauna Loa but at other locations across the island of Hawaii. If all went according to plan, his results would represent a major contribution to the study of the earth's shape and density, known as geodesy.

Wilkes included the naturalist Charles Pickering and the horticulturalist William Brackenridge in the Expedition, but there was one scientist who was noticeably absent. The geologist James Dana, destined to pioneer the science of volcanology, had been assigned to the *Peacock*. It was an astonishingly self-serving decision on the part of Wilkes, who apparently did not want the talented scientist to overshadow his own accomplishments at Mauna Loa. (Prior to the *Peacock*'s departure, Dana had been able to make a brief visit to Hawaii, spending just a single day at the volcano of Kilauea.) For this particular expedition, Wilkes would have the island and its volcanoes to himself.

"I look upon [the climb up Mauna Loa] as being one of the great works of my cruise," he wrote Jane. "It requires no small exertion to accomplish it, but I have not much fear if the naked natives will hold out against the cold of its summit." As always, uppermost in Wilkes's thoughts was what this "novel and arduous enterprise" would do for his reputation. When he returned from the top of Mauna Loa, he confidently told Jane, "No one will be able to take away my fame."

Wilkes had employed the services of a leading Hawaiian missionary and doctor by the name of Gerrit Judd to organize the party of more than two hundred natives required to carry the equipment and provisions. Although the climb promised to be difficult, Wilkes was not about to go without some of the comforts he had come to expect aboard the *Vincennes*. His retinue included his steward, cook, his Chilean servant Juan, and, of course, Sydney. To make sure Judd had someone to talk to while he performed his experiments, Wilkes also brought along the American consul Peter Brinsmade. Since Wilkes had promised to pay him several times his annual missionary's salary for his efforts, Judd was particularly anxious to please the man whom he deferentially referred to as "the Commodore." Wilkes was delighted to discover that Judd had provided primitive sedan chairs for both himself and the consul, and he even sketched a drawing for Jane, showing him seated proudly on a parasol-equipped chair mounted on two poles shouldered by four natives. The Hawaiians, he told Jane, referred to him as *"Komakoa,"* or Great Chief, and "considered it a high honor to be thus employed."

But even the normally humorless Wilkes recognized the absurdity of the scene. As he and Brinsmade took up the rear, the diminutive Dr. Judd led a procession that included not only two hundred native bearers, but also their wives, children, and mothers-in-law. In addition to the pendulum clock, which required ten men, the natives lugged a small cannon for high-altitude sound experiments, the panels of the portable house, boxes of miscellaneous equipment, tents, and untold numbers of calabashes of food and water. There was even a herd of livestock that included a multitude of goats and one large, rowdy steer. "Little Dr. [Judd] sprang upon his horse, a lame one," Wilkes wrote Jane, "and off he hobbled full of importance & business as the adjutant of our party. I laughed until the tears came into my eyes. So would you have done." For Wilkes, this adventure was to provide a much-needed diversion. "I [was] most contented," he wrote, "by feeling I was getting rid of [the] ship for a month at least and all its cares, duties, noise, etc. etc."

Since Mauna Loa is so wide, it is impossible to see the summit from its base; as a consequence, the volcano appeared to be much lower than it actually was. "From Hilo, Mauna Loa looks as if one might walk over its smooth surface without difficulty," Wilkes wrote; "there is, indeed, so much optical deception in respect to this mountain that it served to give us all great encouragement." Instead of marching directly up Mauna Loa, Wilkes planned first to visit the crater of Kilauea to the southeast. Although just over four thousand feet high, Kilauea (pronounced Key-la-WAY-ah) is the most active volcano in the world, and from Hilo, Wilkes could see "the silvery cloud which hangs over it by day." As night came on, the fires beneath this pillar of steam gave the cloud a reddish hue, providing a haunting, almost biblical destination point for the climbing party.

The incline was not steep, but the coarse basalt over which they walked was making short work of their shoes, and Wilkes sent down orders to the *Vincennes* for additional shoes and leather sandals for the natives. Three days later, with Kilauea not far ahead, they reached the upper edge of a dense stand of trees. "[O]n turning its corner," Wilkes wrote, "Mauna Loa burst upon us in all its grandeur. . . . The whole dome appeared of a bronze color, and its uninterrupted smooth outline was relieved against the deep blue of a tropical sky. Masses of clouds were floating around it, throwing their shadows distinctly on its sides. . . . I now, for the first time, felt the magnitude of the task I had undertaken."

A group of ten sailors, including Charlie Erskine, Joseph Clark, and the quartermaster Tom Piner, pushed ahead to Kilauea. Erskine and his friends sat with their feet dangling over the crater's edge, transfixed by the bubbling pools of bright-red lava, one of which sent up jets fifty to seventy-five feet in the air. Erskine estimated that the crater, known to scientists as a caldera, was "seven times as large as Boston Common"—about two by three miles across and a thousand feet deep.

A sailor named Bill Richmond began, in Erskine's words, "to spin a yarn about the kind of purchase he could rig in order to hoist one of the big icebergs we had seen in the Antarctic seas so as to drop it into this volcano. What a sizzling it would make!" It was dark by the time the rest of the expedition arrived. Wilkes immediately voiced his displeasure with Charlie and his compatriots. "He called us a 'pack of foolish virgins,'" Erskine remembered, "and said 'I don't believe you could find half a dozen landlubbers so silly as to perch themselves there.'" Wilkes ordered the men to move away from their dangerous roost and make camp for the night.

The next day Wilkes and Dr. Judd decided to get a closer look at Kilauea. An eruption in 1832 had filled the caldera with solid lava to within six hundred feet of the top. Later that same year, the middle of this new crater floor had collapsed, leaving a six-hundred- to one-thousand-foot-wide rim that had become known as the Black Ledge. It was now possible to use the Black Ledge as a kind of ramp down to the caldera floor. "The crackling noise made in walking over this crisp surface (like a coating of blue and yellow glass) resembles that made by treading on frozen snow in very cold weather," Wilkes wrote. "Every here and there are seen dark pits and vaulted caverns, with heated air rushing over them. Large and extended cracks are passed over, the air issuing from which, at a temperature of 180 degrees, is almost stifling."

The Black Ledge's sharp crust cut the men's shoes, but it was Sydney that suffered the most. The pads of the dog's feet were so severely injured that he would be lame for several days.

A portion of the Black Ledge had partially collapsed, and Wilkes and his party scrambled down the fractured pieces of basalt to the caldera floor. They were now close enough to the pools of lava that the soles of their shoes began to smoke as the tips of their walking sticks caught fire. Their guide warned that a lava pool could suddenly overflow in a matter of seconds. Wilkes judged it "one of the most horrible deaths ... [to be] cut off from escape by the red molten fluid." When one of the nearby lava pools began to percolate ominously, they decided it was time to retreat to the Black Ledge.

Later, Gerrit Judd would return to the crater floor of Kilauea. Wilkes wanted a sample from one of the lava pools for the Expedition's collection, and Judd, always eager to please his leader, offered to give it a try, taking with him a frying pan lashed to a long pole. As a precaution against the tremendous heat, he wore thick woolen socks and leather sandals over his shoes, as well as gloves. He had worked his way down into a hollow that was between twenty and thirty feet *below* what Wilkes called "the great fiery lake" in the southern portion of the crater. He was climbing up black rocks that were so hot that his spit bounced off them as it would on a griddle. Above him he could see jets of lava shooting up twenty-five feet in the air and then dropping down into the lake. If the pool should overflow, he would be immediately burned to death. Quite sensibly, he ordered the natives in his party to retreat to higher ground. He was about to follow them when he heard a peculiar sound about fifty feet away. Instead of fleeing in panic, Judd went to have a closer look. "In an instant, the crust was broken asunder by a terrific heave," Wilkes wrote, "and a jet of molten lava, full fifteen feet in diameter rose to the height of forty-five feet, with a most appalling noise." Judd began to run for it, but realized that he was now under a ledge of rock, with nowhere to go on either side of him. The heat had become so intense that it was impossible for him to look in the direction of the lava; the rocks beneath his feet were shaking in anticipation of what he assumed would be another explosion of lava. "Although he considered his life as lost," Wilkes wrote, "he strove, although in vain, to scale the projecting rock."

By this time his native companions were in full retreat. Judd called out urgently for help, and one of them turned back. Judd saw the arm of his good friend Kalumo extended toward him over the ledge, but before he could grab it, another jet of lava rose up in the air above their heads. Scorched by the searing heat, Kalumo withdrew his hand. Judd cried out, and Kalumo once again put out his hand. This time Judd grabbed it and was quickly pulled onto the ledge. "Another moment," Wilkes wrote, "and all aid would have been unavailing to save Dr. Judd from perishing in the fiery deluge."

Even though he had barely escaped with his life, Judd refused to quit. The crater was now full of bubbling lava, and after securing the pole with the frying pan attached to it from one of the natives, he returned to the edge of the pool and dipped the pan into the lava. "The cake he thus obtained," Wilkes wrote, "(for it resembled precisely a charred pound-cake), was added to our collections."

Judd had been badly burned around his wrists and elbows and wherever his shirt had touched his skin. But his injuries were nothing compared to Kalumo's. His "whole face was one blister," Wilkes wrote, "particularly that side which had been most exposed to the fire." Wilkes estimated that the crater that had almost claimed Judd was approximately two hundred feet in diameter and thirty-five feet deep and had filled in less than twelve minutes. In honor of the doctor's heroism, Wilkes named it Judd's Lake.

That night they all watched what Wilkes called "this mighty laboratory of nature" from the safety of the caldera's edge. "The streams were of a glowing cherry-red color," he wrote, "illuminating the whole crater around; the large lake beyond seemed swelling and becoming more vivid, so that we expected every moment to see an overflow from it of greater grandeur. . . . The sight was magnificent, and worth a voyage round the world to witness."

Before they departed for Mauna Loa, Judd insisted that the natives' family members, who had severely depleted the Expedition's provisions, return to Hilo. It had also become clear to Wilkes that the natives, with just a tapa worn as a shawl, were not equipped to withstand the cold temperatures of the volcano's summit. In anticipation of their inevitable desertion, Wilkes sent a message to the *Vincennes* to send up fifty men and a complement of officers, along with additional provisions.

Soon after leaving Kilauea, they reached a section of uneven ground that made it impossible for the natives to carry Wilkes's and Brinsmade's chairs. "My legs I confess regretted the change," Wilkes wrote. He quickly became convinced that the guide, Puhano, who had led both Douglas and Lowenstern to the summit, had taken the wrong route. "I therefore, in company with Mr. Brinsmade, took the lead, compass in hand."

By the end of the day they had climbed into the clouds. That evening the temperature dropped to 43°F–more than forty degrees lower than it had been at Hilo. By the afternoon of the following day, December 19, they were beyond the tree line. "All the ground was hard, metallic-looking lava," Wilkes wrote. The featureless landscape made it difficult for them to mark a trail. Wilkes ordered his men to collect branches from the few shrubs they passed so that they might be used as "fingerposts" to designate the path ahead. By three P.M., they had reached an altitude of 6,071 feet. "[E]ven light loads had become heavy," Wilkes wrote, "and those of any weight, insupportable." They were desperately low on food, but water was now their chief concern. They possessed a mere six gallons for over three hundred people. Wilkes ordered them to make camp.

That night, the horticulturalist William Brackenridge, one of the most robust members of the Expedition, came down with what Wilkes termed "a violent attack of mountain-sickness." Nausea and headaches are only a few of the symptoms of what is known today as hypoxia, a reaction to the reduced levels of oxygen at high altitudes that affects individuals without respect to their physical conditioning. Cold and dehydration are also known to aggravate the symptoms. That night, Wilkes wrote, "we all began to experience great soreness about the eyes, and a dryness of the skin."

The natives were particularly hard hit, and many of them began to question Wilkes's motives. "[T]hey never knew of anyone having gone up this mountain before," he wrote, "and thought me mad for taking so much trouble to ascend it." The next day was a Sunday, and Dr. Judd conducted a religious service. While several natives went below for some calabashes of much-needed water, Wilkes and his companions used the day of rest to acclimate themselves to the change of altitude. They also had the opportunity to enjoy the view, which in an age before recreational mountain climbing and air travel was unlike anything they had ever seen. Beneath them were the clouds, "all floating below us in huge white masses, of every variety of form." Beyond and above the clouds was the horizon line, where the greenish sweep of the sea blended seamlessly with the "cerulean blue" of the sky. "The whole scene reminded me," Wilkes wrote, "of the icy fields of the Southern Ocean." Around three P.M., as the sun began to settle in the west, the clouds started to move up the mountainside, and "finally," Wilkes wrote, "we became immersed in them."

Soon after setting out the next morning, December 21, from what Wilkes called Sunday Station, the ascent became much steeper. "[T]he whole face of the mountain consisted of one mass of lava," Wilkes wrote, "that had apparently flowed over in all directions from the summit." The sun beat down on the black rock, and the men found their desire for water "redoubled" since the previous day. Wilkes had originally planned on using the snow at the volcano's summit to provide water for his men. But the summit was still eight thousand feet above them, requiring a hike of two, perhaps three more days. Around noon, Wilkes called a temporary halt. "Most of the party were now lying on the rocks," he wrote, "with the noonday sun pouring on them; a disposition to sleep, and a sensation and listlessness similar to that procured by seasickness, seemed to prevail." Judd offered to climb ahead in search of snow, and Wilkes gladly sent the doctor on his way. For his part, Wilkes had no choice but to succumb to exhaustion: "I enjoyed as sound an hour's sleep on the hard lava as I have ever had."

They climbed another two miles before making camp near a large cave, which provided excellent shelter for the natives. This would become known as the Recruitment Station. As darkness descended, there was no sign of Dr. Judd. Fires were lit, and in a few hours Judd appeared, bone weary and with a snowball in his hands. He had climbed for about four and a half hours, roughly halfway to the summit, before he reached snow. He reported that the drifts appeared to be melting fast. It would require a long hard day of hiking if they were to have water the next day. That night, despite the grim conditions, Charlie Erskine and his fellow sailors made the best of it in the shelter of the cave, "singing, laughing, and joking, as if on a picnic party." "Place the sailor in any situation you will," Charlie insisted, "you cannot deprive him of his mirth and gayety." Tom Piner, the elderly quartermaster and a devout Christian, told his young companions that they were now "as near to heaven as we ever would be unless we mended our ways."

On the morning of December 22, Wilkes left Lieutenant Thomas Budd in charge of the Recruitment Station as he pushed on with a party of twelve natives and seven men, including his steward and servant. Throughout the day, the temperature continued to drop, and Wilkes kept the natives ahead of him so that they couldn't desert. By the afternoon it was just 25°F and blowing a gale from the southwest. The natives were now in danger of freezing to death. Wilkes ordered them to deposit their loads in the lee of a nearby wall of rocks, then granted them permission to return to the station below. "[T]hey seemed actually to vanish," he wrote. "I never saw such agility displayed by them." Soon the natives on the trail below began to desert en masse. "The mountain became . . . a scene of confusion," he wrote, "being strewn with instruments, boxes, pieces of portable houses, tents, calabashes, etc."

Wilkes was left with only his guide and nine men. A snowstorm was coming, the temperature had dropped to 18°F, and many of them had become stricken with a severe case of altitude sickness. Wilkes described it as "a violent throbbing of the temples and a shortness of breath, that were both painful and distressing." Although they found it difficult even to move, Wilkes ordered them to start building a shelter out of the coarse blocks of lava (which they referred to as clinkers) strewn about the mountainside. Soon they'd constructed a circular enclosure, with a piece of canvas serving as the roof. They hung blankets along the inside walls, "which I hoped," Wilkes wrote, "would keep us from being frozen." Wilkes's steward had some tea in his knapsack, and after making a small but serviceable fire, they enjoyed what food they had. "The supper being ended," Wilkes wrote, "we stowed ourselves away within the circular pen; and while the men kept passing their jokes about its comforts, the wind blew a perfect hurricane without." That night the temperature dropped to 15°F. They were at an altitude of 13,190 feet.

Around four A.M., their canvas roof collapsed, dumping a large quantity of snow into the shelter. They did their best to restore the roof, but all of them were now extremely cold. "I need scarcely say," Wilkes wrote, "I passed a most uncomfortable night."

The next morning one of the men found a calabash of provisions that had been abandoned by the natives. After what the sailors termed "a comfortable breakfast," they set out around eleven A.M. They soon discovered that the upper portion of the volcano was, in Wilkes's words, "a mass of clinkers." "[I]t . . . continued snowing in squalls," he wrote, "with a keen southwest wind driving in our faces; the ground being covered a foot deep with snow, rendered it more dangerous and irksome to pass over such loose and detached masses."

They reached the caldera of Mauna Loa in the early afternoon. Although not as active as Kilauea, the volcano's proportions stunned Wilkes and his men: "The very idea of standing on the summit of one of the highest peaks in the midst of this vast ocean, in close proximity to a precipice of profound depth, overhanging an immense crater . . . would have been exciting even to a strong man," Wilkes wrote; "but the sensation was overpowering to one already exhausted by breathing the rarefied air, and toiling over the lava which this huge caldron must have vomited forth in quantities sufficient to form a dome sixty miles in diameter, and nearly three miles in height."

Wilkes had entertained hopes of descending into the crater that afternoon but quickly realized that the snow and high winds required them to make camp. By four P.M. they'd pitched a tent about sixty feet from the ledge of the crater. Since it was impossible to drive stakes into the rock, they used blocks of lava to secure the tent's ropes. Once the tent had been set up, Wilkes ordered the men, with the exception of his steward and servant, to return to their previous encampment. Wilkes intended to spend his first night on the summit of Mauna Loa much as he did in the cabin of the *Vincennes,* accompanied by only his steward and his trusted servant Juan.

That night the storm picked up. "Our fire was dispersed," Wilkes wrote, "candles blown out, and the tent rocking and flapping as if it would go to pieces, or be torn asunder from its fastenings, and disappear before the howling blast. I now felt that what we had passed through on the previous night was comfort in comparison to this. The wind had a fair sweep over us, and as each blast reached the opposite side of the crater, the sound which preceded its coming was at times awful; the tent, however, continued to stand, although it had many holes torn in it, and the ridge-pole had chafed through its top."

The next morning they were unable to light a fire. With four inches of snow on the ground, Wilkes decided that the three of them should wait until assistance arrived from below. Around eleven A.M., Judd and Charles Pickering reached the summit. Judd opened the tent door and found Wilkes and his attendants wrapped in their blankets.

Judd had some bad news. All the natives had deserted. "I was glad to hear it," Wilkes later wrote Jane, "for I could not help pitying their forlorn condition in such bitter weather. This put me in better spirits, greatly to [Judd's] surprise. . . . I became merry, got something to eat and comforted myself that my sailors would be along soon and be all the help I could wish for, & so it happened."

Over the next few weeks, a series of supply stations was established between the summit and the *Vincennes* that sent a steady stream of provisions and men to what Wilkes called Pendulum Peak. By the end of December, there were enough men on the summit to finish the construction of a virtual village comprising a dozen structures, each surrounded by its own stone wall, with a much larger wall encircling the entire outpost. Several days of fine weather greatly facilitated their efforts but also showed Wilkes the incredible variations in temperature encountered at this altitude–ranging from 13°F at night to 92°F in the noonday sun. For Wilkes, this was troubling, since his pendulum experiments must be conducted at a constant temperature. He must do everything in his power to insulate the pendulum house.

After erecting the house's wooden walls, he placed a thick, hair-cloth covering both inside and out; he then surrounded the entire house with a heavy-duty canvas tent. But this did not provide sufficient protection. In addition to the fluctuations in air temperature, Wilkes became convinced that there was a "hollow tunnel or cavern" beneath the house that made it difficult to retain warmth at night. He decided to thatch the pendulum house, placing dry grass procured from Hilo between the house and the tent and over the lava floor. By January 5, he was satisfied that he could maintain a temperature of 40°F inside the house, and the pendulum experiments were begun.

Three days later on January 8, they were socked with another storm. "At 10 pm I was unable to proceed with the pendulum observations," Wilkes wrote, "for such was the fury of the storm that the journeyman-clock, with a loud beat, although within three feet of my ear, could not be heard. I was indeed apprehensive that the whole tent, house, and apparatus would be blown over and destroyed." Later that night the wind began to moderate, and by the next morning Wilkes resumed his experiments. Then, on January 10, they were hit with the highest winds of the Expedition.

"I will not say that I never saw it blow so hard," Charlie Erskine later remembered, "but I never saw it blow any harder. For fear of some damage to the instruments we were ordered to run out and take them down. We had no sooner got them stowed away snug in their cases than our camp was struck by a terrific hurricane which raised the roof of the pendulum house high into the air and scattered its fragments on the sides of the mountain. The other house was demolished and several valuable instruments badly injured. Pieces of canvas from our tents, spread out as big as table-cloths, might be seen floating in the air. The wind was so violent that it was impossible to keep our footing, so we laid down and clung closely to the side of the mountain."

As the sailors lay pinned to the jagged summit of Mauna Loa, they kept up their usual banter. "Amidst all this Jack had his jokes, you may be sure," Erskine wrote. "You might hear one sing out, 'I say, old gruffy, my lad, did you ever fall in with anything like this off Cape Cod? 'No, my hearty, it even beats Cape Horn.' Another would shout, 'I've seen it blowing like blue blazes, but this is a regular blow-hard, hard enough to blow Yankee Doodle on a frying-pan.'"

The next morning, Erskine was astonished to see that "the Star Spangled Banner" was still waving from the flagpole. "I felt proud to know that my country's flag . . . had been borne by brave men, north, south, east, and west, and waved to the breeze in as high an altitude as the flag of any other nation."

The following night, after reassembling the scattered pieces of the pendulum house, Wilkes finally completed his experiments. Even though there was close to half a foot of snow on the ground, he resolved to assist in surveying the interior of the crater the next day, January 12. The wind had died to next to nothing and a brilliant equatorial sun shone down on the pure white snow. Wilkes made several observations with a theodolite, but as the sun climbed in the sky, he found it increasingly difficult to concentrate on his work. "The weather was still and calm," he wrote, "and a deathlike stillness prevailed, which I dreaded to break, even by making a remark to my companions upon the splendor of the scene before us. The sight was surpassingly grand." In the distance, sandwiched between the deep blue of the ocean and the white haze of the sky, were the islands of Maui and Kahoʻolawe. They also had clear views of the surrounding peaks of Hualalai and Mauna Kea. "I can never hope again to witness so sublime a scene," Wilkes wrote, "to gaze on which excited such feelings that I felt relieved when I turned from it to engage in the duties that had called me to that spot."

When Wilkes returned to the camp, he discovered that a party of forty natives had taken advantage of the break in the weather to climb to the summit. They had heard that Wilkes was willing to pay them well for helping to disassemble the village of Pendulum Peak and carry the equipment down the mountain. As the temperature began to plummet that evening, Wilkes realized that he had to provide shelter for the natives. The pendulum house was the largest building on the mountain, and after packing up the clock and pendulum, Wilkes ordered the natives to spend the night on the house's bed of dry grass. He also ordered Joseph Clark to etch "Pendulum Peak, January 1841" into the lava. Clark subsequently asked that "U.S. Ex. Ex." be added "in order that there might be no mistake as to who had been there."

That night, Wilkes began to feel a peculiar sensation, "as if cobwebs had passed over my face and eyes." As the pain in his eyes grew progressively stronger, his sight began to dim. He soon realized he was suffering from snow blindness, a condition in which the surface of the eye has been sunburned. Wilkes was convinced he would never see again. "I felt forcibly the horror of probable blindness," he wrote.

He took some consolation in knowing that it had not afflicted him until after he had completed all his appointed tasks. Despite his sufferings, he insisted that they leave the next morning as scheduled, even if he had to be led down the mountain. Luckily, his condition began to improve, and he was able to put in a full day of hiking. By five P.M., they had descended all the way to Sunday Station at an altitude of six thousand feet, where they found "the soft and delightful temperature of spring." "I cannot venture to describe," Wilkes wrote, "the effect this produced on us after our three week's sojourn on the cold, bleak, and barren summit." Despite the improved weather, Wilkes was exhausted. Even after several natives had administered the "loomi-loomi," described by Wilkes as "a gentle kneading of the limbs, which has a great tendency to restore the circulation, and relax the muscles and joints," he remained "fairly broken down."

While Wilkes and his compatriots had been battling hurricanes and altitude sickness atop Mauna Loa, the officers and men left on the *Vincennes* had taken full advantage of their commander's absence. "Nearly all day the Ship Has Been filled with yellow *Hores*," the taxidermist John Dyes wrote. A phonetic speller, the disapproving Dyes provided a graphic description of a typical day aboard the *Vincennes* at Hilo: "After [the Hawaiian women] Had Regaled themselves in the Wardroom & Paid their Respects to some of the Gentlemen Rooms in private tha Vissited the Steerage Where the Same Scene took place from those tha visited the men on the Birth Deck & the Black Cookes Wher the Same

Biseness were carried on, tha then went back into the Wardroom & Steerage where the young Gentelmen as tha are termed gallivanted them around the Deck to the Laughter & Sneers of all hands."

Reynolds's friend Passed Midshipman William May, supposedly conducting observations ashore, lived for three months "in a straw hut by the side of a purling stream," where, he proudly wrote Reynolds, his nights were spent "resting in the arms of a delicious little Kanacca girl, who first gave up to me her Virgin Charms." Even the ship's chaplain Jared Elliott succumbed to the island's temptations. Instead of a native girl, Elliott's attentions were directed toward the wife of a missionary. "If anyone had behaved to you as he has behaved," Wilkes wrote Jane, "I should certainly have kicked him out of doors." Elliott, whom May described as "a wolf in sheep's clothes," was eventually dismissed from the squadron and sent home in disgrace.

Although he was well aware of the chaplain's transgressions, Wilkes appears to have remained oblivious to the illicit goings-on aboard his flagship. By the time he returned to the *Vincennes* in March, after completing yet another round of pendulum experiments, he was already looking ahead to what he considered to be the most ambitious and difficult part of the Expedition: the survey of the Columbia River.

CHAPTER 12

The Wreck of the Peacock

THE WEST COAST of North America was up for grabs in 1841. Although American citizens had begun to settle throughout the region, both California to the south and the Oregon territory to the north (extending well beyond the present border between Washington and British Columbia) were under the control of foreign powers. Mexico, which had won its independence from Spain in 1821, possessed California while Oregon, although officially under joint occupation by the United States and Great Britain, was in effect ruled by the powerful English conglomerate, the Hudson's Bay Company. Given the HBC's extensive system of trading posts, farms, and forts, the British had even had the audacity to suggest that their boundary should extend as far south as the Columbia River.

The history of discovery in the region, particularly when it came to the Columbia, favored the United States. Cook had spent a considerable amount of time in the Pacific Northwest, but had not found the Columbia River. In 1792, one of Cook's junior officers, George Vancouver, returned to lead a survey of the coast. Although Vancouver would explore the Strait of Juan de Fuca and discover and name Puget Sound, he sailed past the wall of breakers at the mouth of the Columbia without suspecting that a huge river existed on the other side. "The sea had now changed from its natural to river-coloured water," Vancouver wrote, "the probable consequence of some streams falling into the bay. Not considering this opening worthy of more attention, I continued our pursuit to the northwest."

Later that same year, in May 1792, three hundred years after Columbus arrived in America, a humble sea otter trader from Boston by the name of Robert Gray also detected evidence of a strong flow of freshwater along the coast. Unlike the British explorer, Gray thought it was worthy of more attention, particularly if it might yield him some additional otter pelts. Taking advantage of a break in the weather, the thirty-seven-year-old captain managed to sail the 212-ton sloop *Columbia Rediva* over the wave-whipped bar. Once within the six-mile-wide river mouth, Gray found a new world that rivaled anything discovered by Columbus.

At that time of year, the river would have been roiling with salmon, many of them more than five feet long. As he gradually felt his way up the river, Gray was astounded by the size of the trees—some as high as three hundred feet. A merchant instead of an explorer, Gray was most interested in the pelts offered to him by the Clatsop, Tillamook, and Chinook Indians living along the river. By the time he had sailed just fifteen miles, Gray had accumulated 150 otter, 300 beaver, and several hundred other animal furs. Later that summer, after successfully recrossing the bar, Gray encountered Vancouver and told the explorer about the river. Vancouver dispatched a lieutenant to the bar, who eventually ventured almost a hundred miles upstream. The fact remained, however, that an American merchant captain had outdone a government-sponsored explorer from the most powerful maritime nation on earth.

By the time Lewis and Clark spent the winter of 1805–6 at Fort Clatsop near the mouth of the Columbia, the river had been visited by close to a dozen American ships. In 1811 the New Yorker John Jacob Astor launched his plan to establish the trading post of Astoria. Although the War of 1812 forced Astor to sell Astoria to the British, who renamed it Fort George, the recorded history of the river, as its name would suggest, began with Captain Gray's *Columbia*.

Wilkes's awkward meeting in Fiji with Captain Belcher had made it clear that the British considered the region their own. "The Officers of Belcher's vessels, like true Englishmen, heard with surprise that we intended to Survey that Coast . . . ," William Reynolds wrote. "You may be sure that when Belcher reaches England his Government will do something towards increasing the Colony they have there already.... They want a large slice of the Main and if we do not take care, they will be in the Columbia River before us, and we may get them out, if we can."

When the *Porpoise* returned from her sweep through the Tuamotu and Society Islands on March 24, 1841, Wilkes was seething with more than his usual anxiety and impatience. If it had been possible, he would have left immediately for the Pacific Northwest. Unfortunately, the *Porpoise*'s bottom was in need of recoppering, requiring that they remain in Honolulu for another ten days.

Ringgold and his officers soon realized that their commander was motivated by something more than a need to reach the Columbia River in a timely fashion. Word had made its way to Oahu that the U.S. naval vessels *St. Louis* and *Yorktown* were due to arrive shortly. No one knew for certain if Wilkes had improperly assumed his rank, but everyone had his suspicions and could only wonder what would happen if the squadron were to encounter a naval vessel commanded by a legitimate captain. "I feel curious to know the fate of the proud Swallow tail," wrote the *Porpoise*'s first lieutenant Robert Johnson, referring to the commodore's pennant.

The *Yorktown* was captained by John Aulick, an officer who had objected so vehemently to Wilkes's appointment that he had attempted to intimidate Wilkes during a private meeting in Washington. If there was an officer in the U.S. Navy who would delight in calling Wilkes's bluff, it would be Captain Aulick. In a letter to Jane, Wilkes claimed to be unconcerned about the possible threat. "I should rejoice to meet him with my broad Pendt. Flying," he insisted. "Before I get home I shall be fairly set down as Comdr." As of the end of March, however, Wilkes's promotion had not yet come through, and he apparently thought it best to postpone, if not avoid altogether, a meeting with his nemesis. On April 5, the *Vincennes* and the *Porpoise* escaped safely from Honolulu and were on their way to the Columbia River, where they were to meet the *Peacock* and the *Flying Fish* at the end of the month.

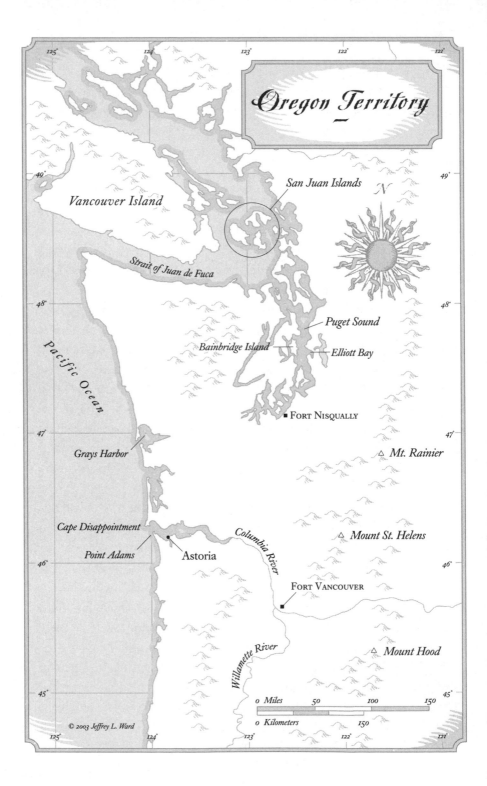

Oregon Territory

Vancouver Island

San Juan Islands

N

Strait of Juan de Fuca

Puget Sound

Bainbridge Island

Elliott Bay

Pacific Ocean

■ Fort Nisqually

Grays Harbor

△ Mt. Rainier

Cape Disappointment

Columbia River

△ Mount St. Helens

Point Adams

Astoria

Fort Vancouver

Willamette River

△ Mount Hood

| 0 Miles | 50 | 100 | 150 |

| 0 Kilometers | | 150 |

© 2003 Jeffrey L. Ward

✦ ✦ ✦

After a passage of just twenty-two days, Wilkes sighted the fog-shrouded fist of basalt known as Cape Disappointment on April 28. Stretching for six miles to the south was a continuous line of breakers, where the milky waters of the Columbia River collided with the blue swell of the Pacific. "Mere description can give little idea of the terrors of the bar of the Columbia," Wilkes wrote. "[A]ll who have seen it have spoken of the wildness of the scene, and the incessant roar of the waters, representing it as one of the most fearful sights that can possibly meet the eye of the sailor."

Even today, now that a series of dams has done much to tame the fury of the Columbia, the waters between Cape Disappointment and Point Adams are a war zone. The river might be compared to a colossal 1,243-mile-long water cannon firing, on average, 150 billion gallons of water a day into the ocean surge of the Pacific. The resulting impact

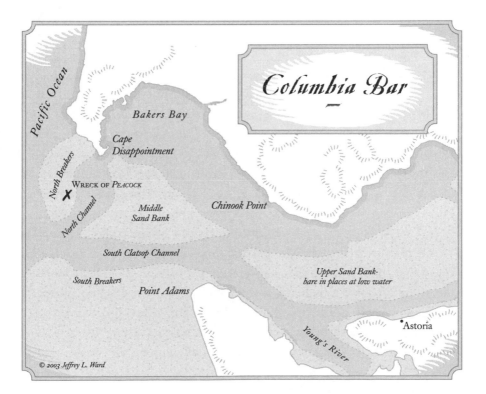

is stupendous. A modern-day Columbia River pilot likens it to "two giant hammers smashing into each other." It is the only river in the United States where incoming vessels are required to use a river-bar pilot. Navigational guides rank it as the third most dangerous river entrance in the world, and the Coast Guard station at Cape Disappointment today averages one rescue mission a day. Since Captain Gray first discovered the river, the chaotic waters stretching across its mouth have claimed more than two thousand shipwrecks; at least seven hundred people have drowned.

In 1841, before dams, jetties, channel buoys, and motor power had begun to domesticate the river, mariners regarded the Columbia as nothing less than a malevolent monster. Waves at the bar were known to reach a hundred feet, and ships had waited as many as eleven weeks before conditions moderated to the extent that their captains dared to risk crossing the bar. Even then, things could go terribly wrong. Two of the thirty-five ships supplying the Hudson's Bay Company had been lost and twenty-six sailors drowned. "Perhaps there have been more lives lost here, in proportion to the number of those who have entered this river," a traveler wrote in the 1830s, "than in entering almost any harbor in the world."

Wilkes had brought along a man from Honolulu who claimed to be a Columbia River pilot. He also had sailing directions that had come to him indirectly through Captain Belcher. On Cape Disappointment and Adams Point, the Hudson's Bay Company had trimmed the branches of several tall, conspicuously situated trees to help mariners locate the elusive channel across the bar. Unfortunately, the high seas raging across the river mouth when Wilkes arrived made it impossible to attempt a crossing.

That night, as the *Vincennes* and the *Porpoise* wallowed in the turbulence outside the bar, Wilkes decided on a change of plan. Too impatient to wait for conditions to moderate at the bar, he would head north up the coast. Even though his orders limited him to the Columbia River and San Francisco Bay, he would sail to the Strait of Juan de Fuca and, heading east and then south, survey the inland coastline all the way to Puget Sound. It was an audacious, typically impulsive decision on

Wilkes's part. But before he could begin to survey the region that would one day contain the cities of Seattle, Tacoma, and Olympia, Wilkes nearly lost it all on the appropriately named Destruction Isle.

At night in a dense fog, both the *Vincennes* and the *Porpoise* were sailing up the coast with their studdingsails set. When sailing along a dangerous shore, it was common practice to ready the anchor cables in case of emergencies. Wilkes, who judged the coast to be at least forty miles to the east, ordered that the hawse holes (through which the anchor cables were led) be closed; it would make the deck drier in the high seas. That night Wilkes was awakened by the cry of "Rocks Ahead!" An undetected current had swept them to the east. The two vessels were immediately rounded up and were soon struggling against mountainous seas that threatened to dash them against the rocks. "The moment we found ourselves in deep water," William May later wrote Reynolds, "a tremendous bustle of bending cables and giving orders ensued."

On May 2, at 6:30 P.M., exactly forty-nine years after Vancouver, the *Vincennes* and the *Porpoise* anchored in the Strait of Juan de Fuca. They were soon surrounded by canoes of natives in conical grass hats who asked "whether we were Boston or King George's ships"—national designations that dated back to the days when American fur trading was dominated by Boston merchants. Over the last few months, Wilkes's attitude toward the captive Fijian chief Veidovi had softened considerably, and Veidovi was now allowed on the *Vincennes*'s deck. "It was amusing to us," Wilkes wrote, "to observe the contempt our prisoner . . . entertained for these Indians, which was such that he would hardly deign to look at them."

As the two vessels made their way through Admiralty Inlet and into Puget Sound, Wilkes marveled at the contrast between this inland waterway and the mouth of the Columbia. "Nothing can exceed the beauty of these waters, and their safety: not a shoal exists . . . that can in any way interrupt their navigation. . . . I venture nothing in saying there is no country in the world that possesses waters equal to these." Today, there are no fewer than four U.S. Navy bases on Puget Sound; none exists on the Columbia River.

At the Hudson's Bay Company outpost of Fort Nisqually, situated between modern Tacoma and Olympia, Wilkes made initial contact with the powers-that-be in the Pacific Northwest. Relations would prove surprisingly cordial between the Americans and the HBC throughout the squadron's time in the territory, and Wilkes quickly went to work, sending surveying parties throughout Puget Sound and beyond, as two log cabins were built to replace the pendulum houses damaged on the summit of Mauna Loa. When Wilkes received word from an HBC employee that the *Peacock* had arrived at the bar, he resolved to travel overland down to the Columbia, where he would lead the officers of the *Peacock* and the *Flying Fish* in the survey of the river.

But when he reached Astoria on May 23, after an arduous five-day journey by horse and canoe, he was disappointed to discover that he had received erroneous information. The *Peacock* and the *Flying Fish* had not yet arrived. They were now more than a month overdue.

Wilkes would later admit to having felt a strong sense of trepidation back in early December when he drew up the sailing instructions for the *Peacock*'s and the *Flying Fish*'s cruise to the central Pacific. He was well aware of Hudson's deficiencies as a surveyor. He was also concerned that his second-in-command lacked the discipline, judgment, and determination to complete the cruise in the allotted time. As they all knew, the Expedition's highest priority was the survey of the Columbia River, and Wilkes could only hope that Hudson would break off the cruise in time to reach the Pacific Northwest between April 15 and May 1. His orders could not have been more explicit: "it must not be later than the latter date."

By May 1, the *Peacock* and the *Flying Fish* were still thousands of miles from the west coast of North America. "This cruise of now, more than six months," Reynolds wrote, "has had less to redeem it, than any other, I ever made." Hudson had wasted days searching out nonexistent islands and spent just hours surveying new discoveries. At Tabiteauea (known to them as Drummond Island) in the Gilbert or Kiribati Group, the squadron encountered hostile natives armed with stingray-tipped spears and swords studded with shark teeth. Despite unmistakable evidence to the contrary, Hudson insisted that the natives were harmless and led a party ashore. Sure enough, a sailor was lured away from the group and never seen again. In retaliation, Hudson attacked the village the next day, killing an estimated twenty natives. "More War!" Reynolds wrote. "It seems to me, that our path through the Pacific is to be marked in blood."

The cruise was particularly exasperating for those aboard the schooner. While the officers of the *Peacock* were allowed to visit native villages, Hudson almost never permitted those aboard the *Flying Fish* to go ashore. In the last 180 days, Reynolds had spent exactly twelve hours and fifteen minutes on land. "This Schooner kills me," he wrote. "No more exercise to be had, than a large bird might find in a *small* cage, and without this I cannot enjoy life. No society & no books. It worries my very soul, with nothing around us, but Sea & sky."

There was one member of the Expedition, however, for whom the last six months had provided plenty of food for thought: the geologist James Dana. Having seen what an extremely young volcanic island looked like in Hawaii, Dana could now identify the relative age of an island by the amount of erosion it exhibited. By the end of the cruise, he had begun to recognize an unmistakable pattern: each island chain possessed a distinct chronology, with the oldest island at one end of the chain and the youngest at the other. "There is a system in their arrangements," he wrote, "as regular as in the mountain heights of the continent." It is now believed that chains of volcanic islands are formed as the Pacific plate moves over what are called "hot spots"–stationary heat sources emanating from deep within the earth. Although the theory of plate tectonics would not be posited until the twentieth century, Dana's recognition of the linear pattern of island chains was a first, crucial step toward formulating this revolutionary concept.

Not until May did the lethargic Hudson finally order the *Peacock* and the *Flying Fish* to start sailing east. Contrary to Wilkes's instructions, which insisted that he sail directly to the Pacific Northwest, Hudson decided to stop at Honolulu for provisions before continuing on to the Columbia River. On June 13, they spied the green island of Oahu. It was, Reynolds wrote, "as good a sight for our eyes, as ever the first glimpse of the New World, was to the vision of Columbus." They were now almost two months behind schedule, with more than two thousand miles between them and the Columbia River.

By the end of May, Wilkes decided to leave Purser Waldron at Astoria to wait for the *Peacock* while he and Drayton visited Hudson's Bay Company headquarters at Fort Vancouver, approximately one hundred miles up the Columbia. There he met Dr. John McLoughlin, a tall, imposing figure who served as the company's chief factor. Wilkes, traveling by canoe with just a handful of servants and an artist, met McLoughlin in a deceptive guise. Instead of the commodore of a four-vessel squadron, Wilkes looked more like a curious fact-gatherer intent on visiting American settlers in the Willamette River valley to the south. For McLoughlin, it was a most nonthreatening introduction to the Ex. Ex. By the time the survey of the Columbia River was under way in August—an undertaking that was hardly in the HBC's best interests—enough goodwill existed between the company and the Expedition that the squadron was allowed to do as it pleased. All in all, it would prove to be a masterful, even if inadvertent, diplomatic performance on Wilkes's part.

As Drayton continued up the Columbia, Wilkes traveled south up the Willamette River, where he met with recently arrived American missionaries and farmers who complained of the HBC's unchallenged authority in the region. By the middle of June, he was back at Fort Vancouver. There was still no word from the *Peacock* and the *Flying Fish*. Wilkes was becoming convinced that they had met with some kind of accident. As soon as he completed his survey of the Columbia, he would have to mount a massive search operation. For now, he would return to Fort Nisqually and finish his pendulum experiments.

By the beginning of July, his experiments had been completed. Excellent progress had also been made on the survey of Puget Sound. It was time for a Fourth of July celebration. That morning, two brass howitzers were brought ashore to the observatory, where they were fired twenty-six times, once for each state of the union. "The reports of the guns not only astonished the natives," Charlie Erskine remembered, "but waked up the red-coats in the fort, who came running up to the observatory with the Indians, nearly out of breath, to inquire the cause of the racket. We pointed to our country's flag, which was so proudly waving in the breeze over the observatory. . . . They then called us a crew of crazy Americans."

Around nine o'clock, the officers and men of the *Vincennes,* dressed in white shirts and trousers, were mustered on the deck and landed on shore. A procession was formed, with Wilkes and his officers at the head, followed by the port and starboard watches, the marines, and a fifer and drummer. Striding proudly beside the master-at-arms, clearly enjoying his first time ashore since his arrest, was Veidovi, along with Wilkes's dog Sydney.

For Wilkes, whose relations with his officers and men had been so acrimonious and difficult, it was a day like no other. "It was truly gratifying," he wrote, "to see them all in such good health and spirits, not a man sick, and their clothes as white as snow, with happy and contented faces." That night, he and his officers had dinner together for the first time in more than a year. The pendulum house had been transformed into a banquet hall and the feasting continued until well past midnight. What might have been a night of unalloyed celebration was inevitably tempered with talk of the *Peacock.* "It was impossible to conjecture her fate," Wilkes wrote, "yet her continued absence and detention beyond the time of her anticipated arrival, naturally excited many fears and surmises, which as the time passed on, made each one [of us] more certain that some disaster had befallen them."

The *Peacock* and the *Flying Fish* left Honolulu on June 2. Prior to their departure, Hudson had told Reynolds and the schooner's commander, Passed Midshipman Samuel Knox, that he intended to use the schooner to locate the channel across the Columbia River bar before he risked the much larger, and deeper, *Peacock.* As a consequence, the two vessels sailed to the Pacific Northwest in tandem, with the ship carrying short sail so as not to lose the *Flying Fish.* Not until Sunday, July 18, after a passage of forty-six days—more than twice as long as it took the *Vincennes* and the *Porpoise*—did the *Peacock* and the *Flying Fish* finally reach the mouth of the Columbia. They were now almost three months late.

As the fog began to clear that morning, the officers of the *Flying Fish* made preparations for the arrival of Captain Hudson. When Knox discovered that his dress uniform had been eaten by mice, Reynolds gloated that he had left *his* uniform safely tucked away in a drawer aboard the *Peacock;* but Knox was to have the last laugh.

As far as the officers of the schooner were concerned, the conditions were not favorable for crossing the bar. There was a heavy swell running, and the breakers at the river mouth were dangerously high. The *Peacock* was well to weather of them, and instead of sailing down to deliver Hudson to the *Flying Fish,* the ship steered straight for the breakers ahead. "[I]t would be useless to deny that *we* had a presentiment that disaster & distress, or death, would happen to some of the vessels, or to some of us . . . ," Reynolds wrote. "I never could get rid of this feeling, and, like the others, could only hope for the best."

A sense of foreboding also seems to have possessed the *Peacock*'s captain. Hudson had told Wilkes of his concern about the Columbia River bar as early as the previous fall in Honolulu. His dread of the Columbia may have contributed to his now being three months behind schedule. But the *Peacock*'s lateness only added to her captain's anxieties, especially given the prospect of having to explain himself to the judgmental Wilkes. When finally faced with the breakers that had been figuring so prominently in his thoughts for the last eight months, Hudson appears to have panicked. Instead of using the schooner to search out the channel as he had previously planned, he decided to save a few hours by sailing boldly across the bar in the *Peacock*. His rashness in Antarctica had nearly sunk the ship; his officers and men could only hope that they would be luckier this time.

At 11:30 A.M., approximately seven miles from Cape Disappointment, Hudson called "All Hands to Work Ship into Port." With his copy of the sailing directions in his hand, he walked to the forward part of the ship, where he would divide his time between the forecastle and the foreyard, as Lieutenant George Emmons climbed up to the foretop yard. The directions indicated that they should head east for Cape Disappointment until Chinook Point bore east-northeast. But just as they reached the proper bearing, they encountered a steep, violent sea. Hudson became convinced that they were too far to the south. He wore the ship around and headed for a section of smooth water that he took to be the channel.

The *Peacock* forged ahead against the ebbing tide. After five minutes, they were almost abreast of Cape Disappointment, approximately two miles to the north. Some of the men had even begun to believe that they just might make it, when the *Peacock*'s keel struck bottom as the bow burrowed into the sand. The helm was immediately put a-lee in an effort to turn the ship back out to sea. The yards and sails were also brought into play, but there was no longer any way to control the *Peacock;* she was stuck fast on the bar as waves burst against the ship's sides. All the sails were quickly furled, and Lieutenant Emmons was dispatched in the cutter to see if there was any hope of pushing the ship through to deeper water. The building seas nearly capsized Emmons's boat, but he did manage to cast the lead. The *Peacock,* he regretted to inform Hudson, was aground for good.

As the waves continued to build, the ship began to bounce up and down on the hard sand of the bar. Part hobbyhorse, part jackhammer, the *Peacock* was pounding so severely that Hudson feared the ship might soon begin to break apart. Behind them, they could see the *Flying Fish* hovering just beyond the breakers, "like a child watching the agonies of its parent without being able to afford any relief." "We saw the sea of wild foam she was among," Reynolds wrote, "*& we gave her up for lost, from that moment.*" Knox ordered the helmsman to steer for the disabled ship, but Hudson would have none of it and raised the signal flag indicating danger. "With very sad & heavy hearts we stood to seaward & hove to," Reynolds wrote.

Back aboard the *Peacock,* conditions were worsening. The bucking of the hull was whipping the masts back and forth, and to ease the strain, the royal and topgallant yards were lowered to the deck. By now the waves were too wild to permit them to take to the boats. Until the seas moderated, they were trapped aboard the *Peacock.* Hudson was tempted to cut away the masts to ease the motion of the hull, but since the yards were used to lower the boats, this would have left them with no way to escape from the wreck–assuming that the waves would eventually begin to diminish. The hold had begun to fill with water, and Hudson organized two gangs to keep the pumps working around the clock.

The ship was now broadside to the waves, which crashed against the topsides and drenched the men on deck. In hopes of relieving the strain on the hull, Hudson used the port fore yardarm to lower an anchor over the side. With the anchor in place, the sea pushed the *Peacock*'s stern around, and she was soon bow-first to the waves. By now the tide was approaching dead low and there was only nine feet of water under the main chains. The shoaling sand began to raise havoc with the rudder, wrenching it back and forth so severely that the iron tiller broke off seven inches from the rudder head. Soon the rudder had gnawed a gaping hole through the bottom of the hull.

At 8:45 P.M. the anchor cable broke. The ship swung sideways to the seas and was soon being blasted by the waves. This time the starboard anchor was let go, and once again, the *Peacock* swung gradually into the swell. This provided some temporary relief, but by midnight the ship was being tossed about so violently that the timbers and planking had begun to pull apart. They could see sand in the hold of the ship, and Hudson determined that it was useless to keep the pumps going. At two A.M. a huge wave broke over the port bow, stoving in the port bulwarks at the waist of the ship and flooding the spar deck. In an attempt to drain the water, they chopped a hole in the starboard bulwarks.

What the officers and crew of the *Peacock* didn't know was that they had a special advocate among the small crowd of onlookers gathered at the bluff on Cape Disappointment. Although the *Vincennes*'s purser Robert Waldron had long since left Astoria, his black servant John Dean had remained to keep an eye out for the ship and schooner. As dawn approached, Dean organized a rescue party of Chinook Indians that included one of the river's two native pilots. At daybreak they headed out in a canoe, and by six A.M. they were alongside the *Peacock*. Perhaps miffed that a boatload of Indians led by a young African American had been able to venture across seas that he had considered impassable, Hudson did not choose to mention Dean's rescue party in his official report. Dean would take the artist Alfred Agate and his portfolio of drawings and paintings; the purser William Speiden, who clutched the ship's accounts and moneybox; and the dismissed surgeon Charles Guillou. By seven A.M. the waves had quieted to the point that Hudson judged it safe to begin launching the ship's boats.

Hudson insisted that the officers and men take only the clothes on their backs. The scientifics were the one exception, and with their journals in their arms, Dana, Peale, Hale, and Rich climbed into one of the boats. The charts and surveying equipment were loaded into another while the marines and some of the sailors were crowded into the third and fourth boats, and they were off. The more than sixty officers and sailors left aboard the ship watched the boats' progress across the turbulent river with the knowledge that their own lives depended on the boats' safe–and speedy–return.

Later that morning Emmons was able to get another load of people ashore, but by noon, when he returned to pick up the remaining officers and sailors, the seas had built back up again. The *Peacock*'s side-to-side motion had become so severe that she was in danger of capsizing. Hudson ordered that the masts be cut away with an ax. Beginning with the foremast, the spars fell, one after the other. On the stump of the mizzen, Hudson raised the American flag union down–a sign of distress.

"This led me to believe that the ship was going to pieces," Emmons wrote, "and I redoubled my efforts to get through the surf to her." One of the boats reared so high on a wave that it toppled end over end, tossing the crew headlong into the boiling sea. One sailor broke a hip, several others were also injured, but all were rescued by the boat led by Lieutenant DeHaven. Realizing that there was no hope of reaching the *Peacock* in these conditions, Hudson had his men switch the flag to union up. Emmons understood immediately that he and the others were to return to shore. "Seeing how useless my efforts were," he wrote, "and that by continuing to persevere, I was not only risking the means but jeopardizing the lives that were looked to for success, I turned back. And with feelings that I will not attempt to describe nor shall I soon forget."

Even without her masts, the *Peacock* continued to beat against the bar. Hudson could only wonder how much longer the ship would last, but this did not prevent him from ordering his men to eat their dinner on the wave-washed deck. Ever so gradually, the waves began to diminish until Emmons was able to reach the ship in the early evening. Only after all the remaining officers and sailors had been transferred into the boats did Hudson leave the ship. It was dark by the time they reached the sanctuary of Bakers Bay, tucked inside Cape Disappointment. In the glow of several shoreside fires, the *Peacock*'s officers and crew gathered together and gave their captain three heartfelt cheers.

The next morning Emmons ventured out to see what was left of the ship. The hull and deck had been pulled apart, scattering hundreds of specimens and artifacts to the wind and waves. Only the ship's bowsprit could be seen above the water, pointing pathetically into the sky. For Emmons, who as a midshipman had been assigned to the *Peacock* back in 1828 when she had been first launched in New York, it was a particularly moving sight. "Thus have I witnessed the beginning and end of the *Peacock*...," he wrote. "[T]here is some consolation in knowing that after the many narrow risks she has run this cruise that her fate has finally been prolonged until reaching her native shore."

For the last two days, the officers and men of the *Flying Fish* had been left to flit nervously back and forth along the outskirts of the bar, helpless witnesses to the destruction of the *Peacock*. The immense height of the seas had made it impossible for them to determine how many, if any, had escaped from the wreck alive. But when they saw Emmons's boat rowing toward them on July 20, they knew, for the first time, that at least *someone* had survived. "I was too impatient *to wait*," Reynolds wrote, "& jumping on the taffrail, screamed at the top of my voice, *to know if all were saved?* There was one moment of silence & suspense, ere the answer came back. The very sea seemed stilled. *All hands safe on shore & well!* Hurrah! Hurrah! There was no controlling it. The feeling *would burst out,* and there was another hearty cheer!"

With the help of Old George, a one-eyed Chinook Indian whom Reynolds described as "the queerest looking pilot I ever put my eyes on," the *Flying Fish* soon crossed the bar and joined the castaways at Bakers Bay. John Dean had presented Hudson with the orders Wilkes had prepared weeks before, instructing him to begin the survey of the river. It was an opportunity for Hudson to redeem himself, in some measure, for the loss of the ship. Instead, he chose to take the majority of his crew up the river to Astoria, where they would wait in idleness until Wilkes's arrival. "If Captain Hudson possessed the gumption to conduct a survey," Reynolds wrote, "his place would have been on board this Schooner, *at once,* driving on with all the boats & finishing [the survey of the] bar, while the weather was fine." Instead, Reynolds and Knox were left alone at Bakers Bay.

Ever since the Fourth of July, Wilkes had been in seemingly ceaseless motion. With his observations at Nisqually completed, he took over the leadership of the surveys of Puget Sound. As each day brought no word of the *Peacock,* he drove himself and his men harder and harder since it now looked as if they would have to perform the survey of the Columbia on their own. "In this state of feeling," Wilkes wrote, "the officers of the *Vincennes* showed a highly commendable spirit, and aware that additional labors were thus to be thrown upon them, strained every nerve to avoid any further loss of time."

Although Vancouver had surveyed much of the region forty-nine years earlier, Wilkes would leave his own indelible, if largely unappreciated, stamp upon the land. Almost three hundred Washington place names can be attributed to the Ex. Ex. For example, Elliott Bay along the eastern shore of Puget Sound was named for Midshipman Samuel Elliott and is the site of modern-day Seattle. Even Veidovi (whom Wilkes called "Vendovi") would have an island named for him. Despite Wilkes's reputation for self-glorification, not a single island, cove, or strait is named for the commander of the Ex. Ex.

By July 27, the squadron had made its way to the San Juan Islands, the labyrinth of more than 450 islands and reefs that lay scattered over the international water boundary between British Columbia and the United States. The forty-ninth parallel had already been discussed as a possible boundary between the two countries, and Wilkes quite rightly realized that if this did become the case, these islands would be of special interest. That afternoon Passed Midshipman William May arrived from Nisqually with a letter informing Wilkes of the loss of the *Peacock*. "This news, although bad," Wilkes wrote, "was a great relief to me; for I had feared not only the loss of the vessels, but had apprehensions for the lives of the persons on board. A heavy load that had long hung over my mind was removed."

Wilkes spent the next day finishing up the survey of the San Juans and deciding how the squadron should spend the rest of its time in the Pacific Northwest. He had once hoped to send an overland party as far east as the headwaters of the Yellowstone River on the other side of the Rocky Mountains. This would have allowed him to connect the Expedition's surveys with previous surveys of the interior. He now realized it was too late in the season to attempt such a journey. Lieutenant Johnson had returned from a trip across the Cascade Mountains. Prior to leaving on another overland expedition, this time to Grays Harbor on the coast, Johnson fell into an altercation with Wilkes similar to what used to happen on an almost continual basis in the early days of the Expedition. Johnson had given a Bowie knife pistol belonging to the naturalist Charles Pickering to an HBC employee as a gift. When Pickering complained, Wilkes insisted that Johnson clear all subsequent gift-giving with Passed Midshipman Eld. Since this would require him to defer to a subordinate officer, Johnson refused to embark on the expedition to Grays Harbor, and Wilkes had him arrested.

Johnson was now confined to quarters and Eld was on his way to Grays Harbor, but there was yet another, much more important expedition to organize: a more than eight-hundred-mile-long overland journey from the Columbia River to San Francisco Bay. Wilkes decided that Lieutenant George Emmons was the man to lead this expedition, and as the *Vincennes* and the *Porpoise* made their way out of the Strait of Juan de Fuca and down the coast, he drew up the necessary orders. Then, of course, there was the matter of the survey of the Columbia River, which he assumed Hudson and his officers would have already begun by the time he reached the bar.

On August 6, Hudson received word in Astoria of Wilkes's arrival at the bar. That evening, after the *Flying Fish* delivered him to the *Vincennes*,

Hudson had a long talk with the Expedition's leader. In his official report, Wilkes would have nothing but praise for his second-in-command's handling of the cruise to the Central Pacific, even finding no fault with Hudson's conduct during the wreck of the *Peacock*. In his journal, however, he would record his frustrations. It was Hudson's inability to prioritize the Expedition's goals that truly rankled him. "[S]uch a waste of force, time and object," he wrote, "I would not have believed it." Wilkes had vowed to himself that he would not allow his dissatisfaction with Hudson's performance to interfere with their friendship, but future events would make it a difficult promise to keep.

Given what had happened to the *Peacock*, Wilkes decided it was too much of a risk to bring the *Vincennes* across the bar. Instead, he would use the *Porpoise* during the survey of the river while Ringgold sailed the *Vincennes* to San Francisco Bay, where the squadron would reconvene once the survey had been completed. The next morning Knox was temporarily transferred to the *Porpoise* to act as her pilot, leaving Reynolds in command of the *Flying Fish* for the first time in the Expedition. The schooner was to follow the brig across the bar, and both vessels were to sail to Astoria. For a twenty-five-year-old passed midshipman, this was a position of considerable responsibility, especially since it involved negotiating the waters of one of the world's most dangerous rivers. Making the assignment all the more tension-filled was that Reynolds had a considerable audience; the *Flying Fish* had been crammed with sailors from the *Vincennes*. Luckily, he had the help of George, the one-eyed Chinook pilot.

They made it safely across the bar, but with all the people aboard, the little schooner was so weighted down that she was having a difficult time keeping up with the brig, which soon disappeared in the mist up ahead. Then George, with a broad grin stretched across his face, tapped Reynolds on the shoulder. There was the *Porpoise,* aground beside a sandbank. "George was much elated . . . ," Reynolds wrote. "[A]s we passed near to the Brig I sent the Launch to her assistance, & I chuckled as much as George did, to find myself sailing ahead of the grand Commodore."

As they approached Astoria, the sun began to show through the clouds. Although Astoria was the oldest nonnative settlement in the region, the trading post had fallen on hard times. Fort Vancouver (not far from modern Portland) had become the trading center on the river, reducing Astoria (renamed Fort George by the British) to just a few permanent structures. For Americans, however, Astoria–recently popularized in a best-selling book by Washington Irving–was visible proof of the impressive breadth of American mercantile ambitions. "It did certainly hurt my eyes to see the red banner of England flying over *our* possessions," Reynolds wrote, "and I do most devoutly trust that the day will soon come for it to be struck in [this] region forever."

In the last few days, an inspiring change had come to Astoria. The officers and men of the *Peacock* had been busy erecting a collection of crude buildings that included a barbershop, a ninepin alley, and a bakery. Reynolds could see the houses "spread over the sunny side of the hill, with the big ensign of the *Peacock,* waving over the largest shantee." With considerable pride, Reynolds guided the *Flying Fish* into the anchorage. "And so I had the honor of anchoring the first public vessel of the United States, in the waters of this famous place."

Wilkes soon discovered that Hudson had done virtually nothing when it came to furthering the survey of the river. It also became apparent that the *Peacock*'s officers and men had not yet recovered from the trauma they'd experienced at the bar. "I at once inaugurated the strictest discipline," Wilkes wrote, "and with all my energies thrown into the work, I soon made an impression upon them."

They began at Bakers Bay just inside the bar. One evening early on in the survey, Wilkes learned that the HBC's chief factor Dr. McLoughlin had arrived in Astoria to negotiate the sale of a brig that might serve as a replacement for the *Peacock.* Even though it was almost dark and fog had begun to appear about the edges of the shore, making navigation on the river virtually impossible, Wilkes resolved to sail immediately for Astoria in the *Flying Fish.*

It had been almost two years since Reynolds had last been on a vessel with the Expedition's commander. "I really felt the cold shiver run all through me," Reynolds wrote, "on finding myself once more alongside of C.W. You might as well bring holy water, near the Devil. *He,* that is, C.W. or the devil either, for there can't be much difference." Then Wilkes—the unfeeling, tyrannical demon—did a surprising thing. By now it had begun to rain, and noticing that Reynolds was without a coat, Wilkes turned and asked "if I had no Pea Jacket?" It was an unmistakable and, coming from Wilkes, extraordinary gesture of concern, but Reynolds was having none of it: "as if he *could* wheedle me into the belief that *he cared for my comfort*," he wrote in his journal.

Wilkes quickly negotiated the purchase of the brig, which he renamed the *Oregon,* then continued with the survey. While Knox and Reynolds surveyed the bar in the schooner, Wilkes would survey the river between Astoria and Fort Vancouver. On August 18, he left Astoria with a group of boats, leaving Hudson to follow close behind in the *Porpoise.* A few hours later, Hudson ran the *Porpoise* so hard aground that it was feared she would not be floated off till the following spring tide. Finally, after a delay of two days, Hudson managed to free the brig. "I would be happier and more efficient doing the work myself with two assistants," Wilkes grumbled in his journal.

Although Wilkes and Hudson continued to avoid a direct confrontation, there was little doubt that tensions were simmering between the two officers. Beginning with the near sinking of the *Peacock* in Antarctica, Hudson, initially regarded as the best seaman in the squadron, had experienced mishap after mishap. His inability to learn even the rudimentary principles of surveying had made him an object of derision even among his own officers. "[I]t is a truth that the *boys* in this Squadron," Reynolds wrote, "are employed on duties, that are beyond the capacity of . . . Cap H." For Hudson, whose son William Junior was a midshipman in the squadron, the last few weeks had been especially humiliating, and on August 25, he attempted to strike out at the man whose undeniable proficiency cast a glaring light on his own failings.

When Wilkes boarded the *Porpoise* after a long day of survey work, he was shocked to discover that his broad blue commodore's pennant had been replaced by the coach whip of a lieutenant commander. He asked the officer of the deck why the change had been made. The officer explained that Hudson, who was standing just a few feet from

Wilkes, had ordered the switch. By replacing the swallow-tail pennant, Hudson had publicly confirmed what all suspected to be the case—that Wilkes was a commodore in name only. Barely able to contain his rage, Wilkes ordered that his pennant be immediately hoisted to the mast-head. "It shows," he wrote that evening, "how much [Hudson] feels his situation under me. . . . I little thought he would venture upon such an expedient with me, after all that has passed between us. . . . I have little doubt myself that he is ashamed of it."

At the end of August, Emmons, along with Eld, who had just com-pleted his survey of Grays Harbor, left on their overland journey to San Francisco. In early September, Wilkes agreed to the linguist Horatio Hale's request that he be detached from the Expedition so that he could continue his work among the native peoples of the region. It wasn't just the amazing variety of languages that Hale wanted to explore further; there was also a storehouse of oral traditions unlike anything else he'd encountered. Given that the region was soon to be overrun by thou-sands of white settlers, Hale's work with the native peoples of the Pacific Northwest would prove to be one of the most enduring achieve-ments of the Expedition.

As Wilkes pushed on with the survey between Astoria and Van-couver, eventually charting close to a hundred miles of river, Reynolds and Knox struggled to make sense of the ever-shifting sands and cur-rents of the Columbia's lower reaches. "For more than three weeks we toiled on, solitary and alone . . . ," Reynolds wrote. "[W]e were sick & tired of the Mouth of the Columbia, as well we might be. Besides the duty was very dangerous. Once we came within an ace of having to abandon the Schooner & take to the boats, and in fact almost every mo-ment was attended with infinite risk."

They had a brief respite when they took the schooner up to Asto-ria for provisions. Previous to the arrival of the squadron, Astoria had been the somewhat lonely residence of the Birnie family. In recent days the Birnies' many young children had become closely attached to the surgeon Charles Guillou and the Expedition's newest outcast Robert Johnson, who renamed the collection of temporary shacks "Bobville." In early October, with the arrival of Wilkes and the rest of the squadron,

Bobville came to a sudden end. Now that the survey of the upper part of the river was complete, it was time to sail for San Francisco.

Once the *Porpoise* and the *Oregon* had been safely taken across the bar, Wilkes ordered that they wait until he finished the survey of the inner portion of the river mouth in the *Flying Fish*. Over the course of the next few days Wilkes continued to make unmistakable overtures to Reynolds. "He seemed at this time," Reynolds wrote, "to manifest great consideration towards *me,* as if desirous to obliterate the remembrance of the past. We had no intercourse together, since he hurried me out of the *Vincennes,* and now as the cruise [w]as near its end, he imagined that a few smooth words, false & hollow though they be, will be sufficient to wipe away all sense of the thousand outrages, we have groaned under during his tyrannical reign."

One morning Wilkes sent out Knox and Midshipman Blair to record soundings, leaving Reynolds in command of the schooner. "Now, the duty on which he sent Knox," Reynolds wrote, "belonged to me, and it was evident to all, that he was *trusting* the Schooner to *me,* to flatter me up to the top of his bent. I thank my stars, that I am not of so *gullible* a nature, as to be so easily duped." Reynolds, as passionate as the man he had come to loathe, would never forgive Wilkes for not being the ideal leader he had naively believed him to be at the beginning of the voyage. Even though Wilkes had proven himself as capable as Hudson was ineffectual during the survey of the Columbia, Reynolds refused to alter his opinion of his commander.

Reynolds's feelings were surely encouraged by the surgeon Charles Guillou, who had become one of his closest friends in the squadron and who was already preparing to bring charges against Wilkes at the end of the voyage. But there were others, such as Henry Eld and the geologist James Dana, who would come to recognize that Wilkes, despite his obvious faults, was a remarkably resilient and resourceful survivor. "The more I see of him," Eld would later write his father, "the more I am impressed with his indomitable perseverance & tenacity[,] 'like a cork he cannot be sunk.'"

Why then did Wilkes attempt to win over Reynolds—a lowly and still very angry passed midshipman? There is always the possibility that

Wilkes honestly regretted that relations between the two of them had become so embittered, especially in light of his deteriorating relationship with his former confidant William Hudson. But there is also the possibility that, as Reynolds suspected, Wilkes had belatedly come to realize that for political reasons he now needed all the friends he could get—particularly if they were as articulate and popular as William Reynolds.

Events were unfolding back in Washington that did not bode well for Wilkes's return to the United States. A packet of mail had recently arrived at Fort Vancouver containing letters from several of the officers whom Wilkes had dismissed. They gleefully reported to their friends in the squadron that the secretary of the navy was lending a sympathetic ear to their tales of Wilkes's outrages. In recounting this unsettling development to Jane, Wilkes insisted that "my conscience . . . acquits me of having done anything that would cause even a tinge to my cheek." Still, if there should be charges brought against him, no matter how frivolous, "I should be rather inclined to court a full investigation of all my acts [if] it became necessary."

For his part, Reynolds already took for granted that charges would be brought against the commander of the Ex. Ex. "Captain Wilkes has preferred charges against so many of his Officers (and they in return have done him the like favor)," he wrote his father, "that the difficulties can only be settled by a General Court Martial, after our return." As far as he was concerned, there was no question which side was going to win: "The Evidence in every case will I am sure be dead in favor of the Officers."

On October 9, the *Flying Fish* crossed the Columbia bar for the last time. Wilkes had decided that the schooner would not be accompanying the *Porpoise* and the *Oregon* to San Francisco. Instead, Knox and Reynolds were to put the finishing touches on the survey of the outer edge of the bar, then survey a portion of the coast to the south before sailing to Oahu. After rendezvousing in Honolulu, the squadron would return to the United States via Singapore and the Cape of Good Hope, a voyage of some 22,000 miles. (Wilkes had hoped to stop at Japan, but now realized that there wasn't sufficient time if they were to return by May 1842.)

As Wilkes was being rowed from the schooner to the *Porpoise,* Knox asked if he might take the *Flying Fish* back to Astoria to refit. The last year of near-constant service had reduced her sails to rags; almost all her running rigging needed to be replaced. Having been so forcefully rebuffed by Reynolds, Wilkes was not about to assent to Knox's request, no matter how legitimate it might be. "Refit at sea" was his lofty reply. "This was about as practicable," Reynolds wrote, "as it would be for a half drowned man to mend his clothes in the water." Reynolds seemed almost relieved by his commander's return to his old despotic ways; it was so much easier to hate a man who was, as he recorded in his journal, "a headstrong, obstinate, ignorant fool."

Two weeks later the officers and men of the *Flying Fish* were, in Reynolds's words, refitting "with a vengeance." With no other vessels to help them, it had taken ten days to complete the survey of the bar. By then it was too late in the season to survey the Oregon coast. They had already decided to sail for Oahu when, in a furious gale on October 25, their forestay broke. Since the forestay held up both of the schooner's masts, they were in imminent peril of becoming a dismasted wreck. "We did not think it *too* uncharitable," Reynolds wrote, "to wish that 'the man' who told us *'to refit at sea,'* had been lashed to the said stay, when it blew away."

Once they'd repaired the stay, the wind shifted to the west, transforming the rocky coast of Oregon into a lee shore. Over the next few days, a succession of gales would shred their already tattered sails to ribbons and push them terrifyingly close to the wave-battered rocks. Only after they'd patched together a makeshift mainsail were they finally able to put Oregon behind them for good.

By that time, Wilkes had already arrived at Sausalito Bay. The town of Yerba Buena, now known as San Francisco, comprised just a few out-of-repair buildings that were, according to Wilkes, "not calculated to produce a favorable impression on a stranger." But if the town wasn't much, the harbor was "one of the most spacious, and at the same time safest ports in the world." Wilkes predicted that if it did not become a part of the United States, the region would one day combine with the Oregon territory to become "a powerful maritime nation [that would] control the destinies of the Pacific."

By the end of October the overland party led by Emmons and Eld had arrived and the survey of San Francisco Bay had been completed. Wilkes had learned that recently elected president William Henry Harrison had died, putting John Tyler in office. "This is all the news we have," he wrote Jane, "and amuse ourselves with wise and potent arguments as to what our fate will be under the newcomers into power." Whatever the situation in Washington, Wilkes was convinced that he now had the Expedition firmly under control, ending a letter to his wife with these supremely confident, eerily impersonal words: "For myself, I am ready to meet all and everybody. . . . I am superior and master now of all & the storms are hushed. Few will venture to put themselves in array against me. The Expedition I go for and he who attempts to frustrate its actions or course must and shall rue the day he ever made the attempt."

On November 1, against the advice of the harbor pilot, who warned of the possibility of seas breaking at the bar, Wilkes ordered the squadron to depart with the ebbing tide. Around sunset, the already light wind deserted completely. As the tide began to change, the squadron anchored, with the *Porpoise* and the *Oregon* just beyond the bar and, as it would turn out, with the *Vincennes,* which was once again flying Wilkes's commodore's pennant, coming to rest almost precisely over it. The seas remained quiet until ten P.M., when "without any apparent cause," according to Wilkes, the swell began to increase ominously. By midnight, the *Vincennes* was in the midst of her own private tempest: huge rollers pitched the ship so violently that when she swung broadside to the swell, Wilkes feared for the masts. By two A.M. waves of over thirty feet were battering the ship, bursting over the bow and threatening to tear loose the anchor chain. At 3:30 A.M. an immense breaker flooded the spar deck, stoving in boats and hurling spare spars in every direction. Just at that moment a marine named Joseph Allshouse was climbing up a ladder to the deck. A spar slammed into him, and three hours later he died of internal injuries.

Not until eight A.M. did it become possible to raise the anchor. A few miles away, the *Porpoise* and the *Oregon* had been blessed with a quiet night, and both crews were amazed to learn of the *Vincennes*'s ordeal. Allshouse was quickly buried at sea, and Wilkes, the Stormy Petrel, ordered the squadron to begin the first leg of the long sail home.

CHAPTER 13

Homeward Bound

A FTER MORE THAN THREE YEARS at sea, Wilkes was finding it difficult to conceive of a reality beyond the taut discipline of the four vessels under his command. From his perspective, the Expedition was already an unqualified triumph. Having successfully neutralized a possible French threat, he could now claim to have discovered a new continent. Although his survey of Fiji had come at a terrible price, it would surely be recognized as a wondrous and valuable achievement. His climb up Mauna Loa was the stuff of legend, but, as he well knew, what the American people would be most interested in were his surveys of the Pacific Northwest and California.

The nation that had once looked to the Appalachian and Rocky Mountains as its natural western boundaries was becoming increasingly convinced that its dominion should extend all the way to the Pacific. A group of American settlers had arrived in Oregon in 1841; by the spring of 1842 another group would be headed west. What the American people wanted more than anything else was information about this new, untapped territory, and no one currently possessed more charts, maps, sketches, and detailed writings about the west coast of North America than the commander of the Ex. Ex. This, he decided, would be his trump card. If, for some reason, the naval and political leaders in Washington, D.C., refused to provide him with the accolades he deserved, he would withhold "this desired information until I see how they are about to reward me." It was extortion, pure and simple, not to mention a shocking and unlawful abuse of his government's trust, but this was how the egocentric mind of Charles Wilkes worked. Warning Jane that his plan was "entre nous," he asserted that "there is nothing like having the whip in my own hands."

In Honolulu, where the squadron stopped briefly for provisions and repairs before continuing on to Manila, Singapore, and eventually home, Wilkes received unsettling indications that his control over the Expedition's legacy was not as total as he had assumed. His archenemy John Aulick, captain of the USS *Yorktown,* had just left Honolulu ten days before. According to Aulick, it was widely reported back in the United States that Wilkes had lost his grip on both the Expedition and himself. Fearing that Wilkes had gone "crazy," a friend of Aulick's even called on Jane "to ask if such was not the fact." For Wilkes this was distressing and humiliating news, but it got worse.

In New Zealand, Aulick encountered the British explorer James Ross, just back from his own southern cruise. With a copy of Wilkes's chart spread out before them, Ross had asserted that his two ships had sailed over an area where the Americans had claimed there was land. Heading east, Ross had sailed into what is known today as the Ross Sea, eventually establishing a new southern record of 78°04'. Instead of a continent, Ross believed that Antarctica was made up of a group of islands and attributed the Americans' claims to their lack of experience with "the delusive appearances in these icy regions." These were damaging, if not crippling, claims, especially coming from the acknowledged master of high-latitude exploration. But to have Aulick, an officer of the U.S. Navy, taking such obvious pleasure in undercutting the achievements of a fellow American was truly reprehensible.

Wilkes had originally planned to sell the *Flying Fish* in Hawaii. But realizing that the schooner would aid in the survey of the reef-strewn Sulu Sea between the Philippines and Malaysia, he decided to retain her services—much to the distress of William Reynolds, who along with Samuel Knox had grown weary of sailing in the open sea in such a small craft. "[W]ith the sweet & calm resignation that has become our distinguished characteristic," Reynolds sarcastically wrote, they began laying in stores for the more than five-thousand-mile voyage to Manila, where they were to meet up with the *Vincennes.* The two brigs, the *Porpoise* and the newly acquired replacement for the *Peacock*, the *Oregon*, were to investigate the currents to the east of Japan, then sail through the China Sea to Singapore at the southern tip of the Malay Peninsula. Once the entire squadron had rendezvoused at Singapore that winter, they would sail for home. Wilkes had solemnly pledged that they would arrive at the navy yard in New York no later than May 31, 1842.

As far as Reynolds was concerned, the work of the Expedition was finished; all that remained was a long, dull sail home, and he had assured his family that they now had nothing to worry about when it came to his safety. But in January, just a few days from Manila, Reynolds came as close as he would ever come to perishing at sea.

Knox, the schooner's commanding officer, insisted that the current would slacken as they approached Manila, allowing them to steer directly for the port without fear of being swept ashore. Although Reynolds objected strongly to the proposal, Knox, the son of a Boston harbor pilot, insisted that he was right. At 11:30 that night, as both Reynolds and Knox slept in their bunks, leaving the watch to Passed Midshipman Joseph Sanford, the lookout saw breakers off the bow. Reynolds bounded to the deck in his nightshirt. "The sight was frightful," he wrote, "and at the first glance, it seemed impossible we should be saved. The night was very dark, yet we could see the land & the horrible breakers, oh! so close. . . . The wind fairly howled in its violence, and the swell was enormously high, increased twofold by the shoalness of the water, for *now*, we were *in the rollers & could see the bottom*. It was do or die, and most likely would do *and* die."

If they were to drive the schooner through the waves, they needed more sail. Even though she was already staggering under the lone foresail, they raised the mainsail and jib. "The masts switched like willows," Reynolds wrote, "and the water came over the bows, just as it falls over a *mill dam*, ashore, in torrents. . . . Had she not been the most glorious model of a sea boat that ever *was* built, she could not have borne this sail an instant, but she was true as gold." Once they reached the safety of Manila, Reynolds realized that this incident had frightened him more than even the near-loss of the *Peacock* in Antarctica. "Roused out of a sleep, to be drowned in five minutes, without hope, is rather appalling to any man . . . ," he reflected. "Death cannot be worse than the fright, for the abandonment of hope is death itself." The incident off the Philippines so troubled him that it would be one of the few events of the Expedition that he could not bring himself to describe in a letter to his family.

For Reynolds, Manila stood as the symbol of a fallen empire. A once-prosperous Spanish port, whose gold-laden galleons had annually voyaged across the Pacific to and from Acapulco, the Philippine capital had fallen into neglect with the waning of Spain's global influence. The port's decline, however, had done nothing to lessen the beauty of its women. Reynolds and his fellow officers could not help but gawk at the young ladies they saw passing on the streets. He found himself irresistibly edging toward a resolution: "I am almost tempted to make & record a vow, 'never to wander again unless Mrs. Reynolds sails in company.'"

On January 21, the *Vincennes* and the *Flying Fish* weighed anchor. As she straggled behind the flagship, the schooner passed a merchant vessel, just four months out of Boston, whose captain offered a pile of newspapers. Reynolds was making his leisurely way through one of the papers when he came upon the latest list of navy promotions. Since he felt he was, at the very least, three years away from a promotion, he began to examine the list with only the mildest interest–until he found *his* name among the lieutenants. "I was confounded," he wrote. "Joy and surprise made me dumb! I had not had even the shadow of a hope for such good fortune. . . . Yet here, I had made a Lieut, more than a month ago! I screamed the glorious news aloud, but the utterance nearly choked me. I never felt so proud or happy in all my life."

Making Reynolds's elation all the sweeter was that Wilkes's name was not on the list. He took out a pen and ink, drew a thick black line around the pertinent paragraph, and folded the paper so that the page remained in full view. Then he sent the paper to Wilkes aboard the *Vincennes.*

The crew of the *Flying Fish* arrived in Singapore to discover that the two brigs had preceded them by three weeks but that the *Vincennes,* which had failed to meet them at two prearranged rendezvous points, had not yet arrived. Reynolds and his companions were delighted to have the opportunity to explore this busy, cosmopolitan port, where merchant vessels from no fewer than twenty-four "Asiatic nations," including the "Chinese, Hindoos, Malays, Jews, Armenians, [and] Parsees" mixed with vessels from Europe and America.

The *Vincennes* followed just a few days later. Wilkes was in a "great uproar," claiming that the *Flying Fish* had failed to meet him at a third rendezvous point. Both Knox and Reynolds were mystified since their written orders only mentioned two points of rendezvous. Instead of speaking directly with Knox, who was one of his most faithful officers, Wilkes angrily ordered a court of inquiry to investigate the actions of the *Flying Fish*'s commander. The court, comprising Ringgold, Carr, and Alden, with Emmons acting as the judge advocate, would exonerate Knox, but the breach between Wilkes and his officers was now complete. "This act of [Wilkes's]," Reynolds wrote, "was as black a deed as any that have disgraced him during the cruise."

It was also the act of a man who had just received dreadful news from home. In Singapore Wilkes found forty-two letters waiting for him from Jane. The latest was dated July 15, 1841–a month later than any other letter received in the squadron; for once, Wilkes had the freshest news from the United States. Jane reported that a large number of objects from the Ex. Ex. had already arrived in Washington and that a geologist with no familiarity with the Expedition's aims had been allowed to ransack the collections. Wilkes and the scientific corps had been assured that the crates would remain untouched until their return. "They have broken their faith and in all probability ruined half our results," he wrote.

The news concerning his promotion was also not good. Jane had even dared to question the wisdom of his having flown the pennant of a commodore. "[P]ray, how can you join sides against me . . . ," he demanded. "I feel proud of having borne [the pennant] with triumphant sweep the world over. . . . My only fault was I did not hoist it the moment I left [Norfolk]." It infuriated Wilkes to know that while he received only criticism from his nation's leaders–not to mention his wife–the commanders of competing European expeditions had already received their just rewards. He had heard that d'Urville had been promoted to admiral on his return to France; similar honors had been promised to Ross, while his official standing had, if anything, lessened since leaving Norfolk. With the return of the Expedition's disgruntled officers to the United States, the secretary of the navy, who had formerly addressed him as a lieutenant commandant, now referred to him simply as Lieutenant Wilkes. "I serve a glorious country," he wrote Jane, "but an administration the shabbiest on Earth." In desperation, he urged Jane to speak to her *"influential friends"* concerning his promotion.

But the most disturbing news from his home on Capitol Hill was of a more personal nature. Wilkes's sister Eliza, Jane reported, was not doing well. As was to be expected, word of her son's death had been a devastating blow. Wilkes had sent her a miniature of Wilkes Henry from Honolulu, but he had not been able to bring himself to write her about the boy's passing, and he worried what her reaction to him would be when he saw her for the first time since the tragedy. Wilkes's brother Henry offered some comfort, writing that Eliza was "gradually reviving from the deplorable loss." "God bless you my dear C.," he continued. "May the wound you have received experience the healing effect of time before this [letter] comes to hand. And may you also have the good fortune to find someone who will in some degree supply the place of dear W."

But for Wilkes, there would be no possibility of compensation. For the last three years he had been looking forward to the day when he would be reunited with Jane and their four children. In Singapore, he learned that at least one of them would not be there when he returned. His eldest son Jack, just fourteen, had decided that he wanted to follow in his absent father's footsteps; with Jane's permission, he had secured a midshipman's appointment and would soon be on his way to Brazil. For Wilkes, who had come to see the navy as a thankless, even malicious employer, it was terrible news. "You cannot look upon this as I do . . . ," he wrote. "I could write you much more my dear dear Jane upon this subject, but it would give you pain and me too. . . . I cannot [conceal] from you it has given me great pain."

✦   ✦   ✦

At Singapore, the Expedition lost one of its most trusted and stalwart members: the *Flying Fish*. A survey determined that the schooner was suffering from structural problems that made a passage around the Cape of Good Hope a dangerous proposition, and no one wanted the beloved schooner to follow the *Sea Gull* to the bottom of the ocean. Since Knox was preoccupied with Wilkes's court of inquiry, Reynolds was left with supervising the transfer of the vessel to her new owner–an Englishman who claimed she would make a "beautiful yacht" but who secretly planned to use her, it was rumored, as an opium smuggler. After cleaning her out, Reynolds lowered the American ensign from the *Flying Fish*'s masthead. "I had the same sort of regard for her that a man must entertain for a gallant horse that has carried him safely through the fight, & I almost repented that the poor old craft had been so rudely bartered away."

On February 26, the squadron weighed anchor and began to thread its way through the mass of Chinese junks thronging the waters of Singapore. From the maintop of the *Vincennes,* Charlie Erskine caught a final glimpse of the *Flying Fish:* "As we passed her with a strange commander and crew on board, and a foreign flag at her mast-head floating to the balmy breeze, every bosom was filled with sadness." Of the original six-vessel squadron, only the *Vincennes* and the *Porpoise* were now left; of the original 346 men, a little over half remained, with the losses to desertion, death, and dismissal having been made up by recruitments in Sydney, Honolulu, and other ports. By the end of the voyage, a total of 524 men would have served on the Ex. Ex.

The crew of the *Flying Fish* was dispersed among the *Vincennes,* the *Porpoise,* and the *Oregon,* which was now commanded by Wilkes's former first lieutenant Overton Carr. Much to his relief, Reynolds had been reassigned to the *Porpoise.* "I should have got the Hydrophobia on board the *Vincennes,* with C. W.," he wrote. Not until March 1 did Wilkes officially recognize Reynolds's promotion. He also issued orders to the commanders of the *Porpoise* and the *Oregon.* While the *Vincennes* sailed directly for New York, with brief stops at Cape Town and the island of St. Helena, the two brigs were to take a three-thousand-mile detour to Rio de Janeiro, where they were to perform some trivial observations and pick up a small number of additional specimens. Reynolds branded this "a diabolical arrangement." Just as he had done prior to the squadron's final assault on Antarctica, Wilkes had scripted it so that his flagship would be the first on the scene. After a voyage of almost four years, Reynolds and his compatriots would be forced to arrive in New York at least a month after the *Vincennes.* "[W]e never shall be reconciled to it," he wrote. "[A] disagreeable remembrance of it will haunt me for ever, along with the feeling of hatred which I shall cherish for its author."

But for Charlie Erskine and his fellow sailors aboard the *Vincennes,* these were happy times. "All life and gayety on board," he wrote, "and bright visions of home were before us. The weather was fine, the wind fair, and our gallant ship had all the sail on her that she could possibly carry. She made thirteen and a half knots for five days in succession." One afternoon Charlie noticed that three older seamen were enjoying a nap on the deck and using Wilkes's dog Sydney as a pillow. "I hunted up a bone and placed it about a foot from the dog's nose," he wrote. "As soon as Sydney got a smell of the bone he suddenly sprang up, and the sleepers' heads came down on deck with a thump. . . . [I]f they had known who the culprit was, I verily believe they would have thrown me overboard." But if life aboard the *Vincennes* was now better than it had ever been, Charlie would never forget the shocking brutality that had become commonplace under Wilkes's command. "I had seen as good men as ever trod a ship's deck, lashed to the rigging–made spread eagles of–and flogged." He resolved that he would never again sail on a naval vessel. "I had had enough of the navy during [the last four years] to last me a lifetime."

On March 2, tragedy struck the *Vincennes.* George Porter, the same sailor who had narrowly escaped death three and a half years ago when a rope wrapped around his neck, succumbed to a fever he had caught in Singapore. "He belonged in Bangor, Maine," Charlie remembered, "and how eagerly he looked forward to going home and seeing all the loved ones there! Poor George!"

Three weeks later, Benjamin Vanderford, the Salem bêche-de-mer captain who had served as the Expedition's pilot and interpreter in Fiji, also fell ill. Always a heavy drinker, he began to hallucinate, and after falling into horrifying convulsions, he quickly lost consciousness and died. For Veidovi, the Fijian chief, it was a shattering loss. Vanderford had promised to serve as his protector once they reached the United States. Veidovi retreated to his berth and from that day forward showed a "total disregard of everything that passed around him."

Meanwhile, back in Washington, D.C., Robert Pinkney, the latest officer to return from the Expedition under arrest, had recently arrived in town, and the newly appointed secretary of the navy Abel Upshur was shocked by the lieutenant's account of a commander who proudly insisted that he was above the law. In his annual address Upshur had vowed to do everything he could to stop abuses on the part of the service's superior officers. Wilkes sounded like just the kind of commander who needed to be made an example of. (That he was the leader of an expedition mounted by Jacksonian Democrats only encouraged Upshur, who was part of John Tyler's Whig administration.) Given the seriousness of Pinkney's accusations, Upshur decided that he could not put Wilkes on the promotion list for that spring.

In March, Jane Wilkes received a letter from Dr. John S. Wily, a family friend and former navy surgeon. "You have no time to lose," Wily urged. "Should your husband be left out of the new batch [of promotions], he is irretrievably injured. Take no denial. The principle on which the Secretary is acting is totally subversive of naval discipline and legally wrong. A man is innocent till found guilty, but here we see a death blow given to an officer when absent on duty by a discontented subaltern, whose charges may be trivial, malicious, or unfounded, and against which he has no means of defending himself. . . . Go to Senators, as many as possible. Say if Charles is to be tried, let him be tried; but not *condemned now* which is virtually the case. . . . I would almost rather he was dead, than so shamefully dishonored."

Jane would do exactly as Wily suggested, even writing a memorandum in which she detailed her efforts on her husband's behalf. Twice Jane visited Secretary Upshur. By the second visit, Upshur had had enough of Jane's passionate advocacy and told her, she later wrote, that "if I urged the matter any further I should ruin my husband." Jane responded with a letter of apology for her "too urgent appeal," stating, "I therefore will wait patiently until the decision of his peers shall (as it most assuredly will) restore my husband to his full standing in the service to which his whole life has been devoted."

Back aboard the *Vincennes,* Wilkes was doing everything he could to return to the United States as quickly as possible. Although it looked as if he would not make the May 31 deadline, he still had hopes of returning before the Senate adjourned for the summer. "I shall push hard to get home...," he had written Jane from Singapore, "and I am in hopes [Congress] will sit late."

During a brief stop at Cape Town, Wilkes visited the observatory made famous by the astronomer Sir John Herschel. Here he came across a new British chart that showed the tracks of Ross's and d'Urville's voyages to Antarctica but made no reference to his own. Still worse, it was clear to Wilkes that Ross had used information from the chart he had sent him. "[T]he truth will come out one of these days," he insisted in his journal. After another quick stop at St. Helena, where the officers dutifully visited the home where Napoleon had spent his last days in exile, they were off for the final sprint to New York.

On May 16 Wilkes issued a general order requiring that a committee composed of Hudson, Emmons, and the naturalist Charles Pickering collect from each and every officer "all Journals, rough notes, writings, memorandums, drawings, sketches, paintings, as well as all specimens of every kind collected or prepared since leaving the United States." Even though this had been the policy from the very beginning, it was not a popular order. To have spent four years of one's life on a voyage round the world and to have nothing left to show for it seemed unnecessarily harsh, especially since there was already more than enough material in the Expedition's collections. Emmons possessed a Fijian bow and arrow that had been taken during the bloody boat fight off Malolo.

"But here they go," he wrote bitterly, "and if the Government wants them I have not another word to say." Adding to the resentment of Emmons and others was the rumor that Wilkes was harboring an extensive collection of his own in a cabinet given to him by the consul in Singapore.

As the officers reluctantly turned over their specimens and artifacts, the gun deck of the *Vincennes* became crowded with crates and boxes. Reynolds's volatile friend William May, whom Wilkes had recently named master of the ship, was loath to give up a box of shells he had procured at Fiji after the *Vincennes*'s purser had declined to buy it. On the top of the box, May wrote out "Purchased at Public Sale after the Comdr of the Ex. Ex. had refused them." When Wilkes saw the box, he immediately assumed May was attempting to mock his order. He called May into his cabin and demanded that he remove the words from the top of the box. May responded that *"he would do no such thing,"* and Wilkes ordered him to leave the cabin and consider himself under suspension. Even though Wilkes had made attempts to mend fences with May (just as he'd done with Reynolds at the Columbia River), he now determined to draw up formal charges against the passed midshipman.

As the month of June approached, Wilkes's tension level was reaching an almost unbearable pitch, and he pushed his ship and his men as hard as he had at any point during the voyage. Despite near gale-force winds, he insisted that no sails should be shortened without his approval. On June 1, the always reliable George Emmons was the officer of the deck. Of all the Expedition's officers, no one had given more of himself than Emmons. In Fiji he had spent more days in an open boat than anyone else; at the Columbia bar he had supervised the successful rescue of the *Peacock*'s crew; just a few weeks later, while suffering from malaria, he had braved hostile native tribes, grizzly bears, and uncooperative guides to complete a grueling overland expedition to San Francisco. If there was an officer who deserved Wilkes's gratitude, it was George Emmons.

But when Emmons sent an officer to Wilkes's cabin "to inform him that I was fearful our spars or rigging might give away if we continued under the same sail," the commander of the Ex. Ex. ridiculed the lieutenant's concern by insisting that he make more sail. Emmons dutifully set the fore topgallant sail and the jib. Under the increased strain, the *Vincennes* parted her bobstay–the chain that led from the tip of the bowsprit down to the cutwater at the bow's waterline. Without the bobstay, the *Vincennes* would quickly lose the bowsprit. Emmons had no choice but to put the helm up and begin to reduce sail. Wilkes erupted from his cabin, appearing on deck "very much excited, &" according to Emmons, "immediately commenced giving his orders in a manner that put all order & system of carrying on duty out of the question. . . . I, however, did not partake of his excitement and continued to repeat his orders–that he might not accuse me of disrespect–and at the same time see what a mess he had got every thing in, until he finally ordered me below & sent for the 1st Lieut." Of course, First Lieutenant Walker did exactly what Emmons had attempted to do–shortening sail and replacing the bobstay before bringing the ship back on course under reduced sail.

By the morning of June 9, the *Vincennes* was approaching the foggy coast of the United States. At noon of the next day, she anchored off Sandy Hook, where a steamer came alongside and began towing the ship into New York Harbor. The question that concerned all aboard the flagship was what Wilkes would do with his broad pennant. Reynolds was not on hand to witness the scene, but others would later tell him about Wilkes's final act as Commodore of the U.S. Ex. Ex. "Curiosity was now on tip toe among the officers of the *Vincennes* to see how this bravado would terminate," he wrote. Would Wilkes dare anchor at the navy yard with the pennant flying or would he replace it with the coach whip of a lieutenant commander? "He did neither," Reynolds wrote. "His impudence–great as it was–could not carry him through the first alternative. His bloated pride would not allow him to adopt the other." As the ship approached the Battery, Wilkes called the crew to muster and "expressed to them my thanks for the manner in which they had conducted themselves during the cruise." A salute was fired, his pennant was hauled down, and Wilkes turned over the ship to Hudson. Hitching a ride with the pilot, Wilkes was able to slip ashore without having to confront the officer whom Reynolds termed "the *real Commodore* of the Station."

✦   ✦   ✦

Wilkes might call himself the discoverer of Antarctica, as well as the surveyor of Fiji and the Columbia River, but for many of his officers, none of these accomplishments seemed to matter anymore. Of the disaffected, no one was more embittered than William Reynolds. By the time he reached Rio de Janeiro, his feelings for his commander had become a dark obsession that threatened to permanently disfigure his once balanced, sensitive, and ebullient personality. "[Wilkes] has done wrongs that he can never repair," he wrote. "He has in the gratification of his *personal* prejudices, his own venom & spite, inflicted injuries on men whose shoes he is unworthy to unloose, that can never be wiped away . . . ! There is not a dissembler in existence more vile or more depraved than the same Mr. Lieutenant Charles Wilkes, whom I once thought was every thing pure and honorable."

Reynolds's anger made it impossible for him to recognize the magnitude of what the Expedition had accomplished. He thought only of the odious Wilkes. "Not one hope has been realized," he insisted. It was only in the context of the suffering he and his fellow officers had endured that Reynolds could compare the Expedition to anything else in American history: "I look upon the hardships, dangers & servitude that we have undergone in this Expedition as parallel in their extent to the worst years of the 'Revolutionary War' & if its operations had been protracted for 48 months longer, every one of us would have been *expended,* from a *wearing out* of the system." Although he had since gained some of the weight back, Reynolds, almost six feet tall and already rail thin at 147 pounds when the cruise began, had dropped to just 135 pounds—"enough to have satisfied a dozen Shylocks," he wrote his family. "I am thin as a shadow, and ugly as thin. My general title of '*Old* Reynolds,' is no misnomer. I look old & feel accordingly."

And yet despite everything, the fact of the matter was that they had experienced the adventure of their lives. Rio de Janeiro marked their complete circumnavigation of the world. They had literally gone where no man had gone before, and while Reynolds might not appreciate it, others could not help but be in awe of what he and his shipmates had achieved. Reynolds reported that the officers of the *Delaware* stationed at Rio "looked at me as if I were a natural curiosity. They had not seen *an Explorer* in full bloom."

They left Rio de Janeiro on May 22. The *Porpoise* passed close to the *Delaware*'s stern and Reynolds was delighted to hear her band playing "'Sweet Home' as loud as they could blow." Frequent calms and head-winds prolonged the return to New York. Not until early July did they reach the navy yard, and to Reynolds's considerable anguish he was re-quired to keep watch aboard the *Porpoise* for several more days. He soon learned that Veidovi had died the day after the *Vincennes*'s arrival, "in consequence," the *New York Herald* explained, "of having no human flesh to eat." A few days later the *Herald* reported that the surgeons at the navy hospital where Veidovi had died had "already cut off his head, and it has been laying in pickle for several days." Soon after, the Fijian's fleshless skull became a permanent part of the Expedition's collection.

On the morning of the Fourth of July, two young men came aboard the *Porpoise*, both of them looking for Lieutenant William Reynolds. It wasn't until one of them asked, "Which of you, is it?" that Reynolds knew the man's voice to be that of his older brother Sam. After four long years, the two brothers didn't recognize each other.

Sam and his friend took William ashore to see some of the holiday celebration in New York. By July 6, he had been granted a leave of ab-sence and spent the night at the American Hotel. Then it was on to Lancaster, Pennsylvania. *"The return home!,"* he recorded on the last page of his journal, "cannot be written here."

Part Four

CHAPTER 14

Reckoning

WILKES ARRIVED in Washington on June 13, 1842. His house on the hill was "almost as I had left it." His wife and children—including Janey, Edmund, and Eliza—could not have been more pleased to see him. But the absence of his eldest son Jack "made a void in my little flock," he noted sadly.

He had once dared to assume that if he should successfully complete his mission, a grateful nation would shower him with praise and recognition. He had fashioned out of disaster one of the largest, most sophisticated scientific and surveying enterprises the world had ever seen. He had found a new continent, charted hundreds of Pacific islands, collected tons of artifacts and specimens, and explored the Pacific Northwest and the Sulu Sea. And he had now returned to find that nobody in New York, Washington, or, it seemed, the entire nation apparently cared.

Jane could not conceal her concern for her husband. He had left a youthful, ambitious forty-year-old man. He had been gone four years but had aged at least ten. His eyes had sunk deep into his skull; he had a cough that wouldn't go away; but as she knew better than anyone, his travails had not yet ended. "She was aware," Wilkes wrote, "that an onslaught would be made upon me and an endeavor made to cast all my service into the Shade."

Washington had changed dramatically in the last four years. When Wilkes had left in August 1838, the Jacksonian Democrats had been in power. Now with the Whig John Tyler as president, Wilkes's former allies had been thrust to the sidelines. At a time when political differences were at their height, Tyler was not about to dwell on the achievements of an expedition mounted by the previous administration. But there was more than party politics at work. Tyler's secretary of state, Daniel Webster, was in the midst of delicate negotiations with the British government concerning the boundary between Maine and Canada. It had been briefly feared that the two countries might even go to war over the border dispute. Tyler had hopes that Webster might be able to expand his negotiations to include the border in the Pacific Northwest, and the last thing he wanted in the summer of 1842 was for Wilkes to call attention to the importance of that region to the American people. As a result, Tyler and his secretary of the navy, Abel Upshur, had instituted a news blackout when it came to the results of the Expedition. Whereas President Van Buren and his secretary of the navy, James Paulding, had regularly published Wilkes's reports, with Van Buren proudly announcing the discovery of Antarctica in his annual address in 1840, no official mention of the Expedition had been made in almost a year. To Wilkes's considerable dismay and indignation, the administration had no interest in the findings he had earlier assumed would win him every concession and accolade he might desire.

The navy had also changed in the last four years. Reform was in the air. Secretary of the Navy Upshur had vowed to protect junior officers suffering under a captain's immoderate and tyrannical rule. Just a few months before he had restored to duty a lieutenant who had been put under arrest by Commodore Charles Morgan of the Mediterranean Squadron. Both Lieutenant Robert Pinkney and Surgeon Charles Guillou claimed that Wilkes was guilty of far worse outrages against his officers. Subjecting the leader of the Ex. Ex. to an extensive court-martial proceeding would not only serve Upshur's agenda within the department, it would make it difficult, if not impossible, for Wilkes to trumpet the findings that the Tyler administration wanted kept under wraps.

Wilkes, however, was determined that the Expedition—and, of course, himself—would get the recognition they deserved. As it so happened, on the very day he arrived in Washington, there was a meeting scheduled of the newly created National Institute for the Promotion of

Science. Spearheaded by former secretary of war Joel Poinsett, the man who had chosen Wilkes to command the Expedition, the National Institute, a forerunner of the Smithsonian Institution, had been awarded custody of the Expedition's collections. Wilkes had joined the Institute by mail during the voyage, and he now realized that the organization might provide him with a way to circumvent the Tyler administration. Wilkes hurriedly made his way to the meeting, where Poinsett enthusiastically heralded his return and proposed that he deliver a lecture about the voyage later in the month.

In the days ahead, Wilkes began to marshal support from influential Democrats while formally announcing his return to the Tyler administration. He had already been counseled by his brother-in-law in New York to control his emotions as best he could. "Let Charles by all means keep cool," James Renwick wrote Jane. "His friends will be sufficiently indignant, he must conciliate." But when Wilkes first met Secretary Upshur, he was anything but conciliatory. "[The secretary's] reception of me was very cold," he wrote. "He never offered to shake hands with me, nor requested me to take a seat. I felt indignant at such treatment and my spirit rose." Wilkes proceeded to take a seat, and as he launched into a furious soliloquy condemning the action that the Navy Department had taken against him, Upshur sat silently in his chair, nervously taking off and putting back on his reading glasses. Wilkes ended his diatribe by warning Upshur that he was about to lose "the brightest feather he could put into his bonnet" if he continued on this course. Immediately following the meeting, Wilkes wrote Upshur requesting that a general court of inquiry be called to investigate his conduct during the Expedition. He knew that if he could win a favorable result in the more informal circumstances of a court of inquiry, his case would never go to trial.

He had also been advised to appeal directly to the White House. "As to the President," Renwick cautioned, "he can be counseled and not driven." But once again, Wilkes's attempts at diplomacy failed miserably. On the evening he called on the president, Wilkes found Tyler with a dozen of his cronies, seated around a fireplace, squirting tobacco juice into the fire. "I was literally struck [dumb] with surprise to find myself in such a company at the President's House," he wrote. "It was exactly like a Virginia or North Carolina bar room, and after the chair was brought forward, the President said, 'be seated, Sir,' and this was all the recognition I got of my presence." Wilkes was convinced that Tyler had no idea who he was; either that or he was "determined to ignore all that had anything to do with the Expedition." Seething with hurt and anger, Wilkes excused himself from the room.

He next sought out John Quincy Adams. Although no Democrat, Adams had been a supporter of the Expedition from the very beginning; he was also a trustee of the National Institute, and Wilkes poured out his soul to the seventy-five-year-old congressman and former president. He told Adams that Tyler's and Upshur's reception had "overpowered him; and all the anxieties and cares and sufferings of the whole [four] years were as nothing to the anguish he had endured within the last five days." He also complained that while he had been denied a promotion, an officer he had placed under arrest had been awarded one that spring. "I said little in answer to him," Adams wrote in his diary, "but must wait to hear the statements of the other side."

On June 20, just a week after his arrival in Washington, Wilkes spoke before a crowd of more than four hundred at a special meeting of the National Institute held in the hall of the new Patent Office Building. On hand was a who's who of political dignitaries, including Secretary of the Navy Abel Upshur. It was an unusual and challenging situation for a naval officer, but Wilkes claimed to have been "glad of the opportunity of giving a truthful account of the operations we had been engaged in." He began in a typically combative manner, recounting how disheartening it had been for himself and his officers and men to discover how little was known of the Expedition's achievements upon their return. Holding nothing back, he made sure "to throw the blame where it belonged on those who were there present & seated near me." Wilkes now had the audience's undivided attention, and he proceeded to tell them the story of the U.S. Ex. Ex. "Throughout the account," he wrote, "there was a marked interest and an audible approval when I closed."

Once the applause had died down, Charles Wickliffe, Tyler's postmaster general, leapt to his feet and began to take Wilkes to task for his criticisms of the current administration. This brought the influential senator William Preston, a Democrat from South Carolina, into the fray, speaking in Wilkes's defense. But it would be John Quincy Adams who would carry the day. Refusing to be drawn into the political sniping, he drew attention to the Expedition's many remarkable accomplishments. Upshur, who was a trustee of the Institute, was politically astute enough to realize that he must act to contain the damage Wilkes had managed to inflict. Once Adams had finished, the secretary of the navy praised Wilkes's speech and proposed that he provide a written synopsis of the voyage. A friend of Wilkes whispered in his ear that "I could desire nothing more gratifying," particularly when Upshur concluded by saying "that the results of the Expedition were highly valuable and honorable, not to this country alone, but to the whole civilized world." But Wilkes remained unconvinced. "I had seen enough of him to know what a deceitful rogue he was."

The very next day, Upshur went on the attack, informing Wilkes by letter that his request for a general court of inquiry had been denied and that "A court martial will be called at the earliest convenient time." By this point Wilkes had submitted a report to Upshur on the Oregon territory. As might be expected, Wilkes took a militant position regarding a possible U.S.-Canadian boundary, insisting that it lie at 54°40', far enough north to include not only the Strait of Juan de Fuca but also Vancouver Island. Fearing that this would have an incendiary effect on the ongoing negotiations with Britain, Upshur did everything he could to delay the report's distribution to Congress, finally insisting that the report remain confidential and not, as Wilkes's supporters had hoped, be published and distributed to the American people that summer.

Even as Upshur worked to quash attempts to publicize the Expedition's results, he moved to strengthen the government's case against Wilkes, taking the extraordinary measure of ordering Dr. Charles Guillou to report to Washington on June 27. Upshur granted Guillou unrestricted access to the Navy Department's files, and for five days the surgeon labored to expand and bolster his charges against the leader of the Ex. Ex. All this time, Wilkes waited impatiently for the court-martial he had been led to believe was imminent. Upshur, of course, was stalling until Guillou had finished assembling seven charges against his former commander. Now, with Pinkney offering an additional four, he informed Wilkes that he would have to wait another three weeks, when a general courts-martial would be convened in New York, where "[you] must take your chances with others whom it is contemplated to bring to trial."

But if Upshur was confident that he had built a strong case against him, Wilkes knew that the secretary was without a crucial source of information. Prior to his departure from the *Vincennes,* Wilkes had collected and boxed all his officers' journals, as well as many other crucial papers, and brought them with him to Washington, where they remained in his sole possession. Not until the middle of July did Upshur realize that Wilkes had these important documents. "You will send to the Department as soon as practicable after the receipt of this letter," Upshur wrote on July 15, "the Journals of all the officers and Scientific Corps." When Wilkes showed the secretary's letter to Senator Silas Wright, a Democrat from New York, Wright smiled and asked him when it would be "practicable" for him to turn over the journals. "Never" was Wilkes's reply. Wright laughed "and said that was right."

When he wasn't preparing for the impending courts-martial, Wilkes continued to promulgate, in the only way presently available to him, the accomplishments of the Expedition. That summer he transformed his house into a miniature museum, and on July 9, in between speeches on the House floor, John Quincy Adams stopped by for a look. "[A]t the earnest and repeated entreaties of Lieutenant Wilkes," he recorded in his diary, "I went over to his house and inspected a great number of the drawings collected during the exploring expedition—portraits of men, women, and children, of the ocean, and Feejee Islands. Fishes, birds, plants, shells, and navigating charts are in great profusion, more than I had time to examine."

The courts-martial were scheduled to begin on July 25 aboard one of the finest ships of the line in the U.S. Navy, the *North Carolina,* lying off New York's Castle Garden. The masts of the huge ship towered above the rest of the vessels in the harbor. "The morning was beautiful," a reporter from the *New York Herald* wrote, "the sun shining in unclouded splendor, and the soft and gentle breezes producing the most pleasing and agreeable sensations as we were being conveyed to the vessel. The ship itself was in beautiful trim, the deck as white as snow, being covered with awnings to shelter those on board from the otherwise insupportable heat of the sun, and crowded with the seamen and marines pursuing their various occupations. . . . Anon the boatswain's shrill whistle sounded, announcing the arrival of a boat with some of the officers detailed for the Court, when the guards and marines and the watch fell in, and gave them a salute as they made their appearance on deck."

There were thirteen officers of the court, including nine commodores, two commanders, and two lieutenants. Although Wilkes would later claim that it had been a "picked court," there were several members who were disposed to look kindly on him. Commodore Charles Ridgely had assisted him during the preparation of the Ex. Ex., fitting out the *Flying Fish* and the *Sea Gull* with great dispatch at the New York Navy Yard. Commodore Jonathan Downes had been equally helpful at the Boston Navy Yard. Wilkes had asked that the officers against whom he had brought charges—William May, Robert Johnson, Charles Guillou, and Robert Pinkney—be tried before him; then his case would finally be called. "The evidence in the course of these trials," the *Herald* reported, "is expected to bring to light many, if not all the proceedings of the celebrated exploring expedition, which have hitherto been like a sealed book to the citizens of these United States, who are deeply interested in all which occurred. . . . [T]he readers of the *Herald* will be furnished with a report of the proceedings day by day, which will be distributed all over the country." For better or worse, the nation's first significant exposure to the U.S. Ex. Ex. would be by way of the often vituperative testimony given during the five courts-martial, each held one after the other over the course of the next month and a half.

Lieutenant Samuel Francis "Frank" Du Pont was the youngest member of the court and no stranger to the antagonisms that could develop between a commander and his officers. Two years earlier, while serving aboard the *Ohio* in the Mediterranean, Du Pont and three other lieutenants had been placed under arrest and sent home after running afoul of Commodore Isaac Hull, who accused them of disrespect. Secretary Paulding would later exonerate Du Pont and the other lieutenants, but the 1840s would become infamous as a decade in which outbreaks between captains and lieutenants became distressingly commonplace. When the *Cyane* returned after a three-year cruise in 1841, nearly every officer was court-martialed, including the captain. Much of the dissension could be traced to the lieutenants' dissatisfaction over their prospects for promotion. Commodore Hull, for example, had become a captain at the age of thirty-three; in 1842 a lieutenant was well into his forties before he could expect a promotion, and he inevitably began to resent the "Old Man" on the quarterdeck. As he anxiously awaited news from Washington concerning *his* promotion, Du Pont was predisposed to look with sympathy toward the complaints of the Expedition's junior officers.

By the second day of the trial of William May, it had become obvious to Du Pont that something out of the ordinary had occurred between Wilkes and his officers during the four years of the Ex. Ex. "One of the witnesses examined today," he wrote his wife, "showed by his manner & tone, as well as the force of his words, that bitter & heartburning hostility which pervades the officers of the Exploring Exp. against their commander. The Court is crowded with them, hanging on every word that is said with an intensity of interest & feeling that I have never seen equaled. I have seen frequently excitement on shipboard, & in Squadrons, but the indignation which seems to pervade these young men, must have sprung from some cause not usual in the Service. They are the handsomest & most prepossessing fellows you can well conceive."

One of these prepossessing fellows was the accused's best friend, William Reynolds. After finally being sprung from the *Porpoise* in early July, he had rushed home to Lancaster, Pennsylvania. In Rio de Janeiro he had received a letter from his sister Lydia reporting that their neighbor Rebecca Krug "is still single and as much admired as ever." By the time he returned to New York two weeks later to testify at May's court-martial, he and Rebecca were approaching, if they had not already reached, an understanding. Before the summer was out, they would be married.

Wilkes had brought two charges against May. In addition to accusing him of disrespect during their confrontation over the box of sea shells at the end of the voyage, Wilkes reached back more than two years to when May had burst into his cabin after learning that Reynolds had been transferred from the *Vincennes* to the *Peacock*. May was represented by his brother, a lawyer from Washington, who claimed that the earlier charge should be barred by the statute of limitations, suggesting that Wilkes had only introduced it "as a menace to the accused." The court was cleared to give the judges the opportunity to decide on the protest in private. When the court was reopened, the judge advocate, a young naval officer named Charles Winder, announced that the first charge had been eliminated. For Reynolds, who could not help but take the charge very personally, it was a hopeful sign.

The trial hinged on whether May had spoken to Wilkes in an insulting manner, and for much of the next two days, witnesses were paraded before the judges to testify as to the general character of both May and Wilkes. May was universally regarded as an energetic and cooperative officer, although some, such as Samuel Knox, did acknowledge that he "is easily excited."

The vast majority of the testimony, however, concerned Wilkes. Lieutenant Walker was asked, "what is his general manner and tone of voice when excited or offended?—and is he quickly excited or offended?" Walker's answer was repeated word-for-word in both the court-martial records and the *Herald:* "In reply to the first part of the question, I would say, that, under such circumstances, his manner is *violent, overbearing, insulting, taxing your forbearance to the last degree to endure it.* As to the second part, he is capricious and often easily excited."

Knox may have had some criticisms of May, but they were nothing compared to his description of Wilkes: "His manner and tone of voice when excited was rather incoherent, and rude withal. He is quickly excited, and offended and his general conduct towards the officers is overbearing." Lieutenant Alden's testimony was more reasoned and insightful than most. When asked if Wilkes was only responding to provocation when he spoke to an officer in an offensive manner, Alden had an interesting answer: "No sir, in most cases directly the contrary; I have noticed that those the most attentive to their duty would fall under his displeasure the soonest; those that tried the hardest to do their best." As Alden recognized, Wilkes's intense insecurity meant that he inevitably felt threatened by his most capable officers; it was the loyal but barely competent ones, such as Carr and Hudson, who won his unstinting praise. Finally, toward the end of the day, Reynolds got his chance to join the chorus of the disaffected: "his tone and voice, when excited," he testified, "was very passionate, harsh, unofficer-like, and insulting. He is easily offended, and his general manner to his officers is extremely harsh and disagreeable."

As was becoming obvious to all, Wilkes had an almost preternatural ability to get under an officer's skin. But as Du Pont increasingly began to appreciate, Reynolds and his compatriots had lacked the maturity to effectively combat Wilkes's peculiar and highly sophisticated form of psychological warfare: "[T]here does not seem [to have been] a man of any experience or knowledge to contend with such difficulties, among them." Instead of strengthening May's cause, the cumulative effect of all the Wilkes bashing inevitably began to work to their enemy's advantage. Where the officers came off as young and overwrought, Wilkes remained, according to Du Pont, "perfectly self possessed," while his "broken & wretched" appearance spoke eloquently of the sufferings he had endured over the last four years.

The following day saw testimony from Wilkes and several of his more loyal officers. Hudson, Du Pont remarked, was "universally condemned [in the Navy] for the loss of his ship & his having waived his rank to go with Wilkes, of whom he's said to have been much afraid." Hudson's testimony would do nothing to redeem him in the eyes of his fellow officers. At one point he would insist, "I don't recollect a solitary act of rudeness or insult on [Wilkes's] part that I have seen or has come to my knowledge." But later, when asked if he had heard Wilkes "make use of profane and violent language," Hudson would lamely admit, "I think I have."

"I am more & more convinced," Du Pont wrote his wife that

evening, "that all the charges brought against these younger men are but trivial, or come from trivial circumstances, & those against Wilkes himself are not much more serious. He was a disagreeable, overbearing, & disgusting commander, but I doubt if he has transcended his authority, & the whole matter could easily have been arranged [through a court of inquiry] by the Secretary." The truth was that a navy secretary with a political ax to grind had used the petty complaints of five officers as an excuse to mount a series of courts-martial that worked to the detriment of not just Wilkes but the entire Expedition. The Ex. Ex. and the nation it represented had been ill served by Abel Upshur.

On Saturday, July 30, May's brother delivered his closing statement, known as the defence. This handwritten document has become part of the permanent record in the Navy Courts-Martial Records at the National Archives. Most of May's defence is written in one hand and describes in thorough but unexceptional detail what occurred between May and Wilkes regarding the box of shells. There are a few pages, however, in which the handwriting appears to be that of May's articulate friend William Reynolds. In these pages, Reynolds rises above the pettiness of the proceedings to address what was for him the real issue of the trial: Wilkes's failure of character. One paragraph in particular stands as a lasting testament to the feelings of the squadron's most eloquent officer: "Little did I dream when I volunteered for duty in the Exploring Expedition, how it would result for me. . . . But it is the quality of our nature to be fallible & its misfortune that we are too often the victims of deceit. I had not then learned the philosophy which teaches that he who would attempt enterprises of great command, must begin his government by laying its foundations in his own breast, in control of his own passions & that he who would survey the world must first sound the depth & shallows of his own character."

At the conclusion of May's defence, the court was cleared for two hours while the judges came to their decision. "As is usual with courts martial," the *Herald* reported, "the decision of the court cannot be made public until it has been approved by the President, the members being all sworn to secrecy." It was on to the trial of Lieutenant Robert Johnson.

✦   ✦   ✦

Wilkes had arrested Johnson for refusing to lead the expedition from Puget Sound to Grays Harbor. Johnson's lawyer, who all agreed was one of the best they'd seen in a navy court-martial, chose to ignore the fact that Johnson had improperly given away a government-issue pistol. Instead, it was Wilkes who was put on trial as Johnson's lawyer pulled apart his account of the confrontation between himself and the lieutenant on the deck of the *Vincennes*. It had occurred during what is always a hectic, noisy, and distracting time aboard a sailing vessel—the weighing of the anchor. As the men worked the capstan and the huge anchor rose up out of the water amid the deafening screech and clatter of chain, Wilkes and Johnson had squared off. For Wilkes it was all black and white: either Johnson was going to lead an expedition to Grays Harbor or he was going to be guilty of disobeying orders. For Johnson, it was much more complicated. Wilkes had inserted a clause in his orders requiring him to gain Passed Midshipman Henry Eld's approval before he dispensed with any more government property. In the navy, an officer was not supposed to submit to the judgment of an inferior officer, and Johnson wanted to discuss this aspect of Wilkes's order. But Wilkes was in a hurry; he was already annoyed at Johnson; and rather than talking it over with him, he placed Johnson under arrest.

Johnson's attorney asked Wilkes, "Have you during your experience in the service known of an instance of an officer receiving an order containing a clause similar in character to the one referred to?" Wilkes admitted that he had known of "no such instance in the Naval Service." But, he continued, the U.S. Ex. Ex. was unlike any operation the navy had ever mounted before. In fact, he had received "private instructions" directing him that "rank was not to be regarded on special duties on the Exploring Expedition." Johnson's attorney pressed Wilkes to reveal the nature of these mysterious instructions. Reluctantly, Wilkes told of the letter he had received in Honolulu from Secretary Paulding that urged him to put down "Cabals of discontented officers." Johnson's attorney demanded that the letter be made part of the public record, but Wilkes claimed "there were portions of these instructions relating to private matters between myself and Mr. Paulding." At the court's insistence,

Wilkes was required to make available only the relevant portions of the letter the following day.

"You are engaged in a great undertaking," Paulding had written, "which has excited the interest of the civilized world, and is looked upon by all your countrymen with great solicitude as one which, if successful in its objects, will redound to the credit of the United States. For that success you are in a great degree personally responsible, and are, in my opinion, fully justified in enforcing those measures which you believe best qualified to ensure the attainment of the great objects of the expedition." Later in the letter, Paulding specifically stated that "the fantastical claims of rank" were not to interfere with the Expedition's goals.

Paulding's letter would be reprinted in newspapers across the country, and at least one naval officer would angrily insist that the secretary's instructions were at odds with that most sacred of institutions—rank. No wonder the Expedition's officers had become embroiled in controversy; a voyage organized on such misguided principles was doomed to failure. It was a theme that would be returned to more than once in the days ahead.

Shortly after the reading of Johnson's defence on August 2, the judges turned their attention to the trial of surgeon Charles Guillou. Guillou was accused, among other things, of failing to account for the disappearance of a tiny metal mortar used in mixing medicines; he had also torn out several pages from his journal, claiming that they contained "private matter." In a blistering protest of Wilkes's charges, Guillou's counsel pounced on the commander's earlier unwillingness to divulge the full contents of Paulding's private letter as proof that Guillou's mutilation of his journal had been justified, but the protest was denied. As the trial dragged on, it was revealed that much of Guillou's refractoriness had to do with Wilkes's refusal to grant him a promised promotion. This did not absolve him, however, of having failed to obey several of his superiors' orders. Guillou admitted as much, insisting that "if he had done any thing wrong it had arisen from misapprehension of [naval regulations]."

Guillou was regarded by Reynolds and his friends as an extremely intelligent and capable officer, and expectations were high for his final defence. On Saturday, August 6, the fourth day of his trial, the great cabin of the *North Carolina* was crowded with spectators. Many of the officers brought along their wives to witness what was to be a lively and damaging attack on the commander of the Ex. Ex. But Guillou's defence proved a disappointment. The best the *Herald* reporter, whose sympathies were clearly with the officers, could say about the defence was that it was "somewhat long." Since Guillou would be the chief accuser in Wilkes's court-martial, it did not bode well for that trial's eventual outcome.

The court-martial of Robert Pinkney began with visual aids. One of the six charges Wilkes had brought against the lieutenant claimed that he had not properly followed his instructions when surveying the south shore of Upolu, requiring that the squadron return to the island more than a year later to redo the survey. Wilkes held up two charts—one based on Pinkney's flawed survey; the other showing what it looked like after it had been done properly. He also read a letter from Pinkney in which the officer admitted to destroying his journal in Tonga. But the testimony of the day was overshadowed by the announcement that at 9:30 the next morning, William May's sentence would be read on the quarterdeck of the *North Carolina*.

The following day the quarterdeck was filled with people, some, according to the *Herald*, "attracted by curiosity, and others by sympathy for the accused, whom they judged from the reports of the evidence . . . to be quite innocent of any disrespect to Lieutenant Wilkes, besides having formed the opinion that Lieutenant Wilkes was a tyrannical and overbearing officer, and very insulting in his deportment to his subordinate officers."

At precisely 9:30 the gig of Commodore Matthew Perry, commanding the steam frigate *Missouri*, came alongside the *North Carolina*. Perry was received with "all the honors," and Passed Midshipman William May was ordered to come forward. Standing in the center of what was described as "a wondering circle of Middies, Lieutenants, Captains, and Commodores, besides a goodly number of civilians," May waited as Perry unfolded the letter he had received from the secretary of the navy. To the surprise of everyone but the judges, May had been found guilty of disrespect to a superior and sentenced to a public reprimand. "The offense of which you have been found guilty," Perry read, "although it involves no moral turpitude, strikes at the foundation of all discipline. A respectful deportment is part of the duty of obedience, and obedience is the first law of military service. It is impossible, therefore, that the Department can fail to look with displeasure on the conduct of an officer who so far loses his self-control as to suffer himself to be betrayed into disrespect to his superior." The letter was handed to May, the crowd dispersed, and by ten A.M. Pinkney's trial had resumed.

As the day of his own court-martial approached, Wilkes did his best to ignore Upshur's repeated demands that he turn over "the *whole* of the Books and Instruments, etc. used by the Exploring Expedition." Finally, in early August, he responded, "your order will be obeyed the very moment I am relieved from the ominous and responsible situation in which I am placed and can attend to them in person."

It was during Pinkney's trial that the judge advocate attempted to force Wilkes's hand. While testifying about the survey at Upolu, Lieutenant George Sinclair requested that he have the opportunity to consult his journal. It was the moment the judge advocate had been waiting for. "I have a letter," he declared, "from the Secretary of the Navy, in which he says that he has sent Lieutenant Wilkes three orders to deliver up those journals, none of which he has regarded."

Since there was little the court could do about the matter that day, the trial continued, with Sinclair stating, to the amusement of everyone but Wilkes, that the Expedition's surveying instructions were so poorly written that "the more I read them the less I understood them." The following morning, Wilkes requested that he be given the opportunity to respond to the *Herald*'s account of the previous day's testimony. The president of the court, Commodore Stewart, reminded Wilkes that what was printed in a newspaper had nothing to do with the testimony allowed by the court. Wilkes blurted out that it was the *Herald*'s statement concerning his not having turned over the Expedition's journals that he wished to counter. Stewart repeated his earlier statement, to which Wilkes replied that "he cared little about what the newspapers said, *he was thickskinned so far as they were concerned.*" The following day, the *Herald* would report that Wilkes subsequently used testimony that had appeared in the newspaper to assist him in examining a witness, "thus acknowledging the *correctness* of the reports which the reporter understood him to impugn at the commencement of the proceedings." Wilkes had managed to anger not only the judge advocate and the judges, but also the popular press, and his own trial had not yet begun.

On Saturday, August 13, Pinkney's counsel, the Expedition's assistant surgeon James Palmer, read his defence. The trial had shown that Wilkes was willing to go to any length and pursue just about any course if it would strengthen his case against the lieutenant, a perfectly competent officer against whom Wilkes had taken a violent and inexplicable dislike. Over and over again during the Expedition, Pinkney claimed, Wilkes "tried to goad me into rebellion." But why? Pinkney had a theory, and it involved the issue of rank.

From the very beginning, the officers of the Ex. Ex. had recognized that the schooners were "of all vessels, most likely to distinguish themselves on the Exploring Expedition." "The history of the *Flying Fish*'s first Antarctic cruise," Pinkney continued, "and the subsequent survey of the mouth of the Columbia by Lieutenant Knox, justify all the hopes which were entertained of those admirable schooners." But instead of putting the *Flying Fish* and the *Sea Gull* under the command of his senior lieutenants, Wilkes had assigned them to passed midshipmen. "[T]he obstinacy with which he maintained a decision so injurious to the Lieutenants," Pinkney insisted, "and so little in accordance with his own solemn assurances, to be guided, in all appointments, by rank alone, at once annihilated confidence." Pinkney claimed that when the *Sea Gull* was lost off Cape Horn, it made even Wilkes aware of the injustice of his actions, and he placed Pinkney, a senior lieutenant, in command of the remaining schooner. "[B]y this act, Lieutenant Wilkes tacitly acknowledged his former error," Pinkney maintained. "The mortification which he seemed to suffer from this circumstance, is the sole cause to which I can trace his strange animosity to me during my subsequent service in the Squadron." It was a difficult theory to sell to a military tribunal, but it came as close as anyone had so far to unlocking the motivations of the Expedition's commander. Reynolds would subsequently send a copy of Pinkney's defence to his father back in Pennsylvania. "It is certainly an able one," he wrote, "& must have hit Wilkes very hard. Even thro' his *'thick skin.'*"

What Pinkney and Reynolds had no way of knowing was that prior to the Expedition's departure, Wilkes had also been denied what he perceived to be his due–an acting appointment to captain. Although many of Wilkes's subsequent actions were indefensible, the truth was that Paulding and Secretary of War Poinsett had failed to give him a rank commensurate with his responsibilities as leader of the Expedition. It was inevitable that a man of Wilkes's temperament would turn his hurt and frustration on his senior lieutenants, and it was with the dismissal of Craven and Lee that the unraveling of his relationship with his officers began. One can only wonder how differently the voyage might have turned out if the Expedition's young and insecure commander had been given the rank he deserved at the outset.

Wilkes's court-martial was scheduled to begin on August 17, just four days after the conclusion of Pinkney's. In the interim, William Reynolds intended to get married. "I do not expect this announcement to surprise you much," he wrote his father on August 14, "as I mentioned to you that if I could make such an arrangement, I should adopt it, without delay." Two days later, Reynolds and Rebecca Krug were married in Lancaster; Reynolds's sister Lydia was a bridesmaid. Almost immediately following the ceremony, the couple was on their way to New York City to spend their honeymoon at Wilkes's court-martial.

Upshur had ordered that Wilkes must return to Washington and retrieve the requested journals and documents before the trial could begin, but Wilkes's counsel Philip Hamilton claimed that the secretary's order required his client "to produce evidence to be used against himself on the trial, contrary to all the rules of law and evidence." The long journey to Washington and back would also "deprive him of his right to a speedy trial." Besides, Wilkes had already sent "a confidential agent" to

Washington to obtain the journals, which should be arriving in New York in the next few days. Reluctantly, the court agreed to continue with the trial.

Reynolds was dismayed that Guillou's charges against Wilkes and their myriad specifications were as long-winded and disorganized as his defence had been. When read in the courtroom, they made for a confusing litany of accusations: illegally attacking natives, excessively punishing sailors and marines, falsely claiming to have seen Antarctica, dressing as a captain, flying a commodore's pennant, refusing to forward Guillou's letters to the secretary of the navy, along with a host of other allegations. "We all regret that Guillou's charges were so *wordy*," Reynolds wrote his father. "We think he has weakened his grounds very much. We would have been better satisfied had he stuck to the Strongest part of his known wrongs, & let other matters alone. There are some errors in his dates, also, which entirely destroy some & weaken other specifications." Luckily, Pinkney had kept his charges brief and to the point, and Reynolds was confident that they "can all be proved."

On the second day of the trial, Wilkes reported that after a thorough search of his home, the man he had sent to Washington had returned with only a few of the requested logs and none of the documents. He was now certain that he had forwarded the papers to the Navy Department when the Expedition was still at sea. When Guillou testified that he knew for a fact that the documents were not in the department's files, Wilkes's counsel turned the surgeon's testimony against him by asking how he had gained such an intimate knowledge of the Navy Department. Guillou had no choice but to admit that he had spent close to two weeks at the department under the orders of the secretary of the navy "to furnish the Judge Advocate with information upon the subject of the accusations I had made against Lieutenant Wilkes." When one of the court's judges voiced his concern about possible "collusion between the Secretary of the Navy, the Judge Advocate, and Doctor Guillou, in preparing the charges," even Wilkes's detractors had to admit that the Navy Department had lent credence to his claims that a nefarious cabal had tried, and was continuing to try, to undermine him and the Expedition.

The case against Wilkes began to look even more suspect when the judge advocate appeared the following morning with one of the disputed log books under his arm and shamefacedly admitted that he had had it all along. Du Pont now wished for a "riper lawyer" in the role of judge advocate. Many in the courtroom—both behind the bench and in the gallery—were annoyed that the judge advocate had not stricken the charges related to the actions taken against natives at Fiji and elsewhere. Just about every officer in the Expedition, including Reynolds, felt that while these measures had been lamentable, they had been completely justified. Wilkes's instructions had stated that, unless it was a case of self-defense, he should refrain from any violent encounters. When the judge advocate asked Lieutenant Robert Johnson if the attack on Malolo "was necessary for self defense," he heatedly responded, "It was not self-defense. I was ordered to go on shore to revenge my messmates, who were murdered at the island before our arrival."

Wilkes's attorney Philip Hamilton recognized an opportunity to win sympathy for his client. George Emmons was asked to describe what he found when he first landed at Malolo. "On arriving there we found the bodies of Lieutenant Underwood and Midshipman Henry on the beach, close to the water. Midshipman Henry was entirely naked, and Lieutenant Underwood had on a pair of thick canvas trousers they could not tear off. They were both wounded in the head. All the crew were wounded, and one of the men was crazy on the beach."

Hamilton: "Did not Lieutenant Wilkes endeavor to restrain the seamen from killing the inhabitants of Malolo?"

Emmons: "He did."

Hamilton: "Have you not expressed a belief that Lieutenant Wilkes was moderate in his punishment of the inhabitants?"

Emmons: "I thought so at the time, and have often said so. I received an order from Lieutenant Wilkes on that day to cease hostilities and felt mortified, because I thought they had not been punished enough."

Hovering over the court-martial, but left unstated throughout the many days of testimony, was the close connection between Wilkes and one of the officers killed at Malolo. It was a rare example of restraint that was calculated to work to Wilkes's advantage, for all knew that his nineteen-year-old nephew had died on that beach.

While the focus of Pinkney's charges was much narrower than Guillou's, the incidents, when contrasted with the life-and-death exploits at Malolo and elsewhere, inevitably came across as petty and inconsequential. The near-collision between the *Flying Fish* and the *Vincennes* in the Tuamotus was rehashed over and over again as more than half-a-dozen officers testified as to whether or not Wilkes had been guilty of using the phrase "God damn it" when addressing Pinkney. In each instance, Hamilton would attempt to prove that the witness's testimony had been influenced by his dislike of Wilkes.

Hamilton had a more difficult time countering the charges of excessive punishment–particularly when it came to the four marines who had refused to reenlist in Hawaii. Passed Midshipman George Colvocoresses (nicknamed Colvo) told how he had taken the marines from the prison in Honolulu to the *Vincennes*. "They were brought to the gangway and punished with the cat, receiving, I think a dozen though not till they had been asked if they were willing to return to duty. And their reply was 'no!'" Hamilton asked George Sinclair which officers in the Expedition had spoken of Wilkes's "reputation for cruelty." "I have heard all the officers of the squadron, with but few exceptions so speak of him," Sinclair replied.

Captain Isaac McKeever–the officer who had persuaded Wilkes to take on his nephew as sailing master of the *Vincennes* before the squadron left for the South Pacific–returned the favor by testifying that there had not been enough time for Wilkes to try the sailors and marines caught drinking in Callao. Wilkes was therefore justified in whipping each of them more than the allotted dozen lashes.

Wilkes's attorney was most successful in portraying Wilkes as a tireless and hardworking commander. Assistant Surgeon John Fox claimed that Wilkes "devoted his whole time to the duties of the squadron, and did not reserve to himself more than five hours a day for sleep. He was irregular in his sleep, so as to injure his health; the length of time he went without sleeping was extraordinary." Even Wilkes's avowed enemies acknowledged that he was "remarkably attentive to his duties."

There was one charge that Wilkes had no choice but to admit to. When Overton Carr was asked if he had been ordered to replace Wilkes's coach whip with a commodore's pennant shortly after leaving Callao, Hamilton interrupted Carr's testimony to say that Wilkes freely acknowledged that he had flown the pennant and worn a captain's uniform. His officers would have to wait until his defence before they heard his rationale for elevating himself in rank.

On Saturday, August 27–ten days into Wilkes's court-martial–the trial took on a new life. That morning the judge advocate announced that he would devote the rest of the proceedings to proving that Wilkes had deliberately lied about sighting Antarctica on January 19, 1840. Two years earlier President Van Buren had staked the reputation of the nation on Wilkes's claim by officially announcing the discovery of a new continent. If Wilkes had lied, he had dishonored not only himself but the entire United States of America. "The Judge Advocate took his seat," the *Herald* reported, "arranged his papers, and prepared for the examination of the witnesses, with the air of one who was determined to use every effort to elicit the *whole truth,* if possible, on this most important specification."

The first witness was James Alden, the watch officer when Wilkes claimed he first sighted land. Alden testified that once the squadron had returned to Sydney, Wilkes had attempted to convince him that he had seen land on the nineteenth when he was certain he hadn't. It wasn't until January 28, Alden insisted, that they saw land for the first time. It was damning testimony, difficult to refute, but Hamilton did the best he could. He asked Alden why, on January 31, he had recommended that Wilkes abandon their pursuit of Antarctica. "We had been constantly beset by ice and in a gale of wind for the greater part of two days," he testified. "The ship was in imminent peril of being lost constantly. It required all hands a greater part of the time. The sick list was large; and the medical officers were the cause, by their reports, of our being called on for our opinion." Wilkes, of course, had overridden the officers' and medical staff's recommendation and continued on. Now that he had established that Wilkes had persevered in spite of his officers, Hamilton asked, "Did you ever hear any officer say Lieutenant Wilkes was a d—d lucky fellow, or words to that effect and that it was no further use of opposing him? Was not that remark made when in sight of land?" Although the question was labeled as hearsay and struck from the record, the implication was clear; Wilkes had been struggling against both the elements and his officers, whose hatred for their commander was so intense that they had been *disappointed* by the discovery of Antarctica. Wouldn't men so inclined be willing to deny earlier reports of sighting land?

Then Hamilton called the gunner John Williamson to testify. Williamson claimed that on the morning of January 19, Wilkes had questioned him if he thought he saw land in the distance. "If it isn't land," Williamson had responded, "I've never seen land." To many, Williamson's testimony seemed highly suspicious; at the very least, it demonstrated the dysfunctional nature of Wilkes's command. Instead of consulting his fellow commissioned officers, Wilkes had been forced to leave the quarterdeck and approach a gunner on the gangway.

But as the judge advocate proceeded to prove, it really made no difference whether or not Wilkes had seen land on the morning of the nineteenth. Three days earlier, on January 16, two young passed midshipmen had become the first to see what would later be recognized as the continent of Antarctica. Even though William Hudson had refused to acknowledge it and Wilkes had done his best to ignore it, the fact remained that these two young men had rescued the nation's honor–if not Wilkes's and Hudson's–through their discovery. The judge advocate called William Reynolds to the stand and asked him to describe what he had seen from the masthead on that historic day.

Reynolds: "I saw what I supposed to be high land on the morning of the 16th about 11 o'clock from the masthead, with Mr. Eld. We were looking at it an hour before we went below to report, and then procured a spyglass, and looked until we became satisfied that it was land. We went below and reported it to the officer of the deck, and Lt. Eld to Capt. Hudson. I could see the land from deck, but not so distinct as

ABOVE: Street scene in Honolulu.
From the Narrative, *courtesy Smithsonian Institution Libraries*

RIGHT: Standing at the edge of the crater at Kilauea on the island of Hawaii. *From the* Narrative, *courtesy Smithsonian Institution Libraries*

BELOW: The encampment atop Mauna Loa known as Pendulum Peak. *From the* Narrative, *courtesy Smithsonian Institution Libraries*

Warriors from the island of Tabiteauea in the Gilbert or Kiribati Group, where the Expedition once again attacked a native village, this time in retaliation for the disappearance of a sailor. *From the* Narrative, *courtesy Smithsonian Institution Libraries*

BELOW: The wreck of the *Peacock*. Here the ship's boats attempt to return to the wreck after delivering a portion of the crew to Bakers Bay, just inside Cape Disappointment at the northern edge of the river mouth. As one of the boats capsizes in the heavy seas at the bar, the crew of the schooner *Flying Fish* watches helplessly from just beyond the bar. *From the* Narrative, *courtesy Smithsonian Institution Libraries*

BELOW: Bakers Bay inside Cape Disappointment, where the *Peacock*'s crew sought temporary refuge. Sketch by Henry Eld. *Courtesy Beinecke Rare Book and Manuscript Library, Yale University*

Astoria, near the mouth of the Columbia River—the oldest permanent white settlement on the West Coast of the United States. The *Peacock*'s ensign is shown flying over the temporary shelters built by her shipwrecked crew. *From the* Narrative, *courtesy Smithsonian Institution Libraries*

LEFT: The interior of a Chinook dwelling. The Chinooks were the leading native traders in the Columbia River region. They developed a patois in their dealings with European and other native peoples that came to be known as the Chinook Jargon. The Expedition's linguist, Horatio Hale, provided the first written description of the language. *From the* Narrative, *courtesy Smithsonian Institution Libraries*

RAMSEY.

GEORGE.

Ramsey and his brother George, the two Chinook pilots who assisted the Expedition in navigating the treacherous waters of the Columbia River. *From the* Narrative, *courtesy Smithsonian Institution Libraries*

Fort Vancouver, located approximately
a hundred miles up the Columbia
River, was headquarters of the
Hudson's Bay Company.
From the Narrative, *courtesy*
Smithsonian Institution
Libraries

The Expedition's
officers attempt to
measure a giant pine
in the primeval forest
near Astoria. This tree
turned out to be
thirty-nine and a half
feet in circumference,
and was estimated to
be at least 250 feet
high. *From the* Narrative,
courtesy Smithsonian Insti-
tution Libraries

Northern California's Mount Shasta, as seen by the overland expedition led by
Lieutenant George Emmons from the Columbia River to San Francisco Bay.
From the Narrative, *courtesy Smithsonian Institution Libraries*

The *Vincennes* at the San Francisco bar. After a night of being pummeled by seas that approached forty feet in height, the squadron's flagship joined the *Porpoise,* the newly acquired *Oregon,* and, once they'd reached Hawaii, the *Flying Fish* for the passage to New York via the Cape of Good Hope. *From the* Narrative, *courtesy Smithsonian Institution Libraries*

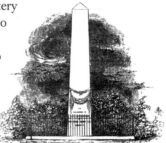

RIGHT: Cenotaph erected at Mount Auburn Cemetery in Cambridge, Massachusetts, in memory of the two officers killed in Fiji "while promoting the cause of science and philanthropy." Also listed were the two officers lost aboard the *Sea Gull* off Cape Horn; not mentioned were the twenty-four sailors and marines who also died during the Expedition. *From the* Narrative, *courtesy Smithsonian Institution Libraries*

Charles Wilkes in the years after the voyage, during which he lived in Washington, D.C., and oversaw the publication of the scientific reports and charts that would prove to be the Expedition's most enduring legacy. *Courtesy Library of Congress*

William Reynolds in the 1840s. Reynolds would be moved to write a seventy-eight-page critique of Wilkes's conduct during the Expedition that took issue with many of the statements made in the five-volume *Narrative* of the voyage. Although unpublished, Reynolds's manuscript, along with his two-volume private journal, provides a fascinating window on the Expedition. *Anne Hoffman Cleaver Collection*

ABOVE: The interior of the National Gallery at the Patent Office in Washington, D.C., where the Expedition's collections were displayed in the 1840s and '50s before being transferred to the Smithsonian Institution. *Courtesy National Portrait Gallery, Smithsonian Institution*

NARRATIVE

OF THE

UNITED STATES

EXPLORING EXPEDITION.

DURING THE YEARS

1838, 1839, 1840, 1841, 1842.

BY

CHARLES WILKES, U.S.N.,

COMMANDER OF THE EXPEDITION,
MEMBER OF THE AMERICAN PHILOSOPHICAL SOCIETY, ETC.

IN FIVE VOLUMES, AND AN ATLAS.

VOL. I.

PHILADELPHIA:
LEA & BLANCHARD.
1845.

LEFT: The title page of volume one of Wilkes's *Narrative. Courtesy Smithsonian Institution Libraries*

An admiral at last. Charles Wilkes, the Stormy Petrel, in 1866–hero of the *Trent* Affair, but also leader of the nearly forgotten U.S. Exploring Expedition. *Courtesy Naval Historical Center*

Another admiral. William Reynolds and his wife, Rebecca, who had honeymooned during Wilkes's court-martial.
Anne Hoffman Cleaver Collection

Charles Erskine, Exploring Expedition veteran and author of *Twenty Years Before the Mast.* On the back cover of the second edition, published in 1896, Charlie included this image of a hand clutching the colt, an apparent reference to the whipping that Charles Wilkes had inflicted on him when he was just sixteen years old. *Author's Collection*

aloft. I pointed out the direction of the land to the officer of the deck, Lt. Budd. He didn't seem to think it was land, and didn't send anyone to the masthead to make further observation. I waited on deck some time, expecting Captain Hudson would come up; he didn't come up, and I went below. We then tacked ship and stood off from the barrier, and there was no entry made in the log or notice taken of the report, much to my disappointment and mortification."

Judge Advocate: "Were you then, and are you now, convinced it was land?"

Reynolds: "I was convinced that it was land at the time, am now so convinced, and never doubted it."

The true goat in this account was William Hudson, who was subsequently subjected to a heated and humiliating series of questions by the judge advocate. Not only were Hudson's competence and intelligence brought into question, it was even suggested that he had willingly doctored his report to the secretary of the navy so as to corroborate Wilkes's claims. "The whole matter is *horrid* in a national point of view," Du Pont wrote a friend. "[M]y mind is clearly made up as to the *moral bearing & integrity* which the matter involves—though to me, Hudson stands if possible in a more unenviable light than Wilkes. Alden's testimony tells the whole story; & to my mind the 19th was the blankest day as far as log books & Journals can show, of the whole week or ten days previous to discovery."

But if Wilkes's honesty had been brought into serious doubt, the judge advocate was unable, in the end, to prove incontrovertibly that he had lied. When it came to the reputation of the Expedition, however, the damage had been done. Wilkes's hunger for glory had permanently tainted what might otherwise have been recognized as one of the most courageous feats of exploration of the nineteenth century.

After almost three weeks, it finally came time for Wilkes's defence. "The room was crowded with spectators," the *Herald* reported, "among whom were many ladies." One of them was Rebecca Reynolds, just back from a brief weekend visit to West Point, from which her husband's younger brother John had recently graduated. Wilkes had gone to the trouble and expense of having his defence printed—a pamphlet of "56 closely printed pages," according to the *Herald*. Wilkes was only able to read a portion of it before his voice gave out and he handed the pamphlet over to Hamilton. "This gentleman bungled so much in his delivery," Reynolds wrote his father, "and spoke in such monotonous & hurried tones that we wondered whether he could be reading a production of his own."

The defence began by relating how Wilkes had returned from the Expedition "to find that I had already been condemned in my absence." He went on to describe the circumstances he had struggled under during the voyage. "A cabal . . . existed," he asserted, "to thwart all the objects of the Expedition, which were not consistent with the ease of the gentlemen who composed it." "I did not spare myself," he continued. "I feel no derogation to my character to admit that I did not spare others when the public service was promoted." His problem with his officers, he explained, related to two diametrically opposed theories of discipline. In a blatant attempt to appeal to the sympathies of the senior members of the court, Wilkes claimed that he subscribed to the "old discipline of the service." "I avow myself, and shall ever be found, opposed to the new idea that authority is to be derived from the *steerage* and *wardroom,* and that officers are to be shown the instructions of their commander, and be civilly asked if they will perform their duty." If Wilkes was a throwback to an earlier and harsher era, he was proud of it. "[T]he work we have executed . . . is enormous," he maintained. "I attribute it to the discipline that has prevailed, and which the laws, rules and regulations of the naval service allow."

He claimed that the only charge that caused him "the least anxiety" was that of excessive punishment, but he was confident that it had been proven that the floggings "were absolutely necessary for the good order and discipline of the service." When it came to the discovery of Antarctica, he now chose to acknowledge and, in fact, acclaim the sighting of land on January 16. But in Wilkes's version of the discovery, Reynolds played no part in it. Without once mentioning his name or his testimony, Wilkes only referred to Eld's description of the sighting. "If ever the testimony of a witness was calculated to produce an impression on the court," he insisted, "it was that of Mr. Eld"—even though Reynolds had made essentially the same remarks earlier in the trial.

He also attempted to explain why he had been forced to rely on the testimony of a noncommissioned officer when it came to proving he had seen land on the morning of January 19. "Those who are unacquainted with the isolation in which the etiquette of the navy places the commander of a strictly disciplined ship of war," he wrote, "may express surprise that no interchange of opinion on the subject of land took place between myself and the officers. Such discipline being maintained, we had little communication." He branded the judge advocate's accusation that he had purposely lied about seeing land as a "wanton and unprovoked assault" on his reputation.

Wilkes saved his most creative arguments for the charge concerning his having flown a commodore's pendant and worn a captain's uniform. "I admitted the facts stated in the specification," he maintained, "but deny that I am therefore guilty of 'scandalous conduct unbecoming an officer.'" The navy regulations read: "No officer shall wear a broad pendant of any kind, unless he shall have been appointed to command a squadron, or vessels on separate service." "Mine was the command of a squadron," he insisted, "and that regulation, if law, is my authority for using the pendant." His argument was somewhat slipperier when it came to the matter of wearing a captain's uniform. There was nothing on the current books that gave him the authority, he admitted, but there were some new regulations under consideration that read, "When an officer shall receive an acting appointment to fill a vacancy from the Secretary of the Navy, in conformity with these regulations, he may assume the uniform, and annex his acting rank to his signature." What Wilkes neglected to mention, however, was that Poinsett and Paulding had specifically refused to give him an acting appointment. Still, given the trouble that the issue of rank was currently creating in the service, it was not difficult to appreciate Wilkes's need to find a way to assert his authority over the rest of the squadron's officers. For Reynolds and his friends, it was distressing in the extreme to think that what had been regarded as such an outrageous abuse of privilege during the Expedition might now be viewed as a mere bending of the rules.

As he approached the end of his defence, Wilkes could not help but make a few personal references. He slammed Upshur for making a court-martial out of what so clearly should have been a court of inquiry and for giving Guillou "unprecedented" access to the files of the Navy Department. He blasted Pinkney for daring to impugn the competence of the officers of the *Sea Gull* in his defence. "I might contrast the intelligence, attention to duty, and untiring activity of the lamented Reid and Bacon with all that is opposite in the character of Lieutenant Pinkney." He claimed that the judge advocate's conduct during the trial had revealed a level of "ignorance and prejudice [that] had it not been publicly exhibited could not have been believed to exist."

Finally, he appealed to the judges as a "brother officer," even as he wrapped himself in the American flag. "[A] bare verdict of not guilty is far less than the nation has a right to require at your hands," he insisted. "Its honor, its glory, the untarnished luster of its unconquered flag, have all been assailed through me. With you rests the power of vindicating that honor, exalting that glory, and wiping off any stain which these proceedings have cast upon that banner."

A few days after the conclusion of the trial, the editor of the *New York Herald,* James Gordon Bennett, delivered his judgment in an editorial. "Lieutenant Wilkes and his associates have exhibited some weaknesses," he wrote, "but it may be justly doubted whether any circumnavigator, after a four years' cruise round the world, ever returned home with fewer really tangible causes of complaint." If there was a villain in this trial, it was Upshur, who should have investigated the loss of the *Peacock* and the *Sea Gull* rather than wasting the court's time with so many trivial charges. "Mr. Wilkes is sensitive and quick-tempered; but did Columbus, or Cook, or Vancouver, Ross, or any other, come out as easily? This temper should be somewhat overlooked in his arduous and responsible duties. . . . No doubt Wilkes has made mistakes in some small matters, but has he not overshadowed these by his other manly qualities, energies, and conduct as commander of the expedition? Is not the whole exposition a disgrace to the navy?"

Reynolds was deeply worried about the fate of Guillou and

Pinkney. Although Johnson had been acquitted, word had leaked out that Guillou had been found guilty and sentenced to dismissal from the navy. But since he had performed such faithful service for the secretary of the navy, Upshur had made it known that if Guillou assembled as many letters of support as possible, there was a good chance President Tyler would commute the sentence. Guillou did just that, procuring letters from just about every officer in the squadron, along with letters from many influential politicians. On September 28, Tyler issued his verdict: "the sentence is mitigated by conviction to suspension without pay or emoluments for twelve months from the date of the sentence." Pinkney would also be found guilty and suspended from duty for six months. For Reynolds, the wait for word of Wilkes's sentence was agonizing. "I shall be in a perfect fever, until I know the result of his sentence," he wrote his father, "and I shall be like to die if the sentence be not a severe one."

On September 22, Upshur issued the verdict. Wilkes was found not guilty on all charges except for illegally flogging the sailors and marines. For that, his only punishment was a public reprimand. "The sentence will astonish you," Du Pont had written a friend, "but it will be no assessment of the way the man is estimated *as a man*." Reynolds and his friends were thunderstruck, but Wilkes was not about to celebrate. "Wilkes's extreme arrogance," Du Pont wrote, "& conviction that he would not only be acquitted, but it would [be] accomplished with a flourish of trumpets & a swipe at his accusers, has thus rendered his sentence doubly severe to himself."

Du Pont carefully studied Wilkes's reaction as the exhausted, sickly, and proud explorer listened to Upshur's reprimand: "The country which honored you with a command far above the just claims of your rank in the navy, had a right to expect that you would, at least, pay a scrupulous respect to her laws. The rebuke, which by the judgment and advice of your associates in the service, she now gives you, for having violated those laws in an important particular, involving the rights of others of her citizens, will be regarded by all as the mildest form in which she could express her displeasure."

"Wilkes was cut to the very soul by his sentence & the wording of the reprimand," Du Pont wrote. "He writhed severely under it & swears vengeance against Upshur."

The voyage had ended; five courts-martial had been heard; but as the Expedition's scientists and artists were well aware, there was still much work to be done. There were collections to be analyzed, reports to be published, but first and foremost, there was a narrative to be written. The battle for control of the Expedition's legacy was about to begin. For Charles Wilkes, it would be the battle of his life.

CHAPTER 15

This Thing Called Science

I N EUROPE there was a long-standing tradition by which the expedition's commander penned his own narrative. But Secretary Abel Upshur had other ideas. He had decided that a literary friend of his from Virginia named Robert Greenhow should chronicle the voyage. By this point, Wilkes had gained the support of a new and powerful ally in Senator Benjamin Tappan, a Democrat from Ohio and an amateur conchologist. During a dinner party back in March 1840, Tappan had fallen into conversation with then Secretary of the Navy James Paulding, who had promised some of the Expedition's shells for the senator's collection. Whether or not Wilkes ever provided him with the shells, Tappan took up the lieutenant's cause soon after his arrival in Washington. As chairman of the Senate's Joint Library Committee, Tappan was in a position to thwart Upshur's attempts to appoint Greenhow as author of the Expedition's narrative. With Tappan's help, Wilkes maintained possession of the officers' journals and was able to begin work on his book that fall.

But Upshur wasn't through with Wilkes yet. At the beginning of the Expedition, Wilkes had instructed his purser to pay him as if he were the captain of a squadron. Soon after his court-martial, he was informed by a naval auditor that he should have been paid as a lieutenant-commandant and that he owed the government more than twelve thousand dollars. "I was well aware it was done with a view of harassing me," Wilkes wrote. Not until years later, long after Upshur was no longer secretary, was the matter finally settled in Wilkes's favor.

Then there was the issue of his promotion. Shortly after his trial had ended, Wilkes mounted an effort to gain his long-anticipated captaincy. Arguing that it was general practice in Europe to reward the commander of a successful expedition, Wilkes pressed hard for the promotion. But Upshur remained unmoved. That fall, Hudson was promoted to commander. But not Wilkes. Not until the following July would Wilkes become a commander. He would have to wait another *thirteen years,* until September 14, 1855, before he was finally awarded the rank that he had felt was his due when the squadron first sailed in 1838.

Wilkes knew that his book constituted just a small part of the work that lay ahead. No one had anticipated that one voyage could have possibly generated such a massive amount of material. The number of ethnographic objects alone was staggering: four thousand pieces, a third more than the total number of artifacts collected during *all three* of Cook's voyages. Indeed, the ethnographic collection of the U.S. Ex. Ex.—including war clubs from Fiji, feathered baskets from California, exquisitely carved rattles from the Northwest Coast, fishhooks from Samoa, and flax baskets from New Zealand—is now thought to be, according to anthropologist Adrienne Kaeppler, the largest ever made by a single sailing expedition.

Even larger than the ethnographic collection was the number of pressed plants accumulated by the botanist William Rich, the horticulturalist William Brackenridge, and the naturalist Charles Pickering: 50,000 specimens of 10,000 species. There were also more than a thousand living plants, plus seeds for an additional 648 species. Titian Peale had brought back a total of 2,150 birds, their skins ready to be mounted for display, along with 134 mammals and 588 species of fish. The geologist James Dana, who had also taken over the department of the conchologist Joseph Couthouy, had collected 300 fossil species, 400 species of coral, and 1,000 species of crustacea, along with what was described as an "immense" number of duplicates. There were 208 "spirit jars" of insects and zoological specimens, along with 895 envelopes containing 5,100 larger specimens.

In addition to all the *stuff* brought back by the Expedition, there was an equally awe-inspiring amount of data. The Expedition's linguist Horatio Hale had amassed notebooks of observations that were unprecedented in their scope and thoroughness, while the naturalist Charles Pickering's voluminous and wide-ranging journal stood as a monument to the incredible diversity of the peoples and places visited over the last four years. Then there were the charts–a total of 241 of them, outdoing the achievements of any previous surveying expedition. Laid down in these charts, with a precision rarely before seen, were 280 Pacific islands, including the first complete chart of the Fiji Group; 800 miles of the Oregon coast; a 100-mile stretch of the Columbia River; the overland route from Oregon to San Francisco; and 1,500 miles of the Antarctic coast. But Wilkes and his officers had also assembled mountains of meteorological, astronomical, magnetic, and oceanographic information. "The results of the expedition were larger and more complex than anyone could have imagined," writes William Goetzmann, the foremost historian of American exploration, "and they outran the intellectual resources of the country."

In 1842, the United States lacked the national institutions required to store, analyze, interpret, and display a collection of this magnitude. In truth, even the most scientifically advanced nations in the world, Germany, France, and England, would have been hard-pressed to handle the returns of the U.S. Ex. Ex. But there was reason for hope. In 1838 an emissary had arrived in New York with the proceeds from the estate left by the Englishman James Smithson for the establishment of a new kind of institution. Beyond Smithson's stipulation that his money–more than half a million dollars in gold coin (worth approximately eleven million in today's dollars)–be used for "the increase and diffusion of knowledge," no one was sure what this institution should be. Some argued that it should be a national observatory; others said it should be a university, a library, perhaps a museum. A stalemate ensued and the Smithson bequest lay idle. In an attempt to force Congress's hand, former secretary of war Joel Poinsett created the National Institute for the Promotion of Science, the organization that hosted Wilkes's first lecture about the voyage. Central to Poinsett's ambitions for his fledgling institute were the collections of the U.S. Ex. Ex. If he could establish the

Institute as the collections' caretaker, he was hopeful that he could persuade Congress to assign the interest from the Smithson bequest to the Institute, which would then become, by default, the nation's museum.

Poinsett, with the help of outgoing secretary of the navy Paulding, arranged for the Expedition's collections to be directed to Washington, where he secured space in the newly built Patent Office Building. He then hired a curator and staff to begin the job of unpacking the Expedition's crates and preparing the specimens for display. But as soon as Wilkes arrived in Washington, he realized that the Institute had made a mess of the collections. Prior to being shipped to the United States, each crate of specimens had been carefully catalogued using a color-coded number and letter system that keyed the objects to the scientists' field notes. Since the Institute's curator was without the catalogue lists, he had no way of determining what was in each crate unless he opened it up and looked inside. Soon the Expedition's collections were in chaos. Titian Peale was horrified to find that a taxidermist had combined the skins of a male and female bird of the same species into a single bird. James Dana discovered that some of the more delicate marine organisms he had collected had been taken out of their bottles of preservative, dried, and then stuck with pins.

Even though the Institute's curator was fired in September and Charles Pickering was brought on to supervise the collection, Wilkes and the scientists remained leery. For his part, Senator Tappan believed that the Expedition's collection should remain a government-subsidized entity unto itself, and he secured the necessary funding from Congress for that. Pickering began to reassemble the Expedition's scientists in Washington. Soon they were unpacking the collections and preparing the objects for exhibition in the Patent Office's huge, 265-foot-long Great Hall.

Pickering provided an early and much-needed rallying point for the Expedition's scientists, but he had little interest in being the head of what was rapidly becoming the country's first national museum. Pickering was a scientist, not a curator. It wasn't the objects themselves that were important, he insisted, it was the knowledge that could be derived from those objects. In Pickering's view, the Expedition's greatest achievements were yet to come since a scientist's true role was not simply to collect and exhibit objects, but to study them. In July, Pickering resigned as superintendent of the collection so that he could continue researching the book he was planning to write about the races of man.

Tappan immediately replaced Pickering with Wilkes. As his conduct on the voyage amply demonstrated, Wilkes had no apparent fear of overcommitting himself. In addition to writing the narrative, he was also directing the production of the Expedition's charts—yet another enormous task for which he had assembled a team of officers that included Expedition veterans Thomas Budd, Overton Carr, Joseph Totten, Frederick Stewart, the artist Joseph Drayton, and eventually Henry Eld. Undaunted by his already considerable responsibilities, Wilkes took charge of the exhibition in the Great Hall of the Patent Office.

One of Wilkes's first acts was the installation of a sign over the hall's entrance that read COLLECTION OF THE EXPLORING EXPEDITION in large gold letters. He then went about overhauling the exhibits—moving the cases into areas of the hall with better light and posting signs that helped visitors find their way around this huge room of specimens and artifacts. Accustomed to the immaculate condition of a man-of-war, Wilkes showed little tolerance for visitors who insisted on using chewing tobacco in this hall of wonders. When the placement of spittoons at the base of columns did little to keep the tobacco juice off the floor, he hired a man, equipped him with a bowl of water and a large sponge, and directed him to follow anyone who dared chew "the weed." "No party could withstand the operation of the man with the sponge," Wilkes proudly reported, "and the custom was greatly abated if not wholly abolished and the Hall kept clean."

The Collection of the Exploring Expedition became wildly popular. Over the course of the next decade, more than a hundred thousand people made their way each year to the Patent Office. Ralph Waldo Emerson, who was in town on a speaking engagement, judged the exhibit to be, with the sole exception of the Capitol building, "the best sight in Washington."

In the back of the Patent Office Building was a greenhouse, where William Brackenridge presided over hundreds of living plants. Many influential Washingtonians, including President Tyler's wife, assumed that these tropical seedlings would be made available to them for their private gardens, but Wilkes instructed Brackenridge to deny all requests for plants. One congressman became so angered that he threatened to stop the Expedition's funding, but Wilkes stood firm. "The restriction was carried out," he wrote, "and our plants preserved."

In January 1843, William Reynolds, who had just spent his first Christmas at home in eleven years, traveled to Washington to lobby in Congress for the extra pay that had been promised the Expedition's officers. He stayed at the house of William May, who had just been promoted to lieutenant. The two friends traveled to Baltimore to attend the wedding of Lieutenant George Emmons. Reynolds reported to Henry Eld, who was then stationed in New York, that there were "a dozen Explorers who graced the occasion. We had a merry time, you may be sure. The very idea of seeing Old George spliced–to me, it was an ocean of fun." During the ceremony it became apparent that Emmons had escaped from the *Peacock* with more than his life, for there he stood, resplendent in the dress uniform he had "preserved with so much cunning & forethought from the wreck of the *Peacock*."

These dozen explorers had a bond that would unite them for the rest of their lives–a bond made all the more powerful by their shared loathing for their former commander. Reynolds undoubtedly knew that Eld was one of the few officers whose relations with Wilkes were almost cordial, but he could not help but vent his own bitter emotions in his letter. He revealed that he had run into Wilkes while in Washington and "had the Supreme gratification of cutting him dead" by refusing to acknowledge his presence. Marriage and the passage of time had done nothing to assuage the vehemence of Reynolds's feelings for Wilkes. He closed his description of their meeting with a denunciation that outdid anything in his journal: "God everlastingly damn him!"

Reynolds would never admit it, but Wilkes had taught him well over the last four years. He had taught him how to hate.

+   +   +

When he wasn't stalking the Great Hall of the Patent Office or over-seeing the completion of the Expedition's charts or finishing up a final round of pendulum experiments, Wilkes worked on his narrative. In addition to his own journal of the cruise, he consulted those of his officers and the scientific corps. He claimed to have been amused rather than angered by the many "malicious remarks" he came across, resolving that his own narrative would be "truthful and free from all vituperation." Inevitably, however, he could not resist the opportunity to settle some scores with his officers, particularly the ones who had spoken against him during the court-martial.

With Jane serving as his "amanuensis," he wrote at what can only be described as a ferocious pace. "I am afraid you're pushing it so hard," his sister Eliza wrote him in April, "[that] you are making a toil out of what should be a pleasure." By the winter of 1844, he was approaching the end of a manuscript that had swelled to three thousand pages. Wilkes considered it "a monument to my exertions in overcoming all impediments."

In late February, he and Jane were invited to attend a gala event aboard the *Princeton,* a new propeller-driven warship that had been equipped with an experimental weapon known as the "Peacemaker." Constructed out of wrought iron and weighing close to ten tons, this "Monster Cannon" had been designed by John Ericsson (who would later gain fame for his ironclads in the Civil War) and was being promoted in naval circles by Captain Robert Stockton. Stockton had invited President Tyler and his cabinet, along with a host of influential senators and diplomats, to a demonstration on the Potomac River, and after being entertained in the cabin with wine and champagne, they were all invited on deck to witness the firing of the great gun.

Since Secretary Abel Upshur had been responsible for funding this expensive vessel, he was offered a prime spot, only a few feet from the Peacemaker. Wilkes later claimed that he held "many misgivings" about the safety of this wrought-iron gun, and he urged Jane and their friends to watch from amidships. "The gun was fired," Wilkes wrote, "but instead of its noise and [the] whistling of its far [flung] shot, a cloud of the

blackest smoke arose & scarcely any report." The breech of the experimental cannon had exploded, hurling a deadly spray of metal fragments
into the crowd. Wilkes ran forward to offer assistance and soon discovered that Upshur and seven others had been killed. "He went to his
[grave] with all his Sins upon him," Wilkes wrote, "and I admit I could
not mourn his loss."

While Wilkes wrote the text, Joseph Drayton assembled the hundreds
of illustrations that would grace the Expedition's narrative—steel en-
gravings and woodcuts based on paintings and drawings by the artist
Alfred Agate, who often worked from sketches provided by the Expedition's officers, as well as the naturalist Titian Peale. The Library Committee had decided that the five volumes of Wilkes's narrative were to
be volumes of the highest possible quality. Bound in dark green morocco, hand-sewn and gilt-edged, they were to be stamped in gold with
the seal of the United States. The Committee insisted that only a hundred copies of the narrative be published, making them, according to
the estimates of one historian, "some of the most expensive books in the
history of American printing."

Recognizing an opportunity for personal gain, Wilkes insisted that
the narrative be copyrighted in his name and that he be given free use
of the illustrations in future editions. Since the government had paid for
the Expedition, as well as for the writing and illustration of the book,
many naval officers viewed this as an outrageous windfall for Wilkes, especially when his own commercial edition of the narrative appeared almost simultaneously with the publication of the government's edition.
However, when the matter was finally investigated by Congress, Wilkes
was allowed to keep his copyright.

Upon the publication of the *Narrative of the United States Exploring
Expedition* in the fall of 1844, many navy officers were shocked to discover that Wilkes had used an official publication of the government to
excoriate some of the very same officers upon whom the success of the
Expedition had depended. Lieutenant Alden, who had dared to deny
seeing Antarctica on the morning of January 19, was a particular target.

Wilkes even suggested that Alden was responsible for the death of Underwood and Henry. He also felt compelled to pad the book with information from secondary sources, much of it with little or no bearing on the voyage.

And yet there were times when the narrative would take flight, especially when Wilkes quoted freely, but often without attribution, from the journals of his more articulate officers and scientists. Even his own prose could sometimes rise to the occasion. His description of the battle to survey the Antarctic coast is riveting. His description of the burial of Underwood and Henry is wonderfully sad. But these patches of clarity only made it all the more achingly obvious how good a book this *could* have been. "A work of oppressive dimensions has been constructed," wrote the naval officer Charles Davis in the *North American Review,* "and the real narrative of the cruise, a story of surpassing interest, is crushed under a weight of irrelevant matter."

Despite its failings, Wilkes's *Narrative* garnered plenty of positive reviews and sold surprisingly well; fourteen different editions would be published in the years prior to the Civil War. The book would also have an impact on some of America's most important and influential writers. James Fenimore Cooper, an old family friend of the Wilkeses, would integrate information from the *Narrative* into at least two of his sea novels. Herman Melville would purchase his own set of Wilkes's work, and scholars have found traces of the U.S. Exploring Expedition throughout his masterpiece *Moby-Dick.* Melville appears to have been most taken with the book's illustrations. For example, his description of Ishmael's Polynesian companion Queequeg has been attributed to an engraving of a tattooed Maori chief in volume two. In an age before the widespread use of photography, the pages of the *Narrative* provided a visual link with the exotic world of the South Pacific (as well as Antarctica and the Pacific Northwest) that no other American book could match.

For many readers, it was Wilkes's description of the Oregon territory and California that was of the greatest interest. James Polk had won the presidential election in 1844, partly on the basis of the expansionist slogan "Fifty-four forty or fight," which as Wilkes had urged two years earlier in his repressed report to Congress, called for the annexation of the entire Oregon territory. But once again, events would transpire to distract the American people from a proper appreciation of the Expedition's findings. Almost coincidental with the appearance of the *Narrative* was the publication of another account of a government expedition to the American West, this one led by the army officer John C. Frémont. Frémont's narrative about his overland journey to the Columbia River and then on to California was everything Wilkes's wasn't. Ghostwritten by his wife, who had a gift for romantic, overwrought prose, Frémont's tale involved his readers in a glorious quest to unlock the mysteries of the West, and in the spring of 1845 Frémont gained the kind of fame that Wilkes had been craving all his life.

Just when he had hoped to command the country's attention with the publication of his own great book, Wilkes was distressed to discover that his past was about to catch up with him. Not long after the conclusion of his court-martial back in the summer of 1842, the four marines he had confined and repeatedly flogged in Honolulu sued him for damages. Not until two and a half years later, in the spring of 1845, would their case be heard in U.S. Circuit Court in Washington. The trial attracted yet another crowd of Exploring Expedition veterans, but this time, in addition to the officers and scientists, there would be a significant number of marines and sailors in the gallery. After eight days, the jury found that Wilkes had been "justified in all his acts save that of imprisonment in a foreign port and neglect." Two of the plaintiffs were awarded just $500 in damages.

The marines were not the only ones who wanted Wilkes to suffer, in some way, for his sins. After a long cruise in the Mediterranean, William Reynolds returned home to discover that Wilkes had maligned him and his fellow officers in his *Narrative*. Reynolds, with the help of twelve others, would spend the next several months preparing a memorandum to Congress demanding that Wilkes retract the slurs from future editions of his book. The memorandum would eventually be published along with a rebuttal from Wilkes that enraged Reynolds all the more, especially when the Joint Library Committee voted not to alter Wilkes's *Narrative* in any way. "[T]he only result of our appeal by

Memorial to Congress," Reynolds complained to James Alfred Pearce, Tappan's replacement as head of the Library Committee, "has been to afford the person of whose slanders we complained, opportunity to repeat them, with additional grossness, under the sanction of a congressional document." Reynolds would then embark on yet another refutation of Wilkes's *Narrative* that would expand to seventy-eight single-spaced manuscript pages and never be published.

In June 1846, the Oregon question was finally resolved with the signing of the Buchanan-Pakenham treaty, establishing the boundary between the U.S. and British Canada at the forty-ninth parallel. This compromise was supported by the influential senator Thomas Hart Benton, who happened to be the father-in-law of the explorer John Frémont. Benton took an active role in touting Frémont's accomplishments and as part of this promotional campaign felt compelled to question and criticize the explorer he viewed as one of his son-in-law's chief rivals–Charles Wilkes. In his *Narrative,* Wilkes had insisted that the mouth of the Columbia River was exceedingly dangerous. Benton, on the other hand, was convinced that the river provided a safe and accessible anchorage. In the summer of 1846 he put together a pamphlet attacking Wilkes's claims, and since it offered an opportunity to malign Wilkes, Reynolds, along with the other two officers from the *Flying Fish,* gladly agreed to contribute to the publication.

Reynolds knew better than anyone that the bar was a frightful piece of water, and yet for the purposes of the pamphlet he was willing to state that "By the erection of a few plain and conspicuous beacons, the sailing directions for the Columbia will be more simple, and may be more easily comprehended, than those for the principal seaports on our eastern coast." That the entrance to the Columbia River is regarded to this day as one of the most dangerous in the world is a disturbing indication of how severely Reynolds's judgment had been distorted by his feelings for the leader of the Ex. Ex. In response, Wilkes would publish a cool and devastating letter that used testimony from the officers' own journals against them.

The continuing battle between Wilkes and his officers would take on another even more distressing dimension. Soon after the death of

Underwood and Henry in Fiji, the officers had created a fund to build a monument to their fallen comrades. Wilkes's family desperately wanted the monument to be located at a cemetery in Brooklyn, New York, so that Henry's mother and sister might regularly view it. The officers, however, insisted that the twenty-foot-high white marble obelisk be constructed at Mount Auburn Cemetery in Cambridge, Massachusetts, since it was closer to Underwood's widow. This skirmish would go to the officers.

With the publication of his narrative behind him, Wilkes turned his attention not only to writing his own scientific reports, which included his two-volume atlas of charts and the volumes on *Meteorology, Hydrography,* and *Physics,* but to overseeing the publication of the other fourteen reports. It would become a lifelong endeavor. When Senator Tappan retired as chairman of the Library Committee in 1846, congressional funding for the reports became harder and harder to find. "I had more trouble and difficulty in securing the appropriation annually," Wilkes wrote, "than I experienced in the command of the Expedition."

A nation that had prided itself in its democratic scorn of book-learning was reluctant to acknowledge that publishing volumes about "bugs, reptiles, etc." was a necessary expense. When asked to vote on yet another appropriation to pay for the seemingly never-ending publications of the Exploring Expedition, one vexed senator complained, "I am tired of all this thing called science here." But for decade after decade, the U.S. Ex. Ex. would not go away. Wilkes's relentless and combative personality was perfectly suited to being a nettle in the side of government. He would often be as much of an annoyance to the scientists he was supposedly championing as he would be to the congressmen he hounded for appropriations, but it is doubtful whether there was anyone else in America who could have accomplished so much.

With the appearance of each new scientific report, the status of the United States in the international scientific community (once nearly nonexistent) would climb a little higher. In its reliance on fieldwork unhindered by the usual Victorian biases, Horatio Hale's report on languages broke new ground in what would eventually become known as the field of ethnography. James Dwight Dana proved to be the "racer" of the scientists, publishing four comprehensive and essential reports over an eleven-year period. His report on *Crustacea,* in which he identified more than five hundred new species of lobsters, crabs, shrimps, and barnacles, would reinvent the field. Charles Darwin offered Dana his highest praise, insisting that if Dana had "done nothing else whatever, it would have been a *magnum opus* for life. . . . I am really lost in astonishment at what you have done in mental labor. And, then beside the labor, so much *originality* in all your works." What makes this all the more remarkable is that Dana, who would eventually become a professor at Yale, was a geologist. When it came to his volume on geology, in which he offered evidence to support Darwin's theory about the formation of coral atolls, the response was just as enthusiastic. The German Alexander von Humboldt, whose expedition to South America at the end of the eighteenth century had inspired generations of explorers and scientists, claimed that Dana's work represented "the most splendid contribution to science of the present day."

Not all of the reports came as quickly or were as well received. Charles Pickering's long-awaited *The Races of Man* was judged by Oliver Wendell Holmes to be "the oddest collection of fragments that was ever seen, . . . amorphous as a fog, unstratified as a dumpling and heterogeneous as a low priced sausage." At Wilkes's insistence, Titian Peale's *Zoology* would be withdrawn prior to publication in 1848 due to its many taxonomical errors. Ten years later, once the volume had been overhauled by John Cassin of the Academy of Natural Science, the report was reissued as *Mammology and Ornithology*. It has since been called "a triumph of new science." The biggest disappointment of the scientific corps would be the botanist William Rich, who lacked the erudition and analytical skills to tackle a collection as big as the Expedition's. The botany reports would eventually be divided up among close to half a dozen different scientists, with the renowned Asa Gray taking the leading role.

Gray had almost shipped out with the squadron in 1838, but the offer of a professorship at the University of Michigan had given him second thoughts. In the years since, he had moved to Harvard and established himself as America's preeminent botanist. His high professional standing meant that he had little tolerance for what one scientist called Wilkes's "quarter deck insolence." As had been the case during the Expedition, Wilkes could be infuriatingly dictatorial and obtuse, but in just about every instance, the scientists finally succeeded in getting their way.

There is no question that Wilkes's unceasing advocacy of the Expedition's publications contributed to a growing realization in Washington that scientific pursuits such as geology, botany, anthropology, and meteorology were crucial to the progress of the nation. Almost in spite of itself, Congress began to see the wisdom and necessity of paying for expeditions on a scale that would have been inconceivable in the era of Lewis and Clark. As the country's population moved west, so did a succession of sophisticated surveying expeditions, all of which, in the tradition of America's first exploring and surveying expedition, took along at least one scientist. Between 1840 and 1860, the federal government would publish sixty works associated with the exploration of the West while subsidizing fifteen naval expeditions around the world. The expenditure for these expeditions and other scientific publications would be enormous, representing somewhere between one-quarter to one-third of the annual federal budget. Not even the race to the moon in the 1960s generated a financial commitment to science that rivaled the decades after the U.S. Ex. Ex.

Gradually, but inevitably, the Exploring Expedition would be eclipsed by the very historical forces that it had helped to set in motion. Foreshadowed by Frémont and made an accomplished fact by the discovery of gold in California in 1848, the interest of the American people shifted from the frontier of the sea to the frontier of the West. Instead of whalers, sealers, China traders, and Polynesian natives, it was now mountain men, pioneers, cowboys, and Indians who captured the American imagination. Even though the Ex. Ex. had had such an early and vital role in the exploration of the Oregon territory and California, the nation would quickly lose all memory of the fact that Wilkes and his men had been the first Americans to chart Puget Sound, the Columbia

River, and San Francisco Bay. Turning from the oceans of the world, the American people looked to the interior of their own continent, and in the tales of western exploration and conquest that would soon become part of the nation's mythology there was no place for Wilkes and the U.S. Ex. Ex.

CHAPTER 16

Legacy

A T THE OUTBREAK of the Mexican War in 1846, Wilkes was unable to secure a position that he thought commensurate with his standing in the navy and elected to remain in Washington. Reynolds was assigned to the *Allegheny,* a new steamship that would be plagued with mechanical problems. As he was forced to sit on the sidelines at the navy yard in Norfolk, his old shipmate James Alden took part in the capture of Vera Cruz and Tabasco; William May was wounded in action, while Reynolds's younger brother John served gloriously at Monterrey and Buena Vista and ended the war as a major.

After repairs were finally completed in the winter of 1848, the *Allegheny* steamed for South America. It was during this cruise that Reynolds's health suddenly began to fail. The constitution that had withstood four years of abuse during the Ex. Ex. fell prey to the unmistakable symptoms of tuberculosis: chills, fever, and night-sweats. His wife Rebecca had recently lost her mother, sister, and brother to the disease. "Wonder if I am to get the Conzumption and die!" he wrote in his journal.

In the years ahead, Reynolds's condition would continue to deteriorate. After a winter at a sanatorium in Florida, he requested a year's leave of absence from the navy, and in September 1851 he set sail for the place that he had called his "second home" during the Exploring Expedition—Hawaii. Rebecca followed a year later, and the couple, who would remain childless, spent the next few years on a one-hundred-acre farm on the island of Kauai.

Reynolds would eventually try to return to active duty on a store-ship in Valparaiso, but poor health once again required him to return to Hawaii, where he assumed the post of naval storekeeper at Honolulu. By now, both his parents were dead, and he had come into a modest inheritance. In Honolulu he met up with an old friend from the Exploring Expedition. In 1852 Charles Guillou resigned his commission to become head of Honolulu's Marine Hospital, and the two former explorers would live out the decade together in the tropical setting they had first come to know with the U.S. Ex. Ex.

By the summer of 1848, Charles and Jane Wilkes had become one of Washington's more socially prominent couples. In December of 1845, they held a party to celebrate the publication of Wilkes's *Narrative* that attracted some of the city's most distinguished citizens. But it was just one of the many social engagements that had become a regular part of their lives together. As if to compensate for their four-year separation during the Expedition, Jane was almost always at her husband's side. "[H]er gay & pleasant manner made her popular in the Society," Wilkes wrote. "We really had a . . . delightful time."

That summer, however, they decided to spend a few months apart. Jack had recently enrolled in the new Naval Academy at Annapolis. Jane and the girls, now seventeen and ten, wanted to spend the summer in Newport, Rhode Island, while Wilkes determined to take his youngest boy, Edmund, on a trip to North Carolina. He and Jane had recently inherited a portion of a mining operation near Charlotte, and Wilkes and Edmund would use it as an excuse to tour the South. After inspecting the mine, they would head north and meet up with the rest of the family in Newport.

For the trip, Wilkes purchased "a very nice traveling wagon" that he outfitted with shelves and boxes for provisions, clothes, and books. "Our intention was to travel from point to point," he wrote, "and picnic the whole way." After saying good-bye to Jane and the girls at the train station in Washington, they made their gradual way south, pulled along by two cream-colored horses. By August they had arrived in North Carolina.

Unbeknownst to Wilkes, Jane had fallen while changing trains in Trenton, New Jersey, and badly hurt her leg. A doctor in New York insisted that it was only a bruise, but several weeks later in Newport, Jane began to feel ill. She took to her bed, and three days later was dead–the apparent victim of blood poisoning.

Wilkes was at the mine when he saw his fifteen-year-old son coming toward him on horseback. "It was a damp muggy day," he remembered, "calculated to depress the spirits of any one." Edmund had picked up a packet of letters in Charlotte, and when Wilkes reached for them, he felt a sudden twinge of fear. "I broke the seals and my worst apprehensions were realized–she had died in New Port about a week before." Unable to read any further, Wilkes gave the letters to his son, saying, "We have lost everything, our best and dearest object in Life." Once back in their hotel room in Charlotte, Wilkes sat on his bed, unable to speak, as Edmund clung to him and wept. "My brain seemed on fire . . . ," he wrote. "I felt shipwrecked indeed."

In 1852, four years after Jane's death, Wilkes moved his family to a house on Lafayette Square that had once been owned by Dolley Madison. That same year he returned to Newport to tend to Jane's grave, where he planted some of her favorite flowers. Back in Washington, he realized that he was in need of a change. "I was very dispirited . . . ," he wrote. "My dear Girls were all in all to me, but they could not supply the want and prevent the desolation I felt, and it became evident to me that a new life was essential to my happiness."

Living nearby in Washington was a young widow named Mary Lynch Bolton, whose husband, Commodore William Bolton, had served on Wilkes's court-martial board. Bolton had died about the same time Wilkes had lost Jane, and the widower now began to consider the widow as a possible bride. "I often trembled for my success," he wrote, "and finally through my perseverance succeeded in being accepted. A new life at once opened to me." Eliza took to her new mother immediately; Janey was initially less receptive, but soon all of them had settled into a contented domesticity. Five years later, in 1859, Mary gave birth to a daughter; Wilkes was sixty-one.

✦ ✦ ✦

After more than a decade at the Patent Office Building, the collection of the Ex. Ex. found a new and permanent home. Congress had finally established the Smithsonian Institution in 1846 with the understanding that it would take over stewardship of the Expedition's collection. But the Institution's first secretary, the scientist Joseph Henry, saw the Smithsonian as a research organization, and one of his first moves was to refuse the Expedition's collection. Like Charles Pickering, Henry was for original research, not the maintenance and display of a momentous pile of artifacts that would require a large, expensive building and sizeable staff. Henry was part of a young group of scientists who were replacing the amateur collectors of the previous era, and he wanted to reserve as much as possible of the Institution's resources for the practice of new science—for laboratories and the publication of results, not specimen cases.

But there were some influential congressmen who were determined that the Smithsonian Institution would become America's national museum. In spite of Henry's protestations, bids went out to architects for a palatial new building. The winner turned out to be Wilkes's nephew James Renwick, Jr., whose ornate Norman design is still known today as the "Castle on the Mall." By 1850, it was clear that Henry needed an assistant, and although Titian Peale was a leading candidate for the job, Henry hired the much younger Spencer Baird from Dickinson College. Baird's personal natural history collection was big enough to fill two boxcars, and he looked with enthusiasm to the possibility of expanding the Smithsonian's holdings, particularly since the many expeditions into the American West were sending back a steady stream of specimens and artifacts to Washington.

Reluctantly, Henry realized that he had no choice but to surrender to the inevitable. In 1858, when the Smithsonian finally acquired the objects of the Exploring Expedition, the Institution's collection had already grown to the extent that the Ex. Ex. objects accounted for just one-fifth of the Institution's total natural history holdings. But no one could deny that the addition of the Expedition's collection added immeasurably to the Smithsonian's importance and prestige. The larger space of the Smithsonian's hall allowed Baird to expand and refresh the original Ex. Ex. exhibit, and much as Wilkes had done at the Patent Office fifteen years before, the words NATIONAL MUSEUM OF THE UNITED STATES were placed above the entrance to the hall. In the words of William Stanton, whose book about the Expedition stands as the definitive account of how science in America was forever changed by the Ex. Ex., "[the] Great National Expedition had created a great national museum."

There were other national institutions whose genesis can be traced to the Exploring Expedition. By this point, Brackenridge's plants in the greenhouse behind the Patent Office had been moved to a new structure located at the foot of Capitol Hill that is now the home of the U.S. Botanic Garden, while the more than four million specimens currently in the National Herbarium began with the dried plants brought back by the Ex. Ex. Soon after Wilkes's return to the United States, the Depot of Charts and Instruments and its small observatory were moved from his home on Capitol Hill to a new location in Washington that became the predecessor of the Naval Observatory and the U.S. Hydrographic Office.

Suddenly it was possible for a scientist to earn a living in the United States—something that had been almost unimaginable when the Expedition had first sailed. This may have been the Expedition's—and its leader's—greatest contribution. "Without Wilkes's incredible energy and Byzantine mind," Stanton writes, "the Expedition's achievements might have been no more lasting than the wake of its ships upon the waters of the world. . . . By putting science into government and government into science he had made it possible for the American scientist to live by his profession—like other respectable people."

But the Expedition's scientific impact was not wholly institutional. It had an indirect, but nonetheless crucial role in introducing Darwin's theory of evolution to the United States. About the same time that Commodore Matthew Perry was establishing diplomatic relations with Japan in 1853, the navy, with the assistance of the Smithsonian and the Coast Survey, sent out an exploring expedition to the North Pacific, led by Wilkes's former lieutenant Cadwallader Ringgold. In many ways it was the Ex. Ex. redux. Included in the squadron of five vessels were the *Vincennes* and the *Porpoise*. There was a botanist named Charles Wright. And like its great predecessor, the North Pacific Expedition would be controversial. Once in China, Ringgold began to act strangely. Instead of pushing on to the north, he remained in port, ceaselessly repairing his vessels. Finally, Commodore Perry, just back from Japan, interceded and, declaring Ringgold "insane," relieved him of command.

Wilkes's beloved *Porpoise* would be lost with all hands in a typhoon, but Charles Wright eventually returned to Cambridge, Massachusetts, where Asa Gray was given the opportunity to examine the botanist's notes. Gray recognized similarities between several Japanese plants described by Wright and those from the East Coast of the United States. The evidence seemed clear that these species of plants–from opposite sides of the earth–had at some point in the distant past come from a common ancestor. Several years later, in 1858, when Darwin sent Gray advance proofs of *On the Origin of Species*, Gray recognized that his own observations validated Darwin's work, and he would become America's foremost promoter of the theory of evolution.

Cadwallader Ringgold was not the only Ex. Ex. officer who would lead a major naval operation in the years preceding the Civil War. Soon after the discovery of gold in California, James Alden returned to his old haunts in California and the Pacific Northwest and expanded on the Expedition's original surveying efforts, this time under the aegis of the Coast Survey. In 1857–58, William Hudson commanded the steamer *Niagara* in an unsuccessful attempt to lay the first telegraph cable across the Atlantic Ocean.

During the 1850s America became involved in an English obsession: the hunt for the lost expedition of Sir John Franklin, who had sailed in 1845 in search of the Northwest Passage and never returned. In the years after Franklin's disappearance, many English explorers, including Wilkes's old rivals James Ross and Edward Belcher, led expeditions into the Arctic, their efforts encouraged by Franklin's widow and the offer of prize money. It had been briefly rumored that Wilkes would lead an American voyage to find Franklin, but his health and personal situation precluded it. Instead, Lieutenant Edwin DeHaven, the same man whose inclusion in the Ex. Ex. at Callao had so angered Wilkes's junior officers, led a privately financed two-vessel expedition north. In a conscious evocation of America's first Exploring Expedition, DeHaven was given an ensign from the *Peacock*. Whether or not the flag of the wrecked exploring vessel proved a curse, this and the next four U.S. voyages to the Arctic–all of which took along the *Peacock*'s flag–would be, in varying degrees, unsuccessful.

DeHaven's surgeon was a dashing, physically frail aristocrat from Philadelphia named Elisha Kent Kane. Even though the expedition accomplished little, Kane wrote a narrative of his experiences amid the arctic ice that became a best-seller. In the tradition of Frémont (or at least of Frémont's wife), Kane's book made real the weird and frightening world of a wilderness. He also wrote quickly, and he was soon on his way back into the northern ice in 1853, this time as the expedition's commander. Kane proved to be a far worse leader of men than even Wilkes, but he did not have to suffer the indignity of a court-martial. After being saved by a rescue ship commanded by yet another Ex. Ex. veteran, Lieutenant H. J. Hartstene (sent home by Wilkes aboard the *Relief*), Kane set to work on *Arctic Explorations in the Years 1853, 54, 55*. The public was enthralled, and *Arctic Explorations* became one of the biggest selling travel books of all time.

Once again, Wilkes watched as another explorer received the accolades that had been denied him. At least he could take some consolation in knowing that the U.S. Exploring Expedition was now almost universally referred to (when, of course, it was referred to at all) as the Wilkes Expedition. Still, deep down he knew that he had never achieved the fame he had originally envisioned for himself as a boy in New York. Then, in 1860, at the age of sixty-two, he got his second chance: the Civil War.

In August 1861 Wilkes was given what he craved–command of a vessel. The steam sailer *San Jacinto* was on station along the west coast of Africa, and he was ordered to deliver her to Philadelphia. Quickly reverting to his old, impetuous ways, Wilkes decided, instead, to go in search of rebel privateers.

He eventually made his way to the West Indies, where he learned that two Confederate commissioners, James Mason and John Slidell, were in Cuba, awaiting passage to England on the British vessel *Trent*.

By this time, Wilkes had been instructed to join Commodore Samuel Du Pont's impending attack on Port Royal, where the North hoped to establish a base of operations off the coast of South Carolina. But he had other ideas. He would remove the rebel diplomats from the British ship. That there was no legal precedent for such an act did not greatly concern Wilkes, who hastily consulted several books of international law and convinced himself that the seizures were justified.

On November 8, 1861, the *San Jacinto* lay in wait off the Bahamas. "It was a beautiful day and the sea quite smooth," Wilkes wrote. "The lookout descried the smoke of the Steamer, and it was then time to inform my officers of my intentions." Wilkes positioned the *San Jacinto* in the path of the *Trent* and fired a warning shot. The British vessel stopped, and Wilkes ordered First Lieutenant Donald Fairfax to board the *Trent* and return with the commissioners. Despite being slapped in the face by Slidell's daughter, Fairfax succeeded in arresting the diplomats, and the *San Jacinto* was soon on her way north. Wilkes described it as "one of the most important days in my naval life."

It was a brazen and illegal grab for celebrity, but it worked. When Wilkes arrived in Boston, he had already been declared a hero. A nation that was still reeling from a Confederate victory at Bull Run was desperate for some good news. Wilkes and his officers were whisked away to a reception at Faneuil Hall, where Boston's mayor extolled Wilkes for his "sagacity, judgment, decision, and firmness." As the joyous mob cheered, Wilkes affected humility: "I have only to say that we did our duty to the Union and are prepared to do it again." He would shake so many hands that day that his fingers became covered with blisters. "[A] pretty severe punishment," he wrote, " for the honor of a public reception."

As the city debated the legality of his actions (the author and lawyer Richard Henry Dana claimed the *Trent* was "a lawful prize"), there was a run on books of maritime and international law. Then it was on to New York, where the president of the city's historical society remarked, "It is, sir, your prerogative to make history; ours to commemorate it." When Wilkes finally returned to Washington, President Lincoln assured him "that I had kicked up a breeze, but he intended to stand by me and rejoiced over the boldness, as he said, of my act." But as an outraged British government threatened to enter the war on the side of the Confederates, the Lincoln administration was forced to hand over Mason and Slidell. Convinced that "my conduct had been correctly American," Wilkes "felt a glow of shame for my country."

Just as he had done so many times during the Exploring Expedition, Wilkes's subsequent actions would sabotage everything he had so far achieved. His new status as a hero won him the rank of acting rear admiral (marking the fulfillment of Mammy Reed's prophecy), and in September 1862 he took command of a "flying squadron" in the Caribbean that was to search out and capture the notorious raiders *Alabama* and *Florida*. The assignment had been forced upon Navy Secretary Gideon Welles, who had already seen enough of Wilkes's reckless arrogance. "He is very exacting toward others," Welles recorded in his diary, "but is not himself as obedient as he should be. . . . He has abilities but not good judgment in all respects. Will be likely to rashly assume authority, and do things that might involve himself and the country in difficulty, and hence I was glad that not I but the President and the Secretary of State suggested him for that command."

As Welles had predicted, Wilkes almost immediately began to make trouble for himself and his country. Claiming that he was without sufficient means to achieve his goals, Wilkes detained several U.S. naval vessels intended for other stations. He took particular delight in occuring the plushly appointed *Vanderbilt*. "This is the vessel for me," he wrote his wife. "She has speed and all the appliances for comforts I am entitled to."

He also repeatedly violated the neutrality of ports throughout the Caribbean, and soon Washington was swamped with protests from Spain, France, Denmark, Mexico, and Britain. The final straw, as far as Welles was concerned, was Wilkes's apparent greed. Instead of searching out raiders, he spent most of his time taking blockade-runners. Since each captured vessel earned him a significant amount of prize money, he was, he boasted to his wife, "filling my pockets" even as he served his country. But on June 1, 1863, Welles chose to recall him. In his annual report, the secretary chastised the former hero for detaining the *Vanderbilt* when she might have otherwise succeeded in taking the *Alabama*.

Furious at this public censure, Wilkes wrote Welles a scathing letter of protest. When Wilkes sent the letter to *The New York Times,* the secretary ordered an inquiry and eventually a court-martial. Wilkes was found guilty on all counts and suspended for three years from the navy. Lincoln commuted his sentence to one year, but Wilkes would never again see active duty.

When the war broke out, William Reynolds returned as quickly as he could to Washington. His health was still poor, but he desperately wanted to serve his country. He spent much of 1862 in a frantic search for a cure, visiting doctors in Baltimore, Philadelphia, and Newport. In October he was made a commander on the reserve list and assigned to the storeship *Vermont* at Port Royal. In the summer of 1863, he learned that his brother John, now a general, had been killed during the first day of the Battle of Gettysburg. About this time, Reynolds's health miraculously began to improve. By the end of the war, his weight had climbed from a low of just 123 pounds to 188. He was put back on the active list, and in the next ten years he would more than make up for the time he had lost to tuberculosis.

Promoted to captain, he was put in command of the *Lackawanna* and ordered to set sail for the Pacific. On August 28, 1867, 1,134 miles to the west of Hawaii, he claimed the Midway Islands–discovered just eight years before by American mariners–for the United States. With the advent of steam power, coaling stations became a priority for a nation with global ambitions. It was the first time, Reynolds proudly pointed out, that his country had "added to the domain of the United States beyond our own shores, and I sincerely hope that this instance will by no means be the last of our insular annexations."

Once back in Washington in 1869, he would be named president of ordnance; in 1873 he was promoted to rear admiral; twice he would serve as acting secretary of the navy. His meteoric rise to the top of his profession was capped by his being named commander of the Asiatic Station. His flagship, the 3,281-ton *Tennessee,* displaced more than the entire squadron of the U.S. Ex. Ex.

At some point, Reynolds was moved to return to the journals he

had kept during the Exploring Expedition. At the end of his private journal, he made a list of the officers with whom he had served. His friend
William May, he noted, had died in 1861; Henry Eld, with whom he
had first sighted Antarctica, had died of yellow fever in 1850, as had the
surgeon John Whittle; his friend James Alden had been named a commodore in 1866. Reynolds did not have the space to note that Alden
had served with Farragut at the battle of Mobile Bay in 1864. Alden was
leading the fleet in the attack when he saw a ship ahead of him hit a
mine (then known as a torpedo) and begin to sink. Instead of continuing on, Alden—as he had done on the beach at Malolo—hesitated. In
command of the ship behind him was Admiral Farragut, who shouted
out, according to legend, "Damn the torpedoes. Full steam ahead!"

Reynolds noted that Overton Carr had been "Disgraced during the
war 1864." The conchologist Joseph Couthouy was "killed 1863 in the
Service." A host of others, including Robert Pinkney and George Sinclair, had become "Rebels." His friend Charles Guillou had eventually
settled down as a pharmacist in New York City. In addition to himself,
a significant number of the officers would reach the rank of admiral—
Alden, Emmons, Case, Craven, and Lee. Then, of course, there was the
Expedition's commander.

Soon after the war, Wilkes bought fourteen thousand acres of land in
Gaston County, North Carolina, that contained an ironworks. It proved
to be a bad investment, and in January 1874 the property was sold at
auction. During this period, he took up, once again, the cause of the Expedition's reports. He was able to secure a small amount of funding to
publish his own *Hydrography* and a botany report, but when in 1876 the
Library Committee requested that it "be removed from its responsibility for the work," the publications of the U.S. Ex. Ex. came to an official
halt.

Left unpublished was a huge report on fishes, to which the noted
Harvard scientist Louis Agassiz had devoted the last years of his life.
For the most part, however, the unfinished reports represented no great
loss to science, even if Wilkes told his son Jack that his *Physics* volume
would have been the most important of the Expedition's publications.

This seems to have been yet another one of his hollow boasts. His *Hydrography* report had contained several misguided theories about winds and current, and soon after the Expedition's return, the British pendulum expert Francis Baily had informed Wilkes that based on the data he had sent him, he could only conclude that Wilkes had made some modification to his pendulum that had ruined his results. This meant that his heroic climb up Mauna Loa had been all for nothing. No wonder Wilkes had taken so long to finish his report on *Physics*.

Instead of science, Wilkes devoted most of his energies after the war to his own legacy. For four years he would write obsessively about his past. His *Autobiography* is a fascinating document in which his paranoia, vanity, and vindictiveness are given full play. To the very end, Wilkes remained incapable of controlling his worst impulses, and the big book that was to redeem his reputation stands as a monument of an altogether different sort, ending, in typical fashion, with a tirade against Navy Secretary Gideon Welles. On February 8, 1877, at the age seventy-eight, Wilkes died at his home on Lafayette Square. Many obituaries referred to him as the hero of the *Trent* Affair but made no mention of his having led the U.S. Exploring Expedition.

In the same year that Charles Wilkes died, William Reynolds suffered a seizure at Yokohama, Japan. He and Rebecca returned to their house on H Street in Washington, just three blocks from his former commander's residence on Lafayette Square. Reynolds died two years later at the age of sixty-three.

Unlike Wilkes, the Stormy Petrel who was always in some kind of trouble with his superiors, Reynolds ended his career as the consummate insider. The Navy Department appointed a committee of admirals, who, accompanied by a marine band, transported Reynolds's coffin to the Washington train station, where it began the long journey home. Once in Lancaster, his body lay in state in the full dress uniform of an admiral, with the ensign from the *Tennessee* draped over the coffin. A long line of carriages followed the hearse to the cemetery, where Reynolds was laid to rest beside his brother John. Like Wilkes before him, his obituary would speak of all that he had done during the Civil

War and after, but make no mention of the voyage that had meant so much to him.

It was left to Charlie Erskine, the cabin boy who had almost dropped a belaying pin on Wilkes's head, to have the last word. In 1890, he published a book, *Twenty Years Before the Mast*–quite an accomplishment for a retired sailor who had been unable to read or write when the Expedition began. Charlie had a series of cards printed up, in which he described himself as "one of two survivors of the U.S. Exploring Expedition around the world, 1838–42, under Com. Charles Wilkes." He also had his own personal collection of Expedition artifacts that included nine war clubs from Fiji that he had procured from the Smithsonian back in 1859.

Charlie's book revealed a side of the Expedition that would have otherwise been lost. For Wilkes and Reynolds, the Ex. Ex. had been about the officers who led it, not the lowly sailors who did most of the work. Reynolds was made livid with rage when Wilkes refused to treat him like a gentleman, but showed no concern for the sailors who were whipped on an almost daily basis. When a reform movement threatened to do away with corporal punishment in the 1840s, Reynolds wrote the Navy Department, insisting that an officer's "power resides alone in the prompt & certain application of the lash."

Charlie, needless to say, had a very different attitude toward the lash, and *Twenty Years Before the Mast* stands as a testament to the countless sailors who suffered in anonymity. "As the sailor lives, so he dies," he wrote in the final chapter. "There is no audience but those who share his dangers. He lies down afar from home and friends, with no one to tell to the world the story of his battles, so bravely fought, though lost; no one to witness his suffering, or note the courage with which he faced his last moment."

With the publication of his book, Charlie had ensured that at least one sailor's story would not be forgotten. Fifty-three years after Wilkes had callously whipped this handsome and trusting boy, a kind of justice had at last been served.

Epilogue

FOR YEARS TO COME mariners around the world would rely on the charts of the U.S. Exploring Expedition. The British and French governments incorporated Wilkes surveys into the charts issued by their hydrographic offices. As late as the 1920s, the U.S. Navy was still using Wilkes charts of the Pacific. During World War II, when battle plans were being drawn up for the invasion of a speck of coral known as Tarawa, it was discovered that the only available chart of the island was made by the Ex. Ex. more than a hundred years before.

And yet, when it came to what Wilkes considered "the greatest discovery of the century," his efforts were almost universally dismissed well into the 1900s. In truth, Wilkes hadn't technically discovered Antarctica since British and American sealers had glimpsed, and even ventured on, the Antarctic Peninsula as early as the 1820s, if not before. What Wilkes had done was much more difficult. By mapping a 1,500-mile section of coastline, he became the first to establish the continental proportions of the land to the south.

Unfortunately, the controversy surrounding Wilkes's court-martial made it impossible for his own country to take any pride in his accomplishment. Then, in 1847, Wilkes's British rival James Ross published a narrative of his own voyage south. Taking up where the doubts raised by the court-martial had left off, Ross questioned whether Wilkes had really found a continent. "I feel myself quite unable to determine in a satisfactory manner," he wrote, "how much of the land was really seen by him with the degree of certainty that gives indisputable authority to discovery." Ross was willing to credit Dumont d'Urville (who died in a tragic train accident soon after his return to Paris) with having set foot on land (whether it was a continent or an island remained to be seen), but he refused to acknowledge any of Wilkes's claims.

With the exception of the Expedition's own charts, no British or American maps referred to Wilkes's findings throughout the 1860s. If it hadn't been for German mapmakers, who were the only ones to record the American claims and adopted the name of Wilkes Land, all trace of Wilkes's achievement might have been lost. Even as a series of British and Australian explorers—including Robert Scott, Ernest Shackleton, and Douglas Mawson—walked across the continent that Ross had thought did not exist, Wilkes received no credit for his discoveries. What these explorers only gradually came to appreciate was the difficulty of judging distances in the clear, dust-free atmosphere of Antarctica. Objects that look just three to four miles away can be as many as thirty to forty miles distant. There is also the phenomenon of "looming," in which a temporary refraction of light makes it possible to see objects that are far below the horizon—sometimes as many as two hundred miles away. When in 1929 Mawson returned to a section of Wilkes Land that he had charted the year before, he was dismayed to discover that he had been off by as many as seventy miles in latitude. By this time the coordinates of many of Ross's land-sightings had also proved in error, and Mawson would begrudgingly acknowledge that Wilkes "had come in for an undue amount of censure."

Finally, in 1958–59, the Australian National Antarctic Research Expedition made an aerial reconnaissance of a portion of Wilkes Land. As was to be expected, it was found that Wilkes had consistently underestimated the distance between the *Vincennes* and the coast. However, where he had been able to get close to land, in the case of the Knox Coast and Piner Bay, his chart had been dead on. What impressed the Australians was the accuracy of Wilkes's estimate of longitude—an extremely difficult thing to calculate at high latitude, not to mention aboard a storm-tossed sailing vessel. The photographic evidence also indicated that Wilkes had faithfully distinguished between what he took to be the overall contours of a continent and where he had actually seen land. Contrary to Ross's insistence that his chart was nothing more than a fabrication, Wilkes was found to have "adhered to high standards of cartographic integrity."

"After more than a century," writes Antarctic expert Kenneth Bertrand, "during which disparagement was most often his reward, there can now no longer be any doubt of the greatness of his achievement."

Wilkes had been his own worst enemy. His aching need for praise and control drove him to some astounding accomplishments but had also led him to commit acts that earned him almost universal censure and scorn. Wilkes needed, more than anything else, someone to rein him in, to be, as he described his wife Jane, "my moderation." Once the Expedition left Norfolk, Wilkes found himself alone with the torment and compulsions that had seethed within him since childhood. Without Jane to domesticate his demons, he could no longer play the part of the talented, passionate man of good feeling–the role that had won him the affection and loyalty of Reynolds and his fellow officers. He must be who he actually was–a scared and needy lieutenant of very limited experience and nautical ability and yet who yearned to be a hero. If he had any hope of seeing the Expedition to its conclusion, he must reinvent himself. The leader who emerged from the breakdown in Rio de Janeiro was almost unrecognizable to his officers: a haughty, unfeeling tyrant who abused and mocked the very men he had once treated as his friends.

But would the Expedition have been more successful if it had been led by a cooler, more capable captain? Probably not. The scientist James Dana was in a unique position to judge such things. Prior to the Expedition, he had served as a teacher to midshipmen in the Mediterranean and was therefore highly knowledgeable when it came to the workings of the U.S Navy. He had had four years to observe Wilkes as a leader and several more to see how he supervised the publication of the Expedition's reports when he answered his friend Asa Gray's queries about his former commander: "Wilkes although overbearing with his officers, and conceited, exhibited through the cruise a wonderful degree of energy and was bold even to rashness in many of his explorations. I know so well what Naval officers very generally are, that I much doubt if with any commander that could have been selected, we should have fared better, or lived together more harmoniously and I am confident that the navy does not contain a more daring explorer, or driving officer."

It wasn't the Expedition or its long and fruitful aftermath that went wrong; it was what happened immediately following its return to the United States. If Wilkes had been able to handle the return in a more calculated and tactful manner, everything might have worked out differently. Even at that late hour, even after all the outrages he had committed, it would have still been possible for him to save the Expedition's reputation. But for Wilkes to have accomplished this late-inning rescue, he would have needed the right kind of advice—especially in the last critical months prior to the *Vincennes*'s arrival in New York. There are strong indications that as the survey of the Columbia River drew to a close, Wilkes began to realize that he needed just this kind of assistance, and the person he turned to was William Reynolds.

Reynolds possessed all the sensitivity, charm, and discretion that Wilkes lacked. He was also a talented writer. With Reynolds acting as Wilkes's partner rather than foe, the Expedition might have had the reception and the narrative it deserved. But it was not to be. If it was not too late to save the Expedition, it was too late to reclaim Wilkes's and Reynolds's friendship. And so, on a rainy summer night on the Columbia River, as Wilkes and a jacketless Reynolds stood side-by-side on the deck of the *Flying Fish*, the United States Exploring Expedition began its long, sure slide into obscurity.

NOTES

ABBREVIATIONS

ACW *Autobiography of Rear Admiral Charles Wilkes,* Department of the Navy, 1978

DU Duke University

FMC Franklin and Marshall College

KSHS Kansas State Historical Society

LOC Library of Congress

LRWEE Letters Relating to the Wilkes Exploring Expedition, Rolls 1–7 of the National Archives microfilm, Records Relating to the United States Exploring Expedition Under the Command of Lt. Charles Wilkes, 1836–1842 (Microcopy 75)

MV *Magnificent Voyagers: The U.S. Exploring Expedition, 1838–1842,* Smithsonian Institution Press, 1985

NA National Archives

For anyone wanting to know more about the U.S. Exploring Expedition, the best place to start is William Stanton's *The Great United States Exploring Expedition.* Wonderfully written and researched, Stanton's book approaches the Expedition in terms of its contribution to the rise of science in America. *Magnificent Voyagers,* an illustrated catalogue of a 1985 exhibition at the Smithsonian Institution edited by Herman J. Viola and Carolyn Margolis, is much more than a catalogue, containing articles that analyze the Expedition from a multitude of perspectives. An earlier book, David B. Tyler's *The Wilkes Expedition,* is also useful, as is the important group of essays about the Expedition published by the American Philosophical Society in *Centenary Celebration: The*

Wilkes Exploring Expedition of the United States Navy, 1838–1842. Daniel Henderson's biography of Wilkes, *Hidden Coasts,* makes good use of Wilkes's own writings but seems reluctant to criticize or evaluate its subject. William H. Goetzmann's *New Lands, New Men: America and the Second Great Age of Discovery* investigates the impulse to explore by sea and land that culminated in the Expedition and the many U.S. expeditions to the West that followed. Echoing observations made by William Stanton in *The Great United States Exploring Expedition* as well as Stanton's earlier and seminal investigation of science and race in nineteenth-century America, *The Leopard's Spots,* Barry Alan Joyce assesses a portion of the scientific legacy of the Expedition in *The Shaping of American Ethnography: The Wilkes Exploring Expedition, 1838–1842.* Alan Gurney's *The Race to the White Continent: Voyages to the Antarctic* examines the Exploring Expedition in the context of the other European voyages to Antarctica, while Kenneth Bertrand's *Americans in Antarctica* and Philip Mitterling's *America in the Antarctic to 1840* are also essential reading. Frances Barkan's *The Wilkes Expedition: Puget Sound and the Oregon Country* provides an excellent account of the Expedition's accomplishments in the Pacific Northwest.

Only a hundred copies of the fifteen published scientific reports of the Exploring Expedition were printed by the U.S. government. The Smithsonian Institution Libraries has recently digitized *all* these publications, a mammoth undertaking that makes these exceedingly rare works available to a general audience for the first time. To view these fascinating, stunningly illustrated reports, as well as the original edition of Wilkes's *Narrative,* go to http://www.sil.si.edu/digitalcollections/usexex/.

Wilkes's five-volume narrative of the Expedition is a padded, uneven read, but parts of it, particularly his description of the assault on Antarctica, are exhilarating. Wilkes's personality is best revealed in his not always reliable, but always self-serving *Autobiography of Rear Admiral Charles Wilkes* (ACW). William Reynolds is well served by *Voyage to the Southern Ocean,* a collection of the letters he wrote home during the Expedition edited by Anne Hoffman Cleaver, a Reynolds descendant, and E. Jeffrey Stann. Reynolds's public and private notebooks from the Expedition, as well as his letters written during the Expedition, are at Franklin and Marshall College (FMC). An edition of Reynolds's private journal, edited by myself and Thomas Philbrick, will be published by Penguin in 2004.

The scientist and artist Titian Peale's journal has been published in a magnificently illustrated volume edited by Jessie Poesch, while the officer George Colvocoresses and the sailors Joseph Clark and Charles Erskine each published accounts during their lifetimes. Just a year after the return of the Expedition, the surgeon James Palmer published a narrative poem titled *Thulia: A Tale of the Antarctic*, about the exploits of the schooner *Flying Fish*, which also includes a prose account of the cruise.

Anyone interested in braving the massive amount of unpublished material connected with the Expedition should consult Daniel C. Haskell's indispensable *The United States Exploring Expedition, 1838–1842 and Its Publications 1844–1874*, published by The New York Public Library in 1942. Most of the existing officers' logs, letters, and courts-martial records are at the National Archives (NA) in Washington, D.C., although the Library of Congress and the Smithsonian Institution also have much Ex. Ex. material. The twenty-three officer journals at the National Archives are available on microfilm as Records Relating to the United States Exploring Expedition Under the Command of Lt. Charles Wilkes, 1836–1842 (Microcopy 75), Rolls 7–25. A good number of the officers retrieved their journals at some point after the Expedition; as a result, many of the journals are now scattered among various repositories, the locations of which are listed in the bibliography; these journals are also available on microfilm. The courts-martial records related to the Expedition are also available on microfilm from the National Archives, Microcopy 75, Rolls 26 and 27.

In 1978 an important cache of Wilkes material was donated to Duke University. Used here for the first time in a book-length examination of the Ex. Ex., the Wilkes Family Papers at Duke contain dozens of letters Wilkes wrote to his wife Jane during the Expedition, as well as letters from Jane, their children, Wilkes's brother Henry, his brother-in-law James Renwick and others. Other important collections of Wilkes papers are at the Kansas State Historical Society (KSHS), the Library of Congress (LOC), and the Wisconsin Historical Society.

PREFACE: YOUNG AMBITION

My thanks to Jane Walsh, an anthropologist at the Smithsonian Institution, for providing me with the total weight of the Expedition's collections. I have inherited the concept of the sea as America's first frontier from my father, Thomas Philbrick, whose *James Fenimore Cooper and the Development of American Sea Fiction* describes how the country's fascination with the sea was reflected in the popular literature of the first half of the nineteenth century. See also my foreword to *American Sea Writing: A Literary Anthology*, edited by Peter Neill, Library of America, 2000, pp. xiii–xvii. I am also indebted to Daniel Boorstin's concept of "sea paths to everywhere" in *The Discoverers*, particularly the chapter "A World of Oceans," pp. 256–66. As John Noble Wilford points out in *The Mapmakers,* Lewis and Clark were instructed to locate "the most direct and practicable water communication across the continent for the purpose of commerce," p. 225. For my comparison of Cook's second voyage to the voyages of earlier explorers, I am indebted to Boorstin's *The Discoverers,* pp. 280–89. For an account of British exploration before and immediately following Cook, see Glyndwr Williams's "To Make Discoveries of Countries Hitherto Unknown: The Admiralty and Pacific Exploration in the Eighteenth Century," in *Pacific Empires,* edited by Alan Frost and Jane Samson, pp. 13–31. William Goetzmann provides the statistics concerning the number of European expeditions to the Pacific in *New Lands, New Men,* p. 268.

For an excellent overview of the many accomplishments of the U.S. Ex. Ex., see Herman Viola's "The Story of the U.S. Exploring Expedition" in MV, pp. 9–23. In an 1841 report, Secretary of the Navy Abel Upshur stated his ambitious goal to expand the U.S. Navy until it was at least "half the naval force of the strongest maritime power in the world." At that time the American navy included eleven ships of the line, seventeen frigates, eighteen sloops, two brigs, nine schooners, three storeships, and three receiving ships in commission. See Claude Hall's *Abel Parker Upshur,* p. 127. For information on China's and Portugal's exploratory efforts, see Boorstin's *The Discoverers,* pp. 156–95. Gavin Menzies provides an intriguing, if perhaps overstated, account of Chinese exploration in *1421: The Year China Discovered America* (2003).

Secretary of the Navy James Paulding's instructions outlining the intended destinations of the Ex. Ex. are in volume one of Charles Wilkes's *Narrative,* pp. xiii–xxiii. According to Geoffrey Smith in "Charles Wilkes" in *Makers of American Diplomacy,* edited by Frank Merli et al., the Ex. Ex. was the "last global voyage wholly dependent upon sail," p. 14.

William Reynolds's enthusiastic words about the Ex. Ex. are from the October 29, 1838, entry of his private journal. On the Lewis and Clark Expedition as a model of good leadership, see James Ronda's "'A Most Perfect Harmony': The Lewis and Clark Expedition as an Exploration Community" in *Voyages of Discovery,* edited by James Ronda, pp. 77–88. William Reynolds's enthusiastic remarks about the Expedition and Wilkes appear in his private journal, recorded on October 29, 1838.

Samuel Clemens's memories of Wilkes the explorer were prompted by his reading the obituary of Wilkes's widow, Mary, in 1906; in *Mark Twain's Autobiography,* vol. II, pp. 120–21. Thoreau's reference to the Expedition appears in the final chapter of *Walden,* p. 560, in *The Portable Thoreau,* edited by Carl Bode,

Penguin, 1977. For an examination of Thoreau's wide reading in the literature of exploration, see John Aldrich Christie's *Thoreau as World Traveler.* In the pamphlet *The Stormy Petrel and the Whale,* David Jaffé argues that Wilkes was a major inspiration for Ahab in *Moby-Dick.* Jaffé cites Melville's reference to "young ambition," p. 21, and elsewhere says of Wilkes, "Clearly, here was a man who could have been a great national hero for any one of a dozen incredible exploits. But the hero was a tarnished one. Melville must have perceived in a sudden flash that here was a great man with a tragic flaw—a will that was unbending to the point of fanaticism or monomania," p. 18.

CHAPTER I: **THE GREAT SOUTH SEA**

For an account of how the names "South Sea" and "Pacific" came into being, see Ernest Dodge's *New England and the South Seas,* p. 10; Herman Melville also provides an interesting version of this naming process in his lecture "The South Seas," in *The Piazza Tales and Other Prose Pieces, 1839–1860,* pp. 411–12. In the *Autobiography of Rear Admiral Charles Wilkes, U.S. Navy, 1798–1877* (subsequently referred to as ACW), Wilkes writes that "the adventures of discoveries" had possessed him since "my early boyhood." He continues, "Indeed, it was this strong bias which led me to sea & the naval Service. I had indulged in the idea of procuring distinction and a craving after the excitement and scenes which such an enterprise would offer," p. 337. Bernard Smith in *European Vision and the South Pacific* discusses how exploration in the first half of the nineteenth century was predominantly by sea instead of land, p. 2.

Wilkes speaks of his traumatic separation from his father in ACW, pp. 7–8; he describes the witch, Mammy Reed, in ACW, pp. 4–5; he writes of having "no other companions than my books and teachers" in ACW, p. 12. Dodge's *New England and the South Seas* contains a good account of the sea otter trade, pp. 22–25; 57–65. Even before the secret of sea otter furs became public knowledge, an American who was part of Cook's expedition, John Ledyard, mounted a personal campaign to send a trading venture to the Northwest. He even traveled to France, where he won the support of Thomas Jefferson and John Paul Jones, but it wasn't until 1787, when a group of six New England merchants enlisted Captains John Kendrick and Robert Gray, that an American sea otter voyage became a reality. When Astor died in 1848, he was considered to be the richest man in the United States; his great grandson, also named John Jacob Astor, would have the distinction of going down with the *Titanic* in 1905. Edmund Fanning, who sold the *Tonquin* (named for the gulf that would become famous during the Vietnam War) to Astor, wrote about the ship's demise in *Voyages to the South Seas, Indian and Pacific Oceans,* pp. 137–50. F. W. Howay in "The Loss of the *Tonquin*" compares various known accounts of the disaster and tells of how the story eventually made its way east.

For an account of the naval side of the War of 1812, see William Fowler's *Jack Tars and Commodores.* Daniel Henderson in *Hidden Coasts* describes the celebrations New Yorkers regularly gave naval heroes during the War of 1812, pp. 9–10. Wilkes relates Mammy Reed's prediction that he would one day be an admiral in ACW, p. 4. James Fenimore Cooper's pessimistic words about Wilkes's chances of getting a midshipman's appointment are in ACW, p. 37. Wilkes speaks of his "hankering after naval life" in ACW, p. 16. He describes his first voyage on a merchant vessel in ACW, pp. 20–28. Wilkes's revealing statement about how his "tastes were not in unison" with a life at sea is in ACW, p. 29. Wilkes speaks of the death of his father in ACW, p. 37. Wilkes relates his impressions of Commodore William Bainbridge in ACW, pp. 41–42. Bainbridge may have been an unfortunate role model for Wilkes. Although an acknowledged hero of the War of 1812, Bainbridge had also suffered his share of defeats and was known as "Hard Luck Bill." See Craig Symonds's "William S. Bainbridge: Bad Luck or Fatal Flaw?" in *Makers of the American Naval Tradition,* edited by James Bradford, pp. 97–99. Wilkes's statement concerning the "debauchery" typical of a naval vessel is in ACW, p. 45. His confession that he "had but few friends" among the officers of the vessels on which he served early on in his career is in ACW, p. 104. He speaks of his long-standing love of Jane Renwick in ACW, pp. 106–7.

Wilkes describes his cruise to the Pacific aboard the *Franklin* in ACW, pp. 109–43. He tells of meeting Captain Pollard in ACW, pp. 168–70. For another account of the Wilkes-Pollard meeting, see my *In the Heart of the Sea,* pp. 207–10. William Cary's narrative *Wrecked on the Feejees* was found in manuscript in an attic in the town of Siasconset on Nantucket and published a few years later in 1887. Walter Whitehall's *The East India Marine Society and the Peabody Museum of Salem* speaks about the sandalwood trade and also includes the memorial written in 1834, pp. 12–13. Amasa Delano describes the killing of seals in his *Narrative of Voyages and Travels,* pp. 306–7. My information on Nathaniel Palmer's encounter with Bellingshausen is based largely on the chapter "Lands Below the Horn" by Robert Morsberger and W. Patrick Strauss in *America Spreads Her Sails,* edited by Clayton Barrow, Jr., pp. 21–40. Davis's and Burdick's sealing voyages to the Antarctic Peninsula are analyzed in Kenneth Bertrand's *Americans in Antarctica, 1775–1948,* pp. 89–101. The 1828 memorial from the citizens of Nantucket is included in J. N. Reynolds's *Address on the Subject of a Surveying and Exploring Expedition*, pp. 165–66.

CHAPTER 2: THE DEPLORABLE EXPEDITION

For information about John Barrow, see Fergus Fleming's *Barrow's Boys: The Original Extreme Adventurers*, pp. 1–12. A. Hunter Dupree writes about the disappointing aftermath of the Lewis and Clark Expedition in *Science and the Federal Government*, pp. 27–28. In his 1825 Inaugural Address, John Quincy Adams speaks of how European voyages of discovery have not only brought glory to their nations but contributed to "the improvement of human knowledge." He continues, "We have been partakers of that improvement and owe for it a sacred debt, not only of gratitude, but of equal or proportional exertion in the same common cause," in *Messages and Papers of the Presidents, 1789–1897*, volume II, edited by James Richardson, p. 312.

As early as 1811, President James Madison had selected the sealer Edmund Fanning to lead a small exploring expedition to the Pacific. Unfortunately, the outbreak of the War of 1812 meant that what would have been known as the Fanning Expedition never left port. Prior to that, in 1790, a Maryland surveyor named John Churchman unsuccessfully attempted to convince Congress to fund a voyage to Baffin Bay off the west coast of Greenland to conduct magnetic experiments; see Dupree's *Science and the Federal Government*, pp. 9–11.

Elmore Symmes speaks of John Symmes's stint in St. Louis in "John Cleves Symmes, The Theorist" in *Southern Bivouac*, p. 558. For an account of *Terra Australis Incognita*, see Jacques Brosse's *Great Voyages of Discovery*, pp. 14–16. As Reginald Horsman relates in "Captain Symmes's Journey to the Center of the Earth" in *Timeline*, Symmes read Cook's *Voyages* when he was just eleven years old; Horsman also describes what it would have been like for a ship to sail into the "great verges," p. 8. As Horsman also relates, a novel entitled *Symzonia: A Voyage of Discovery*, purportedly based on a sea captain's journal of a voyage into the interior of the earth, was published in 1820. E. F. Madden provides a brief overview of the holes in the poles in "Symmes and His Theory," in *Harper's New Monthly Magazine*, pp. 740–49. The Symmes petition was presented by R. M. Johnson of Kentucky and appears in *Debates and Proceedings in the Congress of the United States*, 17th Congress, 1st Session, p. 278. A second petition from an Ohio delegation was presented to Congress on February 7, 1823, in *Debates and Proceedings*, 17th Congress, 2nd Session, p. 191.

For information on Jeremiah Reynolds, who despite being a famous person of his day has virtually slipped through the cracks of history, I have depended on R. B. Harlan's *The History of Clinton County, Ohio*, pp. 580–85, and Henry Howe's *Historical Collections of Ohio*, pp. 431–33. Instead of his relationship with Symmes, it has been Reynolds's connection to Edgar Allan Poe that has interested most scholars; see Robert F. Almy's "J. N. Reynolds: A Brief Biography with Particular Reference to Poe and Symmes" in *The Colophon*, pp. 227–45, and Aubrey Starke's "Poe's Friend Reynolds" in *American Literature*, pp. 152–59. In *Remarks on a Review of Symmes' Theory*, Jeremiah Reynolds speaks of Weddell and the open polar sea, then continues, "suppose, like Weddell, under some fortuitous circumstances, the icy circle should be passed, a few days press of sail would reach the 90°, where anchor might be cast on the axis of the earth, our *eagle* and *star-spangled* banner unfurled and planted, and left to wave on the very pole itself, where, amid the novelty, grandeur, and sublimity, of the scene, the two little vessels would turn once around in twenty-four hours," p. 72.

A letter from Jeremiah Reynolds on the subject of "an Antarctic Expedition" appears in Doc. No. 88, House of Representatives, 20th Congress, 1st Session, pp. 3–4. A series of memorials and letters of support (from such notables as Commodore Thomas ap Catesby Jones and Secretary of the Navy Samuel Southard) are included in Rep. No. 209, 20th Congress, 1st Session. Reynolds's 1828 report on uncharted islands and shoals is in Doc. No. 105, House of Representatives, 23rd Congress, 2nd Session. In a letter dated June 22, 1838, Wilkes's old naval friend Lieutenant R. R. Pinkham, a Nantucketer, charges that Reynolds's report "was copied word for word, from the *Nantucket Inquirer*, after Jenks [editor of the newspaper], Thornton, and myself had spent months in collecting [the information]" (KSHS). The launching of the "strong and splendid discovery ship *Peacock*" is described in the *New York Mirror*, October 4, 1828, p. 106.

Wilkes tells of his chance meeting with Jane and her mother at a chemistry lecture in ACW, p. 209. For the relationship between science and the U.S. government, see A. Hunter Dupree's *Science and the Federal Government*, as well as Robert Bruce's *The Launching of Modern American Science, 1846–1876*, George Daniel's *American Science in the Age of Jackson*, and Nathan Reingold's "Definitions and Speculations: The Professionalization of Science in America in the Nineteenth Century" in *The Pursuit of Knowledge in the Early American Republic*, edited by Alexandra Oleson and Sanborn Brown, pp. 33–69. For information concerning Ferdinand Hassler, I have depended on Ferdinand Cajori's *The Checquered Career of Ferdinand Rudolph Hassler*, as well as Albert Stanley's "Hassler's Legacy" in *NOAA Magazine,* pp. 52–57. For information on Wilkes's brother-in-law James Renwick see the *Dictionary of American Biography* and ACW, pp. 724–27. Wilkes describes his relationship with Hassler in ACW, pp. 216–25.

Wilkes's October 5, 1828, letter to Secretary of the Navy Samuel Southard is in Collection 250, Box 28, Folder 11 of the Southard Papers at the Princeton University Library. Jeremiah Reynolds's October 28, 1828, letter to Southard, in which he describes Wilkes's and Renwick's "spirit of dictation," is also at Princeton. Senator Hayne's arguments against the 1829 expedition are in No. 94 of 20th Congress, 2nd Session.

For information on the South Sea Fur Company and Exploring Expedition, see Edmund Fanning's *Voyages Round the World,* pp. 478–91, which includes a report from the expedition's leader, Benjamin Pendleton; see also William Stanton's *The Great United States Exploring Expedition* (subsequently referred to as Stanton), pp. 26–28. The geologist James Eights's description of the South Shetland Islands is contained in Edmund Fanning's *Voyages to the South Seas,* pp. 195–216. Wilkes tells of being stricken with smallpox in ACW, pp. 285–86. In his introduction to *Voyage to the Southern Ocean,* Herman Viola speaks of how Wilkes's bout with smallpox prevented him from meeting William Reynolds on the *Boxer,* p. xxix. Wilkes describes his surveying duty at Newport, Rhode Island, in ACW, pp. 286–93. He tells of his fallout with Hassler in ACW, pp. 294–96.

For information about the Depot of Charts and Instruments and Wilkes's role in creating what became known as the Capitol Hill Observatory, I have relied on Steven Dick's "Centralizing Navigational Technology in America: The U.S. Navy's Depot of Charts and Instruments, 1830–1842" in *Technology and Culture* and "How the U.S. Naval Observatory Began, 1830–65" in *Sky and Telescope.* Wilkes describes his family's introduction to Washington, D.C., in ACW, pp. 300–303. Harold Langley speaks of the importance of politics to a successful navy career in *Social Reform in the United States Navy, 1798–1862,* p. 23. My discussion of Andrew Jackson's relationship with the U.S. Navy owes much to John Schroeder's *Shaping a Maritime Empire: The Commercial and Diplomatic Role of the American Navy, 1829–1861,* pp. 22–28. Jackson's words of praise concerning the incident at Quallah Batoo are quoted in Schroeder, p. 28.

Jeremiah Reynolds was not only a proponent of science; he was also possessed with a Jacksonian sense of the United States' imperialist destiny: "Our flag should be borne to every portion of the globe, to give to civilized and savage man a just impression of the power we possess, and in what manner we can exercise it when justice demands reparation for insulted dignity"; in *Voyage of the United States Frigate Potomac,* p. ii. For the influence of Reynolds's "Mocha Dick, the White Whale of the Pacific" on Melville, see Perry Miller's *The Raven and the Whale,* pp. 20–22. My references to Reynolds's 1836 "Address on the Subject of a Surveying and Exploring Expedition" are from the edition published by Harpers in 1836; pp. 31, 72–73, 90, 98. My thanks to Susan Beegel and Wes Tiffney for their comments concerning scientific collecting in the nineteenth century. John Schroeder in *Shaping a Maritime Empire* cites Ohioan Thomas Hamer's defense of an exploring expedition, p. 34. Southard's motion to fund "an exploring expedition to the Pacific Ocean and South Seas" was approved by a vote of 44–1 on April 27, 1836; in *Register of Debates in Congress,* 24th Congress, 1st Session, pp. 1298–99; see also pp. 3470–73 for the debates that occurred on May 5, 1836.

For information on Mahlon Dickerson's tenure as secretary of the navy, see W. Patrick Strauss's "Mahlon Dickerson" in *American Secretaries of the Navy,* vol. 1, edited by Paolo Coletta, pp. 155–63. Strauss's "Preparing the Wilkes Expedition: A Study in Disorganization" in *Pacific Historical Review* provides a good, blow-by-blow account of the many missteps associated with the beginnings of the Expedition. Jackson's letters to Dickerson about his interest in the Expedition are in the Letters Relating to the Wilkes Exploring Expedition (LRWEE), National Archives (NA). For an analysis of Commodore Jones's involvement in the Ex. Ex., see Gene Smith's *Thomas Ap Catesby Jones: Commodore of Manifest Destiny,* pp. 70–92.

Wilkes's letters to Dickerson concerning the purchase of instruments in Europe appear in LRWEE. Wilkes's trip to Europe to purchase instruments for the Expedition is chronicled in the dozens of letters he wrote his wife Jane in the Wilkes Family Papers at the Library of Congress; see also Doris Esch Borthwick's "Outfitting the United States Exploring Expedition: Lieutenant Charles Wilkes's European Assignment, August–November, 1836" in *Proceedings of the American Philosophical Society,* which quotes from the November 4, 1836, letter to Jane in which Wilkes refers to *"these giants,"* p. 171. For information on James Ross and his discovery of the magnetic North Pole, see Fergus Fleming's *Barrow's Boys,* pp. 291–92; 334–35. On what was referred to as the "Magnetic Crusade," see John Cawood's "Terrestrial Magnetism and the Development of International Collaboration in the Early Nineteenth Century," pp. 585–86.

The scientist Walter Johnson's February 14, 1837, letter describing the insufficiencies of Wilkes's collection of instruments as well as Charles Pickering's

February 15, 1839, letter about the lack of microscopes and Wilkes's March 18, 1837, letter withdrawing his name from consideration as astronomer are in LRWEE.

In April 1837 the Expedition's newly constructed vessels participated in sea trials. According to Daniel Ammen, who witnessed the trials, "had the object been to build vessels of exceptional slowness the success would have been undoubted"; in *The Old Navy and the New*, p. 28. The rancorous public exchange between Jeremiah Reynolds and Dickerson is reprinted in Reynolds's *Pacific and Indian Oceans*. The reference to the "Deplorable Expedition" appears in the January 25, 1838, issue of the *Long Island Star;* cited in David Tyler's *The Wilkes Expedition* (subsequently referred to as Tyler), p. 19. For an account of the attempts made by the friends of Nathaniel Hawthorne to secure him a position with the Expedition, see James Mellow's *Nathaniel Hawthorne in His Times*, pp. 84–87. For information on the Panic of 1837, I have relied on Arthur Schlesinger's *Political and Social History of the United States, 1829–1925*, pp. 53–61.

Wilkes describes his survey of Georges Bank and his meeting with Nathaniel Bowditch in ACW, pp. 325–30, 360–68. According to Barbara Mc-Corkle in "Cartographic History, 1524–1850" in *Georges Bank*, edited by Richard Backus, "a better survey was not undertaken until 1930–1932," p. 16. Wilkes speaks of his relationship with his cabin boy Charlie Erskine in ACW, pp. 331–33; Erskine's account is in his *Twenty Years Before the Mast*, pp. 10–11. Lieutenant James Glynn in an October 21, 1837, letter to George Emmons describes being cheered at a New York theater; cited in Tyler, p. 1; see also Stanton, p. 54. Stanton describes the heating system in the *Macedonian*, p. 54. In an October 31, 2002, personal communication, the arms expert Charles Thayer describes the genesis of the Bowie knife pistol. Jones designed the pistol and described it as "ideal for penetrating into the interiors of islands inhabited by savages." Jones's attempts to retrieve the Expedition's instruments are detailed in his letters to Poinsett in LRWEE, as is his November 21, 1837, letter of resignation. According to Stanton, word reached Washington of the French voyage to the Pacific and Antarctica in July of 1837, pp. 50–51.

In a May 5, 1838, letter to Wilkes, the naturalist Titian Peale states that "a reduction in the number of members of the Scientific Corps . . . is absolutely requisite as far as regards the beneficial results of the Exped" (KSHS). For information about Joel Poinsett, I have relied on the *Dictionary of American Biography* and Stanton, pp. 60–61. John Quincy Adams's stern words to Poinsett about the Expedition are in the *Memoirs of John Quincy Adams*, volume 9, p. 491. Poinsett's March 1, 1838, letter to Dickerson is in LRWEE.

CHAPTER 3: **MOST GLORIOUS HOPES**

William Reynolds speaks of reading in the Library of Congress in an April 24, 1838, letter to his sister Lydia. Unless otherwise indicated, William Reynolds's letters are located at the Shadeck-Fackenthal Library, Franklin and Marshall College. Reynolds speaks of "the immaculate 'Bowditch'" in a November 19, 1836, letter to Lydia; he writes of Lydia's relationship with Rebecca Krug in an October 30, 1836, letter. He tells of a midshipman being "bilged" in a May 26, 1837, letter. Howard Chapelle provides the dimensions of the *Pennsylvania* in *The History of the American Sailing Navy,* pp. 371–72, 549. Reynolds tells of the *Pennsylvania*'s voyage to Norfolk in a January 6, 1837, letter to Lydia. Herman Viola provides information on Reynolds's family background in his introduction to *Voyage to the Southern Ocean,* pp. xxviii–xxix. Reynolds's letter describing a typical day at the Depot is dated April 24, 1838. In a May 1, 1838, letter he writes of his admiration of Wilkes, and on May 13, 1838, he writes of Wilkes's family seal.

Wilkes recounts how he was awarded command of the Ex. Ex. and then put the squadron together during the spring and summer of 1838 in ACW, pp. 333–59, 370–72, 374. Beverley Kennon's April 13, 1838, letter protesting Wilkes's appointment is in LRWEE. Joseph Smith's April 21, 1838, letter of congratulations to Wilkes is at KSHS. The congressional debates involving Wilkes's appointment are contained in the *Congressional Globe,* 25th Congress, 2nd Session, p. 297.

Lieutenant Matthew Maury, a bitter rival and critic of Wilkes, claimed that Poinsett wanted to offer *him* the same opportunity Poinsett gave Wilkes. Maury wrote a friend that Poinsett had asked him to tell him, without regard to rank, who was the officer most qualified to lead the Expedition. Even though he felt he was the best suited, he gave Poinsett a list of officers with his name at the bottom, claiming he felt he had no right "to draw distinctions among brother officers." Maury said that Poinsett "froze up in disgust . . . and gave Wilkes the command, and so I was the gainer, for I preserved my integrity." Rather than a question of integrity, it may have been a lack of personal courage. Maury was even farther down the list than Wilkes, and his appointment would have inspired an even greater uproar–if indeed Poinsett was seriously considering him for the command. Later in his career, Maury would prove just as politically opportunistic, if not more so, than Wilkes. See Frances Williams's *Matthew Fontaine Maury: Scientist of the Sea,* pp. 114–20.

In volume one of William Hudson's official journal of the Expedition (at the American Museum of Natural History, New York), Hudson was careful to include a copy of Poinsett's June 5, 1838, letter insisting that the Expedition was "purely civil." James Natland's comments about James Dana's religious conversion prior to the departure of the Expedition appear in his "At Vulcan's Shoulder: James Dwight Dana and the Beginning of Planetary Volcanology," pp. 312–39. In an April 3, 1838, diary entry, Secretary of the Navy Dickerson writes, "Mr. Poinsett considered as dying" (The New Jersey Historical Society). An April 7, 1838, letter from Hudson to Wilkes (at Duke University [DU]) reveals that it was Hudson's idea to replace the ships' iron water tanks with casks.

Reynolds's description of how he and May assisted Wilkes in his observations is in a June 17, 1838, letter to Lydia. Wilkes requested the acting lieutenant appointments in a July 11, 1838, letter to Paulding, LRWEE; on the back of the letter Paulding notes the appointments as going to Carr, Walker, Johnson, Hartstene, Alden, Case, Emmons, Perry, Underwood, and Dale. The reference to "refractory and evil spirits" resulting from "senior officers contending among themselves" is from Matthew Fontaine Maury's "Scraps from the Lucky Bag," published anonymously in the *Southern Literary Messenger*, April 1840, p. 235. For an excellent analysis of the issue of rank in the nineteenth-century U.S. Navy, see Donald Chisholm's *Waiting for Dead Men's Shoes: Origins and Development of the U.S. Navy's Officer Personnel System, 1793–1941*, especially Chapter 8, "Movement Toward Rationalization, 1837–44," pp. 167–94; my thanks to John Hattendorf for bringing this source to my attention. In a June 11, 1838, letter to his uncle (at DU), Wilkes's nephew Wilkes Henry writes that "From Mr. Waldron [the purser of the *Vincennes*] I heard that Mr. H. would hereafter be Captn Hudson. It must give you a great deal of pleasure." Wilkes refers to Poinsett's change of heart after his illness in ACW, p. 372; elsewhere in ACW Wilkes describes how Poinsett "left the impression on my mind that it was the intention of the Govt to do it [give him and Hudson acting appointments] just before the departure of the Expedition and I was gulled into the belief it would be done and from day to day anticipated receiving Acg Commissions, but none came," p. 371. Wilkes also claimed that after the Expedition had been concluded Poinsett "admitted to me that it had been a great omission on the part of the Government to have entrusted me with such an important Command without conferring on me the Mantle of a nominal rank," ACW, p. 371. Wilkes's half-joking reference to having Jane come along as his "assistant" was written in July 1838 from Norfolk and is at DU; unless otherwise indicated, all letters between Wilkes and Jane are located at Duke University. Wilkes's July 19, 1838, letter to Poinsett about the acting captain appointments for himself and Hudson is in LRWEE.

In *A Gentlemanly and Honorable Profession,* Christopher McKee provides a detailed description of the preparation of a naval vessel for a presidential visit, p. 123. Edgar Allan Poe's tribute to Jeremiah Reynolds's role in instigating the Expedition is included in his review of a pamphlet about the Exploring Expedition in *Graham's Magazine,* September 1843, pp. 164–65. Jeremiah Reynolds's reference to Wilkes as a "cunning little Jacob" is taken from an anonymous article written by Matthew Maury, in Reynolds's *Pacific and Indian Oceans,* p. 464. William Reynolds's enthusiastic letter to Lydia about the final preparations for the Expedition is dated August 12, 1838. Wilkes's sorrowful letter to Jane about leaving her and the children was written August 11, 1838. The description of Wilkes's captain uniform is taken from the Wilkes Court-Martial Records, Vol. 44, No. 827, p. 26. William Reynolds's description of the "éclat" of the Expedition's officers at the eve of departure is from an unpublished manuscript describing Wilkes's behavior during the Expedition (subsequently referred to as Manuscript) at FMC, p. 1. Wilkes refers to the acting captain appointment as his "shield of protection" in ACW, pp. 370–71. Wilkes's final letter to Poinsett describing his "mortification" is dated August 18, 1838, and is at the Pennsylvania Historical Society. The pilot's report of the high morale of the Expedition's officers appears in the August 25, 1838, *Niles Register.* Wilkes's description of feeling "doomed to destruction" is from his *Narrative of the United States Exploring Expedition* (subsequently referred to as *Narrative*), vol. 1, p. 3.

CHAPTER 4: AT SEA

I have based my description of the squadron's departure on an illustration in Charles Erskine's *Twenty Years Before the Mast,* p. 15. Wilkes claims the *Vincennes* can "do everything but talk" in an April 5, 1840, letter to fellow explorer James Ross, reprinted in the appendix to vol. 2 of the *Narrative,* pp. 453–56. Louis Bolander in "The *Vincennes,* World Traveler of the Old Navy" in *U.S. Naval Institute Proceedings* cites a reference to the cabin of the flagship being a "pavilion of elegance," p. 826. First Lieutenant Thomas Craven's praise of the *Vincennes* is in a June 10, 1838, letter to Wilkes in KSHS. Philip Lundeberg in "Ships and Squadron Logistics" in MV speaks of the alterations to the *Vincennes* and the thirty-six-foot stern cabin, p. 152; he also provides excellent information about the other Expedition vessels. See also Lundenberg's and Dana Wegner's "'Not for Conquest But Discovery': Rediscovering the Ships of the Wilkes Expedition" in *American Neptune,* pp. 151–67. Howard Chapelle discusses the Expedition vessels in *The History of the American Sailing Navy,* specifically mentioning the *Relief*'s innovative use of spencers on all three masts, p. 389. Stanton, who also provides an overview of the Expedition's vessels on the squadron's departure from Norfolk, cites the *Peacock*'s difficulties on the Persian Gulf, p. 75. Hudson discusses his concerns about his vessel in his log. Philip Lundeberg has compiled a useful comparison of exploring vessels in Appendix 1, "Characteristics of Selected Exploring Vessels" in MV, p. 255. Wilkes speaks of his "very distressing thoughts" in ACW, p. 376. A copy of Wilkes's instructions is included in the *Narrative*, vol. 1, pp. xxv–xxxi. Wilkes writes Jane of his "fatigues" on September 2, 1838.

William Reynolds discusses Wilkes's changing uniform; for most of the first year of the voyage, Wilkes's "shoulders, with an excess of modesty, had not even borne the single swab, the only insignia, which his rank as a Lieutenant in the Navy, and as the *'first officer,'* in Command of the Squadron, entitled him to"; Manuscript, p. 17. In a September 1, 1838, letter to Jane, Wilkes writes, "I have made Carr my flag Lieut. . . . and [he] is much with me." In a personal communication (February 9, 2002), William Fowler expresses his doubts about Wilkes's having the authority to name a flag lieutenant. Dudley Pope writes insightfully about the solitude of command, as well as different command styles, in *Life in Nelson's Navy*, pp. 62–64. J. C. Beaglehole in *The Life of Captain James Cook* speaks of Cook's "paroxysms of passion," p. 711. Reynolds mentions that Wilkes "was accustomed to be the guest of the ward room," as well as Wilkes's habit of squishing spiders, in his Manuscript, p. 5. Wilkes describes how he responded to the facial hair challenge in ACW, pp. 384–85. He speaks of his ability to read the characters of his officers in an October 21, 1838, letter to Jane.

Unless otherwise indicated, all of Reynolds's quotations are from his private journal. He writes of the "youthful faces" among the officers in an August 30, 1838, letter to Lydia. In a September 16, 1838, letter to Jane, Wilkes mentions his breakfast with Reynolds and May. In a May 8, 1838, letter to Lydia, Reynolds tells how he was mistaken for his friend May. Wilkes writes Jane of how "very smoothly" his relations with his officers have been in a September 26, 1838, letter. In an October 21, 1838, letter to Jane, he predicts that in a short while "I shall have gained [the officers'] affections and will be enabled to do most anything with them." Charles Erskine describes his contemplated murder of Wilkes in *Twenty Years Before the Mast*, pp. 14–20.

Reynolds refers to the "graceful beauty" of the schooners in a September 6 entry of a letter to Lydia begun on August 30, 1838. George Emmons refers to the schooners as "the pets of the squadron" in the February 5, 1838, entry of his journal (at Yale). In an October 21, 1838, letter to Jane, Wilkes tells of both

Craven's and Lee's pleas to Hudson that they be given command of the schooners. Reynolds describes Wilkes's daily inspection of the schooners in his Manuscript, pp. 4–5. Wilkes's September 13, 1838, order concerning journals is included in the appendix to volume 1 of the *Narrative*, pp. 367–68. Reynolds speaks of the George Porter incident in both his journal and a September 15, 1838, entry in his August letter to Lydia.

For a brief history of Madeira, see Jean Ludtke's *Atlantic Peeks: An Ethnographic Guide to the Portuguese-Speaking Islands*, pp. 233–34. Samuel Eliot Morison discusses Christopher Columbus's relationship to Madeira in *Admiral of the Ocean Sea*, pp. 517–19. The amount of Madeira taken by Cook in 1768 is noted in *The Endeavour Journal of Joseph Banks, 1768–1771*, edited by J. C. Beaglehole, p. 8; my thanks to John Hattendorf for bringing this to my attention. Wilkes tells of the wine he purchased in ACW, p. 388. In a revealing passage in ACW, Wilkes states, "It was surmised that when I had got through my Scientific duties and preparations & was to take command of my own ship and the Squadron, I would be embarrassed and prove a failure, but I felt myself completely at home and gave my attention to all parts essential to the Service," p. 374. As he makes clear in the subsequent description of how he proceeded to frustrate First Lieutenant Craven's attempts to make crew assignments, Wilkes was anything but "at home" on the deck of the *Vincennes*.

Wilkes describes how the squadron searched out doubtful shoals in his *Narrative*, vol. 1, p. 28. For information on bioluminescence, I have depended on Richard Ellis's *Encyclopedia of the Sea*, pp. 36, 95, 255. For information on Magellanic Clouds, I consulted the Web site www.geocities.com/CapeCanaveral/orbit/2. For information on the artists James Drayton and especially Alfred Agate, I have looked to Philip Lundeberg's "Legacy of an Artist Explorer," pp. 1–5. Bernard Smith in *European Vision and the South Pacific* writes about the camera lucida, p. 255. William Reynolds tells of the busy scene on Enxadas Island in a December 4, 1838, letter to Lydia. Wilkes refers to the anxiety he was feeling in Rio in a December 22, 1838, letter to Jane. Doris Esch Borthwick's "Outfitting the U.S. Exploring Expedition" contains a good description of how a pendulum experiment was conducted in the nineteenth century. The description of Wilkes's outburst while performing experiments in Rio is contained in a small daybook kept by William Reynolds, in which he appears to have recorded testimony from the court of inquiry Wilkes later called in Valparaiso, Chile, to investigate the actions of Lieutenant John Dale. Reynolds speaks of the ominous nature of these "little outbreaks" in his Manuscript, p. 6.

In a November 25, 1838, letter to Jane, Wilkes writes, "[Nicholson] calls us all Mr. Hudson, Mr. Wilkes and I spoke to him yesterday about it & told him that if I had a disposition to retaliate, I should call him only Capn Nicolson." Commodore Nicholson's correspondence with Wilkes while the Expedition was at Rio is at KSHS; he makes the comments about Wilkes not being a captain in a January 4, 1839, letter. Wilkes tells of crying during a pendulum experiment in a December 9, 1838, letter to Jane; he tells of his physical collapse in a December 22, 1838, letter to Jane; he also describes the incident in ACW, p. 398.

In a January 2, 1839, letter to Wilkes, Commodore Nicholson writes, "I most sincerely regret we have ever met, as since you have been in this Port, with every disposition on my part to serve and aid you, you have evinced nothing but dissatisfaction." On a copy of Wilkes's correspondence with Nicholson, Secretary of the Navy Paulding scribbled a March 13, 1839, note concerning Wilkes's "tone of feeling which does not seem to be called for by the occasion" (KSHS). William Reynolds writes of Wilkes's "hanging back" when it came to the approach to Cape Horn in his Manuscript, p. 7. Wilkes speaks in detail about his suspension of Craven in ACW, 403–5. Reynolds writes of how some of Wilkes's officers initially defended his actions in his Manuscript, p. 6.

Joseph Couthouy mentions Thomas Piner's comments about "getting into the suburbs" in the February 6, 1838, entry of his journal (at the Museum of Science, Boston). Captain Porter's words about the horrors of rounding Cape Horn are in his *Journal of a Cruise Made to the Pacific Ocean in the U.S. Frigate Essex*, p. 84. For information about tacking a square-rigged ship, I have consulted John Harland's *Seamanship in the Age of Sail*, pp. 181–89.

CHAPTER 5: THE TURNING POINT

James Cook's words upon reaching his Ne Plus Ultra appear in J. C. Beaglehole's *Life of Captain James Cook*, pp. 365–66. When it came to Wilkes's assigning two new commanders to the schooners, he later claimed that a "drinking bout" on the *Flying Fish* contributed to his decision to remove Passed Midshipman Samuel Knox from command, ACW, p. 406. Wilkes tells of how he acted to "astonish" the squadron by dismissing Lee in a February 23, 1839, letter to Jane; in that letter he adds that he was forced "to cut him off by way of example although he is a very good officer as respects to duty." Robert Johnson refers to the "devilish Schooners" in a February 18, 1839, entry in his journal. On Weddell's 1823 record sail south, see Jacques Brosse's *Great Voyages of Discovery*, p. 185. Wilkes tells of their encounter with the whaleship in his *Narrative*, vol. 1, p. 134. Wilkes describes himself in "excellent spirits" in a February 26, 1839, letter to Jane.

Johnson tells about the repair of the *Sea Gull*'s broken gaff in the February 28, 1839, entry of his journal. On the Antarctic Convergence, see Edwin Mickleburgh's *Beyond the Frozen Sea,* p. 22. Johnson speaks of the many penguins and whales in his March 1, 1839, journal entry. Wilkes compares an iceberg to the Capitol building in a March 31, 1839, letter to Jane; he also speaks of his exchange with Ringgold about "adventuring with boldness." The sealer Robert Fildes's description of the South Shetland Islands as a place created by a drunken Mother Nature appears in E. W. Hunter Christie's *The Antarctic Problem,* p. 91. Johnson describes the ice-encrusted state of the *Sea Gull* in a March 5, 1839, journal entry. Wilkes speaks of being "so full of energy" in a May 22, 1839, letter to Jane. Kenneth Bertrand details the route taken by Jeremiah Reynolds's privately funded voyage south in *Americans in Antarctica,* pp. 144–58. Jacques Brosse in *Great Voyages of Discovery* tells of d'Urville's unsuccessful first attempt to sail south in 1837–38, pp. 185–89.

William Hudson complains of the leaky condition of the *Peacock* in a March 11, 1839, journal entry. Titian Peale tells of being awakened by Lieutenant Perry and his snowball in a March 9, 1839, entry. George Emmons tells of William Stewart's fall in a March 10, 1839, journal entry. Hudson describes the Sunday service he conducted in a March 17, 1839, entry. Hudson complains of "this fancy kind of sailing" in a March 17 entry.

All of James Palmer's account of the *Flying Fish*'s sail south appears in "Antarctic Adventures of the United States' Schooner *Flying-Fish* in 1839" in the appendix of *Thulia: A Tale of the Antarctic,* a book-length poem Palmer wrote about the voyage, pp. 65–72. William Walker's account of the voyage appears in the appendix of volume 1 of Wilkes's *Narrative,* pp. 408–14. My description of the formation of grease ice is from the National Imagery and Mapping Agency's *Antarctic Pilot,* p. 18. In *The Antarctic Problem,* E. W. Hunter Christie says that the *Flying Fish*'s voyage was "no mean achievement in so small a vessel so late in the season," p. 135. See also Henderson Norman's "The Log of the *Flying-Fish*" in *U.S. Naval Institute Proceedings,* pp. 363–69.

Reynolds's account of his open-boat survey of Tierra del Fuego is in his journal. Joseph Couthouy's remarks about the sailing characteristics of the launch appear in a March 7, 1839, journal entry. Darwin's remarks about the primitive state of the Yahgans appear in *The Voyage of the Beagle,* p. 213. Bruce Chatwin in *In Patagonia* claims that Darwin "lapsed into that common failing of naturalists: to marvel at the intricate perfection of other creatures and recoil from the squalor of man. . . . For the mere sight of the Fuegians helped trigger off the theory that Man had evolved from an ape-like species and that some men had evolved further than others," p. 128. Johnson tells of walking over the warm crust of Deception Island in a March 12, 1839, journal entry.

Wilkes recounts how Long did not hug the coast (as Wilkes had suggested) during his passage to the Strait of Magellan in ACW, p. 409. James Dana's account of the *Relief*'s near-disaster at the Strait of Magellan is from a March 24, 1839, letter to Robert Bakewell reprinted in Daniel Gilman's *The Life of James Dwight Dana,* pp. 99–103. King's description of the navigational horrors of the Milky Way are contained in Lieutenant Long's March 19, 1839, journal entry; other quotations from Long are from his March 18–20 entries. Pickering's comment about a man's hair turning gray is from his March 18, 1839, journal entry; the other quotes from Pickering are taken from his March 19 and 20 entries. Wilkes recounts Pickering's "philosophic act" in ACW, p. 410. The reference to the *Relief*'s "remarkable escape" is from Gershom Bradford's "On a Lee Shore" in *The American Neptune,* p. 282.

The proceedings of John Dale's Court of Inquiry are contained in the Court-Martial Records, No. 884. In his "General Orders" concerning Dale's Court of Inquiry (reprinted in the appendix to volume 1 of the *Narrative,* p. 421), Wilkes insisted that the mishap was due to Dale's "inexperience" and "want of determined perseverance." Daniel Goleman's comments concerning the "emotional mind" come from his *Emotional Intelligence,* p. 291.

In a March 13, 1839, letter to Jane, Wilkes says that he "suffered much anxiety" as a result of the incident involving Dale at the Strait of Le Maire, adding, "I scarcely ever suffered so much in the same time—when they came on board I immediately suspended Lt. Dale." Reynolds refers to the "turning point" in his Manuscript, p. 16. In a letter to Jane written over the course of June 12–16, 1839, Wilkes refers to the "astonishing" coincidence that all of Jones's officers proved incompetent.

In a June 3, 1839, letter to Jane, Wilkes refers to the officers he will consign to the *Relief* as "useless trash." Reynolds's words about the difficulty of "quieting Captain Long" are from his journal. Wilkes mentions the floggings in his *Narrative,* vol. 1, pp. 232–33; he talks about the loss of the *Sea Gull* on pp. 206–7; he theorizes about how the schooner went down in ACW, p. 411. Reynolds speaks of the "poor fellows" of the *Sea Gull* in a June 30, 1839, letter to Lydia.

Wilkes's reference to giving his officers "the necessary rebuke" is in a May 14, 1839, letter to Jane. He speaks of Carr hanging on to his coattails in a June 12–16 letter to Jane. The statistics about dueling come from Charles

Paullin's "Dueling in the Old Navy" in *U.S. Naval Institute Proceedings,* p. 1157. Christopher McKee in *A Gentlemanly and Honorable Profession* writes eloquently about the "psycho-dynamics" of dueling in the navy; he also claims that Paullin's assertions about dueling are exaggerated, pointing out that the number of deaths attributed to duels accounts for just "one percent of the total number of officers who left the navy before the date," p. 404. Wilkes refers to Wilkes Henry's duel with George Harrison in a June 12–16, 1839, letter to Jane. George Harrison had a reputation in the squadron for hotheadedness; several months later he would be suspended for disrespectful conduct toward Lieutenant Sinclair, who commented on Harrison's apparent hatred for "the whole human race, himself included." Wilkes tells of his conversation with Hudson about Henry and of the officers' letter of support in a July 3, 1838, letter to Jane. The officers' letter is reprinted in the appendix to Wilkes's *Narrative,* vol. 1, p. 422.

Wilkes speaks in praise of Captain McKeever in ACW, p. 412; in a May 22, 1838, letter to Jane, Wilkes mentions that McKeever, unlike Nicholson, refers to him as "Captain Wilkes." Johnson's worries about McKeever's "sinister views" are recorded in a June 29, 1839, journal entry. Reynolds speaks of his despair and anger over Wilkes's decision to take on McKeever's nephew in a June 30, 1839, letter to Lydia.

CHAPTER 6: COMMODORE OF THE PACIFIC

In a July 3, 1839, letter to Jane, Wilkes writes, "I have bought or rather had made a pair of beautiful epaulettes & that I intend to wear them—*keep this to yourself* as I think it now high time to appear in my proper uniform." In a September 12–21 letter to Jane written from Tahiti, Wilkes recounts how he "hoisted the Broad Pendant and . . . my two straps as did Hudson by an order of mine so you see I have had the impertinence to give myself sufficient Dignity at least in appearance." Wilkes refers to this action as "a bold and unwarranted stroke of policy on my part" in ACW, p. 377, but insists that "it was justified under the necessities of the case." Reynolds speaks of Wilkes's "immense" epaulets in his Manuscript, adding, "It is not a little remarkable that the assumption of all this Naval Splendour was deferred until Mr. Wilkes felt himself out of the regions usually infested by American men of war. Perhaps he thought he could carry it more bravely among the breechless savages than amidst the pomp and circumstance of real, full blooded Captains and Commodores, in whose presence he might have been disagreeably reminded of the old fable of the 'Daw in borrowed plumes!'" p. 17. Wilkes's decision to make himself a commodore also fits with what psychologists have termed the "glass bubble syndrome": "People with a narcissistic personality sometimes fantasize consciously and often unconsciously that they are living by themselves in glory, protected from the rest of the world and the common herd by a shield made of something impervious, like a glass bubble. From this vantage point, they can look out at the world with disdain and without fear of challenge"; from *Richard Nixon: A Psychobiography,* by Vamik Volkan et al., p. 98. Wilkes refers to his hoped-for acting appointment to captain as a "shield of protection" in ACW, pp. 370–71.

Reynolds speaks of the mystery of a coral island in a September 12, 1839, letter to Lydia. Titian Peale's comments about the "sorry business" of leaving the scientific corps idle are in an August 14, 1839, journal entry. In contrast to their experiences in the Tuamotus, the scientists had spent a profitable two months in South America, much of it spent hiking into the Andes, where they collected numerous specimens and artifacts. At one point a condor decided that Charles Pickering was the one who should be collected. When the giant bird swooped down with its talons outstretched, the naturalist was forced to fight it off with his Bowie knife pistol.

My description of how Wilkes conducted a survey is based largely on his own "Mode of Surveying the Coral Islands" in the appendix of volume 1 of his *Narrative,* pp. 429–32, as well as "Surveying and Charting the Pacific Basin" by Ralph Ehrenberg, John Wolter, and Charles Burroughs in MV, pp. 165–70. William Goetzmann talks about the speed of Wilkes's survey method in *New Lands, New Men,* p. 276.

Wilkes's order about being kind to natives is reprinted in his *Narrative,* vol. 1, pp. 308–9. Johnson speaks of Sac's enthusiasm for killing penguins in a March 10, 1839, journal entry. Wilkes's words about the encounter with the natives of Reao Atoll (referred to as Clermont de Tonnere) are from his *Narrative,* vol. 1, pp. 312–14. Reynolds's comments on the dignity of the natives are in his journal. Wilkes's pronouncements about the effects of the Expedition's first encounter with Polynesians is in ACW, p. 423; Whittle's outrage is recorded in his journal (at the University of Virginia), p. 48. Couthouy's angry encounter with Wilkes is recorded in an August 31, 1839, entry. Peale's frustrations appear in an August 29, 1839, entry. For an interesting analysis of the tensions between the Expedition's officers and scientists, see Elizabeth Musselman's "Science as a Landed Activity: Scientifics and Seamen Aboard the U.S. Exploring Expedition" in *Surveying the Record,* edited by Edward C. Carter II, pp. 77–101. Reynolds tells of the disintegration of relations between Wilkes and his officers in a December 22, 1839, letter to Lydia. Reynolds includes a copy of Wilkes's order concerning "familiarity among officers of the different grades" in his August 28, 1839, response to Wilkes, in Box 1, Area File 9, RG 45, NA. Reynolds talks about the motivations behind the order in his Manuscript, pp. 26–27. Wilkes writes to Jane of his having "given up inviting the officers to my table" in a September 12–21, 1839, letter.

Reynolds describes Wilkes's behavior at Napuka Atoll (referred to as Wytoohee) in his Manuscript, pp. 24–25. The near-collision of the *Flying Fish* and the *Vincennes* would be seemingly endlessly revisited in both Pinkney's and Wilkes's courts-martial (No. 826 and 827, NA); Wilkes gives his side of what happened in his *Narrative,* p. 332, and ACW, p. 429–30, while Reynolds gives a quite different version in his Manuscript, pp. 22–23; Reynolds also details several incidents that illustrate Wilkes's lack of seamanship, pp. 27–28.

Reynolds questions Wilkes's sanity in a December 22, 1839, letter to Lydia. Wilkes speaks of Jane being his "moderation" in an August 18, 1838, letter. Wilkes brags to Jane about his management of his officers, whom he refers to as "drones," in letters written on June 12–16 and July 3, 1839. In the introduction to ACW, John Kane, Jr., refers to Wilkes as the "Stormy Petrel," p. v. Reynolds talks about Wilkes's tendency to order all hands on deck in his Manuscript, p. 27. The surgeon John Fox testifies to Wilkes's sleeping habits in testimony recorded during Wilkes's court-martial, No. 287, p. 240. Wilkes's writes of his "constant anxiety" in ACW, p. 429.

Jacques Brosse in *Great Voyages of Discovery* recounts how De Brosses coined the term "Polynesia," p. 16. Ernest Dodge tells of Magellan's voyage across the Pacific in *Islands and Empires,* pp. 3–7. For information on Wallis, Cook, Bougainville, and Tahiti, I have relied, in large part on Brosse's *Great Voyages,* pp. 19–42. Dodge discusses the missionaries in Tahiti in *Islands and Empires,* pp. 87–92. Wilkes's memories of the squadron's arrival at Tahiti appear in ACW, p. 424. Wilkes tells Jane about the measures he has taken to eliminate improper relations between his men and the Tahitian women in a September 12–21 letter. Wilkes writes of the scientists' forays into the interior of the island in his *Narrative,* vol. 2, pp. 28–29, 44–47. Charles Pickering writes about the fallacy of applying Western rules to the Tahitians in a September 21, 1839, entry; he speaks about the Tahitians' ability to take advantage of their environment on September 23, 1839; Pickering's journal is at the Academy of Natural Sciences, Ewell Sale Stewart Library. In *New Lands, New Men,* William Goetzmann attributes "the first glimmerings of what came to be known by the end of the nineteenth century as 'cultural relativism'" to Herman Melville, p. 234. But here we see the concept in the writings of both Pickering and

Reynolds, well before the publication of Melville's first novel *Typee* in 1846.
James Dana testifies to the positive shift the scientists experienced once the
squadron reached Tahiti in a February 12, 1846, letter to Asa Gray (at the Gray
Herbarium Archives, Harvard): "The Scientifics had all they desired, after this
first year's doings of which Couthouy so complains." Reynolds records Wilkes's
arrogant words about the impossibility of action being taken against him until
the return of the squadron in his Manuscript, p. 31.

　　Wilkes describes Pago Pago Harbor in his *Narrative,* vol. 2, p. 70. Reynolds
recounts his and Underwood's circumnavigation of Tutuila in his journal.
Wilkes speaks of the *Peacock*'s difficult leave-taking from Pago Pago in his *Narrative,* p. 81; of his own troubles leaving Pago Pago, he simply says, "The moment was a trying one, and the event doubtful; all were at their stations, and not
a word was spoken. Of my own feelings on the occasion I have no very precise
recollection; merely remembering that I felt as if I breathed more freely after
the crisis had passed and we were in safety," p. 87. Reynolds provides two detailed accounts of the near-disaster at Pago Pago—in his journal and in his Manuscript, p. 30. In *Seamanship in the Age of Sail,* John Harland speaks of the
methods of coaxing a ship through a tack in light air, p. 186. Whittle's assessment of Wilkes's "symptoms of confusion and alarm" are in his journal, p. 80.
Reynolds's account of the events that led to his suspension is from his journal.

　　My account of the "almost mutiny" aboard the *Vincennes* has been pieced
together from ACW, pp. 430–31, and Hudson's November 4, 1839, journal entry, pp. 328–30, describing a meeting aboard the *Vincennes* in which Wilkes accused Couthouy of insubordination. According to Hudson, Couthouy urgently
denied "any insubordinate intention" and countered with the claim that many
of Wilkes's officers were refusing to assist the scientists in collecting specimens.
Wilkes was scheduled to meet with the chiefs of Upolu in a few hours and
didn't want to hear any more from Couthouy and told him the meeting was
over. But just as Wilkes prepared to leave his cabin, Couthouy returned, breathlessly insisting that Wilkes should speak to Passed Midshipman William May,
who had refused "to make collections." May soon appeared "in a state of some
excitement," denying Couthouy's accusation. After assuring May that he believed him, Wilkes left for the meeting. Hudson's account clearly indicates that
Wilkes succeeded in putting Couthouy on the defensive. Tyler, p. 115, also
draws on Wilkes's and Hudson's accounts of this encounter but places greater
faith in Wilkes's memory than I have. For more information about Joseph
Couthouy, see Michael Wentworth's "The Naked Couthouy."

　　Reynolds's account of his conversation with Wilkes about his "improper &

disrespectful manner" is from his journal, as is his description of his adventures on Upolu. For information on Horatio Hale, I have depended on Jacob Gruber's "Horatio Hale and the Development of American Anthropology," *The American Philosophical Society,* pp. 9–11, as well as Stanton, pp. 65–66. Ben Finney's *Voyage of Rediscovery* provides a useful analysis of James Cook's emerging awareness that the peoples of Polynesia came from a single source, pp. 6–13. For my account of the birth of Polynesian culture and how that culture was transported to the islands of the Pacific, I have relied on Patrick Kirch's *On the Road of the Winds,* pp. 211–41; the estimate of pre-contact population density on Upolu is from Kirch, p. 312; Kirch also speaks of methods of population control, p. 309; how each Polynesian canoe was "an arkful of biotic resources," p. 303; and the fact that a South Pacific island is not naturally suited to human habitation, pp. 315–16. Finney in *Voyage of Rediscovery* cites Hale's use of Ex. Ex. meteorological data in developing his theory of how the Polynesians pushed east, p. 17. Kirch discusses the predicted sequence of island discoveries, p. 241; he has revised his estimated dates of settlement in *Hawaiki, Ancestral Polynesia: An Essay in Historical Anthropology,* p. 79; my thanks to Paul Geraghty for bringing this source to my attention. Reynolds's concerns about the westernization of Upolu, as well as his reveries about Emma, are in his journal.

Reynolds's account of his run-in with Carr is from his journal. Whittle's grief-stricken words about Reynolds's departure are in a November 11, 1839, entry in his journal, p. 84. Reynolds recounts his excitement about the squadron's arrival at Sydney in his journal; he speaks of Wilkes having received help from his quartermaster in his Manuscript, p. 31.

CHAPTER 7: ANTARCTICA

My description of Antarctica is derived from several sources; many of the statistics come from the modern-day compilation of sailing directions published by the National Imagery and Mapping Agency known as the *Antarctic Pilot,* pp. 18–22, 82, and the *Polar Regions Atlas* published by the Central Intelligence Agency, pp. 35–37, as well as *The Book of the World,* New York: Macmillan Library, 1998, pp. 29, 112–13, and *The National Geographic Atlas of the World,* Seventh Edition, Washington, D.C.: National Geographic, 1999, pp. 122–23; and conversations with retired navy commander Maurice Gibbs, who served as a meteorologist in Antarctica. For information on James Ross, his discovery of the magnetic North Pole, and his preparations for going south, see Fergus Fleming's *Barrow's Boys,* pp. 291–92; 334–35. On the "Magnetic Crusade," see

John Cawood's "Terrestrial Magnetism and the Development of International Collaboration in the Early Nineteenth Century," pp. 585–86.

Wilkes tells what the people of Sydney thought of the U.S. Ex. Ex., especially relative to the Ross Expedition, as well as his own expedition's preparation for the cruise south, in his *Narrative,* vol. 2, pp. 275–77. W. H. Smyth's definition of "martinet" is in his *Sailor's Word Book,* p. 471. The phrase "mask of command" comes from the book of that title by John Keegan. Wilkes tells of the effects of being a martinet in ACW, p. 391. He speaks of being "a *great* man" in a December 10, 1839, letter to Jane. Wilkes describes the difference in leadership styles between himself and Hudson in ACW, p. 403. Reynolds's reference to "Antarctic Stock" is from a March 4, 1840, letter to his mother. Wilkes speaks of the travails of Lieutenant Ringgold in ACW, p. 439, 443–44. Sinclair's mention of the *Flying Fish's* miserable crew is in a December 25, 1839, journal entry.

Wilkes describes squadron logistics at the beginning of the southern cruise in his *Narrative,* vol. 2, p. 283. Reynolds speaks of Wilkes's nefarious strategizing in his Manuscript, pp. 33–34. Sinclair tells of the *Flying Fish's* problems on January 1 in his journal; Reynolds provides the description of Wilkes's interchange with his officers in his Manuscript, p. 35; he also talks of Wilkes's "miserable double dealing," p. 36. Unless otherwise cited, all of Reynolds's descriptions of the Antarctic cruise are from his private journal. Joseph Underwood speaks of the sluggishness of the compass in a January 11, 1840, journal entry. Eld describes Hudson's curiously lackadaisical response to their discovery of land in testimony from Wilkes's court martial, #827, pp. 199 200.

Reynolds gives a fascinating account of Wilkes's propensity to dismiss the input of others: "[Wilkes] was so accustomed to contradict most flatly anyone who approached him with a report or with any subject *that did not originate with himself,* that his officers were really loath to subject themselves to such insolence," Manuscript, p. 41. Wilkes's description of navigating the ice in fog is from his *Narrative,* vol. 2, p. 294; his explanation of why he gave up on the idea of sailing in tandem is on p. 295. My description of the Newfoundland breed of dog is based on information in "Newfoundlands" by Sharon Hope available on the Web site www.k9.com. My thanks to Susan Beegel for bringing this resource to my attention.

Alden's description of the events of January 19, 1840, is from his testimony at Wilkes's court-martial, pp. 153–54; his journal of the voyage is logbook #120 at the Mariners Museum, Newport News, Virginia. Wilkes speaks of his lack of faith in his officers in a January 19, 1840, journal entry. John Williamson's testimony concerning his conversation with Wilkes on January 19 is from Wilkes's court-martial, p. 195. Davis tells of Hudson insisting that he erase the mention of land in testimony from Wilkes's court-martial, p. 195; Hudson also testified about the events of that day, p. 187. Reynolds provides added details about the *Peacock*'s encounter with an iceberg in his March 4, 1840, letter to his mother. The details about the *Peacock*'s chronometers being knocked over and the near crushing of a boat by two icebergs is from Wilkes's *Narrative,* vol. 2, pp. 302, 304; Wilkes also describes Hudson's last desperate attempt to push the *Peacock* through the ice, p. 305. Information on how to reship a rudder comes from John Harland's *Seamanship in the Age of Sail,* p. 302. Reynolds refers to Wilkes as the "hero of Pago Pago" in his Manuscript, p. 39.

CHAPTER 8: A NEW CONTINENT

Unless otherwise indicated, Wilkes's description of the *Vincennes*'s Antarctic cruise after January 23, 1840, comes from his *Narrative,* vol. 2, pp. 309–65. Joseph Underwood tells of his belief that a vessel might be driven further south, "if it were thought to be an object" in a January 22, 1840, journal entry; he describes his square-off with Wilkes in a January 24, 1840, entry. Wilkes speaks in detail about the episode at Disappointment Bay in ACW, p. 443. Reynolds tells of Wilkes's hatred of Underwood in his Manuscript, p. 42. Alden recounts his January 28 conversation with Wilkes about land in his testimony at Wilkes's court-martial, p. 157. Jared Elliott provides information on how the *Vincennes* was handled amid the ice in a February 21, 1840, entry. Reynolds tells of Wilkes's command style in the Antarctic in his Manuscript, p. 40; he also tells of Alden's and Blunt's account of the rescue of seaman Brooks, p. 41; as might be expected, Wilkes's account is quite different; in fact, he claims *he* was the one who first spotted Brooks on the yard, a statement that Reynolds angrily refutes.

For information on the aurora, I have relied on Robert Eather's *Majestic Lights: The Aurora in Science, History, and the Arts,* pp. 3, 51. Wilkes tells of his celebration of the discovery of the continent and some of his officers' disparaging remarks in ACW, p. 443. For information on the unusual clarity of the Antarctic atmosphere and the difficulties it creates in judging distances, see the *Antarctic Pilot,* p. 80. Charles Erskine tells of his experiences on the iceberg in *Twenty Years Before the Mast,* pp. 113–15; he also tells how he learned to read and write, pp. 39, 129. In *New Lands, New Men,* William Goetzmann refers to Wilkes's picture of himself sliding down the ice as "the only recorded instance where Wilkes seemed to have had a sense of humor," p. 206. Kenneth Bertrand in *Americans in Antarctica* mentions Ringgold's misguided decision to head the *Porpoise* north, p. 178. D'Urville's description of his encounter with the *Porpoise* is from his *Two Voyages to the South Seas,* p. 486.

Alden recounts the construction of the chart of Antarctica in his testimony at Wilkes's court-martial, p. 154. Wilkes tells of his "wisdom and perseverance" in a March 7–11, 1840, letter to Jane. Alden recounts Wilkes's speech about the secrecy of their discovery in Wilkes's court-martial, p. 159. D'Urville speaks of the "tough work" of sailing along the ice barrier in *Two Voyages to the South Seas,* pp. 489–90. Alden's testimony concerning his conversation with Wilkes about seeing land on January 19 is from Wilkes's court-martial, pp. 153–54. I am following William Stanton's lead in suspecting that Wilkes altered his journal entry for January 19; see Stanton, p. 173. Hudson unsuccessfully fended off charges that he altered his report to the secretary of the navy at Wilkes's court-martial, p. 185. Wilkes tells of his emotional meeting with Hudson in a March 27–April 5, 1840, letter to Jane. Ringgold speaks of asking Wilkes why he hadn't mentioned discovering land on January 26 in his testimony at Wilkes's court-martial, p. 162. Sinclair's skeptical words about Ringgold's newfound memory of seeing land are from an April 12, 1840, journal entry. Wilkes confesses to Jane that no one on the *Porpoise* and *Flying Fish* was originally aware of land to the south in a March 31, 1840, letter. Wilkes's April 5, 1840, letter to James Ross is included in Appendix XXIV of Wilkes's *Narrative,* vol. 2, pp. 453–56.

CHAPTER 9: **THE CANNIBAL ISLES**

In a March 18, 1840, letter to Jane, Wilkes speaks of his not having received a letter from her in sixteen months, as well as of Hudson having received a letter in Sydney dated the middle of August. His reference to not blaming Jane for the delay is in an August 13, 1840, letter. He speaks of being a "worn out old voyager" in a letter written between March 27 and April 5, 1840. Wilkes mentions the self-imposed distance between himself and Wilkes Henry in an August 18, 1840, letter to Jane.

R. A. Derrick's *History of Fiji* provides a good summary of exploration, shipping, and trade in the group, pp. 64–74. I have depended on Derrick's *The Fiji Islands: A Geographical Handbook* for geographical and cartographic information about the islands. Reynolds speaks of the motivations behind the Ex. Ex.'s survey of Fiji in his private journal, in which he also refers to Wilkes's actions against various officers; he writes of the destruction of his and May's "little palace" in an October 19, 1840, letter to his family. For information about

Congreve war rockets I have depended on Richard Hobbs's "The Congreve War Rockets, 1800–1825," in *U.S. Naval Institute Proceedings,* pp. 80–88.

James Cook's reference to the Fijians' "addiction" to cannibalism is cited in Fergus Clunie's *Fijian Weapons and Warfare,* p. 1. Derrick writes about Tasman, Cook, and Bligh in *A History of Fiji,* pp. 37–47. Reynolds, who speaks of Wilkes's preliminary chart of Fiji in his journal, tells of the pilot's interchange with the Expedition's commander in his Manuscript, p. 47. Wilkes writes of the squadron's arrival in Fiji in his *Narrative,* vol. 3, pp. 45–47. Reynolds's enthusiastic description of Ovalau is in a September 21, 1840, letter to his family. His description of a Fijian warrior is from his journal. Wilkes describes how a Fijian son strangles his mother and father in his *Narrative,* vol. 3, p. 94; he also speaks of the sacrifices that accompanied the launching of Tanoa's canoe, p. 97. Derrick chronicles instances of human sacrifice in *A History of Fiji,* p. 21, as does Clunie, p. 7. The reference to man being the most popular animal food source in Fiji is from Patrick Kirch's *On the Road of the Winds,* p. 160; Kirch also discusses the development of "conquest warfare" in Fiji, p. 160.

Derrick in *A History of Fiji* tells of the impact of Charlie Savage, pp. 44–45; he also speaks of "tame white men," p. 47. Clunie refers to David Whippy's mercenary beginnings in Fiji, p. 92. Wilkes tells of his strategy in contacting Tanoa in his *Narrative,* vol. 3, p. 48, in which he also recounts his climb up Nadelaiovalau, which he refers to as Andulong, pp. 50–52. Wilkes tells of setting up the observatory at Levuka and the organization of Alden's and Emmons's surveying parties in his *Narrative,* vol. 3, pp. 52–53. Wilkes recounts giving Sinclair a "severe rebuke" in ACW, p. 457; Sinclair gives his side of it in a May 11, 1840, journal entry.

Wilkes recounts Tanoa's dramatic arrival in his *Narrative,* vol. 3, p. 54. Derrick in *A History of Fiji* tells about Tanoa's and Seru's decimation of Verata, p. 22. The missionary's account of Seru's torture and eating of two prisoners appears in Clunie, p. 41. In his journal Reynolds refers to the squadron's determination "to have the thing settled" when it came to the question of cannibalism, adding: "I remember reading in some book of travels, the assertion of the author, 'that he considered all the accounts of such a practice among any people, to be fabulous: the bug bear stories of voyagers who delighted in tales of the marvelous: that he did not believe mankind could be so vile, or human nature so degraded: in short, that there was no such thing as a People who fed upon men for the love of it.' If this gentleman, who had such exceeding faith in the goodness of human kind, had been killed in Fegee, *his ghost* would have corrected his notions with a vengeance. (See Quarterly review, Dec. or Sep. 1836.)"

The argument to which Reynolds refers is essentially the same made by William Arens in *The Man-Eating Myth* (1979). See Gananath Obeyesekere's attempt to discount contemporary references to cannibalism in "Cannibal Feasts in Nineteenth-Century Fiji: Seamen's Yarns and the Ethnographic Imagination," pp. 87–109; in *Cannibalism and the Colonial World,* edited by Francis Barker, et al. While Obeyesekere makes the excellent point that the sailors' fears of survival cannibalism at sea contributed to their obsession with native cannibalism, he chooses not to refer to the Expedition's findings concerning cannibalism, even though he is clearly aware of Wilkes's *Narrative.* For a contrasting view, see Marshall Sahlins's "Raw Women, Cooked Men, and Other 'Great Things' of the Fiji Islands," in *The Ethnography and the Historical Imagination,* edited by John and Jean Camaroff.

Wilkes describes his meeting with Tanoa in his *Narrative,* vol. 3, pp. 55–60. Wilkes tells of his meeting with Paddy O'Connell and his decision to abduct Veidovi, whom Wilkes refers to as "Vendovi" (my thanks to Fiji scholar Paul Geraghty for pointing out the proper spelling of Veidovi), in his *Narrative,* vol. 3, pp. 68–69, 104–5. Reynolds recounts how Hudson went about capturing Veidovi in his journal, as does Wilkes in his *Narrative,* vol. 3, pp. 126–36. Wilkes tells of Whippy's concerns about the taking of Veidovi in his *Narrative,* vol. 3, pp. 141–42; his description of how his dog Sydney protected him in Fiji is from ACW, p. 462. Wilkes recounts his meeting with Belcher in his *Narrative,* vol. 3, p. 182; in ACW, pp. 463–64; and in a June 22, 1840, letter to Jane.

Reynolds speaks of Perry's three weeks without orders from Wilkes in his Manuscript, p. 53. In addition to his journal, Reynolds tells of boat surveying duty in a September 21, 1840, letter to his family. Hudson's calculation about the number of miles traveled by the *Peacock*'s boats in Fiji is in his journal, p. 567. Reynolds describes the cannibalism incident aboard the *Peacock* in his journal, while Wilkes tells of Hudson vomiting in an August 10, 1840, letter to Jane. My thanks to Jane Walsh, an anthropologist at the Smithsonian Institution who has worked extensively with the Ex. Ex. collection, for sharing an article in manuscript in which she writes probingly about how the Fijians consciously manipulated the Expedition's officers' and scientists' fears of cannibalism.

James Dana refers to the botanist Rich as "so-so" in a June 15, 1840, letter to Asa Gray in Daniel Gilman's *Life of James Dwight Dana,* p. 122. Wilkes mentions the discovery of a new species of tomato and a stand of sandalwood trees, as well as Horatio Hale's Fijian vocabulary, in his *Narrative,* vol. 3, pp. 306, 309, 325, 341. Derrick cites Hale's reference to Fiji being "the school of arts of the

Pacific Islands," p. 17. For information about Pickering and Brackenridge in Fiji, I have also relied on Richard Eyde's "Expedition Botany: The Making of a New Profession" in MV, p. 30. James Dana tells of how Darwin's insights "threw a flood of light" on his own thinking about coral reefs in the preface to his *Corals and Coral Islands,* p. 7. Daniel Appleman's "James Dwight Dana and Pacific Geology" provides an excellent account of Dwight's use of Darwin's insight about coral reefs, MV, pp. 91–95; Appleman also refers to how Dwight's subsequent work during the Expedition would anticipate the theory of plate tectonics, p. 110.

Wilkes's account of what he did during the four-day gale is in his *Narrative,* vol. 3, p. 239, in which he also provides a detailed account of the incident at Solevu, which he refers to as Sualib, pp. 239–44. My account of the attack on Solevu also relies on the journals of Reynolds and Sinclair; Erskine, who was part of Perry's boat-crew, also tells of the incident in *Twenty Years Before the Mast,* pp. 163–65. James Dana writes of the need to do something more than burn a Fijian village in a June 15, 1840, letter to Asa Gray in Daniel Gilman's *Life of James Dwight Dana,* p. 120.

CHAPTER 10: MASSACRE AT MALOLO

Wilkes tells of organizing the survey of the Yasawa Group in his *Narrative,* vol. 3, p. 247. Sinclair voices his suspicions that Wilkes was mounting a "war party" in a July 15, 1840, journal entry. Wilkes refers to having reached "the top of the hill" in a June 22, 1840, letter to Jane. Reynolds's bitter remarks concerning Wilkes's unwillingness to include him in the survey party are in his journal. Sinclair describes Wilkes's unseamanlike management of the *Flying Fish* in a July 16, 1840, entry; he also expresses his bewilderment and frustrations with his commander on July 17; he mentions Underwood's loss of a mast on July 16. Reynolds details Wilkes's persecution of Underwood in his Manuscript, p. 52. In his journal, William Briscoe, the ship's armorer, included excerpts from Jared Elliott's eulogy for Underwood and Henry, in which Elliott speaks of Underwood's innate politeness. Wilkes tells of being pursued by native canoes to the western shore of Viti Levu in his *Narrative,* vol. 3, p. 259–61. Sinclair expresses his regret that the *Flying Fish* did not sail on to Malolo in a July 24, 1840, journal entry.

My account of the deaths of Underwood and Henry and the attack on Malolo are drawn from Wilkes's *Narrative,* vol. 3, pp. 266–84; as well as the journals of Reynolds, Sinclair, Emmons, Alden, and Briscoe; and Joseph Clark's *Lights and Shadows of Sailor Life*, pp. 149–57. Wilkes writes of being "unfit for further duty" after the massacre at Malolo in an August 10, 1840, letter to Jane, written on the second anniversary of leaving his family in Washington, D.C.; he also mentions finding fault with both Underwood and Alden in this August 10 letter. Reynolds describes the auction of Underwood's possessions in his Manuscript, pp. 52–53, where he also writes of Wilkes's treatment of Veidovi, p. 55. Wilkes tells of having the ship's barber cut off Veidovi's hair in ACW, p. 475. Reynolds describes his and his fellow officers' depressed mental state after the Fiji survey in his journal.

CHAPTER 11: MAUNA LOA

Harold Bradley writes of how Americans dominated whaling in Hawaii in *The American Frontier in Hawaii*, p. 218. Charles Erskine describes how the sailors were dressed when they went out on leave in *Twenty Years Before the Mast*, p. 205. Reynolds recounts how the sailors conducted themselves while on leave in his journal. Erskine tells of writing his first letter to his mother in *Twenty Years*, p. 204. Reynolds recalls reading his mail in Honolulu in a September 21, 1840, letter to his family. I have also drawn upon letters he wrote on October 19, 1840, and November 16, 1840.

Wilkes tells of the "30 or 40 letters waiting for me" in a letter to Jane dated October 2–11, 1840. In two undated private letters to Secretary Paulding at DU, Wilkes informs him of his charges against Lee and Pinkney. "Over half my labours in this service," he writes, "have been driving the officers to their duty." Wilkes would produce a portion of Paulding's encouraging letter of December 14, 1839, as evidence in his court-martial; it was reprinted in the *New York Herald*, August 3, 1842. Wilkes writes of the dismissal of Pinkney, Guillou, and Couthouy in letters to Jane dated November 8–22, November 30, and in an undated letter probably written in November 1840, claiming, "I take great pleasure in driving them up to the mark by whip and spur." The reference to Wilkes "getting delirious" appeared in *Niles Weekly Register*, LVII (December 21, 1839), p. 258. Wilkes claims in a November 8–22, 1840, letter to Jane that Couthouy "has been writing all the lies home to his friend [Jeremiah] Reynolds that have been published." The quotations about senior officers being "immune to any serious punishment" come from Harold Langley's *Social Reform in the United States Navy, 1798–1862*, p. 24.

Wilkes refers to the "all protecting care over me" in a May 22, 1839, letter to Jane. His angry words about Gilliss addressing him "with familiarity" are in an undated letter to Jane probably written in November 1840. In an undated letter probably written in the fall of 1840, he encloses a miniature of himself painted by the artist Alfred Agate that shows him with a captain's two epaulets and asks Jane if she thinks "I am improved in appearance by the addition to my shoulders." Reynolds's words about Wilkes being "either crazy, beyond redemption, or . . . a rascally tyrant" are from his journal. Wilkes writes to Jane of making the Expedition "a brilliant one" in an undated letter probably written in November 1840, in which he also refers to "our promotions." William Reynolds speaks of the news about Antarctica being received "with great Enthusiasm" in a November 16, 1840, letter.

Herman Melville writes of the "judicial severity" practiced by a navy captain in *White-Jacket,* p. 301. A list of the twenty-five instances in which Wilkes inflicted more than twelve lashes on his men is included in the Wilkes Court-Martial file, pp. 19–21. Harold Langley covers the history of flogging in *Social Reform in the United States Navy,* pp. 137–38; he also provides an excellent description of how it was performed, pp. 139–141. Wilkes's treatment of the marines who initially refused to reenlist is documented in his Court-Martial file, pp. 19–21; George Colvocoresses testified concerning Wilkes's actions against the marines, pp. 123–24. Langley writes of the marines' "strange dual situation in regard to flogging," p. 142. George Emmons, who brought charges against the marines Ward and Riley, writes of their and Sweeney's punishments in an October 31, 1840, journal entry. Wilkes speaks of the consul's complaints concerning the behavior of American whalemen and his decision to whip Sweeney and the marines "round the fleet" in his *Narrative,* vol. 4, p. 57. Langley describes flogging round the fleet as a "death sentence" and also speaks of its rarity in the U.S. Navy, p. 142. Admiral W. H. Smyth in the *Sailor's Word-Book* defines flogging round the fleet as "a diabolical punishment," p. 582. My account of the flogging is also based on descriptions provided by Charles Erskine in *Twenty Years,* pp. 208–9; the October 31, 1840, journal entry of John Dyes; and testimony during Wilkes's court-martial from Robert Johnson, p. 145, and Overton Carr, p. 203.

Wilkes writes of the great potential of Pearl Harbor in his *Narrative,* vol. 4, p. 79. Reynolds recounts his last-minute transfer from the *Peacock* to the *Flying Fish* in his journal. For information on Mauna Loa I have relied on the monograph *Mauna Loa Revealed,* edited by J. M. Rhodes and John Lockwood, especially the Preface, xi–xii; and the chapter by Walther Barnard, "Mauna Loa Volcano: Historical Eruptions, Exploration, and Observations (1799–1910)," pp. 1–19. See also *Volcanoes in the Sea: The Geology of Hawaii* by Gordon Macdonald, et al., and Andrew Doughty and Harriett Friedman's *Hawaii: The Big Island Revealed*, pp. 28–29. Victor Lenzen and Robert Multhauf in "Development of Gravity Pendulums in the 19th Century" discuss Bouguer's pioneering use of the pendulum in the Andes in *The Museum of History and Technology*, pp. 307–9. See also John Noble Wilford's account of Bouguer's activities in *The Mapmakers*, pp. 128–30.

James Dana describes his hastily formed impressions of Mauna Loa and Kilauea in a November 30, 1840, letter to Edward Herrick, in Daniel Gilman's *Life of James Dwight Dana*, pp. 124–26. Wilkes writes of his climb up Mauna Loa "being one of the great works of my cruise" in a December 11, 1840, letter to Jane. He writes of his sedan chair and the absurdity of the scene as they set out up the volcano in a January 24, 1841, letter to Jane. Unless otherwise indicated, Wilkes's description of his climb up Mauna Loa, as well as his visit to Kilauea, are from his *Narrative*, vol. 4, pp. 112–75. Wilkes would visit Kilauea a second time after climbing up Mauna Loa; it was during this second visit that Dr. Judd's hairbreadth escape occurred. Roberta Sprague's "Measuring the Mountain: The United States Exploring Expedition on Mauna Loa, 1840–41" in *The Hawaiian Journal of History*, pp. 71–91, is based almost exclusively on Wilkes's *Narrative*. Charles Erskine recounts the yarn about dropping an iceberg in the caldera of Kilauea in *Twenty Years*, pp. 214–15. Wilkes speaks of regretting the loss of his chair soon after departing from Kilauea in a January 24, 1841, letter to Jane.

For information on altitude sickness, I have depended on *Medicine for Mountaineering*, edited by James Wilkerson, pp. 220–26. Erskine describes his and his fellow sailors' "mirth and gayety" in the cave at Recruitment Station in *Twenty Years*, p. 219. Wilkes tells of his reaction to Judd's news of the natives' desertion in a January 24, 1841, letter to Jane. Erskine's description of the hurricane atop Mauna Loa is in *Twenty Years*, pp. 221–22. Wilkes tells of his final examination of the snow-covered caldera of Mauna Loa in his *Narrative*, vol. 4, pp. 159–60. Snow blindness is described in *Medicine for Mountaineering*, p. 285. Wilkes speaks of the "loomi-loomi" in his *Narrative*, vol. 4, p. 166.

John Dyes's account of "yellow Hores" aboard the *Vincennes* is in a March 2, 1841, journal entry, in which he adds, "This has took place several times while her in the Captains Absence." William May writes of his sexual relationship with a native girl in a May 9, 1841, letter to William Reynolds, Box 1, Area File 9, RG 45, NA. Wilkes complains of Chaplain Elliott's behavior in an undated letter to Jane probably written in the fall of 1840.

CHAPTER 12: THE WRECK OF THE *PEACOCK*

An excellent discussion of the joint occupation of the Oregon territory by the United States and Britain is *The Wilkes Expedition: Puget Sound and the Oregon Country,* edited by Frances Barkan, p. 92. For information on the discovery and exploration of the Columbia River, I have relied on William Dietrich's *Northwest Passage: The Great Columbia River,* pp. 67–70, and Timothy Egan's *The Good Rain: Across Time and Terrain in the Pacific Northwest,* pp. 27–29. Vancouver's mention of detecting freshwater along the Oregon coast is cited in Egan, p. 28. Gray's discovery of the Columbia is recounted in John Boit's log, which appears in *Voyages of the Columbia,* edited by Frederick Howay. My thanks to Mary Malloy for providing me with the estimate of the number of ships that had visited the Columbia River prior to Lewis and Clark. William Reynolds writes of the surprise of Belcher's officers when they heard the Ex. Ex. was to survey the Columbia River in a October 19, 1840, letter.

Wilkes was in such a rush to get the *Vincennes* and the *Porpoise* out of Honolulu that he personally oversaw the recoppering of the brig. His lack of knowledge in this area, however, turned the usually straightforward procedure into a comical embarrassment for his officers. In his March 26, 1841, journal entry, George Sinclair writes, "Capt. Wilkes seems to have taken charge of the operation and everything goes on head over heels and is more noise and confusion than would be made in heaving down the whole navy at home." Robert Johnson speculates about Wilkes's commodore's pennant in a March 24, 1841, journal entry: "I can suppose the possibility of the commander of the Expedition having authority to hoist a broad pendant, but it does appear to me strange he should do so without by intimation (at least) of such authority, Subject himself to the Suspicion, which I believe to be general, of an usurpation of dignities which are not his of right." Wilkes writes of meeting Captain Aulick with his commodore pennant flying in a letter to Jane written from March 14–April 4, 1841.

Wilkes's description of the Columbia River bar is in his *Narrative,* vol. 4, p. 293. My description of the Columbia River and the many shipwrecks that have occurred at the bar are based on Dietrich's *Northwest Passage,* pp. 97–109, and Egan's *The Good Rain,* pp. 16–18. See also James Gibbs's *Pacific Graveyard.*

The Columbia River pilot Captain James McAvoy, of the aptly named *Peacock*, compares the collision of waters at the bar to "two giant hammers" in Egan's *The Good Rain*, p. 24; Dietrich cites the reference by the Reverend Samuel Parker to the large number of deaths at the bar, p. 108. Wilkes refers to his decision not to cross the Columbia bar and to survey Puget Sound, as well as the near-disaster at Destruction Isle, in his *Narrative*, vol. 4, p. 294. William May tells of the "tremendous bustle of bending cables" that ensued in a May 9, 1841, letter to William Reynolds, Box 1, Area File 9, RG 45, NA. Wilkes's description of Veidovi's "contempt" for the region's native people is in his *Narrative*, vol. 4, p. 297, as are his words of praise for Puget Sound, p. 305. Dietrich in *Northwest Passage* points out that there are now four navy bases in Puget Sound with none on the Columbia River, p. 109.

My account of Wilkes's activities in the Pacific Northwest owes much to Constance Bordwell's "Delay and Wreck of the *Peacock:* An Episode in the Wilkes Expedition" in *Oregon Historical Quarterly;* also, Edmond S. Meany provides a useful transcription of Wilkes's difficult-to-decipher journal in his "Diary of Wilkes in the Northwest" in *The Washington Historical Quarterly.* Wilkes writes of having "no further difficulties with the officers" in a May 28, 1841, letter to Jane.

Wilkes tells of his concerns about Hudson's ability to complete his assignment in the central Pacific cruise in ACW, pp. 499–500. Wilkes's orders to Hudson are in Appendix VIII of his *Narrative*, vol. 4, pp. 517–19. Reynolds's complaints about Hudson and the six month cruise are from his journal. Daniel Appleman in "James Dwight Dana and Pacific Geology" in MV discusses how Dana's observations of the linear pattern of island chains was "fundamental" to the formulation of the theory of plate tectonics, pp. 106–110. See also Robert Dott Jr.'s "James Dwight Dana's Old Tectonics–Global Contraction Under Divine Direction" in *American Journal of Science*, pp. 283–311.

Bordwell in "Delay and Wreck of the *Peacock*" makes the point that Wilkes's appearance at Fort Vancouver, "attended by a middle-aged draftsman clad in navy fatigues and armed only with a sketchbook," had the effect of reducing the likelihood that the Hudson's Bay Company would perceive the Ex. Ex. as a possible threat to their dominance in the region, p. 135. Charles Erskine describes the Fourth of July celebration at Fort Cowlitz in *Twenty Years Before the Mast*, pp. 235–38. Wilkes recounts how he found the celebration "truly gratifying," as well as his concerns about the *Peacock*, in his *Narrative*, vol. 4, p. 412.

Reynolds's remarks about the importance of the Columbia survey to the

Expedition and the sense of foreboding that gripped himself and the others are from his journal. Wilkes attributes the loss of the *Peacock* to Hudson's "apprehensions and imagination" in ACW, p. 502. My account of the wreck is based primarily on Hudson's journal, a microfilm copy of which is at the University of North Carolina, and Emmons's journal, at Yale, for the days July 18–20, 1841, and Wilkes's *Narrative,* vol. 4, pp. 489–94. Bordwell in "Delay and Wreck of the *Peacock*" also provides a useful description of the wreck, pp. 162–63, as do Stanton, pp. 249–52, and Tyler, pp. 285–99.

Unless otherwise indicated, Reynolds's accounts of his time at the Columbia River are from his journal. Wilkes speaks of the "state of feeling" that led him to drive his officers to complete the survey of Puget Sound in his *Narrative,* vol. 4, p. 478. Drew Crooks provides a detailed account of the Washington place names left by the Ex. Ex. in *The Wilkes Expedition,* edited by Frances Barkan, pp. 96–124. Wilkes recounts first hearing the news of the loss of the *Peacock* in his *Narrative,* vol. 4, p. 484. He speculates as to why Hudson was delayed so long in a July 27, 1841, journal entry. John Frazier Henry, in "The Midshipman's Revenge" in *Pacific Northwest Quarterly,* theorizes that William May introduced two nonexistent islands into the survey of the San Juan Islands, Adolphus and Gordon, so as to embarrass Wilkes, p. 159. Although an intriguing theory, the bogus islands may have also been the result of the hurried nature of the Expedition's survey of the island group in the wake of the *Peacock*'s loss. Wilkes's confrontation with Robert Johnson is detailed in Wilkes's July 17, 1841, journal entry.

Wilkes's frustrations about how Hudson conducted his cruise of the central Pacific are in an August 6, 1841, journal entry. I have found Bordwell's analysis of the mounting tensions between Wilkes and Hudson during the survey of the river especially helpful, pp. 169–73. Wilkes tells of having to start from scratch with the survey of the river in his *Narrative,* vol. 5, p. 113; he speaks of how he labored to "bring things into order" in ACW, p. 503. Soon after Wilkes asked Reynolds about his pea jacket, he decided that it was too dangerous to continue sailing up the river on a foggy night and ordered the *Flying Fish* back to Bakers Bay. "No man in his senses," Reynolds ranted, "would have *started.* Great was our relief, to get rid of him. When we reached the cove, he went ashore & pitched his tent for the night." Wilkes describes the incident with his commodore's pennant in an August 25, 1841, journal entry. Both Stanton, p. 267, and Bordwell, p. 175, speak of the importance of Wilkes's decision to allow the philologist Horatio Hale to leave the squadron and pursue his own interests.

Henry Eld's praise of Wilkes's "indomitable perseverance & tenacity" comes from a letter he wrote to his father after the Expedition on March 16, 1845 (at LOC); cited by Tyler, p. 397. Unlike Reynolds, Eld had maintained a healthy skepticism concerning the Expedition and its leader from the very beginning. Back on August 17, 1838, as the squadron sailed from Norfolk, Virginia, he wrote his father that "all the Zeal that I ever felt for the Service or my country has Evaporated" (LOC). Having never committed himself on a personal level to Wilkes, Eld was able to witness the disintegration of relations between the commander and his officers with an unusual, and much-needed, degree of detachment.

Wilkes writes about his potential difficulties with the secretary of the navy and the possibility of a "full investigation" in an October 18, 1841, letter to Jane. Reynolds predicts that there will be a court-martial at the end of the Expedition in an August 10, 1841, letter to his father. Reynolds compares refitting the schooner at sea to a drowning man mending his clothes in a November 7, 1841, letter. He describes the *Flying Fish*'s difficulties off Oregon in both his journal and a November 7, 1841, letter to Lydia. Wilkes writes about Yerba Buena and San Francisco Bay, as well as the *Vincennes*'s ordeal at the bar, in his *Narrative*, vol. 5, pp. 152, 171, 254–56. He tells of being "master now of all" in an October 18, 1841, letter to Jane.

CHAPTER 13: HOMEWARD BOUND

In a November 22, 1841, letter to Jane, Wilkes reveals his plan to use his findings from the Pacific Northwest to win himself a promotion: "I have no idea of giving up my results until I am satisfied they intend doing what I conceive ought in justice to be done for me." For information concerning how developing American attitudes toward the Oregon territory influenced Wilkes and the Expedition, I have looked to John Wickman's dissertation "Political Aspects of Charles Wilkes's Work and Testimony, 1842–1849," Indiana University, pp. 27–28. Wilkes speaks of John Aulick's claims about his unbalanced mental state and Ross's dismissal of his Antarctic results in two letters written on November 22 and November 27, 1841, both written from Oahu. James Ross would write in detail about his doubts about Wilkes's claims and his meeting with Aulick in *A Voyage of Discovery and Research in the Southern and Antarctic Regions*, pp. 275–90. Wilkes tells Jane to remove Aulick and his family from "the vocabulary of our acquaintance" in a November 27, 1841, letter.

William Reynolds writes of learning that the *Flying Fish* would not be sold in Oahu in his journal; unless otherwise noted, all quotations from Reynolds in this chapter are from his journal. Wilkes tells of the orders he issued to the Expedition's commanders at Oahu in his *Narrative,* vol. 5, p. 265; he also refers to the many "Asiatic nations" at Singapore, p. 374. George Emmons included extensive notes and transcripts from Knox's court of inquiry with the February 19, 1842, entry of his journal. Wilkes responds to the forty-two letters he received from Jane at Singapore in a February 20, 1842, letter. In a November 27, 1841, letter written at Oahu, he mentions his concerns about his sister Eliza: "I am well aware [it] will be a great trial meeting me yet I hope it may do her good. I have often been intending to write to her but could never yet bring myself to the trial." He also writes about Eliza in his letter from Singapore. Henry Wilkes writes about the "deplorable loss" of Wilkes Henry in a February 17, 1840, letter that was sent to Singapore (at DU).

Wilkes tells of his decision to sell the *Flying Fish* in his *Narrative,* vol. 5, pp. 409–10. Charles Erskine describes his emotions on seeing the schooner for the last time in *Twenty Years Before the Mast,* p. 257. William Reynolds provides a statistical analysis of those who served on the Ex. Ex. in his Manuscript, p. 70; he also speaks of how Wilkes found it necessary "to concoct some scheme by which he could divert the other vessels from their homeward course and secure to the *Vincennes* a sufficient start," p. 68. Erskine writes of the "gayety" aboard the *Vincennes* in *Twenty Years,* p. 258, in which he also tells of his trick using the dog Sydney and his decision not to reenter the navy, p. 263, and the death of George Porter, p. 258. Stanton describes the Fijian chief Veidovi as "the most spectacular of the specimens collected," p. 281. Erskine in *Twenty Years* claims that quartermaster Tom Piner's attempts to Christianize Veidovi were so successful that the men started referring to the chief as "The old Christian cannibal, man-eater," p. 194. Wilkes tells of the bond between Veidovi and the interpreter Benjamin Vanderford in his *Narrative,* vol. 5, p. 418. William Briscoe recounts the details of Vanderford's death in his March 23, 1842, journal entry.

For information about Secretary of the Navy Abel Upshur and his general attitude toward abuses by naval officers and by Wilkes in particular, I have depended on Wickman's "Political Aspects of Charles Wilkes's Work and Testimony," p. 23, and Claude Hall's *Abel Parker Upshur,* pp. 161–62. John S. Wily's March 10, 1842, letter to Jane Wilkes, urging her to do everything possible to win her husband a promotion, is at DU, as is Jane's memorandum, written in March 1842, describing her interviews with Upshur and President Tyler. Wilkes writes Jane of his hope of returning before the adjournment of Congress in a

February 20, 1842, letter. He tells of seeing the map of Ross's and d'Urville's voyages to Antarctica at the Cape Town Observatory in an April 15, 1842, journal entry; he tells of the stop at St. Helena in his *Narrative,* vol. 5, pp. 440–41; he writes of ordering the officers to turn over their personal collections in ACW, p. 515, where he also refers to the rumors concerning his having kept a collection for himself, p. 513. George Emmons tells of having to hand over the Fijian bow and arrow in May 16, 1842, journal entry. Wilkes recounts his confrontation with William May over his marked box of shells in a May 23, 1842, journal entry; he speaks of "The state of excitement I now feel" in a June 2, 1842, entry. Emmons describes his final run-in with Wilkes in a June 1, 1842, entry.

Wilkes recounts the *Vincennes*'s return to New York in his *Narrative,* vol. 5, pp. 452–53. Reynolds speaks of the officers' curiosity about how Wilkes would resolve the commodore pennant issue in his Manuscript, p. 69. Although Reynolds doesn't mention it, Wilkes's son Jack was a brand-new midshipman aboard the *Delaware* when Reynolds visited her officers at Rio de Janeiro; see ACW, p. 519. Reynolds refers to his dramatic weight loss during the Expedition as "enough to have satisfied a dozen Shylocks" in a November 7, 1841, letter to Lydia. Anne Hoffman Cleaver and E. Jeffrey Stann in *Voyage to the Southern Ocean* cite a reference Reynolds made in a letter eight years earlier to his having reached five feet ten and a half inches in height, p. 250. Veidovi's death and mutilation are recounted in the *New York Herald,* June 11, 17, 26, 1842. Veidovi's skull subsequently became part of the collections of the Smithsonian Institution. See T. D. Stewart's "The Skull of Vendovi: A Contribution of the Wilkes Expedition to the Physical Anthropology of Fiji."

CHAPTER 14: RECKONING

Wilkes describes his return to his house on Capitol Hill and Jane's knowledge of the "onslaught" that was about to be launched against him in ACW, p. 519. For my account of the political situation in which Wilkes found himself upon his return to Washington, I have looked to John Wickman's dissertation "Political Aspects of Charles Wilkes's Work and Testimony, 1842–1849," pp. 29–41. Secretary of the Navy Upshur's approach to officer relations is described in Claude Hall's *Abel Parker Upshur,* pp. 161–62. Wickman mentions the fact that Wilkes attended a meeting of the National Institute for the Promotion of Science on the same day of his arrival in Washington, p. 31. James Renwick's advice about how Wilkes should gain political support is in a June 19, 1842, letter to Jane at DU. Renwick, along with two of his sons, was involved in the survey on which the eventual Maine-Canada border would be based and therefore had much personal experience with the workings of the Tyler administration. Wilkes tells of his meetings with Upshur and President Tyler in ACW, pp. 520–22. In a June 21, 1842, letter to Wilkes, Upshur refers to Wilkes's June 16, 1842, letter in which he requested a court of inquiry; in Wilkes's Court-Martial records at NA. John Quincy Adams details his meeting with Wilkes in a June 15, 1842, diary entry, in *Memoirs of John Quincy Adams,* vol. 11, p. 177. In addition to Wilkes's account of his speech before the National Institute in ACW, pp. 525–26, I have relied on a story in the June 25, 1842, *National Intelligencer* and Wickman, pp. 36–37.

Upshur's June 21, 1842, letter to Wilkes denying his request for a court of inquiry is in Wilkes's Court-Martial records. Wickman discusses Wilkes's report on Oregon and his "nationalistic remarks concerning the necessity of the 54-40 boundary line," p. 38; he also describes Upshur's "plan of suppression" when it came to the report, pp. 39–41. Upshur's letter to Guillou ordering him to report to the Navy Department was produced during Wilkes's court-martial; Guillou testified that he had made two trips to Washington–during the spring and at the end of June–to assemble materials for the case against Wilkes. Wilkes's July 5, 1842, letter to Upshur complaining of the delay of his trial is in his court-martial records, as is Upshur's July 8, 1842, letter to Wilkes informing him of the date of his trial and the July 15, 1842, letter to Wilkes ordering him to turn over documents relating to the Expedition. Wilkes tells of how he boxed the "most important papers & documents" of the Expedition before leaving the *Vincennes* in ACW, p. 515. Wilkes recounts his conversation with Senator Wright about Upshur's order in ACW, p. 522. John Quincy Adams tells of his visit to Wilkes's house in a July 9, 1842, entry in his *Memoirs,* vol. 11, p. 202.

My account of the courts-martial of William May, Robert Johnson, Charles Guillou, Robert Pinkney, and Charles Wilkes is based primarily on the courts-martial records at NA; the reports in the *New York Herald,* beginning on July 26, 1842, and continuing on an almost daily basis until September 10, 1842; and letters written by Samuel Francis Du Pont on July 25, 27, 29, August 25, 31, September 22, October 6 and 14, 1842, at the Hagley Museum and Library, Wilmington, Delaware. For information on Du Pont's problems with Commodore Hull, I have consulted James Merrill's *Du Pont: The Making of an Admiral,* pp. 128–32, and Linda Maloney's "Isaac Hull: Bulwark of the Sailing Navy" in *Command Under Sail: Makers of the American Naval Tradition, 1775–1850,* edited by James Bradford, pp. 268–69; Maloney also speaks in general terms of the problems that the issue of rank had brought to the U.S. Navy in the 1840s, and specifically refers to the *Cyane,* p. 269.

An August 20, 1842, issue of the *Niles Register* refers to the uproar caused by the reading of Paulding's letter at Johnson's court-martial: "These instructions have been criticized by some with considerable severity." Wilkes's August 7, 1842, letter to Upshur, informing him that he cannot deliver the Ex. Ex. documents in his possession because of the "ominous and responsible situation in which I am placed," is in Wilkes's Court-Martial records. Reynolds praises Pinkney's defence in an August 21, 1842, letter to his father. Herman Viola's epilogue in *Voyage to the Southern Ocean* offers a chronology of the events leading up to Reynolds's marriage to Rebecca Krug and quotes from his August 14, 1842, letter to his father, p. 288; the letter from Lydia referring to Rebecca Krug's continued availability is cited on p. 285. Reynolds refers to the newlyweds' reception in New York in his August 21, 1842, letter to his father, where he also mentions Wilkes's mental state and his disappointment in Guillou's charges. Reynolds's description of Wilkes's defence is in a September 10, 1842, letter to his father. James Gordon Bennett's editorial concerning Wilkes's court-martial is in the September 10, 1842, issue of the *New York Herald.* Guillou's sheaf of letters of support is included as part of his court-martial records, as is President Tyler's commuted sentence. According to Wickman, "The fact that Guillou was the principal witness for the prosecution in Wilkes's trial possibly had something to do with this reversal," p. 71.

CHAPTER 15: THIS THING CALLED SCIENCE

John Wickman in *Political Aspects of Charles Wilkes's Work and Testimony, 1842–1849* discusses Upshur's attempt to have Robert Greenhow write the narrative, as well as Wilkes's relationship with Benjamin Tappan, pp. 51–62. Upshur became angry when Tappan referred to Wilkes as a captain, insisting that Wilkes was only a lieutenant. Tappan responded by reminding Upshur that his own president held a title he did not technically deserve since he had inherited the position after the death of Harrison and had not been formally elected by the American people.

Wilkes refers to the dispute over his pay in ACW, p. 531. In a September 22, 1842, letter to a naval friend, Samuel Du Pont writes, "You will find as soon as

Wilkes knows his Sentence, that the grand intrigue, public and private will be entered into, to raise him to a post Captaincy. We have had the Commercial already out telling what was done in like case for Parry RM, Vancouver, etc. I hope if he succeeds that he will be put at the head of the list." The author of the "Commercial" for Wilkes's promotion was apparently his brother-in-law James Renwick. In a June 19, 1842, letter to Jane Wilkes, Renwick refers to "Poinsett and Paulding's promise to seek for an appointment as Post Captain," and asks for information so that he can write up the case for Wilkes's promotion: "As a beginning I want the date of d'Urville and Charles's striking the icy barrier. The fact of d'Urville's promotion to an admiral, and from what rank, the fact of Ross' promotion and from what rank."

My description of the Ex. Ex.'s collection comes from Adrienne Kaeppler's "Anthropology and the U.S. Exploring Expedition" in MV, pp. 120–42. Richard Eyde in "Expedition Botany: The Making of a New Profession" in MV talks about the size of the botany collection, p. 25. George Watson in "Vertebrate Collections: Lost Opportunities" in MV states the number of birds, mammals, and fish, pp. 48, 69. Stanton provides statistics on the number of fossil species as well as coral and crustacea species, p. 317. Douglas Evelyn in "The National Gallery at the Patent Office" in MV cites Charles Pickering's account of the number of specimens in spirit jars and envelopes, p. 234. Kaeppler in MV describes Horatio Hale's linguistic achievement, which included the first account of Chinook Jargon, "a simplified hybrid language that had emerged on the northwest coast during the eighteenth century in the contacts between European sailors and traders and the Indians of the area," p. 142. Unfortunately, none of Hale's original notebooks have survived; Charles Pickering's are at the Academy of Natural Sciences in Philadelphia. William Goetzmann in *New Lands, New Men* describes the stunning scope and quality of the Expedition's charts, p. 290; he also makes the point that the Ex. Ex. collections "outran the intellectual resources of the country," p. 289. My account of the formation of the Smithsonian Institution is based largely on Nathan Reingold's and Marc Rothenberg's "The Exploring Expedition and the Smithsonian Institution" in MV, pp. 243–53. My thanks to Michael Hill for determining what Smithson's original bequest would have been worth in today's dollars. My account of the Expedition's relationship with the National Institute is based largely on Douglas Evelyn's "The National Gallery at the Patent Office" in MV, pp. 227–42, as well as Stanton, pp. 297–303; Stanton cites Pickering's statement that the Expedition's legacy should not be measured "by producing specimens to which an unfortunate importance has been so often attached but by the communication of facts," p. 297.

Wilkes describes his moves to improve the Ex. Ex. exhibit at the Patent Office in ACW, pp. 528–29. Tyler describes the team Wilkes put together to produce the charts, p. 391. Stanton cites Ralph Waldo Emerson's praise of the exhibit at the Patent Office, p. 301. Wilkes tells of the first lady's unsuccessful attempt to secure plants from the Expedition's greenhouse in ACW, pp. 529–30.

William Reynolds describes his visit to Washington, D.C., in a January 22, 1843, letter to Henry Eld. Wilkes claims to have been amused rather than angered by the "many misstatements and malicious remarks" in his officer's journal in ACW, p. 541, in which he also claims his own *Narrative* was "free from all vituperation," p. 532. James Renwick refers to Jane Wilkes as Wilkes's "amanuensis" in a January 8, 1843, letter to Jane, in which he also speaks of his progress in reading Wilkes's manuscript. Eliza Henry (Wilkes's sister) worries about Wilkes's working too late at night on his book in an April 3, 1843, letter to Wilkes (at DU). Wilkes claims his manuscript reached three thousand pages in ACW, p. 532, where he also describes his book as "a monument to my exertions," p. 533. His description of the explosion aboard the *Princeton* and the death of Upshur is in ACW, pp. 525, 584–87. I have also relied on Claude Hall's description of the incident in *Abel Upshur*, pp. 210–12.

Wilkes attributes "the style and beauty" of the published narrative to Joseph Drayton in ACW, p. 542; Daniel Haskell in *The United States Exploring Expedition and Its Publications* describes what the volumes looked like, pp. 33–34. Wickman claims that the Expedition's publications are "some of the most expensive books in the history of American printing," p. 92; he also discusses Wilkes's insistence on keeping the copyright to the *Narrative*, pp. 90–91. Wilkes tells of the challenge of seeing his big book through the press in ACW, pp. 535–37. Charles Davis's reference to the "oppressive dimensions" of the *Narrative* is in the *North American Review*, vol. LXI, 1845, p. 100; he also refers to the "variety of styles" that are apparent throughout the book. Wickman provides a synopsis of the many, largely positive reviews of the *Narrative*, p. 97. For James Fenimore Cooper's debt to Wilkes's *Narrative*, see W. B. Gates's "Cooper's *The Sea Lions* and Wilkes's Narrative" and "Cooper's *The Crater* and Two Explorers." David Jaffé in *The Stormy Petrel and the Whale* discusses Herman Melville's use of the *Narrative* in *Moby-Dick;* he also points to Ko-Towatowa as the "prototype for Queequeg," p. 43. Melville had a personal connection to the Expedition; before being detached from the squadron at Callao, his cousin Henry Gansevoort had been a passed midshipman on the *Peacock*. During the winter of 1858–59, Melville traveled around the Northeast delivering a lecture about the South Pacific that, as at least one newspaper reporter recognized, contained a veiled criticism of the Ex. Ex.'s attack on the Fijian village of Malolo. Melville termed it an "indiscriminate massacre upon some poor little village on the seaside–splattering the town's bamboo huts with blood and brains of women and children, defenseless and innocent," in "The South Sea" in *The Piazza Tales and Other Prose Pieces, 1839–1860,* pp. 415–16. David Roberts in *A Newer World* describes how Frémont's wife ghostwrote his books and cites Bernard De Voto's statement that Frémont's reports "were far more important than his travels," p. 127; he also tells of how the spring of 1845 marked the height of Frémont's celebrity, p. 138. According to Goetzmann, Frémont was "the explorer as propagandist *par excellence*," p. 172. See also Tom Chaffin's *The Pathfinder: John Charles Frémont and the Course of American Empire.*

The decision in the marines' suit against Wilkes is reported in the May 31, 1845, *Niles Register;* the suit is first mentioned almost three years earlier in the September 17, 1842, *Niles Register.* "Memorial of Officers of the Exploring Expedition" dated January 11, 1847, is in 29th Congress, 2nd Session, Senate, No. 47; the memorialists are William Walker, Robert Johnson, James Alden, John Dale, Edwin DeHaven, A. S. Baldwin, George Sinclair, William Reynolds, Simon Blunt, William May, Joseph Sanford, George Colvocoresses, and James Blair. Wilkes's rebuttal is dated March 3, 1847, and is in 29th Congress, 2nd Session, Senate, No. 217. Reynolds's complaint to James Pearce about the publication of Wilkes's rebuttal is from manuscript material in the archives at FMC, as is his seventy-eight-page critique of Wilkes's *Narrative*. Wickman discusses Thomas Hart Benton's claim that the Columbia River offered a safe port, pp. 105–10. Letters from Reynolds and others concerning this topic appear in "Communications" in 29th Congress, 1st Session, Senate, No. 474; Wilkes's "Statement" is in 29th Congress, 1st Session, Senate, No. 475. Chaffin in *The Pathfinder* discusses yet another dustup between Wilkes and Benton/Frémont in the spring of 1848, this one concerning the accuracy of Wilkes's chart of the California coast, pp. 388–89. Wickman has a chapter about the Wilkes-Frémont feud, pp. 131–50, and claims that Wilkes came out the winner.

In a letter dated February 17, 1841, to Charles Wilkes (at DU), Henry Wilkes says that their sister Eliza and her daughter hope that the memorial to the slain officers will be at Greenwood Cemetery in Brooklyn: "I should think that there will not be any difficulty in having their wishes effected as it is understood that Lieut Underwood though officially of Maine . . . was a resident of this state and considered as belonging to it." For an account of the memorial that was eventually built at Mount Auburn Cemetery in Cambridge, Massachusetts, see Blanche Linden-Ward's *Silent City on a Hill,* pp. 240–41. Wilkes claims that securing the annual appropriation for publication of the Expedition's reports was "more trouble" than the Expedition itself in ACW, p. 546. The senator's frustrated reference to "this thing called science" is quoted by Haskell, p. 23. John J. Audubon, on the other hand, immediately recognized the importance of the Expedition's scientific reports. In the summer of 1842, he wrote young Spencer Baird (destined to become the head of the Smithsonian Institution) that the reports "ought to come to the World of Science at least as brightly as the brightest rays of the Orb of Day during the Mid-summer Solstice. Oh, my dear young friend, that I did possess the wealth of the Emperor of Russia, or of the king of the French; then indeed I would address the Congress of our Country, ask of them to throw open these stores of Natural Curiosities, and Comply with mine every wish to publish, and to *Give Away* Copies of the invaluable Works thus produced to every Scientific Institution throughout our Country, and throughout the World," quoted in Haskell, p. 8.

After the publication of his report, Horatio Hale gave up the study of languages to become a lawyer in Canada. Late in life, he came out of retirement to dispute the findings of Lewis Henry Morgan, whose work with Native Americans and other native cultures had led him to declare that just as biological organisms evolved, so did societies, from the primitive to the more advanced. Hale's work in the South Pacific and in Oregon had made him realize that Morgan was imposing his own value system on cultures that were neither more nor less advanced than Western societies; they were simply different. Not long after in 1887, Hale met Franz Boas, a German anthropologist who had been working in British Columbia and was destined to become a giant in his field. Hale's insistence on the importance of fieldwork and language in the study of man resonated with the young scientist, and when Hale died nine years later, Boas wrote, "Ethnology has lost a man who contributed more to our knowledge of the human race than perhaps any other single student." See Jacob Gruber's "Horatio Hale and the Development of American Anthropology," pp. 5–37, and Stanton, pp. 373–76.

Frederick Bayer in "The Invertebrates of the U.S. Exploring Expedition" in MV quotes Darwin's praise of Dana's report, p. 81. Stanton cites Humboldt's reference to Dana's "splendid contribution to science," p. 372. The unrelenting pace Dana sustained after the Expedition's return finally proved too much for him, and he suffered a nervous breakdown in the late 1850s. Although he would be forced to drastically reduce his output in subsequent years, he still managed to write popular books about coral and volcanoes that drew on his experiences with the Ex. Ex. "If this work gives pleasure to any," he wrote in the preface to *Coral and Coral Islands,* "it will but prolong in the world the enjoyments of the 'Exploring Expedition,'" p. 6.

Even if Oliver Wendell Holmes had no use for Pickering's *The Races of Man,* the report contained, as Stanton demonstrates, insights of the highest order into how the human species had adapted to an extraordinary variety of environments. Pickering was influenced by his friend Samuel George Morton, the chief exponent of what became known as the American School of Anthropology. Morton claimed that each race (of which Pickering counted eleven) was a distinct species and had separate origins. See Stanton, pp. 338–48. Stanton also discusses the difficulties Titian Peale had with Wilkes and the publication of his report and judges John Cassin's revamped version of the report to be "a triumph of new science," pp. 327–29. On William Rich and Asa Gray and the botany reports, see Richard Eyde's "Expedition Botany: The Making of a New Profession" in MV, pp. 25–41, as well as Stanton, pp. 331–37. The botanist John Torrey's reference to Wilkes's "quarter deck insolence" is quoted by Haskell, p. 22.

Goetzmann contends that between one-quarter and one-third of the federal budget in the 1840s and 50s went to the sciences and the arts, p. 178. On the importance of the sea as an American frontier, see Thomas Philbrick's *James Fenimore Cooper and the Development of American Sea Fiction.* Goetzmann also writes insightfully about the "mountain men of the sea," pp. 237–46.

CHAPTER 16: LEGACY

For information on William Reynolds during the Mexican War and while living in Hawaii in the 1850s, I have depended on the epilogue by Herman Viola in *Voyage to the Southern Ocean,* pp. 292–93. My thanks to Reynolds descendant Anne Hoffman Cleaver for sharing with me the letters she possesses written by Rebecca Krug Reynolds. For information on Charles Guillou, I have relied on the biographical sketch by Emily Blackmore in *Oregon and California Drawings,* with a commentary by Elliot Evans, pp. 1–19.

Tyler cites a letter Jane and Charles Wilkes wrote to their son Jack in which they mention the celebration they hosted in December 1845, p. 396. Wilkes writes of the "delightful time" he and Jane had in Washington society in

ACW, p. 533, in which he also tells of his and Edmund's trip to North Carolina in the summer of 1848 and the death of his wife, pp. 637–56. Daniel Henderson in *Hidden Coasts* claims Jane died of blood poisoning, p. 224. Wilkes describes his move to the Dolley Madison house as well as his wooing of Mary Bolton in ACW, pp. 731–34.

My account of the transfer of the Ex. Ex. collection from the Patent Office to the Smithsonian Institution is based largely on Nathan Reingold and Marc Rothenberg's "The Exploring Expedition and the Smithsonian Institution" in MV, pp. 243–53, and Stanton, p. 359. Stanton also writes about the other institutions the Expedition helped to foster and Wilkes's essential role in "putting science into government and government into science," p. 363. For my account of how Ringgold's North Pacific Expedition, as well as the Ex. Ex. before it, made possible Asa Gray's advocacy of Darwin's theory of evolution, I have relied on Eyde in MV, pp. 38, 41; Stanton, pp. 368–70; and Goetzmann, pp. 345–58; as well as Gordon Harrington's "The Ringgold Incident: A Matter of Judgment" in *America Spreads Her Sails,* edited by Clayton Barrow, pp. 100–111, and Allan Cole's "The Ringgold-Rodgers-Brooke Expedition to Japan and the North Pacific, 1853–1859."

For information on the post–Ex. Ex. career of James Alden, William Hudson, and other officers, I have relied on the ZB Files, Operational Archives at the Naval Historical Center. For an account of the laying of the transatlantic cable, see John Steele Gordon's *A Thread Across the Ocean.* On the international search for the lost Franklin Expedition, I have looked to two books by Fergus Fleming, *Barrow's Boys,* pp. 380–425, and *Ninety Degrees North,* pp. 1–91, and Elisha Kane's *Arctic Explorations.*

Wilkes describes his Civil War experiences in ACW, in which he refers to the "beautiful day" on which he took Slidell and Mason from the *Trent,* p. 769, and how his hands became blistered at the celebration at Boston's Faneuil Hall, p. 775; he also quotes President Lincoln's praise of his actions, p. 776. In my account of the *Trent* Affair, I have also relied on Gordon Warren's *Fountain of Discontent: The Trent Affair and Freedom of the Seas,* in which he quotes Wilkes's reference to "one of the most important days in my naval life," p. 22, as well as the Boston mayor's praise of Wilkes and Wilkes's humble response, p. 27, and the New York Historical Society president's commemoration, p. 31. In a November 19, 1861, letter to his father, Charles Francis Adams, Jr., writes from Boston that the *Trent* Affair "created quite a stir and immense delight, though at first every one thought it must be a violation of national law; but [Richard

Henry] Dana crowed with delight and declared that if Lord John made an issue on that, you could blow him out of water," in *A Cycle of Adams Letters, 1861–1865,* edited by Worthington Chauncey Ford, p. 71. On Wilkes's subsequent activities during the war, I have relied on William Jeffries's "The Civil War Career of Charles Wilkes." Jeffries quotes Secretary of the Navy Gideon Welles's diary entries about Wilkes, p. 327, as well as Wilkes's letters to his wife about the "comforts" of the *Vanderbilt,* p. 331, and "filling my pockets" with prize money, p. 335.

My account of William Reynolds's career during and after the Civil War is based on Viola's epilogue in *Voyage to the Southern Ocean,* pp. 296–98. The epilogue in ACW tells of Wilkes's last years after the war, pp. 927–30. Wilkes's son John recorded that the unpublished *Physics* report "was thought by the Admiral to be more valuable than any of the Scientific volumes of the U.S. Ex. Ex.," in Haskell, p. 110. According to Victor Lenzen and Robert Multhauf in "Development of Gravity Pendulums in the 19th Century," Francis Baily "appears to have found [Wilkes's pendulum results] defective because of insufficient attention to the maintenance of temperature constancy and to certain alterations made to the pendulums," p. 318. For information on Louis Agassiz's unpublished report on fishes, see Watson in MV, p. 66. Stanton speaks of some of the absurdities contained in Wilkes's *Hydrography* report, p. 362; he also refers to the many obituaries that made no reference to Wilkes's involvement with the Ex. Ex., p. 363. The obituary describing Reynolds's funeral is from the archives at FMC. For information on Charles Erskine, I am grateful to Daniel Finamore at the Peabody-Essex Museum, who provided me with a copy of Erskine's calling card and a list of the artifacts that were donated to the museum, apparently by his son in the early twentieth century. I am also grateful to Jane Walsh at the Smithsonian Institution, who brought to my attention a November 11, 1859, memo describing the artifacts "Sent by order of Prof. Henry to Charles Erskine care W. Elliot Woodward, Roxbury, Mass," in the Office of Distribution File, Record Unit 120, 1st Series, Volume 3:96, Smithsonian Institution Archives. William Reynolds expressed his fervent support for flogging in a manuscript titled "Response to the circular on naval punishment" at FMC. For an account of the attempt to abolish flogging in the 1840s, and Herman Melville's role in it, see Robert Chapel's "The Word Against the Cat: Melville's Influence on Seamen's Rights." Charlie's reference to the anonymity of the common sailor is from his *Twenty Years Before the Mast,* p. 310.

EPILOGUE

Ralph Ehrenberg, et al., discuss the use of Wilkes charts as late as the invasion of Tarawa during World War II in "Surveying and Charting the Pacific Basin," MV, p. 187. James Ross undercuts Wilkes's Antarctic claims in *A Voyage of Discovery and Research in the Southern and Antarctic Regions,* p. 298. Kenneth Bertrand evaluates Wilkes's discovery of Antarctica in great detail in *Americans in Antarctica, 1775–1948,* pp. 184–90, in which he refers to the difficulty of judging distances in Antarctica. In addition to his words about the "the greatness of his achievement," Bertrand writes, "Time and subsequent exploration have substantiated Wilkes's claim of an Antarctic continent and confirmed his landfalls," p. 190. William Hobbs in "Wilkes Land Rediscovered" tells of the errors Douglas Mawson found in his own mapping efforts of the Antarctic coast, p. 634. He also cites Shackleton's account of his firsthand experience with the phenomenon of polar looming when he sighted Wilkes's Cape Hudson: "This is most weird. All hands saw the headland to the southwest, and some of us sketched it. Now (afternoon), although the sky is beautifully clear to the south-west, nothing can be seen. We cannot have drifted far from yesterday's position. No wonder Wilkes reported land," p. 643. Hobbs writes that "the naming of Wilkes Land came through German sources and that American atlases made no use of it, at least through the forties, fifties, and much of the sixties of the nineteenth century," p. 649. James Dana's letter to Asa Gray is dated February 12, 1846, and is at the Gray Herbarium Archives at Harvard.

SELECTED BIBLIOGRAPHY

UNPUBLISHED SOURCES

Alden, James. Lieutenant. Journal. Logbook #120, Mariners' Museum, Newport News, Virginia.

Anonymous journalist aboard *Vincennes.* Records Relating to the United States Exploring Expedition (Microcopy 75), Roll 10, NA.

Blair, James L. Passed Midshipman. Journal. Yale Collection of Western Americana, Beinecke Rare Book and Manuscript Library.

Briscoe, William. Armorer. Journal. Records Relating to the United States Exploring Expedition (Microcopy 75), Roll 13, NA.

Case, Augustus L. Lieutenant. Journal. U.S. Naval Academy Museum.

Claiborne, Micajah G. L. Lieutenant. Journal. Records Relating to the United States Exploring Expedition (Microcopy 75), Roll 12, NA.

Clark, George W. Midshipman. Journal. Records Relating to the United States Exploring Expedition (Microcopy 75), Roll 25, NA.

Colvocoresses, George M. Passed Midshipman. Journal. Yale Collection of Western Americana, Beinecke Rare Book and Manuscript Library.

Couthouy, J. P. Conchologist. Journal. The Museum of Science, Boston.

Dana, James D. Geologist. Letters to Asa Gray. Archives of the Gray Herbarium Library, Harvard University.

DeHaven, Edwin J. Lieutenant. Journal. Records Relating to the United States Exploring Expedition (Microcopy 75), Roll 24, NA.

Dickerson, Mahlon. Secretary of the Navy. Letters and Diary. Historical Society of New Jersey.

Du Pont, Samuel Francis. Lieutenant and Judge at Courts-Martial. Letters during summer and fall 1842. Hagley Museum and Library, Wilmington, Delaware.

Dyes, John W. W. Taxidermist. Journal. Records Relating to the United States Exploring Expedition (Microcopy 75), Roll 11, NA.

Eld, Henry, Jr. Passed Midshipman. Journal. 2 vols. Yale Collection of Western Americana, Beinecke Rare Book and Manuscript Library.

——. Letters. LOC.

Elliot, Jared Leigh. Chaplain. Journal. 2 vols. LOC.

Elliott, Samuel B. Midshipman. Journal. Records Relating to the United States Exploring Expedition (Microcopy 75), Roll 17, NA.

Emmons, George Foster. Lieutenant. Journal. 3 vols., scrapbook, and sketchbooks. Yale Collection of Western Americana, Beinecke Rare Book and Manuscript Library.

Gilchrist, Edward. Assistant Surgeon. Journal. Records Relating to the United States Exploring Expedition (Microcopy 75), Roll 14, NA.

Green, Ezra. Sailor. Papers. Nimitz Library. United States Naval Academy.

Hartstene, Henry J. Lieutenant. Journal. Records Relating to the United States Exploring Expedition (Microcopy 75), Roll 12, NA.

Holmes, Silas. Assistant Surgeon. Journal. 3 vols. Yale Collection of Western Americana, Beinecke Rare Book and Manuscript Library.

Hudson, William L. Lieutenant, Second-in-Command of Expedition. Journal. Vol. 1 (RF-38-I), American Museum of Natural History Archives, New York; vol. 2, Microcopy, Southern Historical Collection, University of North Carolina.

Johnson, Robert E. Lieutenant. Journal. 2 vols. Records Relating to the United States Exploring Expedition (Microcopy 75), Roll 15, NA.

Knox, Samuel R. Passed Midshipman. Journal. Peabody Essex Museum.

——. Letters. Yale Collection of Western Americana, Beinecke Rare Book and Manuscript Library.

Letters Relating to Wilkes Exploring Expedition, 1836–1842 (Microcopy 75), Rolls 1–6, NA.

Long, Andrew K. Lieutenant. Journal. Records Relating to the United States Exploring Expedition (Microcopy 75), Roll 18, NA.

Maury, Matthew F. Lieutenant. Papers. LOC.

May, William. Passed Midshipman. Letter to Frederick May, 23 October 1840. Box 1, Area File 9, RG 45, NA.

——. Letter to William Reynolds, 9 May 1841. Box 1, Area File 9, RG45, NA.

Pickering, Charles. Naturalist. Journal. 2 vols. The Academy of Natural Sciences, Ewell Sale Stewart Library, Philadelphia, Pennsylvania.

——. Letters. Massachusetts Historical Society. Boston, Massachusetts.

Poinsett, Joel R. Secretary of War. Papers. 10 vols. Historical Society of Pennsylvania.

Reynolds, William. Lieutenant. Public and Private Journals. 2 vols., Letters, Critique, and other materials. William Reynolds Archives and Special Collections, Franklin and Marshall College, Lancaster, Pennsylvania.

——. Letter to Charles Wilkes, 28 August 1839. Box 1, Area File 9, RG45, NA.

Robinson, R. P. Purser's Clerk. Journal. Records Relating to the United States Exploring Expedition (Microcopy 75), Roll 22, NA.

Sanford, Joseph Perry. Passed Midshipman. Journal. Records Relating to the United States Exploring Expedition (Microcopy 75), Roll 19, NA.

Sickels, J. Frederick. Surgeon. Journal. Records Relating to the United States Exploring Expedition (Microcopy 75), Roll 16, NA.

Sinclair, George T. Lieutenant. Journal. Records Relating to the United States Exploring Expedition (Microcopy 75), Roll 21, NA.

Stuart, Frederick D. Captain's Clerk. Journal. Records Relating to the United States Exploring Expedition (Microcopy 75), Roll 20, NA.

Underwood, Joseph A. Lieutenant. Journal. Yale Collection of Western Americana, Beinecke Rare Book and Manuscript Library.

Whittle, John S. Assistant Surgeon. Journal. Alderman Library, University of Virginia.

Wilkes, Charles. Commander. Journals. Records Relating to the United States Exploring Expedition (Microcopy 75), Rolls 7–9, NA.

——. Papers. Kansas State Historical Society, Topeka.

——. Papers. Manuscript Division, LOC.

——. Papers. Manuscript Department, Duke University Library.

——. Papers. Wisconsin Historical Society, Madison.

Wilkes, John. Son of Charles. Letter Books. 7 vols. LOC.

PUBLISHED SOURCES AND DISSERTATIONS

Adams, Charles Francis, ed. *Memoirs of John Quincy Adams.* Vols. 7, 8, 9, and 11. Philadelphia: Lippincott, 1875.

Adams, John, and John Quincy Adams. *Selected Writings.* Edited by Adrienne Koch and William Peden. New York: Knopf, 1946.

Albion, Robert G. "Distant Stations." *United States Naval Institute Proceedings* 80 (1954), pp. 265–73.

——. *Makers of Naval Policy, 1798–1947.* Edited by R. Reed. Annapolis: Naval Institute Press, 1980.

Alder, Ken. *The Measure of All Things: The Seven-Year Odyssey and Hidden Error That Transformed the World.* New York: Free Press, 2002.

Almy, Robert F. "J. N. Reynolds: A Brief Biography with Particular Reference to Poe and Symmes." *The Colophon,* new series, 2(2) (Winter 1937), pp. 227–45.

Ammen, Daniel. *The Old Navy and the New.* Philadelphia: Lippincott, 1891.

Anderson, Bern. *The Life and Voyages of Captain George Vancouver.* Seattle: University of Washington Press, 1960.

Anderson, Charles Roberts. *Melville in the South Seas.* New York: Dover, 1966.

Andrist, Ralph K. "Ice Ahead!" *American Heritage* 17 (1966), pp. 60–63, 92–103.

Anonymous. Review of Reynolds's Address. *North American Review* 45 (1837), pp. 361–90.

——. "Sailing of the Exploring Expedition." *Sailor's Magazine* 11 (1838), pp. 67–68.

Appleby, Joyce. *Inheriting the Revolution: The First Generation of Americans.* Cambridge, Mass.: Harvard University Press, 2000.

Appleman, Daniel E. "James Dwight Dana and Pacific Geology." In *Magnificent Voyagers*. Edited by Herman J. Viola and Carolyn Margolis. Washington: Smithsonian Institution Press, 1985, pp. 89–117.

Backus, Richard H., ed. *Georges Bank*. Cambridge, Mass.: MIT Press, 1987.

Barkan, Frances B., ed. *The Wilkes Expedition: Puget Sound and the Oregon Country*. Olympia: Washington State Capital Museum, 1987.

Barker-Benfield, G. J. *The Horrors of the Half-Known Life: Male Attitudes Toward Women and Sexuality in Nineteenth-Century America*. New York: Harper, 1976.

Barrett, Andrea. *Ship Fever*. New York: Norton, 1996.

——. *The Voyage of the Narwhal*. New York: Norton, 1998.

Barrow, Clayton R., ed. *America Spreads Her Sails: United States Sea Power in the Nineteenth Century*. Annapolis: Naval Institute Press, 1973.

Barry, J. Neilson. "Pickering is Journey to Fort Colville in 1841." *Washington Historical Quarterly* 20(1) (1929), pp. 54–63.

Bartlett, Harley Harris. "The Reports of the Wilkes Expedition, and the Work of the Specialists in Science." *Proceedings of the American Philosophical Society* 82(5) (June 1940), pp. 601–705.

Bayer, Frederick M. "The Invertebrates of the U.S. Exploring Expedition." In *Magnificent Voyagers*. Edited by Herman J. Viola and Carolyn Margolis. Washington: Smithsonian Institution Press, 1985, pp. 71–87.

Beaglehole, J. C. *The Life of Captain James Cook*. Stanford, Calif.: Stanford University Press, 1974.

Beaglehole, J. C., ed. *The Endeavour Journal of Joseph Banks, 1768–1771*. Sydney, Australia: Public Library of New South Wales, with Angus and Robertson, 1962.

Bedini, Silvio A. *Thinkers and Tinkers: Early American Men of Science*. New York: Scribner, 1975.

Belcher, Edward. *Narrative of a Voyage Around the World*. 2 vols. London: Colburn, 1843.

Bellingshausen, Thaddeus. *The Voyage of Captain Bellingshausen to the Antarctic Seas, 1819–21*. 2 vols. Edited by Frank Debenham. London: Hakluyt Society, 1945.

Bellwood, Peter. *Man's Conquest of the Pacific: The Prehistory of Southeast Asia and Oceania*. New York: Oxford University Press, 1979.

——. *The Polynesians: Prehistory of an Island People*. London and New York: Thames and Hudson, 1987.

Bemis, Samuel Flagg. *A Diplomatic History of the United States*. New York: Henry Holt, 1953.

Bernstein, Jeremy. *Ascent: Of the Invention of Mountain Climbing and Its Practice*. Lincoln and London: University of Nebraska Press, 1965.

Berry, Robert Elton. *Yankee Stargazer: The Life of Nathaniel Bowditch*. New York and London: McGraw-Hill, 1941.

Bertrand, Kenneth J. "Geographical Exploration by the United States." In *The Pacific Basin*. Edited by Herman Friis. New York: American Geographical Society, 1967.

——. *Americans in Antarctica, 1775–1948*. New York: American Geographical Society, 1971.

Bixby, William. *The Forgotten Voyage of Charles Wilkes*. New York: David McKay, 1966.

Blair, James, et al. *Communications . . . in relation to the entrance of the Columbia River*. 1846. U.S. 29th Cong., 1. Sess., Senate doc. 474, ser. 478.

Boggs, S. Whittemore. "American Contributions to Geographical Knowledge of the Central Pacific." *Geographical Review* 28 (1938), pp. 177–92.

Bolander, Louis H. "The *Vincennes:* World Traveller of the Old Navy." *U.S. Naval Institute Proceedings* 62 (1936), pp. 825–31.

Boorstin, Daniel. *The Americans: The National Experience*. New York: Random House, 1965.

——. *The Exploring Spirit: America and the New World, Then and Now*. New York: Random House, 1976.

——. *The Discoverers*. New York: Random House, 1983.

Bordwell, C. "Delay and Wreck of the *Peacock:* An Episode in the Wilkes Expedition." *Oregon Historical Quarterly* 92 (1991), pp. 119–98.

Borthwick, Doris Esch. "Outfitting the United States Exploring Expedition: Lieutenant Charles Wilkes' European Assignment, August–November, 1836." *Proceedings of the American Philosophical Society* 109(3) (1965), pp. 159–72.

Boss, Richard C. "They Came on *Porpoise:* A Ship Modeler Explores the U.S. Ex. Ex." Parts 1 and 2, *Nautical Research Journal* 34 (4)(1989), pp. 199–205, and 35(1) (1990), pp. 42–47.

Bradford, Gershom. "On a Lee Shore." *The American Neptune* 12(4) (October 1952), pp. 282–87.

Bradford, James C., ed. *Command Under Sail: Makers of the American Naval Tradition, 1775–1850*. Annapolis: Naval Institute Press, 1988.

Bradley, Harold Whitman. *The American Frontier in Hawaii: The Pioneers, 1789–1843*. Stanford, Calif.: Stanford University Press, 1942.

Brookes, Jean Ingram. *International Rivalry in the Pacific Islands, 1800–1875*. Berkeley: University of California Press, 1941.

Brosse, Jacques. *Great Voyages of Discovery: Circumnavigators and Scientists, 1764–1843*. Translated by Stanley Hochman. New York: Oxford: Facts on File Publications, 1983.

Brown, Stanley. *Men from Under the Sky: The Arrival of Westerners in Fiji*. Rutland, Vt.: Charles Tuttle, 1973.

Bruce, Robert V. *The Launching of Modern American Science, 1846–1876*. New York: Knopf, 1987.

Bryan, G. S. "The Wilkes Exploring Expedition." *Proceedings of the U.S. Naval Institute* 65 (1939), pp. 1452–64.

——. "The Purpose, Equipment and Personnel of the Wilkes Expedition." *Proceedings of the American Philosophical Society* 82 (1940), pp. 551–60.

Bryant, Samuel W. *The Sea and the States: A Maritime History of the American People*. New York: Crowell, 1967.

Burns, Sir Alan. *Fiji.* London: Her Majesty's Stationery Office, 1963.

Burstein, Andrew. *America's Jubilee.* New York: Knopf, 2001.

Cajori, Florian. *The Chequered Career of Ferdinand Rudolph Hassler.* New York: Arno Press, 1980.

Campbell, A. B. *Customs and Traditions of the Royal Navy.* Aldershot: Gale and Polden, 1956.

Carlyle, Thomas. *On Heroes, Hero-Worship and the Heroic in History.* Edited by Carl Neimeyer. Lincoln and London: University of Nebraska Press, 1966.

Carrol, Anne E. "The First American Exploring Expedition." *Harpers New Monthly Magazine* 44 (1871), pp. 60–64.

Carter, Edward C., II, ed. *Surveying the Record: North American Scientific Exploration to 1930.* Philadelphia: American Philosophical Society, 1999.

Cary, William S. *Wrecked on the Feejees.* Fairfield, Wash.: Galleon Press, 1972.

Cawood, J. "Terrestrial Magnetism and the Development of International Collaboration in the Early Nineteenth Century." *Annals of Science* 34 (1977), pp. 551–87.

Central Intelligence Agency. *Polar Regions, Atlas.* Washington, D.C.: National Foreign Assessment Center, CIA, 1979.

Chaffin, Tom. *The Pathfinder: John Charles Frémont and the Course of American Empire.* New York: Hill and Wang, 2002.

Chapel, Robert B. "The Word Against the Cat: Melville's Influence on Seamen's Rights." *American Neptune* 42 (January 1982), pp. 57–65.

Chapelle, Howard. *The History of the American Sailing Navy.* New York: Bonanza, 1949.

Chatwin, Bruce. *In Patagonia.* New York: Penguin, 1977.

Chaubey, N. P. "Effect of Age on Expectancy of Success and on Risk-Taking Behaviour." *Journal of Personality and Social Psychology* 29 (1974), pp. 774–78.

Chisholm, Donald. *Waiting for Dead Men's Shoes: Origins and Development of the U.S. Navy's Officer Personnel System, 1793–1941.* Stanford, Calif.: Stanford University Press, 2001.

Christie, Hunter E. W. *The Antarctic Problem: An Historical and Political Study.* London: Allen and Unwin, 1951.

Christie, John Aldrich. *Thoreau as World Traveler.* New York: Columbia University Press, 1965.

Clark, Joseph G. *Lights and Shadows of Sailor Life, As Exemplified in Fifteen Years' Experience.* Boston: Mussey, 1848.

Clemens, Samuel L. *Mark Twain's Autobiography.* 2 vols. New York: Harper, 1924.

Clunie, Fergus. *Fijian Weapons and Warfare.* Suva, Fiji: Fiji Museum, 1977.

Cole, Allan B. "The Ringgold-Rogers-Brooke Expedition to Japan and the North Pacific, 1853–59." *Pacific Historical Review* 16 (1947), pp. 152–62.

Coletta, P. E., ed. *American Secretaries of the Navy.* 2 vols. Annapolis: Naval Institute Press, 1980.

Collins, Frank S. "The Botanical and Other Papers of the Wilkes Expedition." *Rhodora* 14 (1912), pp. 57–68.

Colvocoresses, George M. *Four Years in the Government Exploring Expedition; Commanded by Captain Charles Wilkes.* New York: Fairchild, 1855.

Commager, Henry Steele. *The Empire of Reason: How Europe Imagined and America Realized the Enlightenment.* Garden City, N.Y.: Doubleday, 1977.

Conklin, Edwin G. "Connection of the American Philosophical Society with Our First National Exploring Expedition." *Proceedings of the American Philosophical Society* 82 (1940), pp. 519–41.

Cook, Warren. *Flood Time of Empire: Spain and the Pacific Northwest, 1543–1819.* New Haven and London: Yale University Press, 1973.

Cooley, Mary E. "The Exploring Expedition in the Pacific." *Proceedings of the American Philosophical Society* 82(5) (1940), pp. 707–19.

Cowen, Robert C. *Frontiers of the Sea: The Story of Oceanographic Exploration.* New York: Doubleday, 1960.

Crain, Caleb. *American Sympathy: Men, Friendship and Literature in the New Nation.* New Haven and London: Yale University Press, 2001.

Crawford, Michael J. "*White-Jacket* and the Navy in Which Melville Served." *Melville Society Extracts* 94 (Sept. 1993), pp. 1–5.

Crosby, Alfred W. *Germs, Seeds and Animals: Studies in Ecological History.* Armonk, N.Y.: M. E. Sharpe, 1994.

Dana, Edward Salisbury. "James Dwight Dana." *American Journal of Science* ser. 3, 49 (1895), pp. 329–56.

Dana, James D. "United States Exploring Expedition." *American Journal of Science and the Arts* 44 (1843), pp. 393–408.

——. "Notes on Upper California." *American Journal of Science and Arts,* ser. 2, 7 (1849), pp. 247–64, 376–94.

——. *Corals and Coral Islands.* New York: Dodd & Mead, 1872.

——. *Characteristics of Volcanoes.* New York: Dodd & Mead, 1890.

Daniels, George H. *American Science in the Age of Jackson.* New York: Columbia University Press, 1968.

Darwin, Charles. "Note on a Rock Seen in an Iceberg in 61 degrees South Latitude." *Royal Geographical Society of London Journal* 9 (1839), pp. 517–28.

——. *The Voyage of the Beagle.* New York: Doubleday, 1962.

Davis, Charles H. "The United States Exploring Expedition." *North American Review* 61 (1845), pp. 54–107.

Deacon, Margaret. *Scientists and the Sea, 1650–1900: A Study of Marine Science.* New York: Academic Press, 1971.

De Camp, Sprague, and Catherine C. De Camp. *The Story of Science in America.* New York: Scribner, 1967.

Deiss, William A. "Spencer F. Baird and His Collectors." *Journal of the Society for the Bibliography of Natural History* 9(4) (1980), pp. 635–45.

Delano, Amasa. *Narrative of Voyages and Travels.* Boston: F. G. House, 1817.

Dening. Greg. *Islands and Beaches: Discourse on a Silent Land, Marquesas, 1774–1880.* Chicago: Dorsey Press, 1980.

——. *Mr. Bligh's Bad Language: Passion, Power and Theatre on the Bounty.* Cambridge, New York, Melbourne: Cambridge University Press, 1992.

Derrick, R. A. *The Fiji Islands: A Geographical Handbook.* Suva, Fiji: Government Press, 1957.

——. *A History of Fiji.* Suva, Fiji: Government Press, 1957.

De Voto, Bernard. *The Course of Empire.* Boston: Houghton Mifflin, 1952.

Diamond, Jared. *Guns, Germs, and Steel: The Fates of Human Societies.* New York and London: Norton, 1997.

Dick, Steven J. "How the U.S. Naval Observatory Began, 1830–65." *Sky and Telescope* 60(6) (1980), pp. 466–71.

——. "Centralizing Navigational Technology in America: The U.S. Navy's Depot of Charts and Instruments, 1830–1842." *Technology and Culture* 33 (1992), pp. 467–509.

Dietrich, William. *Northwest Passage: The Great Columbia River.* New York: Simon & Schuster, 1995.

Dodge, Ernest S. "Captain Benjamin Vanderford of Salem." *Essex Institute Historical Collection* 79(4) (October 1943), pp. 315–29.

——. *Northwest by Sea.* New York: Oxford University Press, 1961.

——. *New England and the South Seas.* Cambridge: Harvard University Press, 1965.

——. *Beyond the Capes: Pacific Exploration from Captain Cook to the "Challenger" (1776–1877).* Boston and Toronto: Little, Brown, 1971.

——. *Islands and Empires: Western Impact on the Pacific and East Asia.* Minneapolis: University of Minnesota Press, 1976.

Dott, Jr., Robert H. "James Dwight Dana's Old Tectonics–Global Contraction Under Divine Direction." *American Journal of Science* 297 (March 1997), pp. 283–311.

Dousset, Roselene, and Etienne Taillemite. *The Great Book of the Pacific.* Translated by Andrew Mouravieff-Apostal and Edita Lausanne. Secaucus, N.J.: Chartwell Books, 1979.

Dulles, Foster R. *America in the Pacific.* Boston: Houghton Mifflin, 1932.

Dumont d'Urville, Jules S-C. *Two Voyages to the South Seas.* Edited and translated by Helen Rosenman. Melbourne, Australia: Melbourne University Press, 1987.

Dupree, A. Hunter. "Science vs. the Military: Dr. James Morrow and the Perry Expedition." *Pacific Historical Review* 22 (1953), pp. 29–37.

——. *Science in the Federal Government.* Cambridge, Mass.: Harvard University Press, 1956.

——. *Asa Gray, 1810–1888.* Cambridge, Mass.: Harvard University Press, 1959.

Duraind, George J. "As California Seemed in '41." *San Francisco Chronicle,* June 4, 1905, Sunday Supplement, p. 3.

Eather, Robert H. *The Majestic Lights: The Aurora in Science, History and the Arts.* Washington, D.C.: American Geophysical Union, 1980.

Edel, William W. "The Golden Age of the Naval Chaplaincy, 1830–55." *Proceedings of the United States Naval Institute* 50 (1924), pp. 875–83.

Ehrenberg, Ralph E., John A. Wolter, and Charles A. Burroughs. "Surveying and Charting the Pacific Basin." In *Magnificent Voyagers*. Edited by Herman J. Viola and Carolyn Margolis. Washington, D.C.: Smithsonian Institution Press, 1985, pp. 165–87.

Ellis, Richard. *Encyclopedia of the Sea*. New York: Knopf, 2000.

Emmons, George F. *The Navy of the United States, 1775 to 1853*. Washington, D.C.: Gideon and Company, 1850.

——. "Extracts from the Emmons Journal." *Oregon Historical Society Quarterly* 26 (1925), pp. 263–73.

Erskine, Charles. *Twenty Years Before the Mast*. Philadelphia: Jacobs, 1896.

Evelyn, Douglas E. "The National Gallery at the Patent Office." In *Magnificent Voyagers*. Edited by Herman J. Viola and Carolyn Margolis. Washington, D.C.: Smithsonian Institution Press, 1985, pp. 227–41.

Eyde, Richard. "Expedition Botany: The Making of a New Profession." In *Magnificent Voyagers*. Edited by Herman J. Viola and Carolyn Margolis. Washington, D.C.: Smithsonian Institution Press, 1985, pp. 25–41.

——. "William Rich of the Great Exploring Expedition and How His Shortcomings Helped Botany Become a Calling." *Huntia* 8(1) (1985).

Fanning, Edmund. *Voyages Round the World*. 1833. Rpt. Upper Saddle River, N.J.: Gregg Press, 1970.

——. *Voyages to the South Seas, Indian and Pacific Oceans*. 1838. Rpt. Fairfield, Wash.: Galleon Press, 1970.

Feipel, L. N. "The Wilkes Expedition: Its Progress Through Half a Century, 1826–76." *Proceedings of the United States Naval Institute* 40 (1914), pp. 1323–50.

Fernandez-Armesto, Felipe. *Civilizations: Culture, Ambition, and the Transformation of Nature*. New York: Free Press, 2001.

Feuer, Lewis S. *The Scientific Intellectual: The Psychological and Sociological Origins of Modern Science*. New York: Basic Books, 1963.

Field, Admiral M. *Hydrographical Surveying, A Description of Means and Methods Employed in Constructing Marine Charts*. 4th ed. London: John Murray, 1920.

Finney, Ben. *Voyages of Rediscovery: A Cultural Odyssey Through Polynesia*. Berkeley, Los Angeles, London: University of California Press, 1994.

Flannery, Tim. *The Eternal Frontier: An Ecological History of North American and Its People*. New York: Atlantic Monthly Press, 2001.

Fleming, Fergus. *Barrow's Boys*. New York: Atlantic Monthly Press, 1998.

——. *Ninety Degrees North: The Quest for the North Pole*. New York: Grove Press, 2001.

Fossi, G. E., and D. Smith. *The Explorations of Antarctica*. London: Cassell, 1990.

Fowler, Henry W. "The Fishes Obtained by the Wilkes Expedition, 1838–1840." *Proceedings of the American Philosophical Society* 82 (1940), pp. 733–800.

Fowler, William M., Jr. *Jack Tars and Commodores: The American Navy, 1783–1815*. Boston: Houghton Mifflin, 1984.

Friedman, Lawrence J., and David Curtis Skaggs. "Jesse Duncan Elliott and the Battle of Lake Erie: The Issue of Mental Instability." *Journal of the Early Republic* 10 (Winter 1990), pp. 493–516.

Friis, Herman R., ed. *The Pacific Basin: A History of Its Geographical Exploration.* New York: American Geographical Society, 1967.

Frost, Alan, and Jane Samson. *Pacific Empire: Essays in Honor of Glyndwr Williams.* Vancouver: University of British Columbia Press, 1999.

Gates, W. B. "Cooper's *The Sea Lions* and Wilkes' *Narrative.*" *Publications of the Modern Language Association* 65 (1950), pp. 1069–75.

——. "Cooper's *The Crater* and Two Explorers." *American Literature* 23 (1951), pp. 243–46.

Gerbi, Antonello. *The Dispute of the New World: The History of a Polemic, 1750–1900.* Translated by Jeremy Moyle. Pittsburgh: University of Pittsburgh Press, 1955.

Gibbs, James A. *Pacific Graveyard: A Narrative of Shipwrecks Where the Columbia River Meets the Pacific Ocean.* Portland, Ore.: Binford and Mort, 1964.

Gilman, Daniel C. *The Life of James Dwight Dana: Scientific Explorer, Mineralogist, Geologist, Zoologist, Professor in Yale University.* New York and London: Harper, 1899.

Goetzmann, William. *Exploration and Empire: The Explorer and the Scientist in the Winning of the American West.* New York: Vintage Books, 1972.

——. *New Lands, New Men: America and the Second Great Age of Discovery.* New York: Viking, 1986.

Goleman, Daniel. *Emotional Intelligence.* New York: Bantam, 1995.

Gordon, John Steele. *A Thread Across the Ocean: The Heroic Story of the Transatlantic Cable.* New York: Walker, 2002.

Gough, Barry. *The Royal Navy and the Northwest Coast of North America.* Vancouver: University of British Columbia Press, 1971.

Gould, R. T. "The First Sighting of the Antarctic Continent." *Geographical Journal* 65 (1925), pp. 220–25.

Graebner, Norman A. *Empire on the Pacific: A Study in American Continental Expansion.* New York: Ronald Press, 1955.

Grattan, C. Hartley. *The Southwest Pacific to 1900.* Ann Arbor: University of Michigan Press, 1963.

Gravelle, Kim. *Fiji's Times: A History of Fiji.* Suva, Fiji: Fiji Times & Herald Limited, 1979.

Gray, Asa. *Letters.* 2 vols. Jane Loring Gray, editor. Boston: Houghton Mifflin, 1893.

Greenberg, John L. *The Problem of the Earth's Shape from Newton to Clairaut: The Rise of Mathematical Science in Eighteenth-Century Paris and the Fall of "Normal" Science.* New York and Melbourne: Cambridge University Press, 1995.

Greene, John C. "American Science Comes of Age, 1780–1820." *Journal of American History* 55 (June 1968), pp. 22–41.

Gruber, Jacob. "Horatio Hale and the Development of American Anthropology." *Proceedings of the American Philosophical Society* 3 (1967), pp. 5–37.

——. "Who Was the *Beagle*'s Naturalist?" *British Journal for the History of Science* 4 (1969), pp. 266–82.

Guillou, Charles F. B. *Oregon and California Drawings, 1841–1847.* With Biographical Sketch by Emily Blackmore and Commentary by Elliot A. P. Evans. San Francisco: The Book Club of California, 1961.

Gurney, Alan. *Below the Convergence: Voyages Toward Antarctica, 1699–1839.* New York and London: Norton, 1997.

——. *The Race to the White Continent: Voyages to the Antarctic.* New York and London: Norton, 2000.

Hafertepe, Kenneth. *America's Castle: The Evolution of the Smithsonian Building and Its Institution, 1840–1878.* Washington, D.C.: Smithsonian Institution Press, 1984.

Hale, Horatio. "Migrations in the Pacific." *American Journal of Science and Arts,* ser. 2, 1 (1846), pp. 317–32.

Hale, Sarah Josepha. "The Wreck of the Peacock." *Godey's Lady's Book* 24 (May 1842), pp. 292–93.

Hamersly, Lewis R. *The Records of Living Officers of the United States Navy and Marine Corps.* Philadelphia: Lippincott, 1870.

Harlan, R. B. *History of Clinton County, Ohio.* Chicago: W. H. Beers, 1882.

Harland, John. *Seamanship in the Age of Sail: An Account of Shiphandling of the Sailing Man-of-War, 1600–1860.* Annapolis: Naval Institute Press, 1984.

Haskell, Daniel C. *The United States Exploring Expedition, 1838–1842 and Its Publications, 1844–1874.* New York: New York Public Library, 1942.

Henderson, Daniel. *Hidden Coasts: The Biography of Admiral Charles Wilkes.* New York: William Sloane, 1953.

Henry, John Frazier. "The Midshipman's Revenge." *Pacific Northwest Quarterly* 73 (1982), pp. 156–64.

——. *Early Maritime Artists of the Pacific Northwest Coast, 1741–1841.* Seattle, London: University of Washington Press, 1984.

Hezel, Francis X. "New Directions in Pacific History: A Practitioner's Critical View." *Pacific Studies* 11(3) (July 1988), pp. 101–10.

Hill, Jim Dan. "Charles Wilkes: Turbulent Scholar of the Old Navy." *U.S. Naval Institute Proceedings* 57 (1931), pp. 868–87.

Hobbs, Richard R. "The Congreve War Rockets, 1800–1825." *United States Naval Institute Proceedings* 94(3) (1968), pp. 80–88.

Hobbs, William H. "Wilkes Land Rediscovered." *Geographical Review* 22 (1932).

——. "The Discovery of Wilkes Land, Antarctica." *Proceedings of the American Philosophical Society* 82 (1940), pp. 561–82.

Hoffmeister, John E. "James Dwight Dana's Studies of Volcanoes and of Coral Islands." *Proceedings of the American Philosophical Society* 82 (1940), pp. 721–32.

Horsman, Reginald. *Race and Manifest Destiny: The Origins of American Racial Anglo-Saxonism.* Cambridge, Mass.: Harvard University Press, 1981.

——. "Captain Symmes's Journey to the Center of the Earth." *Timeline* (October 2000), pp. 2–13.

Horwitz, Tony. *Blue Latitudes: Boldly Going Where Captain Cook Has Gone Before.* New York: Holt, 2002.

Howay, F. W. "The Loss of the Tonquin." *Washington Historical Quarterly* 13(2) (April 1922), pp. 83–92.

Howe, Henry. *Historical Collections of Ohio.* Norwalk, Ohio: The State of Ohio, 1896.

Idyll, C. P., ed. *Exploring the Ocean World.* New York: Thomas Y. Crowell, 1969.

Irmscher, Christoph. *The Poetics of Natural History: From John Bartram to William James.* New Brunswick, N.J.: Rutgers University Press, 1999.

Irving, Washington. *Astoria.* 1836. Rpt. Portland, Ore.: Binford and Mort, 1967.

Jackson, D. D. "Around the World in 1,392 Days with the Navy's Wilkes–and His 'Scientifics.'" *Smithsonian* 16 (1985), pp. 48–62.

Jackson, Ian. "Exploration as Science: Charles Wilkes and the U.S. Ex. Ex., 1838–42." *American Scientist* 73 (Sept.–Oct. 1985), pp. 450–61.

Jaffé, David. *The Stormy Petrel and the Whale.* Washington, D.C.: University Press of America, 1976.

Jeffries, William W. "The Civil War Career of Charles Wilkes." *Journal of Southern History* 3(2) (1945), pp. 324–48.

Jones, A. G. E. *Antarctica Observed: Who Discovered the Antarctic Continent?* Whitby, North Yorkshire, England: Caedmon of Whitby, 1982.

Joyce, Barry Alan. *The Shaping of American Ethnography: The Wilkes Exploring Expedition.* Lincoln and London: University of Nebraska Press, 2001.

Kaeppler, Adrienne L. "Anthropology and the U.S. Expedition." *In Magnificent Voyagers.* Edited by Herman J. Viola and Carolyn Margolis. Washington, D.C.: Smithsonian Institution Press, 1985, pp. 119–47.

Kane, Elisha Kent. *Arctic Explorations: The Second Grinnell Expedition in Search of Sir John Franklin, 1853, 54, 55.* Chicago: Lakeside Press, 1996.

Karsten, Peter. *The Naval Aristocracy: The Golden Age of Annapolis and the Emergence of Modern American Navalism.* New York: Free Press, 1972.

Kazar, John D. "The U.S. Navy and Scientific Exploration, 1837–1860." Ph.D. Dissertation, University of Massachusetts, 1973.

Keegan, John. *The Mask of Command.* New York: Penguin, 1988.

——. *The Price of Admiralty: The Evolution of Naval Warfare.* New York: Viking, 1989.

Kirch, Patrick Vinton. *On the Road of the Winds: An Archaeological History of the Pacific Islands Before European Contact.* Berkeley, Los Angeles, London: University of California Press, 2000.

Krout, Mary Hannah. "Rear Admiral Wilkes and His Exploits." *U.S. Naval Institute Proceedings* 50 (1924), pp. 405–16.

Labaree, B. W., ed. *The Atlantic World of Robert G. Albion.* Middletown, Conn.: Wesleyan University Press, 1975.

Langley, Harold D. *Social Reform in the United States Navy, 1787–1862.* Urbana: University of Illinois Press, 1976.

Lenzen, Victor P., and Robert Multhauf. "Development of Gravity Pendulums in the 19th Century." *Contributions from the Museum of History and Technology,* Bulletin 240, Paper 44 (1964), pp. 302–47.

Leonhart, Joye. "Charles Wilkes: A Biography." In *Magnificent Voyagers.* Edited by Herman J. Viola and Carolyn Margolis. Washington, D.C.: Smithsonian Institution Press, 1985, pp. 189–203.

Linden-Ward, Blanche. *Landscapes of Memory and Boston's Mount Auburn Cemetery.* Columbus: Ohio State University Press, 1989.

Linklater, Andro. *Measuring America: How the United States Was Shaped by the Greatest Land Sale in History.* London: HarperCollins, 2002.

Livermore, Seward W. "American Naval-Base Policy in the Far East, 1850–1914." *Pacific Historical Review* 13 (June 1944), pp. 113–35.

Long, David F. *Diplomatic Activities of U.S. Naval Officers, 1798–1883.* Annapolis: Naval Institute Press, 1988.

Loomis, Chauncey. *Weird and Tragic Shores: The Story of Charles Francis Hall, Explorer.* New York: Modern Library, 2000.

Ludtke, Jean. *Atlantic Peeks: An Ethnographic Guide to the Portuguese-Speaking Atlantic Islands.* Hanover, Mass.: Christopher Publishing, 1989.

Lundeberg, Philip K. "Ships and Squadron Logistics." In *Magnificent Voyagers.* Edited by Herman J. Viola and Carolyn Margolis. Washington, D.C.: Smithsonian Institution Press, 1985, pp. 149–63.

——. "Legacy of an Artist-Explorer." *Pull Together: Newsletter of the Naval Historical Foundation and the Naval Historical Center* 28(1) (1989), pp. 1–5.

Lundeberg, Philip K., and Dana M. Wegner. "Not for Conquest But Discovery: Rediscovering the Ships of the Wilkes Expedition." *American Neptune* 49(3) (1989), pp. 151–67.

MacCartney, Clarence Edward. *Mr. Lincoln's Admirals.* New York: Funk and Wagnalls, 1956.

Macdonald, Gordon A., Agatin T. Abbott, and Frank L. Peterson, eds. *Volcanoes in the Sea: The Geology of Hawaii.* Honolulu: University of Hawaii Press, 1983.

MacKenzie, Alexander S. "Comments upon the Official Correspondence Connected with the Southern Exploring Expedition." *Army and Navy Chronicle* 3 (1836), pp. 337–42.

Madden, E. F. "Symmes and His Theory." *Harper's New Monthly Magazine* 65 (1882), pp. 740–49.

Masling, M. "How Neurotic Is the Authoritarian?" *Journal of Abnormal Social Psychology* 49 (1954), pp. 316–18.

Maury, Matthew Fontaine. *The Physical Geography of the Sea and Its Meteorology.* Cambridge, Mass.: Harvard University Press, 1963.

Mawson, Sir Douglas. "Wilkes's Antarctic Landfalls." *Proceedings, Royal Geographical Society of Australia, South Australian Branch,* Sess. 1932–33, Vol. 34 (1934), pp. 70–113.

——. *The Home of the Blizzard: A True Story of Antarctic Survival.* New York: St. Martin's Press, 1998.

McDougall, Walter A. *Let the Sea Make a Noise: A History of the North Pacific from Magellan to MacArthur.* New York: Basic Books, 1993.

McKee, Christopher. *Edward Preble: A Naval Biography, 1761–1807.* Annapolis: Naval Institute Press, 1972.

——. *A Gentlemanly and Honorable Profession: The Creation of the United States Naval Officer Corps, 1794–1815.* Annapolis: United States Naval Institute Press, 1991.

Mellow, James R. *Nathaniel Hawthorne in His Times.* Boston: Houghton Mifflin, 1980.

Melton, Buckner F., Jr. *A Hanging Offense: The Strange Affair of the Warship* Somers. New York: The Free Press, 2003.

Melville, Herman. *White-Jacket, or The World in a Man-of-War.* 1850. Evanston, Ill.: Northwestern University Press, 1970.

——. *The Piazza Tales and Other Prose Pieces, 1839–1860.* Evanston and Chicago: Northwestern University Press and Newberry Library, 1987.

——. *Moby-Dick, or The Whale.* 1851. Evanston and Chicago: Northwestern University Press and Newberry Library, 1988.

Merk, Frederick. *Manifest Destiny and Mission in American History.* New York: Knopf, 1963.

——. *The Oregon Question.* Cambridge, Mass.: Harvard University Press, 1967.

Merli, Frank, and Theodore Wilson, eds. *Makers of American Diplomacy.* New York: Scribner, 1974.

Merrill, James M. *Du Pont: The Making of an Admiral.* New York: Dodd, Mead, 1986.

Mickelburgh, Edwin. *Beyond the Frozen Sea: Visions of Antarctica.* London: Bodley Head, 1987.

Mill, Hugh Robert. *The Siege of the South Pole.* London: Aston Rivers, 1905.

Miller, Perry. *The Raven and the Whale: The War of Words and Wits in the Era of Poe and Melville.* New York: Harcourt Brace, 1956.

Mitterling, Philip L. *America in the Antarctic to 1840.* Urbana: University of Illinois Press, 1959.

Moring, John. *Men with Sand: Great Explorers of the North American West.* Helena, Mont.: Falcon, 1998.

Morison, Samuel Eliot. *"Old Bruin": Commodore Matthew C. Perry, 1794–1858.* Boston: Little, Brown, 1967.

——. *Admiral of the Ocean Sea: A Life of Christopher Columbus.* 1942. New York: MJF Books, 1970.

Morrell, Benjamin, Jr. *A Narrative of Four Voyages to the South Sea, North and South Pacific Ocean.* New York: Harper, 1832.

Morrison, Dorothy Nafus. *Outpost: John McLoughlin and the Far Northwest.* Portland: Oregon Historical Society Press, 1999.

Musselman, Elizabeth Green. "Science as a Landed Activity: Scientifics and Seamen Aboard the U.S. Exploring Expedition." In *Surveying the Record.* Edited by Edward C. Carter II. Philadelphia: American Philosophical Society, 1999, pp. 77–101.

National Imagery and Mapping Agency. *Sailing Directions: Antarctica.* Bethesda, Md.: National Imagery and Mapping Agency, 1997.

Natland, James H. "At Vulcan's Shoulder: James Dwight Dana and the Beginnings of Planetary Volcanology." *American Journal of Science* 297 (March 1997), pp. 312–42.

Newell, Julie R. "James Dwight Dana and the Emergence of Professional Geology in the United States." *American Journal of Science* 297 (March 1997), pp. 273–82.

Norman, Henderson Daingerfield. "The Log of the Flying Fish." *United States Naval Institute Proceedings* 65(3) (1939), pp. 363–69.

Obeyesekere, Gananath. "Cannibal Feats in Nineteenth-Century Fiji." In *Cannibalism and the Colonial World.* Edited by Francis Barker, Peter Hulme, and Margaret Iversen. Cambridge, England: Cambridge University Press, 1998.

O'Brian, Patrick. *Men-of-War: Life in Nelson's Navy.* New York and London: Norton, 1974.

O'Brien, John. *American Military Laws, and the Practice of Courts Martial; with Suggestions for their Improvement.* Philadelphia: Lea & Blanchard, 1846.

Oleson, Alexandra, and Sanborn C. Brown. *The Pursuit of Knowledge in the Early American Republic: American Scientific and Learned Societies from Colonial Times to the Civil War.* Baltimore and London: Johns Hopkins University Press, 1976.

Padgen, Anthony. *Peoples and Empires: A Short History of European Migrations, Exploration, and Conquest, from Greece to the Present.* New York: Modern Library, 2001.

Palmer, James C. Thulia: *A Tale of the Antarctic.* New York: Samuel Colman, 1843.

Parry, John H. *Trade and Dominion: The European Oversea Empires in the Eighteenth Century.* London: Weidenfeld & Nicolson, 1971.

Paullin, Charles O. "Dueling in the Old Navy." *U.S. Naval Institute Proceedings* 35 (1909), pp. 1155–97.

Peale, Titian Ramsay. "The South Sea Surveying and Exploring Expedition." *American Historical Record* 3 (1874), pp. 244–51, 305–11.

Philbrick, Nathaniel. *In the Heart of the Sea: The Tragedy of the Whaleship* Essex. New York: Viking, 2000.

Philbrick, Thomas. *James Fenimore Cooper and the Development of American Sea Fiction.* Cambridge, Mass.: Harvard University Press, 1961.

Pickering, Charles. *The Races of Man and their Geographical Distribution.* London: H. G. Bohn, 1863.

Pillsbury, J. E. "Wilkes and d'Urville's Discoveries in Wilkesland." *Proceedings of the U.S. Naval Institute* 36 (June 1910), pp. 465–68.

Poe, Edgar A. "Review of J. N. Reynolds's Report on the U.S. Exploring Expedition." *Graham's Magazine* 24 (September 1843), pp. 164–65.

Poesch, Jessie, ed. *Titian Ramsay Peale and His Journals of the Wilkes Expedition.* Philadelphia: American Philosophical Society, 1961.

Poinsett, Joel R. "The Exploring Expedition." *North American Review* 56 (1843), pp. 257–70.

——. "The First Three Volumes of a Narrative of the United States Exploring Expedition." *Southern Quarterly Review* 8 (1845), pp. 1–69.

Ponko, Vincent, Jr. *Ships, Seas, and Scientists: United States Exploration and Discovery in the Nineteenth Century.* Annapolis: Naval Institute Press, 1979.

Pope, Dudley. *Life in Nelson's Navy.* Annapolis: Naval Institute Press, 1987.

Porter, Charlotte. *The Eagle's Nest: Natural History and American Ideas, 1812–1849.* Tuscaloosa: University of Alabama Press, 1986.

Prendergast, Michael L. "James Dwight Dana: The Life and Thought of an American Scientist." Ph.D. Dissertation, University of California, Los Angeles, 1978.

Raban, Jonathan. *Passage to Juneau: A Sea and Its Meanings.* New York: Pantheon, 1999.

Rehn, James A. G. "Connection of the Academy of Natural Sciences of Philadelphia with Our First National Exploring Expedition." *Proceedings of the American Philosophical Society* 82 (1940), pp. 543–49.

Reichelderfer, Francis W. "The Contribution of Wilkes to Terrestrial Magnetism, Gravity, and Meteorology." *Proceedings of the American Philosophical Society* 82 (1940), pp. 583–600.

Reingold, Nathan. "Definitions and Speculations: The Professionalization of Science in America in the Nineteenth Century." In *The Pursuit of Knowledge in the Early American Republic.* Edited by A. Oleson and S. C. Brown. Baltimore: Johns Hopkins Press, 1976, pp. 33–69.

Reingold, Nathan, and Marc Rothenberg. "The Exploring Expedition and the Smithsonian Institution." In *Magnificent Voyagers.* Edited by Herman J. Viola and Carolyn Margolis. Washington: Smithsonian Institution Press, 1985, pp. 243–53.

Reynolds, Jeremiah N. *Remarks on a Review of Symmes's Theory.* Washington, D.C.: Gales and Seaton, 1827.

——. *Voyage of the United States Frigate Potomac.* New York: Harper, 1835.

——. *Address on the Subject of a Surveying and Exploring Expedition to the Pacific Ocean and South Seas.* New York: Harper, 1836.

——. "Leaves from an Unpublished Journal." *New York Mirror* 15(43) (April 21, 1838), pp. 340–341.

——. "A Leaf from an Unpublished Manuscript." *Southern Literary Messenger* 5 (1839), pp. 408–15.

——. "Mocha Dick or the White Whale of the Pacific." *Knickerbocker Magazine* 13 (1839), pp. 377–92.

——. Introduction to *Pacific and Indian Oceans: or, The South Sea Surveying and Exploring Expedition.* New York: Harper, 1841.

Reynolds, William. *Voyage to the Southern Ocean: The Letters of Lieutenant William Reynolds from the U.S. Exploring Expedition, 1838–1842.* Edited by Anne Hoffman Cleaver and E. Jeffrey Stann. Annapolis: Naval Institute Press, 1988.

Rhea, Robert L. "Some Observations on Poe's Origins." *University of Texas Studies in English* 10 (1930), pp. 135–46.

Rhodes, J. M., and John P. Lockwood, eds. *Mauna Loa Revealed: Structure, Composition, History, and Hazards.* Geophysical Monograph 92, Washington, D.C.: American Geophysical Union, 1995.

Richardson, James D., ed. *A Compilation of the Messages and Papers of the Presidents.* Vol. 2. Washington, D.C.: Government Printing Office, 1903.

Riesenberg, Felix. *The Pacific Ocean.* New York: McGraw-Hill, 1940.

Ritvo, Harriet. *The Platypus and the Mermaid.* Cambridge, Mass.: Harvard University Press, 1997.

Roberts, David. *A Newer World: Kit Carson, John C. Frémont, and the Claiming of the American West.* New York: Simon & Schuster, 2000.

Rodgers, John. "James Dwight Dana: A Special Issue of the American Journal of Science." *American Journal of Science* 297(3) (1997).

Rodgers, N. A. M. *The Wooden World: An Anatomy of the Georgian Navy.* Annapolis: Naval Institute Press, 1986.

Ronda, James P. *Voyages of Discovery: Essays on the Lewis and Clark Expedition.* Helena: Montana Historical Society Press, 1998.

Ross, Frank E. "The Antarctic Explorations of Lieutenant Charles Wilkes U.S.N." *Proceedings of the Royal Geographical Society of Australasia, South Australian Branch* 35 (1935), pp. 130–41.

Ross, J. C. *A Voyage of Discovery and Research in the Southern and Antarctic Regions During the Years 1839–43.* 2 vols. New York: David & Charles Reprints, 1969.

Rozwadowski, H. "Small World: Forging a Scientific Maritime Culture for Oceanography." *Isis* 3 (1996), pp. 409–29.

Ruschenberger, William S. W. "Charles Pickering." *Academy of Natural Sciences Proceedings* 30 (1878), pp. 166–71.

Sahlins, Marshall. *Islands of History.* Chicago: University of Chicago Press, 1985.

——. "Raw Women, Cooked Men, and Other 'Great Things' of the Fiji Islands." In *Ethnography and the Historical Imagination.* Edited by John and Jean Comaroff. Boulder, Colo.: Westview Press, 1992.

——. *How "Natives" Think: About Captain Cook, for Example.* Chicago: University of Chicago Press, 1995.

Scarr, Deryck. *Fiji: A Short History.* Laie, Hawaii: Institute for Polynesian Studies, 1984.

Schlee, Susan. *A History of Oceanography: The Edge of an Unfamiliar World.* London: Robb Hale, 1973.

Schlesinger, Arthur Meier. *Political and Social History of the United States, 1829–1925.* New York: Macmillan, 1927.

Schmucker, Samuel M. *The Life of Dr. Elisha Kent Kane, and of other Distinguished American Explorers*. Philadelphia: J. W. Bradley, 1858.

Schroeder, John. *Shaping a Maritime Empire: The Commercial and Diplomatic Role of the American Navy, 1829–1861*. Westport, Conn.; London, England: Greenwood, 1985.

Sellers, Charles Coleman. *Mr. Peale's Museum*. New York: Norton, 1979.

Silverberg, Robert. *Stormy Voyage: The Story of Charles Wilkes*. Philadelphia: Lippincott, 1968.

Slotkin, Richard. *Regeneration Through Violence: The Mythology of the American Frontier, 1600–1860*. Middletown, Conn.: Wesleyan University Press, 1978.

Smith, Bernard. *European Vision and the South Pacific, 1768–1850*. Oxford: Clarendon Press, 1960.

Smith, G. S. "The Navy Before Darwinism: Science, Exploration and Diplomacy in Antebellum America." *American Quarterly* 28 (Spring 1976), pp. 41–55.

Smith, Gene A. *Thomas Ap Catesby Jones: Commodore of Manifest Destiny*. Annapolis: Naval Institute Press, 2000.

Smyth, W. H. *Sailor's Word-Book: An Alphabetical Digest of Nautical Terms*. 1867. London: Conway Maritime Press, 1996.

Snow, Philip A. *Bibliography of Fiji, Tonga and Rotuma*. Coral Gables, Fla.: University of Miami Press, 1969.

Spector, Ronald H. *Eagle Against the Sun: The American War with Japan*. New York: Vintage, 1985.

Sperlin, O. B. "Our First Official Horticulturalist." *Washington Historical Quarterly* 21 (1931), pp. 218–29, 298–305; and 22 (1931), pp. 42–58, 67–69.

——. "Washington Forts of the Fur Trade Regime." *Washington Historical Quarterly* 8 (April 1917), pp. 102–14.

Sprague, R. A. "Measuring the Mountain: The United States Exploring Expedition on Mauna Loa, 1840–1841." *Hawaiian Journal of History* 25 (1991), pp. 71–91.

Stackpole, Edouard A. *The Sea-Hunters: The Great Age of Whaling*. Philadelphia: Lippincott, 1953.

Stanley, Albert A. "Hassler's Legacy." *NOAA [National Oceanic and Atmospheric Administration]* 6(1) (1976), pp. 52–57.

Stann, E. Jeffrey. "Charles Wilkes as Diplomat." In *Magnificent Voyagers*. Edited by Herman J. Viola and Carolyn Margolis. Washington, D.C.: Smithsonian Institution Press, 1985, pp. 205–25.

Stanton, William. *The Leopard's Spots: Scientific Attitudes Towards Race in America, 1815–59*. Chicago: University of Chicago Press, 1960.

——. *The Great United States Exploring Expedition of 1838–1842*. Berkeley, Los Angeles, London: University of California Press, 1975.

——. *American Scientific Explorations, 1803–1860*. Philadelphia: American Philosophical Society Library, 1991.

Starke, Aubrey. "Poe's Friend Reynolds." *American Literature* 11 (1939), pp. 152–59.

Stegner, Wallace. *Beyond the Hundredth Meridian: John Wesley Powell and the Second Opening of the West.* New York: Penguin, 1992.

Stewart, T. D. "The Skull of Vendovi: A Contribution of the Wilkes Expedition to the Physical Anthropology of Fiji." *Archaeology and Physical Anthropology in Oceania* 13(2 & 3) (1978), pp. 204–14.

Stone, Witmer. "Titian Ramsey Peale." *Cassinia* 19 (1915), pp. 1–13.

Strauss, W. Patrick. "Preparing the Wilkes Expedition: A Study in Disorganization." *Pacific Historical Review* 28 (1959), pp. 221–32.

——. "Pioneer American Diplomats in Polynesia, 1820–40." *Pacific Historical Review* 31 (1962), pp. 21–30.

——. *Americans in Polynesia, 1783–1842.* East Lansing: Michigan State University Press, 1963.

——. "Mahlon Dickerson." In *American Secretaries of the Navy.* Edited by Paolo E. Coletta. Annapolis: Naval Institute Press, 1980.

Swisher, Earl. "Commodore Perry's Imperialism in Relation to America's Present-Day Position in the Pacific." *Pacific Historical Review* 16 (February 1947), pp. 30–40.

Symmes, Elmore. "John Cleves Symmes, the Theorist." *Southern Bivouac: A Monthly Literary and Historical Magazine* 2 (1887), pp. 555–66, 621–31, 682–93.

Taylor, E. G. R. *The Haven-Finding Art: A History of Navigation from Odysseus to Captain Cook.* New York: Abelard-Schuman, 1957.

Tent, Jan, and Paul Geraghty. "Exploding Sky or Exploded Myth: The Origin of Papalagi." *Journal of the Polynesian Society* 110(2) (2001), pp. 171–214.

Theroux, Paul. *The Happy Isles of Oceania: Paddling the Pacific.* New York: Ballantine Books, 1992.

Thomas, Nicholas. *Entangled Objects: Exchange, Material Culture and Colonialism in the Pacific.* Cambridge, Mass.: Harvard University Press, 1990.

Thompson, Warren S. "The Demographic Revolution in the United States." *Annals of the American Academy of Political and Social Science* 262 (1949), pp. 62–69.

Topham, Washington. "Dr. Frederick May." *Columbia Historical Society* 31/32 (1930), pp. 307–10.

Towle, E. L. "Science, Commerce, and the Navy on the Seafaring Frontier (1842–61)." Ph.D. Dissertation, University of Rochester, 1965.

Turner, Frederick Jackson. *The Frontier in American History.* 1920. Rpt. New York: Holt, 1962.

Tyler, David B. *The Wilkes Expedition: The First United States Exploring Expedition, 1838–1842.* Philadelphia: American Philosophical Society, 1968.

Valle, James E. *Rocks and Shoals: Order and Discipline in the Old Navy, 1800–1861.* Annapolis: Naval Institute Press, 1980.

Van Alstyne, Richard W. *The Rising American Empire.* New York: Oxford University Press, 1960.

Van Tassel, David D., and Michael G. Hall, eds. *Science and Society in the United States.* Homewood, Ill.: Dorsey, 1966.

Viola, Herman J. "The Story of the U.S. Exploring Expedition." In *Magnificent Voyagers*. Edited by Herman J. Viola and Carolyn Margolis. Washington, D.C.: Smithsonian Institution Press, 1985, pp. 9–23.

Viola, Herman J., and Carolyn Margolis, eds. *Magnificent Voyagers: The U.S. Exploring Expedition, 1838–1842*. Washington, D.C.: Smithsonian Institution Press, 1985.

Walsh, Jane MacLaren. "Cannibalism." Unpublished Manuscript.

Walvin, James, and J. A. Mangan, eds. *Manliness and Morality: Middle Class Masculinity in Britain and America, 1800–1940*. New York: St. Martin's Press, 1987.

Ward, R. Gerard, ed. *Man in the Pacific Islands*. Oxford: Clarendon Press, 1972.

Warren, Gordon H. *Fountain of Discontent: The Trent Affair and Freedom of the Seas*. Boston: Northeastern University Press, 1981.

Waterhouse, Joseph. *The King and People of Fiji*. Honolulu: University of Hawaii Press, 1997.

Watson, George E. "Vertebrate Collections: Lost Opportunities." In *Magnificent Voyagers*. Edited by Herman J. Viola and Carolyn Margolis. Washington, D.C.: Smithsonian Institution Press, 1985, pp. 43–69.

Weber, Gustavus A. *The Coast and Geodetic Survey: Its History, Activities, and Organizations*. Service Monograph of the U.S. Government, No. 16. Baltimore: Institute for Government Research, 1923.

——. *The Hydrographic Office, Its History, Activities and Organization*. Baltimore: The Johns Hopkins University Press, 1926.

——. *The Naval Observatory: Its History, Activities and Organization*. Baltimore: The Johns Hopkins University Press, 1926.

Wentworth, Michael. "The Naked Couthouy." *Athenaeum Items: A Library Letter from the Boston Athenaeum* 126 (October 2001), pp. 8–12.

Westwood, Howard. "Reform in the United States Navy: The Plucking of Officers of the Latter 1850s." *American Neptune* 50 (Spring 1990), pp. 107–18.

Whitehill, Walter Muir. *The East India Society and the Peabody Museum of Salem*. Salem, Mass.: Peabody Museum, 1949.

Wickman, John E. "Political Aspects of Charles Wilkes' Work and Testimony." Ph.D. Dissertation, University of Indiana, 1964.

Wilford, John Noble. *The Mapmakers: The Story of the Great Pioneers in Cartography–From Antiquity to the Space Age*. New York: Knopf, 2000.

Wilkerson, James A., ed. *Medicine for Mountaineering*. Seattle: The Mountaineers Books, 2001.

Wilkes, Charles. *Synopsis of the Cruise of the U.S. Exploring Expedition*. Washington, D.C.: Peter Force, 1844.

——. *Narrative of the United States Exploring Expedition*. 5 vols. 1844. Rpt. Upper Saddle River, N.J.: Gregg Press, 1970.

——. "Report on the Territory of Oregon." *Quarterly of the Oregon Historical Society* 12 (September 1911), pp. 269–99.

——. *Columbia River to the Sacramento*. Oakland, Calif.: Oakland Biobooks, 1958.

——. *Autobiography.* Washington, D.C.: Naval History Division, Department of the Navy, 1978.

Williams, Francis Leigh. *Matthew Fontaine Maury: Scientist of the Sea.* New Brunswick, N.J.: Rutgers University Press, 1963.

Williams, Glyndwr. *The Great South Sea: English Voyages and Encounters, 1570–1750.* New Haven, Conn.: Yale University Press, 1997.

Winchester, Simon. *The Map That Changed the World: William Smith and the Birth of Modern Geology.* New York: HarperCollins, 2001.

Withey, Lynne. *Voyages of Discovery: Captain Cook and the Exploration of the Pacific.* Berkeley: University of California Press, 1989.

Worcester, Dean C. *The Philippine Islands and Their People.* New York: Macmillan, 1899.

Wright, Ronald. *On Fiji Islands.* New York: Viking, 1986.

Young, James Sterling. *The Washington Community, 1800–1828.* New York and London: Harcourt, 1966.

Ziff, Larzer. *Return Passages: Great American Travel Writing, 1780–1910.* New Haven and London: Yale University Press, 2000.

Zweig, Paul. *The Adventurer: The Fate of Adventure in the Western World.* Princeton, N.J.: Princeton University Press, 1974.

PUBLICATIONS OF THE
UNITED STATES EXPLORING EXPEDITION

Agassiz, Louis. *Ichthyology.* Vols. 21 and 22. (Never printed).

Baird, Spencer F., and Charles Girard. *Herpetology.* Vol. 20. Philadelphia: C. Sherman, 1858.

Brackenridge, William D. *Botany. Cryptogamia Filices.* Vol. 16. Philadelphia: C. Sherman, 1854.

Cassin, John. *Mammalogy and Ornithology.* Vol. 8 and Atlas. Philadelphia: C. Sherman, 1858.

Dana, James D. *Zoophytes.* Vol. 7. Philadelphia: C. Sherman, 1846.

——. *Geology.* Vol. 10. Philadelphia: C. Sherman, 1849. With Atlas, New York: George Putnam, 1849.

——. *Crustacea.* Vols. 13–14. Philadelphia: C. Sherman, 1855.

Gould, Augustus A. *Mollusca and Shells.* Vol. 12. Philadelphia: C. Sherman, 1852, 1857.

Gray, Asa. *Botany. Phanerogamia.* Vol. 15. Philadelphia: C. Sherman, 1854.

——. *Botany. Phanerogamia.* Part 2. Vol. 18. (Never printed).

Hale, Horatio. *Ethnography and Philology.* Vol. 6. Philadelphia: C. Sherman, 1846.

Peale, Titian Ramsay. *Mammalia and Ornithology.* Repressed on publication in 1848. Rpt. with an Introduction by Kier B. Sterling. New York: Arno Press, 1978.

Pickering, Charles. *Races of Man.* Vol. 9. Philadelphia: C. Sherman, 1848.

——. *Geographical Distribution of Animals and Plants.* Vol. 19. (Printing never completed; parts 1 and 2 issued by the author privately in 1854 and 1876, respectively).

Sullivant, William, et al. *Botany. Cryptogamia.* Vol. 17. Philadelphia: 1874. (Never officially distributed).

Wilkes, Charles. *Narrative of the United States Exploring Expedition.* Vols. 1–5. Philadelphia: C. Sherman, 1844.

——. *Meteorology.* Vol. 11. Philadelphia: 1851.

——. *Hydrography.* Vol. 23. Philadelphia: 1858.

——. *Physics.* Vol. 24. (Never printed).

ACKNOWLEDGMENTS

From the very beginning, William Stanton, author of *The Great United States Exploring Expedition of 1838–1842*, has been as helpful and encouraging as a fellow author can be. Many thanks, Bill. Without the invaluable research assistance and unflagging enthusiasm of Michael Hill, this book would have taken several more years to write. I also want to thank the staff and trustees of the Egan Institute of Maritime Studies for their steadfast support. Anne Hoffman Cleaver, a descendant of William Reynolds, shared with me the letters and photographs in her possession. Others who generously provided me with materials, leads, and advice were Betsey Welton, Philip Lundeberg, E. Jeffrey Stann, George Peacock (a descendant of Ex. Ex. veteran George Emmons), Diana Brown, Charles Thayer, Christopher McKee, Charles Styer (a descendant of Charles Wilkes), and Harley Stanton.

One of the great pleasures of this project has been the opportunity to work with the staffs of so many noteworthy institutions. Very special thanks to everyone at the Smithsonian Institution, especially Jane Walsh, who met with me several times and gave me a personal tour of the Expedition's ethnographic collections; Leslie Overstreet, who graciously organized a day-long visit with the staff of the institution's Museum of Natural History; and Nancy Gwinn, who as director of the institution's libraries made it all possible. Thanks as well to Martin Kalfatovic, G. Dale Miller, Tracy Robinson, Storrs Olson, James Mead, Warren Wagner, Stephen Cairns, and Frederick Bayer—all at the Smithsonian Institution. Thanks also to Earle Spamer at the Academy of Natural Sciences; Matthew Pavlick and Mark Katzman at the American Museum of Natural History; Edward C. Carter II and Roy Goodman at the American Philosophical Society; Stephen Jones and Taran

Schindler at the Beinecke Rare Book and Manuscript Library at Yale University; Catharina Slautterback at the Boston Athenaeum; Linda McCurdy and Elizabeth Dunn at Duke University; Douglas Halsey, an interpreter with the National Park Service at Fort Vancouver; Ann Upton, Michael Lear, and Christopher Raab at Franklin and Marshall College; Lisa DeCesare at the Botany Libraries of the Harvard University Herbaria; Jeffrey Flannery at the Library of Congress; Cathy Williamson and Josh Graml at the Mariners' Museum; William Fowler and Nicholas Graham at the Massachusetts Historical Society; Carolyn Kirdahy at the Museum of Science, Boston; Libby Oldham at the Nantucket Historical Association; Richard Peuser at the National Archives; Michael Crawford at the Naval Historical Center; Gale Munro at the Naval Historical Foundation; James Lewis at the New Jersey Historical Society; John Hattendorf at the Newport War College; Eleanor Gillers at the New-York Historical Society; Mary Catalfamo at the Nimitz Library at the U.S. Naval Academy; Daniel Finamore and Charity Galbreath at the Peabody Essex Museum; John Delaney, Margaret Sherry Rich, and Anna Lee Pauls at Princeton University; Robert Summerall, James Cheevers, and Dolly Pantelides at the U.S. Naval Academy Museum; Mark Pharaoh at Urrbrare House at the University of Adelaide, home of the Mawson Antarctic Collection; Laura Clark Brown at the University of North Carolina; Michael Plunkett at the University of Virginia; and Suzanne Warner at the Yale University Art Gallery.

I have benefited greatly from the expertise and astute editorial advice of those who agreed to read and comment on my manuscript. Many thanks to William Stanton, William Fowler, Thomas Congdon, John Hattendorf, Robert Madison, Michael Crawford, Jane Walsh, Maurice Gibbs, Susan Beegel, Wes Tiffney, Mary Malloy, Stuart Frank, Paul Geraghty, Michael Hill, and Michael Jehle.

Wendy Wolf at Viking Penguin did a masterful job of editing; thanks once again, Wendy. Thanks also to her assistant, Cliff Corcoran, and to Michael Burke for his copyediting. Thanks to Hal Fessenden for his essential input on the manuscript, as well as to Francesca Belanger for the wonderful design work, to Kate Griggs for all her production help, and to master strategist Gretchen Koss. Thanks to Jeffrey Ward for the maps and to Mark Myers for the illustration of the squadron.

Very special thanks to my agent, Stuart Krichevsky, whose counsel and friendship have meant more to me than he knows. Thanks also to his assistant, Shana Cohen.

This book is dedicated to my father, Thomas Philbrick. He first steered me in the direction of the Ex. Ex., and in addition to transcribing all of William Reynolds's journal, as well as scores of letters written by Charles Wilkes, he brought his years of teaching and writing experience to his careful reading of the manuscript. Also there every step of the way was my mother, Marianne D. Philbrick. Thanks also to my brother, Samuel Philbrick; the years we spent sailing together as teenagers were, for me, the starting point of this voyage of discovery. Finally, my deepest thanks to my wife, Melissa D. Philbrick, and to our children, Jennie and Ethan. Here's to future voyages together.

INDEX